Math in Focus

Singapore Math®
by Marshall Cavendish

Student Edition

Program Consultant
Dr. Fong Ho Kheong

Authors
Dr. Lai Chee Chong
Leong May Kuen
Low Wai Cheng
Yap Shin Tze

Marshall Cavendish
Education

U.S. Distributor

Houghton Mifflin Harcourt.
The Learning Company™

Accelerated
Course
2A

Contents

© 2020 Marshall Cavendish Education Pte Ltd

Contents

Activity

Algebraic Expressions

Chapter Opener

 How do you simplify, expand, or factor algebraic expressions?

RECALL PRIOR KNOWLEDGE

Recognizing parts of an algebraic expression • Evaluating algebraic expressions • Simplifying algebraic expressions • Expanding algebraic expressions • Factoring algebraic expressions • Recognizing equivalent expressions • Writing algebraic expressions to represent unknown quantities

▶ Activity

Chapter

 3 Algebraic Equations and Inequalities

Chapter

4 Linear Equations and Inequalities

Chapter Opener

 How do you solve for a variable in a linear equation with two variables?

RECALL PRIOR KNOWLEDGE

Identifying equivalent fractions • Expressing the relationship between two quantities with a linear equation • Solving algebraic equations • Representing fractions as repeating decimals • Solving algebraic inequalities

 Activity

$$x^2 + x - 1 = 0$$

Lines and Linear Equations

Activity

MATH JOURNAL 341

PUT ON YOUR THINKING CAP! 342

CHAPTER WRAP-UP 344

CHAPTER REVIEW 345

PERFORMANCE TASK 351

Functions

Chapter Opener 355

 How can you represent and interpret a function?

RECALL PRIOR KNOWLEDGE 356

Writing algebraic expressions to represent unknown quantities • Graphing a linear equation using a table of values

Activity

Chapter

 7 Exponents

Chapter Opener

 How do you represent repeated multiplication of the same factor?

RECALL PRIOR KNOWLEDGE

Interpreting the real number system • Adding and subtracting integers
• Multiplying and dividing integers • Finding the square of a whole number
• Finding the cube of a whole number

▶ Activity

Scientific Notation

▶ Activity

Manipulative List

Algebra tiles

Counters

Preface

Welcome!

Math in Focus® is a program that puts **you** at the center of an exciting learning experience! This experience is all about equipping you with critical thinking skills and mathematical strategies, explaining your thinking to deepen your understanding, and helping you to become a skilled and confident problem solver.

What's in your book?

Each chapter in this book begins with a real-world situation of the math topic you are about to learn.

In each chapter, you will encounter the following features:

THINK introduces a problem for the whole section, to stimulate creative and critical thinking and help you hone your problem-solving skills. You may not be able to answer the problem right away but you can revisit it a few times as you build your knowledge through the section.

ENGAGE consists of tasks that link what you already know with what you will be learning next. The tasks allow you to explore and discuss mathematical concepts with your classmates.

LEARN introduces new mathematical concepts through a Concrete-Pictorial-Abstract (C-P-A) approach, using activities and examples.

Activity comprises learning experiences that promote collaboration with your classmates. These activities allow you to reinforce your learning or uncover new mathematical concepts.

TRY supports and reinforces your learning through guided practice.

INDEPENDENT PRACTICE allows you to work on a variety of problems and apply the concepts and skills you have learned to solve these problems on your own.

Additional features include:

RECALL PRIOR KNOWLEDGE	Math Talk	MATH SHARING	Caution and Math Note
Helps you recall related concepts you learned before, accompanied by practice questions	Invites you to explain your reasoning and communicate your ideas to your classmates and teachers	Encourages you to create strategies, discover methods, and share them with your classmates and teachers using mathematical language	Highlights common errors and misconceptions, as well as provides you with useful hints and reminders
LET'S EXPLORE	MATH JOURNAL	PUT ON YOUR THINKING CAP!	CHAPTER WRAP-UP
Extends your learning through investigative activities	Allows you to reflect on your learning when you write down your thoughts about the mathematical concepts learned	Challenges you to apply the mathematical concepts to solve problems, and also hones your critical thinking skills	Summarizes your learning in a flow chart and helps you to make connections within the chapter
CHAPTER REVIEW	Assessment Prep	PERFORMANCE TASK	STEAM
Provides you with ample practice in the concepts learned	Prepares you for state tests with assessment-type problems	Assesses your learning through problems that allow you to demonstrate your understanding and knowledge	Promotes collaboration with your classmates through interesting projects that allow you to use math in creative ways

Are you ready to experience math the Singapore way? Let's go!

The Real Number System

Have you ever been on a Ferris wheel?

A Ferris wheel revolves around its hub, lifting passengers and carrying them in a circle. You need the number π to calculate the distance traveled in one revolution of a Ferris wheel. Common approximations of π include $\frac{22}{7}$ and 3.14. A closer approximation of π is the calculator value 3.141592654.

Look again at the last digit in the approximation of π. Did you know that the exact value of π does not stop there? π belongs to a group of numbers called irrational numbers.

The real number system comprises irrational numbers and rational numbers. In this chapter, you will learn about the numbers that make up real numbers and how to locate them on a number line.

What numbers make up the set of real Numbers?

Name: _____   Date: _____

Recognizing types of numbers

Type of Number	Whole Numbers	Negative Numbers	Fractions	Decimals
Examples	0, 1, 2, 3	$-1, -2, -3$	$\frac{1}{4}, \frac{3}{5}, \frac{19}{10}$	1.3, 2.71

Graph the numbers in the table on a horizontal number line.

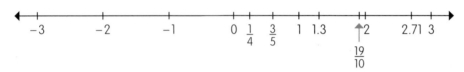

We can also graph the numbers on a vertical number line.

▶ Quick Check

Graph each number on a horizontal number line. Then, order the numbers from least to greatest.

1 $\frac{11}{17}, 1\frac{3}{5}, 0.3, 1.6, \frac{19}{10}$

Comparing decimals

When comparing two decimals, 1.945 and 1.954, you may use a place value chart to determine which decimal is greater.

	Ones		Tenths	Hundredths	Thousandths
1.945	1		9	4	5
1.954	1		9	5	4

The two decimals have the same values in ones and tenths. So, we compare hundredths. In the hundredths place, $4 < 5$. So, 1.954 is greater than 1.945.

You can also use a number line to compare the decimals.

From the number line, you can see that 1.954 lies to the right of 1.945. So, $1.954 > 1.945$.

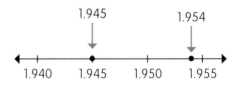

▶ Quick Check

Compare each pair of numbers using <, >, or =. Draw a number line to help you.

2 3.87 ◯ 3.68

3 0.982 ◯ 0.982

4 5.23 ◯ 5.235

Determining absolute values

The absolute value of a number n is denoted by $|n|$.

Examples: $|2| = 2, |-3| = 3$

The absolute value of a number is a measure of its distance from 0.

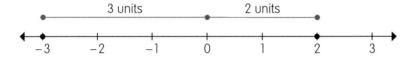

The distance from -3 to 0 is 3 units.

The distance from 2 to 0 is 2 units.

▶ Quick Check

Use the following set of numbers for ⑤ to ⑨.

$34, -23, -54, 54, -60$

⑤ Find the absolute value of each number.

⑥ Which number is closest to 0?

⑦ Which number is farthest from 0?

⑧ Name two numbers with the same absolute value.

⑨ Which number has the greatest absolute value?

Use a number line to find the absolute value of each number.

⑩ $|-15|$

⑪ $|6|$

⑫ $|-2.1|$

Compare each pair of numbers using <, >, or =.

⑬ $|-7| \bigcirc |-72|$

⑭ $|5| \bigcirc |-5|$

⑮ $|-26| \bigcirc |7|$

Comparing numbers on a number line

You can use a number line to compare numbers. On a horizontal number line, the lesser number lies to the left of the greater number. On a vertical number line, the lesser number lies below the greater number.

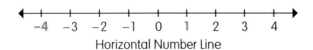

Horizontal Number Line

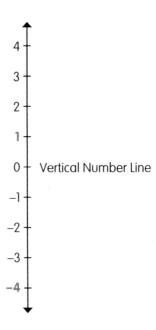

Vertical Number Line

$-4 < 1$, because -4 is to the left of 1 on the horizontal number line, and -4 is below 1 on the vertical number line.

▶ **Quick Check**

Compare each pair of numbers using > or <. Draw a number line to help you.

16 $-3 \bigcirc 5$

17 $-7 \bigcirc -12$

18 $-28 \bigcirc 0$

19 $\dfrac{1}{2} \bigcirc \dfrac{3}{4}$

20 $-1\dfrac{1}{4} \bigcirc 2\dfrac{2}{3}$

21 $-1.23 \bigcirc -1.25$

Using order of operations to simplify numerical expressions

STEP 1 Perform operations within parentheses.

STEP 2 Evaluate exponents.

STEP 3 Multiply and divide from left to right.

STEP 4 Add and subtract from left to right.

Evaluate $(58 - 16) + 7 \cdot 3$.

$(58 - 16) + 7 \cdot 3$
$= 42 \quad + 7 \cdot 3$ Perform operations in parentheses.
$= 42 \quad + 21$ Then, multiply.
$= 63$ Then, add.

▶ **Quick Check**

Evaluate each expression.

22 $75 - (18 + 2) \cdot 3$

23 $15 \cdot (40 \div 8) + 72$

Adding and subtracting fractions

You can add and subtract fractions with unlike denominators.

$$5\frac{2}{3} + 1\frac{3}{4} = 5 + \frac{2}{3} + 1 + \frac{3}{4} \qquad \text{Rewrite the sum.}$$

$$= 6 + \frac{2}{3} + \frac{3}{4} \qquad \text{Add the whole numbers.}$$

$$= 6 + \frac{2 \cdot 4}{3 \cdot 4} + \frac{3 \cdot 3}{4 \cdot 3} \qquad \text{Rewrite the fractions as fractions with a common denominator.}$$

$$= 6 + \frac{8}{12} + \frac{9}{12} \qquad \text{Simplify the products.}$$

$$= 6 + \frac{17}{12} \qquad \text{Add the fractions.}$$

$$= 6 + 1\frac{5}{12} \qquad \text{Write the improper fraction as a mixed number.}$$

$$= 7\frac{5}{12} \qquad \text{Write the sum as a mixed number.}$$

▶ **Quick Check**

Add or subtract. Express each answer in simplest form.

24 $\frac{2}{3} + \frac{5}{4}$

25 $\frac{7}{8} - \frac{2}{3}$

26 $1\frac{1}{4} + 3\frac{2}{5}$

Multiplying and dividing fractions

You can multiply two fractions.

▶ **Method 1**

$$\frac{2}{3} \cdot \frac{3}{4} = \frac{2 \cdot 3}{3 \cdot 4} \qquad \text{Multiply the numerators. Multiply the denominators.}$$

$$= \frac{6}{12} \qquad \text{Simplify the product.}$$

$$= \frac{1}{2} \qquad \text{Write the fraction in simplest form.}$$

▶ **Method 2**

$$\frac{2}{3} \cdot \frac{3}{4} = \frac{\overset{1}{\cancel{2}}}{3} \cdot \frac{3}{\underset{2}{\cancel{4}}} \qquad \text{Divide a numerator and a denominator by the common factor, 2.}$$

$$= \frac{1}{\underset{1}{\cancel{3}}} \cdot \frac{\overset{1}{\cancel{3}}}{2} \qquad \text{Divide a numerator and a denominator by the common factor, 3.}$$

$$= \frac{1 \cdot 1}{1 \cdot 2} \qquad \text{Multiply the numerators. Multiply the denominators.}$$

$$= \frac{1}{2} \qquad \text{Simplify the product.}$$

You can divide a fraction by another fraction.

$\dfrac{3}{4} \div \dfrac{3}{8} = \dfrac{3}{4} \cdot \dfrac{8}{3}$ Rewrite using the reciprocal of the divisor.

$= \dfrac{3}{\underset{1}{\cancel{4}}} \cdot \dfrac{\overset{2}{\cancel{8}}}{3}$ Divide a numerator and a denominator by the common factor, 4.

$= \dfrac{\overset{1}{\cancel{3}}}{1} \cdot \dfrac{2}{\underset{1}{\cancel{3}}}$ Divide a numerator and a denominator by the common factor, 3.

$= \dfrac{1 \cdot 2}{1 \cdot 1}$ Multiply the numerators. Multiply the denominators.

$= 2$ Simplify the product.

▶ **Quick Check**

Multiply or divide. Express each answer in simplest form.

(27) $\dfrac{2}{9} \cdot \dfrac{3}{4}$ (28) $\dfrac{5}{8} \div \dfrac{21}{4}$ (29) $\dfrac{3}{4} \div 1\dfrac{1}{2}$

Multiplying and dividing decimals

Ignore the decimal as you multiply. Then, decide where to place the decimal point in the product.

$$
\begin{array}{r}
\overset{1}{3}.6\,2 \quad \longleftarrow \\
\times \quad\;\; 0.3 \quad \longleftarrow \\
\hline
1\,0\,8\,6 \\
0\,0\,0 \\
\hline
1.0\,8\,6 \quad \longleftarrow
\end{array}
$$

2 decimal places
+ 1 decimal place

3 decimal places

You can express the division expression as a fraction when you divide by a decimal. Then, multiply the dividend and divisor by the same power of 10.

$17.8 \div 0.25 = \dfrac{17.8}{0.25}$ Write division as a fraction.

$= \dfrac{17.8 \cdot \mathbf{100}}{0.25 \cdot \mathbf{100}}$ Multiply both the numerator and the denominator by 100 to make the denominator a whole number.

$= \dfrac{1,780}{25}$ Simplify the product.

$= 71.2$ Divide as with whole numbers.

▶ **Quick Check**

Multiply or divide.

(30) $15.8 \cdot 2.7$ (31) $8.82 \div 0.6$

Representing Rational Numbers on a Number Line

Learning Objectives:
- Find the absolute values of rational numbers.
- Express numbers in $\frac{m}{n}$ form.
- Locate rational numbers on a number line.

> **New Vocabulary**
> set of integers   positive integer
> negative integer   negative fraction
> rational number

THINK

Each of the unknown numbers, A, B, C, and D has one of the following values:

-3.4 $5\frac{3}{4}$ $-\frac{1}{2}$ 2.1

The following clues are given:

$A > D$ $|B| > |C|$

D can be expressed as $\frac{21}{10}$.

Find the values of A, B, C, and D. Then, order them from least to greatest.

ENGAGE

Draw a number line. Graph $\frac{1}{4}$, $-\frac{1}{4}$, 1.65, and -1.65 on your number line.
How did you choose what intervals to use? What do you observe about the numbers you graphed and their distances from zero? Share your observations.

LEARN Find the absolute values of fractions, mixed numbers, and decimals

1. Previously, you learned how to graph whole numbers and negative numbers on a number line. The set of whole numbers and their opposites is called the set of integers.

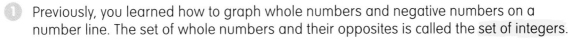

The numbers on the right of 0 are called positive integers. The numbers on the left of 0 are called negative integers. The number 0 itself is neither positive nor negative.

There are gaps between the integers on the number line. These gaps contain fractions.

In the gap between 0 and 1, you can write proper fractions such as $\frac{1}{4}$, $\frac{1}{2}$, $\frac{3}{5}$, and $\frac{9}{10}$.

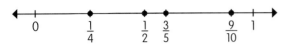

The integer 1 is one unit from 0. So, the fraction $\frac{1}{2}$ must be $\frac{1}{2}$ unit from 0. You can write this distance as $\left|\frac{1}{2}\right|$. The measure of the distance of other fractions from 0 is defined in the same way.

> The absolute value of a positive fraction is just the fraction itself.

Examples: $\left|\frac{1}{4}\right| = \frac{1}{4}$, $\left|\frac{3}{5}\right| = \frac{3}{5}$, and $\left|2\frac{5}{8}\right| = \frac{21}{8}$, because $2\frac{5}{8} = \frac{21}{8}$.

2 Imagine a mirror placed on the number line at the number 0.

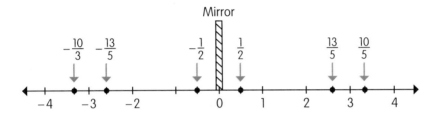

As you look into the mirror, you see the images of the positive integers. These images are the negative integers.

> In a mirror, the distance of an image from the mirror and the distance of the object from the mirror are equal.

In the same way, fractions such as $\frac{1}{2}$, $\frac{13}{5}$, and $\frac{10}{3}$ each has an opposite in the mirror.

The negative fractions are $-\frac{1}{2}$, $-\frac{13}{5}$, and $-\frac{10}{3}$.

The absolute value of a negative fraction is defined as the distance of the negative fraction from 0. You find the absolute value of negative fractions in the same way as for negative integers.

Examples: $\left|-\frac{10}{3}\right| = \frac{10}{3}$, $\left|-\frac{13}{5}\right| = \frac{13}{5}$, $|-1.35| = 1.35$.

So, the distance of $-\frac{10}{3}$ from 0 is $\frac{10}{3}$ units. In the same way, $-\frac{13}{5}$ is $\frac{13}{5}$ units from 0, and -1.35 is 1.35 units from 0.

Practice finding the absolute values of fractions, mixed numbers, and decimals

Solve.

① Find the absolute values of $3\frac{2}{7}$, $-\frac{18}{5}$, and -1.87.

② Graph the three numbers on a number line and indicate their distances from 0. Which number is farthest from 0?

ENGAGE

a How can you express $-\frac{10}{13}$ in another way?

b What other ways can you express $-2\frac{2}{3}$?

Share your ideas.

LEARN Express integers, fractions, and mixed numbers in $\frac{m}{n}$ form

① A rational number is a number which can be written as $\frac{m}{n}$, where m and n are integers with $n \neq 0$. The definition of rational numbers comes from the concept of fractions.

Examples: $1\frac{1}{2} = \frac{3}{2}$. So, $1\frac{1}{2}$ is a rational number.

$3 = \frac{3}{1}$. So, 3 is a rational number.

To express 0 in the form $\frac{m}{n}$, you can write 0 as $\frac{0}{1}$.

For negative fractions, mixed numbers, and whole numbers, the negative integers may be the numerator or denominator.

Examples: $-\frac{2}{9} = \frac{-2}{9} = \frac{2}{-9}$

$-1\frac{1}{2} = \frac{-3}{2} = \frac{3}{-2}$

$-3 = \frac{-3}{1} = \frac{3}{-1}$

TRY Practice expressing integers, fractions, and mixed numbers in $\frac{m}{n}$ form

Write each number as $\frac{m}{n}$ in simplest form, where m and n are integers.

① $11\frac{1}{6}$ ② 48 ③ $-5\frac{4}{12}$ ④ $-\frac{25}{10}$

ENGAGE

Think of a decimal with at least three digits. Find a fraction that is equivalent to your decimal. Use at least two different strategies. Share your strategies.

LEARN Express decimals in $\frac{m}{n}$ form

① Write 30.5 as $\frac{m}{n}$, where m and n are integers with $n \neq 0$.

$30.5 = 30\frac{1}{2}$ Write the integer, 30. Write 0.5 as $\frac{1}{2}$.

$\quad\ \ = \frac{61}{2}$ Write as an improper fraction.

② Write -0.186 as $\frac{m}{n}$, where m and n are integers with $n \neq 0$.

$-0.186 = -\frac{186}{1,000}$ 6 is in the thousandths place. Use 1,000 as the denominator.

$\qquad\ \ = \frac{-93}{500}$ Simplify.

TRY Practice expressing decimals in $\frac{m}{n}$ form

Write each decimal as $\frac{m}{n}$ in simplest form, where m and n are integers with $n \neq 0$.

① 11.5 ② -7.8 ③ 0.36 ④ -0.125

© 2020 Marshall Cavendish Education Pte Ltd

ENGAGE

a Draw a number line and graph $\frac{1}{2}$ and 0.8. On the same number line, graph 0.53 and 1.8.

b Graph $-\frac{1}{2}$, -0.53, $-\frac{4}{5}$, and -1.8 on another number line.

c How can you graph $\frac{1}{2}$, -0.53, $-\frac{4}{5}$, and -1.8 on the same number line? How did you decide what your endpoints should be on the number line? How about your intervals? How did you decide where to graph each point? Explain.

LEARN Locate rational numbers on a number line

1 Locate the rational numbers $\frac{3}{5}$ and -2.4 on a number line.

STEP 1 Find the integers that the rational number lies between.

$\frac{3}{5}$ is a proper fraction so it is located between 0 and 1.

-2.4 is located between -3 and -2.

⚠️ **Caution**

-2.4 can be written as a mixed number, $-2\frac{2}{5}$ or $-2\frac{4}{10}$. Remember that it is a negative mixed number. Make sure that you do not graph -2.4 by counting to the right of 0.

STEP 2 Graph a number line and label the integers.

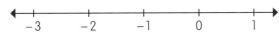

STEP 3 Divide the distance between the integers into equal segments.

Divide the distance between 0 and 1 into 5 equal segments and the distance between -3 and -2 into 10 equal segments.

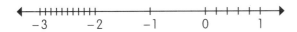

STEP 4 Use the segments to locate $\frac{3}{5}$ and -2.4.

Activity Locating rational numbers on a number line

① Locate each of the following rational numbers on a number line.

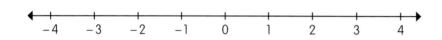

$$-3.6, \quad -\frac{1}{2}, \quad 2.9, \quad 1\frac{1}{4}, \quad 0.25, \quad -\frac{16}{5}, \quad 3.6$$

The rational numbers on the right of 0 are positive.
The rational numbers on the left of 0 are negative.

② **Mathematical Habit 2** Use mathematical reasoning
Explain how you located each rational number on the number line.

③ **Mathematical Habit 3** Construct viable arguments
What is another way to locate the rational numbers on the number line? Explain your answer.

TRY Practice locating rational numbers on a number line

Draw a number line to locate each pair of rational numbers.

1 $\frac{1}{6}$ and $\frac{15}{3}$

2 -0.4 and $\frac{11}{5}$

3 $\frac{12}{15}$ and -1.8

4 $-\frac{5}{15}$ and $-\frac{25}{30}$

INDEPENDENT PRACTICE

Find the absolute value of each fraction. Draw a number line to show how far the fraction is from 0. Write each fraction in simplest form.

1 $\frac{7}{10}$

2 $\frac{18}{8}$

3 $-\frac{5}{13}$

4 $-\frac{48}{15}$

Write each integer or fraction as $\frac{m}{n}$ in simplest form, where m and n are integers.

5 67

6 -345

7 $\frac{25}{80}$

8 $-\frac{264}{90}$

9 $-\frac{14}{70}$

10 $\frac{600}{480}$

Write each mixed number or decimal as $\frac{m}{n}$ in simplest form, where m and n are integers.

11 $7\frac{7}{9}$

12 $-5\frac{1}{10}$

13 $2\frac{5}{12}$

14 $-10\frac{11}{36}$

15 0.4

16 -0.625

17 5.80

18 9.001

19 -10.68

Locate the rational numbers on the number line.

20 $-\frac{1}{4}$, -1.5, 0.8, $\frac{5}{2}$

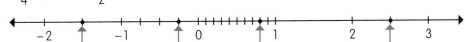

21 $1\frac{7}{10}$, $-\frac{13}{5}$, 2.25, -0.7

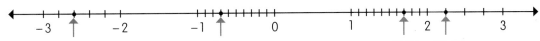

Graph each rational number on a separate number line.

22 $67\frac{1}{8}$

23 $\frac{305}{20}$

24 $\frac{98}{28}$

25 $-\frac{21}{12}$

26 -25.8

27 -45.3

28 A video game gives you 10 minutes to find a treasure. The numbers below show the amount of time left when you have found the treasure for each of eight games. A negative time means you have gone beyond the 10 minutes allotted. Use these data to answer **a** to **h**.

$\frac{23}{8}, 0, -7\frac{1}{5}, 6, -\frac{17}{4}, 8, 7.8, -9.1$

a Order the times from most to least time left using the symbol >.

b Write the absolute value of each number.

c Which number has the greatest absolute value?

d Order the absolute values from least to greatest. Use the symbol <.

e Graph the original numbers on a number line.

f Which negative number in the list is farthest from 0?

g Which positive number in the list is closest to 10?

h Which time is closest to −5 minutes?

Writing Rational Numbers as Decimals

Learning Objectives:
- Write rational numbers as terminating or repeating decimals using long division.
- Compare rational numbers on the number line.

New Vocabulary
terminating decimal
repeating decimal

THINK

Write two possible rational numbers in the form $\frac{m}{n}$ such that $0.125 < \frac{m}{n} < \frac{2}{9}$.

How do you express your numbers as decimals?

ENGAGE

a   List the factors of 100. Now, make a list of fractions that have a denominator that is a factor of 100. Trade your list of fractions with your partner. Write each of your partner's fractions as a decimal. What method did you use? Share your method.

b   Using a nonfactor of 100, write a fraction and find its corresponding decimal. Share your decimal and discuss what type of decimal it is.

LEARN Write rational numbers as terminating decimals using long division

1   In a previous course, you learned to write some rational numbers as decimals.

Examples: $\frac{3}{10} = 0.3$, $\frac{21}{100} = 0.21$, and $5\frac{323}{1,000} = 5.323$.

Any rational number may be written in decimal form using long division.

Since $\frac{1}{4}$ means 1 divided by 4 you can write $\frac{1}{4}$ as a decimal using long division.

```
    0.25      Divide 1 by 4.
4 ) 1.00      Add zeros after the decimal point.
    8
    ──
    20
    20
    ──
     0        The remainder is 0.
```

**Math Talk**

Any fraction whose denominator has only 2s and 5s in its prime factorization can be written as a terminating decimal. Why?

So, $\frac{1}{4} = 0.25$.

The fraction $\frac{1}{4}$ is written as 0.25.

Notice that the long division ends with a remainder of zero. A decimal, such as 0.25, is called a terminating decimal, because it has a finite number of nonzero decimal places.

2 Using long division, write the rational number $6\frac{2}{25}$ as a terminating decimal.

```
       0.08
   25 ) 2.00
       2 00
          0
```

Divide 2 by 25.

Add zeros after the decimal point.

The remainder is 0.

You can also write $6\frac{2}{25}$ as the improper fraction, $\frac{152}{25}$. Then, divide 152 by 25. The answer is the same.

So, $6\frac{2}{25} = 6.08$.

TRY Practice writing rational numbers as terminating decimals using long division

Using long division, write each rational number as a terminating decimal.

1 $\frac{7}{8}$

2 $\frac{19}{4}$

3 $\frac{52}{40}$

4 $10\frac{13}{25}$

ENGAGE

a Write $\frac{9}{2}$ as a decimal. How do you write $\frac{2}{9}$ as a decimal?

b Now, try $\frac{9}{4}$ and $\frac{4}{9}$. What do you notice? Share your observations.

c Think of another two numbers that will result in the same observations in **b** when written in fractions. Share the numbers and fractions.

LEARN Write rational numbers as repeating decimals using long division

1 Since $\frac{1}{3}$ means 1 divided by 3, you can write $\frac{1}{3}$ as a decimal using long division.

```
       0.333
   3 ) 1.000
       9
       10
        9
        10
         9
         1
```

Divide 1 by 3.

Add zeros after the decimal point.

The remainder will not terminate with 0.

So, $\frac{1}{3} = 0.333...$

A repeating decimal, such as 0.333…, has a group of one or more digits that repeat endlessly.

When you divide 1 by 3, the division process will not terminate with a remainder of 0. The digit 3 keeps repeating infinitely. A decimal, such as 0.333…, is called a repeating decimal.

For the repeating decimal 0.333…, the digit 3 repeats itself. You can write 0.333… as $0.\overline{3}$, with a bar above the repeating digit 3. So, 0.333… = $0.\overline{3}$.

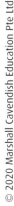

② Using long division, write the rational number $\frac{13}{12}$ as a repeating decimal.

$$
\begin{array}{r}
1.0833 \\
12\overline{)13.0000} \\
\underline{12} \\
1\,00 \\
\underline{96} \\
40 \\
\underline{36} \\
40 \\
\underline{36} \\
4
\end{array}
$$

Divide 13 by 12.
Add zeros after the decimal point.

The remainder will not terminate with 0.

Stop dividing when the digits continue to repeat themselves.

So, $\frac{13}{12}$ = 1.0833...

  = $1.08\overline{3}$

Math Talk
If you see a repeating decimal such as 0.246246..., where 2, 4, and 6 repeat as a group of digits, how do you write the repeating decimal using bar notation?

Activity Classifying rational numbers in decimal form ————————

Work in pairs.

① On a spreadsheet, label four columns with the following column heads.

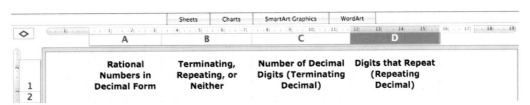

Rational Numbers in Decimal Form	Terminating, Repeating, or Neither	Number of Decimal Digits (Terminating Decimal)	Digits that Repeat (Repeating Decimal)

Enter each rational number below in the first column, labeled "Rational Numbers in Decimal Form." Make sure that the cells in this column are formatted to display decimals up to 8 decimal places.

$\frac{5}{16}$, $\frac{141}{25}$, $-\frac{40}{111}$, $-\frac{15}{16}$, $\frac{14}{5}$, $\frac{1}{8}$, $-\frac{9}{44}$, $\frac{2}{11}$, $\frac{5}{4}$, and $-\frac{40}{9}$.

For example, if you enter $\frac{5}{16}$ into the spreadsheet, the entry will show the decimal form of this fraction.

Determine whether the decimal is terminating, repeating, or neither. Enter either "Terminating," "Repeating," or "Neither" in the second column.

If the decimal terminates, record the number of decimal digits in the third column.
If the decimal repeats, record the repeating digits in the fourth column.

(2) **Mathematical Habit 3 Construct viable arguments**
Did you find any decimals that neither terminated nor repeated? What can you conclude
about the decimal form of a rational number?

TRY Practice writing rational numbers as repeating decimals
using long division

Using long division, write each rational number as a repeating decimal.
Use bar notation to indicate the repeating digits.

1 $\frac{5}{9}$

2 $\frac{11}{6}$

 Using a calculator, write each rational number as a repeating decimal.
Use bar notation to indicate the repeating digits.

3 $\frac{23}{54}$

4 $\frac{78}{37}$

ENGAGE

a Compare $\frac{3}{8}$ and 0.35. Which is greater? What strategies did you use to compare?

b Compare $\frac{2}{3}$ and 0.4. Which is less? What strategies did you use to compare?

c Discuss when you should change fractions to decimals or decimals to fractions in order to
compare them. Use examples to justify your answers.

LEARN Compare rational numbers

1 Compare the two rational numbers, $\frac{3}{4}$ and $\frac{4}{5}$, using the symbols > or <.
Write each rational number as a decimal first.

$\frac{3}{4} = 0.75$ $\qquad \frac{4}{5} = 0.8$

To compare the rational numbers,
we compare their decimal forms, 0.75 and 0.8.

0.**7**5 $\qquad\qquad$ 0.**8**0

Since 7 tenths < 8 tenths, 0.75 < 0.8.

> Compare the corresponding place value
> of two decimals from left to right. Stop at
> the first pair of digits which are different.

You may also use a number line to compare these decimals.

0.75 lies to the left of 0.80.
So, 0.75 < 0.80.

$$\frac{3}{4} < \frac{4}{5}$$

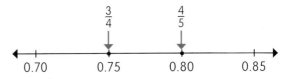

2 Compare the positive rational numbers, $\frac{11}{8}$ and $\frac{15}{11}$, using the symbols > or <.

$\frac{11}{8} = 1.375$ Write each rational number as a decimal.

$\frac{15}{11} = 1.3636...$

$\quad = 1.\overline{36}$

Compare the decimals, 1.375 and $1.\overline{36}$.

From the number line, 1.375 lies to the right of $1.\overline{36}$.

So, $1.375 > 1.\overline{36}$

$$\frac{11}{8} > \frac{15}{11}$$

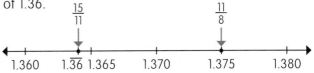

3 Compare the negative rational numbers, $-\frac{2}{11}$ and $-\frac{3}{16}$, using the symbols > or <.

▶ **Method 1**

Compare using a number line.

$-\frac{2}{11} = -0.\overline{18}$ Write each rational number as a decimal.

$-\frac{3}{16} = -0.1875$

Use the absolute values of $-0.\overline{18}$ and -0.1875 to help you graph the decimals on a number line.

$|-0.\overline{18}| = 0.\overline{18}$
$|-0.1875| = 0.1875$

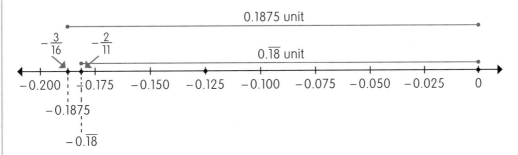

From the number line, -0.1875 lies farther to the left of 0 than $-0.\overline{18}$.
So, $-0.\overline{18} > -0.1875$

$$-\frac{2}{11} > -\frac{3}{16}$$

▶ **Method 2**

Compare using place value.

You can also write an inequality using the absolute value of the two numbers.

$$|-0.\overline{18}| < |-0.1875|$$

The two numbers are negative, so the number with the greater absolute value is farther to the left of 0. It is the lesser number.

$$-0.\overline{18} > -0.1875$$
$$-\frac{2}{11} > -\frac{3}{16}$$

TRY **Practice comparing rational numbers**

Compare each pair of rational numbers using the symbols > or <. Draw a number line to help you.

1. $\frac{24}{7} \bigcirc \frac{10}{3}$

2. $-\frac{3}{5} \bigcirc -\frac{4}{5}$

3. $-10\frac{3}{4} \bigcirc -\frac{41}{5}$

4. $-4.063 \bigcirc -4\frac{1}{6}$

Name: __Nathan__   Date: __9/26/2021__

INDEPENDENT PRACTICE

Using long division, write each rational number as a terminating decimal.

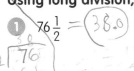

1 $76\frac{1}{2} = \boxed{38.0}$

$2\overline{\smash{)}76}$

2 $-39\frac{2}{5}$

3 $-\frac{47}{10}$ $\boxed{-4.7}$

4 $\frac{5}{16}$

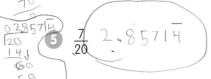

5 $\frac{7}{20}$ $\boxed{2.85714}$

6 $\frac{7}{8}$

Simplify each rational number. Then, use long division to write each rational number as a terminating decimal.

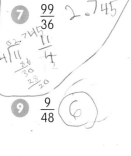

7 $\frac{99}{36}$ 2.745

8 $\frac{12}{15}$

9 $\frac{9}{48}$ $\boxed{6}$

10 $-\frac{132}{8}$

11 $-\frac{48}{50}$ $24\overline{\smash{)}25}$

$\boxed{1.041}$

12 $-\frac{14}{128}$

Using long division, write each rational number as a repeating decimal with 3 decimal places. Identify the pattern of repeating digits using bar notation.

13 $\frac{5}{6}$ $\boxed{1.2}$

$5\overline{\smash{)}6}$

14 $-8\frac{2}{3}$

Write each rational number as a repeating decimal using bar notation. You may use a calculator.

15 $\dfrac{8}{55}$

16 $\dfrac{456}{123}$

17 $-\dfrac{987}{110}$

18 $\dfrac{11}{14}$

19 $-\dfrac{10}{13}$

20 $\dfrac{4,005}{101}$

Refer to the list of rational numbers below for 21 **and** 22 **. You may use a calculator.**

$$-\dfrac{23}{32}, \dfrac{7}{15}, -\dfrac{368}{501}, -\dfrac{19}{26}, \dfrac{37}{44}$$

21 Write each rational number as a decimal with at most 6 decimal places.

22 Using your answers in 21, list the numbers from least to greatest using the symbol <. Graph a number line between −1 and 1 with 0 in the middle. Then, place each rational number on the number line.

Answer the question.

23 **Mathematical Habit 2 Use mathematical reasoning**

Maria tries to compare $-\dfrac{2}{3}$ and $-\dfrac{5}{8}$ using absolute values. She finds their decimal equivalents to be $-0.\overline{6}$ and -0.625, and she knows $|-0.\overline{6}| > |-0.625|$. Explain why Maria must reverse the inequality in her final answer, $-\dfrac{2}{3} < -\dfrac{5}{8}$.

3 Introducing Irrational Numbers

Learning Objective:
• Use rational approximations of irrational numbers to locate irrational numbers approximately on a number line.

New Vocabulary
irrational number

THINK

The dots on a grid are 1 centimeter apart. On a number line, locate the side length of the square drawn on the grid.

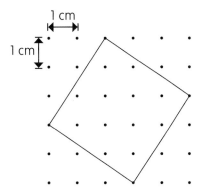

ENGAGE

Find the side length of each square that has the area given.

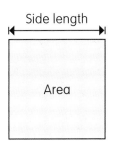

Side length

Area

Area (square units)	1	4	9	16
Side Length (units)				

How does the table of values help you find the side length of a square with an area of 2 square units? How do you use the areas of other squares to locate the value of the side length on a number line? Explain your thinking.

Activity Finding the value of $\sqrt{2}$ using a square ————————————

① Square *ABCD* is made up of 4 smaller squares. The side length of each small square is 1 inch. Find the area of *ABCD*.

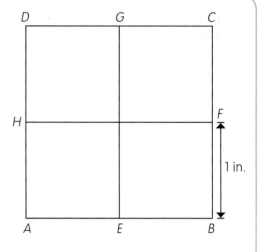

② If there are lines joining the points *EF, FG, GH* and *HE*, state how the areas of squares *ABCD* and *EFGH* are related. Write the area of *EFGH*. Then, express the side length of *EFGH* in exact form.

③ Use your ruler to measure the length of *EF*. How is this measurement different from the length found in ② ?

---

① An irrational number is a number that cannot be written as $\frac{m}{n}$, where *m* and *n* are integers with $n \neq 0$. When written in decimal form, an irrational number is nonterminating and nonrepeating.

Some examples of irrational numbers are π and $\sqrt{2}$.

π = 3.14159265358979323846264338327950…

$\sqrt{2}$ = 1.4142135623730950488016887242 0969…

Math Note

Since the term "rational number" means that the number can be expressed as a ratio of two integers, so the term "irrational number" means that the number cannot be expressed as a ratio of two integers.

② All rational numbers can be expressed as fractions, and you can locate their exact positions on a number line. Irrational numbers, however, do not have exact values. You estimate the positions of irrational numbers by approximating irrational numbers as rational numbers.

③ You can use areas of squares to approximate the values of irrational numbers. Consider $\sqrt{2}$. The area of a square with side length $\sqrt{2}$ units is 2 square units.

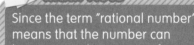

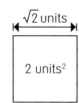

Notice that 2 is more than 1 but less than 4.

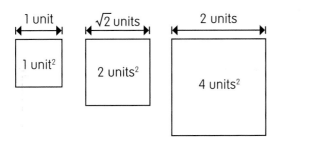

$$1 < 2 < 4$$
$$1 < \sqrt{2} < 2$$

To more accurately locate $\sqrt{2}$ on a number line, you need to determine if $\sqrt{2}$ is closer to 1 or 2. Consider another square with side length 1.5 units.
The area of the square is 1.5^2 square units or 2.25 square units.

1.5 units

2.25 units²

$$1 < 2 < 2.25$$
$$1 < \sqrt{2} < 1.5$$

Since 2 is very close to 2.25, you can conclude that $\sqrt{2}$ is slightly less than 1.5.
The approximate value of $\sqrt{2}$ is shown on the following number line.

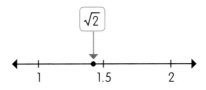

4   Locate $\sqrt{10}$ on a number line using areas of squares.
The area of a square with side length $\sqrt{10}$ units is 10 square units.

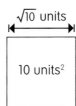

Compare this square with squares of areas 9 square units and 16 square units.

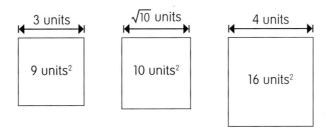

$9 < 10 < 16$
$3 < \sqrt{10} < 4$

Since 10 is very close to 9, you can conclude that $\sqrt{10}$ is slightly greater than 3.
The approximate value of $\sqrt{10}$ is shown on the following number line.

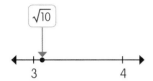

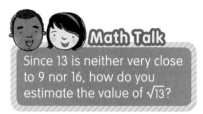

Math Talk

Since 13 is neither very close to 9 nor 16, how do you estimate the value of $\sqrt{13}$?

TRY Practice locating irrational numbers on a number line using areas of squares

Use areas of squares to locate each irrational number on a number line.

1 $\sqrt{34}$

2 $\sqrt{198}$

ENGAGE

Use areas of squares to locate $\sqrt{5}$ on a number line. This method only gives you an approximate value. How do you locate $\sqrt{5}$ more precisely on a number line? Discuss.

LEARN Locate irrational numbers on a number line using a calculator

1. You can use a calculator to locate irrational numbers more precisely on a number line.

2. Locate $\sqrt{5}$ on a number line using a calculator.

STEP 1 Find an approximate value of $\sqrt{5}$ using a calculator, and round the value obtained to 2 decimal places.

$\sqrt{5}$ is 2.24 when rounded to 2 decimal places.

STEP 2 Use the approximate value to identify the numbers, to 1 decimal place, that $\sqrt{5}$ lies between.

$2.2 < 2.24 < 2.3$
$2.2 < \sqrt{5} < 2.3$

STEP 3 Estimate the position of $\sqrt{5}$ in a suitable interval on a number line.

2.24 is about halfway between the interval 2.2 to 2.3 and is closer to 2.2 than 2.3. The approximate value of $\sqrt{5}$ is shown on the following number line.

3. Locate $-\sqrt{61}$ on a number line using a calculator.

STEP 1 Find an approximate value of $-\sqrt{61}$ using a calculator, and round the value obtained to 2 decimal places.

$-\sqrt{61}$ is -7.81 when rounded to 2 decimal places.

STEP 2 Use the approximate value to identify the numbers, to 1 decimal place, that $-\sqrt{61}$ lies between.

$-7.9 < -7.81 < -7.8$
$-7.9 < -\sqrt{61} < -7.8$

STEP 3 Estimate the position of $-\sqrt{61}$ in the interval on a number line.

–7.81 is slightly less than –7.8. The approximate value of $\sqrt{61}$ is shown on the following number line.

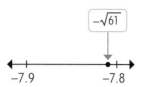

Caution

The number –7.81 is less than –7.8. It should be located to the left of –7.8 on a number line. It should not be confused with positive numbers, where 7.81 is located to the right of 7.8.

TRY Practice locating irrational numbers on a number line using a calculator

 Use a calculator to locate each irrational number on a number line.

1 $\sqrt{28}$

2 $-\sqrt{123}$

INDEPENDENT PRACTICE

Locate each irrational number on a number line using areas of squares.

1 $\sqrt{11}$

2 $\sqrt{24}$

3 $\sqrt{50}$

4 $\sqrt{79}$

5 $\sqrt{164}$

6 $\sqrt{200}$

Locate each irrational number on a number line using a calculator.

7 $\sqrt{6}$

8 $\sqrt{12}$

9 $\sqrt{99}$

10 $-\sqrt{22}$

11 $-\sqrt{128}$

12 $-\sqrt{250}$

Introducing the Real Number System

Learning Objective:
• Order real numbers.

New Vocabulary
real number

THINK

A piece of paper has a length of 29.7 cm and a width of 21.0 cm. Find the paper's length-to-width ratio. Which of the following numbers is closest to the ratio?

$$\frac{7}{5} \quad \sqrt{2} \quad 1.\overline{41}$$

ENGAGE

Using a calculator, locate $\frac{17}{9}$, 2.56, and $\sqrt{7}$ on a number line.

Now, think of another three numbers of different forms and put them in order.

LEARN Order real numbers

① The real number system is a combination of the set of rational numbers and the set of irrational numbers.

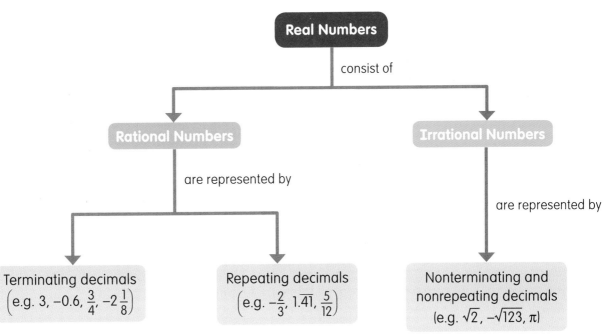

② To compare different forms of real numbers, it is generally easier to convert any non-decimal to decimal form before comparing.

3 Locate the set of real numbers on a number line, and order them from least to greatest using the symbol <.

$$2\frac{4}{7} \quad -\frac{72}{15} \quad -2.3492 \quad \sqrt{\pi}$$

Express each number in decimal form rounded to at least 3 decimal places where appropriate.

$$2\frac{4}{7} \approx 2.571 \qquad -\frac{72}{15} = -4.8 \qquad -2.3492 \approx -2.349 \qquad \sqrt{\pi} \approx 1.772$$

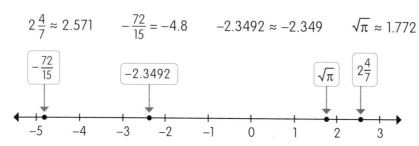

So, $-\frac{72}{15} < -2.3492 < \sqrt{\pi} < 2\frac{4}{7}$.

TRY Practice ordering real numbers

Locate the set of real numbers on a number line, and order them from least to greatest using the symbol <.

1 $\sqrt{10} \qquad -\frac{53}{9} \qquad -\frac{3\pi}{2} \qquad 6.2\overline{86}$

MATH SHARING

Mathematical Habit 6 Use precise mathematical language

Which of the real numbers are rational numbers, and which are irrational numbers? Explain how you arrived at your answer. Represent all the numbers on a number line.

$$2 \qquad -\sqrt{2} \qquad -\pi \qquad \frac{10}{3} \qquad 0.2 \qquad -3$$

5 Introducing Significant Digits

Learning Objectives:
- Determine the number of significant digits in a number.
- Round a number to a particular number of significant digits.

New Vocabulary
significant digit

THINK

A piece of glass is exactly 0.004512 meters thick. State the thickness rounded to 2 decimal places. Would this rounded figure be meaningful to a contractor? What estimated thickness would be meaningful?

ENGAGE

The length of a ribbon is measured using two different rulers.

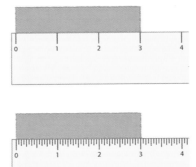

Andy says the length is 3 centimeters. Becky says the length is 3.0 centimeters.
What do you think is the difference in the way that both of them have presented their measurements? Explain your thinking.

LEARN Determine the number of significant digits

1. When you measure a quantity, the precision of your reading depends on the type of measuring instrument used.

   Look at the following measurement.

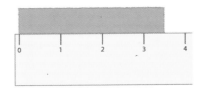

   The ruler indicates that the length of the ribbon is between 3 centimeters and 4 centimeters. You see that the length is at least 3 centimeters. So, the digit 3 is certain.

You can estimate that the digit in the first decimal place is 5 because the length seems to be halfway between 3 centimeters and 4 centimeters. So, the approximate length of the ribbon is 3.5 centimeters, where the digit 5 is estimated.

The length 3.5 centimeters has 2 significant digits. In general, the more significant digits there are, the more precise a measurement is.

2 You use five rules to determine which digits in a number are significant.

Rule 1: Any digit that is not zero is significant.
For example, 3.5612 has 5 significant digits.

Rule 2: Zeroes between non-zero digits are significant.
For example, 60.00103 has 7 significant digits

Rule 3: For decimals, all the trailing zeroes are significant.
For example, 2.500 has 4 significant digits.

Rule 4: Zeroes to the left of the first non-zero digit are not significant.
For example, 0.000482 has 3 significant digits.

Rule 5: For whole numbers, the trailing zeroes may or may not be significant.
For example, 800 has 2 significant digits when rounded to the nearest ten and 1 significant digit when rounded to the nearest hundred.

TRY Practice determining the number of significant digits

Find the number of significant digits in each number.

1 900,045

Refer to Rule 1 and Rule 2.

2 0.0068

3 734.100

© 2020 Marshall Cavendish Education Pte Ltd

Solve.

④ The mass of an object is 5,400 grams after rounding to the nearest 10 grams. State the number of significant digits in the mass.

ENGAGE

Recall and discuss the rules of rounding a number to a particular place value. Use specific examples to explain your thinking. Now, how do you round 123,000 to 1 significant digit? Explain.

Discuss what other numbers when rounded to 1 significant digit gives you the same answer.

LEARN Round whole numbers to a particular number of significant digits

① Round 5,632 to 3 significant digits.

As the fourth significant digit is 2, which is less than 5, you round down.

So, 5,632 rounded to 3 significant digits is 5,630.

> ⚠ **Caution**
> When you round 5,632 to 5,630, be sure to replace the last digit with 0. A common mistake is to completely remove the last digit. In this example, the result would be 536, which is much smaller than the original value.

② Round 345,090 to 4 significant digits.

As the fifth significant digit is 9, which is 5 or more, you round up.

So, 345,090 rounded to 4 significant digits is 345,100.

③ Round 669,420 to 2 significant digits.

As the third significant digit is 9, which is 5 or more, you round up.

So, 669,420 rounded to 2 significant digits is 670,000.

④ Round 43,540,245 to 7 significant digits.

As the eighth significant digit is 5 or more, you round up.

So, 43,540,245 rounded to 7 significant digits is 43,540,250.

> When you round a number to a particular number of significant digits, check that the answer has the same number of significant digits given.

TRY Practice rounding whole numbers to a particular number of significant digits

Round each whole number to the given number of significant digits.

1 627
(2 significant digits)

2 5,030
(2 significant digits)

3 459,610
(3 significant digits)

4 18,455
(4 significant digits)

ENGAGE

You have learned to round a whole number to a particular number of significant digits.
Now, how do you round 0.0123 to 1 significant digit? Explain.

Look back at when you rounded 123,000 to 1 significant digit. How is rounding to a significant digit different in decimals than it is in whole numbers? Discuss.

LEARN Round decimals to a particular number of significant digits

1 Round 0.023461 to 3 significant digits.
As the fourth significant digit is 6, which is 5 or more, you round up.
So, 0.023461 rounded to 3 significant digits is 0.0235.

2 Round 0.0005549 to 2 significant digits.
As the third significant digit is 4, which is less than 5, you round down.
So, 0.0005549 rounded to 2 significant digits is 0.00055.

3 Round 1.00308 to 5 significant digits.
As the sixth significant digit is 8, which is 5 or more, you round up.
So, 1.00308 rounded to 5 significant digits is 1.0031.

© 2020 Marshall Cavendish Education Pte Ltd

④ Round 32.401 to 4 significant digits.

As the fifth significant digit is 1, which is less than 5, you round down.

So, 32.401 rounded to 4 significant digits is 32.40.

Caution

32.401 rounded to 4 significant digits is 32.40 and not 32.4.

⑤ Round 589.54 to 3 significant digits.

As the fourth significant digit is 5 or more, you round up.

So, 589.54 rounded to 3 significant digits is 590.

⑥ The length of a parallelogram is 13.54 centimeters and the height is 8.22 centimeters.

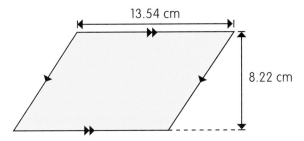

13.54 cm

8.22 cm

a Calculate the area of the parallelogram.

Area of parallelogram = 13.54 · 8.22
= 111.2988 cm²

Area of a parallelogram = Base · Height

b State the area of the parallelogram to 3 significant digits.

The area of the parallelogram to 3 significant digits is 111 square centimeters.

TRY Practice rounding decimals to a particular number of significant digits

Round each decimal to the given number of significant digits.

① 0.00914073
(4 significant digits)

② 24.00963
(5 significant digits)

③ 32.018
(3 significant digits)

④ 2,560.58
(4 significant digits)

Solve.

⑤ The radius of a circle is 2.53 centimeters.

   a Find the area of the circle. Use 3.14 as an approximation for π.

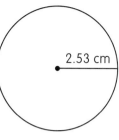

2.53 cm

Area of circle = πr^2

   b Find the area of the circle to 3 significant digits.

LET'S EXPLORE

The average distance from Earth to the Sun is about 149,600,000 kilometers. How many of the trailing zeroes could be significant? Explain.

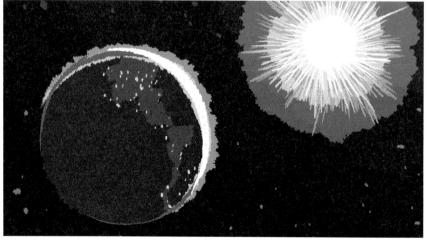

INDEPENDENT PRACTICE

Find the number of significant digits in each number.

1 7,294

2 56,001

3 0.0700

4 3.008

5 600.0

6 0.0045

7 0.505

8 10.400

Round each whole number to the given number of significant digits.

9 9,591
(2 significant digits)

10 613,256
(4 significant digits)

11 17,447
(3 significant digits)

12 10,300
(2 significant digits)

13 2,490,983
(4 significant digits)

14 350,216
(4 significant digits)

15 75,000
(3 significant digits)

16 675,348
(1 significant digit)

Round each decimal to the given number of significant digits.

17 0.5482
(1 significant digit)

18 1.0023
(2 significant digits)

19 36.82073
(5 significant digits)

20 0.04945
(3 significant digits)

21 830.7
(3 significant digits)

22 5.129
(2 significant digits)

23 3.38049
(4 significant digits)

24 0.0999
(2 significant digits)

Solve.

25 Evaluate $5.68 \times \frac{19.3^2}{6.251} - 0.982 \times 41.4$. Give each answer to the given number of significant digits.

    a 1 significant digit   b 2 significant digits

    c 3 significant digits   d 5 significant digits

26 The distance between San Antonio and San Diego is 1,100 miles after rounding to the nearest 100 miles. State the number of significant digits in the distance.

27 John measures the volume of a liquid using the measuring cylinder shown. The smallest division in the scale represents 2 millimeters. He recorded his reading as 42.5 milliliters. How would you know that his reading is incorrect?

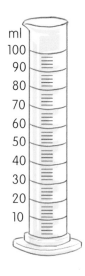

 28 The length of a rectangle is 23.46 centimeters and the height is 11.68 centimeters.

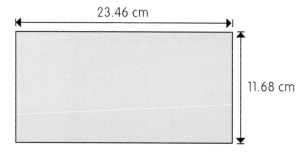

    a Find the area of the rectangle.

    b Find the area of the rectangle to 3 significant digits.

29 How many seconds are in a month of 30 days? Give your answer to 3 significant digits.

Adding Integers

Learning Objectives:
- Add integers with the same sign.
- Add integers to their opposites.
- Add integers with different signs.

> **New Vocabulary**
> zero pair
> additive inverse

THINK

a Will the sum of two integers be always greater than each of the integers? Why do you think so?

b Discuss what possible patterns you can observe when adding two integers. Give examples to justify your observations.

ENGAGE

a In a golf game, par is considered the number of strokes a player needs to get to the hole. Par is scored as 0 points. Playing one under par is considered a score of –1. Alex was playing golf. On the first hole, he scored two over par. On the second hole, he scored three under par.

Use to show Alex's score on the first two holes.

b Name two possible par results of each round to achieve a score of –2.

c If Alex scored two under par at his first hole, what are the possible pars he should have for the next two holes to achieve a total score of –3?

LEARN Add integers with the same sign

1 You can use counters to represent integers.

⚪ represents + 1 and ⚫ represents – 1.

You can use counters to represent the positive integer 3 and the negative integer – 2.

⚪⚪⚪ ⟶ 1 + 1 + 1 = 3

⚫⚫ ⟶ (– 1) + (– 1) = – 2

2 Evaluate – 1 + (– 3).

▶ **Method 1**
Add using counters.

⚫   (– 1)
    +   ⟶   ⚫⚫⚫⚫ – 4
⚫⚫⚫ (– 3)

So, (– 1) + (– 3) = – 4.

▶ Method 2

Add using a number line.

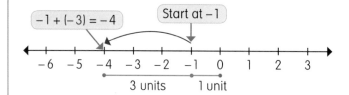

Start at − 1. Then, add − 3, a jump of **3 to the left** to reach − 4.

Distance of sum from 0: $|-1| + |-3| = 1 + 3$
$$= 4$$

You move in a negative direction, so the sum is negative.

$$-1 + (-3) = -4$$

> When you add integers with the same sign on a horizontal number line:
> • move to the right, or in the positive direction, to add a positive integer.
> • move to the left, or in the negative direction, to add a negative integer.

> How do you evaluate $(-1) + (-3)$ using a vertical number line?

▶ Method 3

Add using absolute values.

First, add the absolute values of the two negative integers.

$|-1| + |-3| = 1 + 3$ Add the absolute values.
$\qquad\quad = 4$ This is the distance of the sum from 0.

Then, decide whether the sum is positive or negative.

$-1 + (-3) = -4$ Use the common sign, a negative sign, for the sum.

> When you use absolute values to add integers with the same sign, first add their absolute values, and then use the common sign.
>
> The sum of positive integers is positive.
> The sum of negative integers is negative.

Adding integers with the same sign

(1) **Mathematical Habit 5** Use tools strategically
Use two different methods to illustrate each solution.

a $2 + 3$ b $(-2) + (-3)$ c $-4 + (-1)$

(2) **Mathematical Habit 2** Use mathematical reasoning
Explain how to add two integers with the same sign. How are the absolute values of the addends related to the sum?

(3) **Mathematical Habit 3** Construct viable arguments
Is the sum of positive integers always positive? Is the sum of negative integers always negative? Explain your answer.

TRY Practice adding integers with the same sign

Evaluate each sum.

1 $-3 + (-5)$

2 $-15 + (-7)$

3 $-18 + (-22)$

ENGAGE

1. Choose an integer. Trade with your partner. Use to show how you would add the number your partner chose and its opposite.

   What can you say about the sum of a number and its opposite? Explain your thinking.

2. A kettle of water at room temperature was boiled. After boiling, the water was left to cool down back to room temperature. Use a number line to find the total change in temperature.

LEARN Add integers to their opposites

1. You have learned that each integer has an opposite.
   For example, the opposite of 1 is – 1. 1 and – 1 form a zero pair.

   Remove one zero pair.

   zero pair

   You write 1 + (– 1) = 0.

2. Evaluate 2 + (– 2).

   ▶ **Method 1**
   Add using counters.

   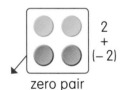

   Remove two zero pairs.

   zero pair

   2 + (– 2) = 0

   > **Math Note**
   > **Commutative Property of Addition:**
   > If a and b are integers, then
   > $a + b = b + a$. Hence, 2 + (–2) and
   > (–2) + 2 give the same answer.

   ▶ **Method 2**
   Add using a number line.

   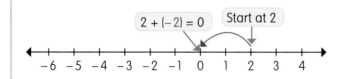

   2 + (– 2) = 0   Start at 2

   Start at 2. Then, add – 2, a jump of **2 to the left** to reach 0.

   2 + (– 2) = 0

   2 and – 2 are called additive inverses because 2 and its opposite – 2 have a sum of zero.

   > **Math Talk**
   > Write a rule for the sum of a number and its additive inverse. How are the absolute values of a number and its additive inverse related?

③ There are real-world situations in which opposite quantities combine to make zero. Examples of real-world situations involving opposite quantities include:

a A hydrogen atom has a charge of zero, because it contains one positively charged proton and one negatively charged electron.

b You put a 3-ounce stone on a scale and then remove it.
The overall change in weight on the scale is 0 ounces.

c You heat up an oven, and then turn it off so that it returns to room temperature.
The overall change in temperature is 0°F.

d You ride 50 feet up in an elevator and ride 50 feet back down.
Overall, your change in position is 0 feet.

TRY Practice adding integers to their opposites

Evaluate each sum.

1 $-5 + 5$

2 $9 + (-9)$

3 $-21 + 21$

ENGAGE

The temperature recorded at 5 A.M. was -12°F. The temperature rose to 13°F at 4 A.M. What was the change in temperature? What was a possible temperature recorded at noon?

LEARN Add two integers with different signs

Activity Exploring addition of integers ————————————————————

Work in pairs.

⬤ represents +1 and ⬤ represents − 1.

⬤ + ⬤ represent a zero pair.

① Use counters to add two integers with different signs.

  a Evaluate 3 + (− 2).

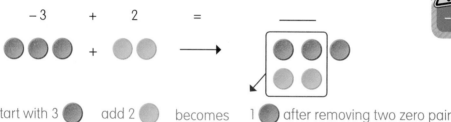

$$3 \qquad + \qquad (-2) \qquad = \qquad \_\_\_\_\_$$

Start with 3 ⬤ add 2 ⬤ becomes 1 ⬤ after removing two zero pairs.

  b Evaluate (− 3) + 2.

$$-3 \qquad + \qquad 2 \qquad = \qquad \_\_\_\_\_$$

Caution

$-3 + 2 \neq -5$

Start with 3 ⬤ add 2 ⬤ becomes 1 ⬤ after removing two zero pairs.

② Use counters to evaluate each sum.

  a 7 + (− 2) and (− 7) + 2   **b** (− 8) + 5 and 8 + (− 5)

③ **Mathematical Habit 2** **Use mathematical reasoning**
Explain how to add two integers with different signs. How are the absolute values of the addends related to the sum?

1 Suppose the temperature was − 8°F at 7 A.M. Five hours later, the temperature has risen 10°F. Find the new temperature.

Temperature at 7 A.M.

As the temperature rose, you can find the new temperature by finding − 8 + 10.

Evaluate − 8 + 10.

▶ **Method 1**

Add using counters.

$$-8 + 10 \longrightarrow \quad 2$$

Remove eight zero pairs

− 8 + 10 = 2

The new temperature is 2°F.

► **Method 2**

Add using a number line.

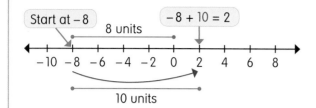

Start at − 8. Then, add 10, a jump of **10 to the right** to reach 2.

Distance of sum from 0: $|10| - |-8| = 10 - 8$
$$= 2$$

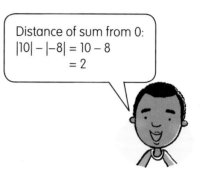

Distance of sum from 0:
$|10| - |-8| = 10 - 8$
$$= 2$$

$-8 + \mathbf{10} = -8 + \mathbf{8} + \mathbf{2}$
$$= \quad 0 + 2$$
$$= \quad 2$$

The new temperature is 2°F.

► **Method 3**

Add using absolute values.

First, find the difference between the absolute values of the two integers.

$|10| - |-8| = 10 - 8$ Subtract the lesser absolute value from the greater one.
$$= 2 \qquad\quad \text{Simplify.}$$

Then, decide whether the sum is positive or negative.

$-8 + 10 = 2$ Use the sign of the addend with the greater absolute value, the positive sign of 10.

The new temperature is 2°F.

When you use absolute values to add integers with different signs, first subtract the lesser absolute value from the greater one, and then use the sign of the integer with the greater absolute value.

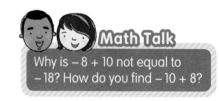

Math Talk

Why is − 8 + 10 not equal to − 18? How do you find − 10 + 8?

TRY Practice adding two integers with different signs

Evaluate each sum.

①   − 11 + 6.

②   − 10 + 3

③   11 + (− 25)

© 2020 Marshall Cavendish Education Pte Ltd

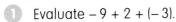 **ENGAGE**

In a game, you start out with 15 points. At each turn, you pick a card. 3 points are awarded for a blue card picked and 5 points are deducted for a red card picked. Alan had a total of 14 points at the end of 5 turns. How many blue and red cards did he pick?

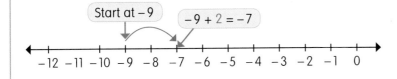 **LEARN** Add more than two integers with different signs

1 Evaluate $-9 + 2 + (-3)$.

▶ **Method 1**

Add using a number line.

Start at -9 $-9 + 2 = -7$

$\begin{array}{ccccccccccccc} & | & | & | & | & | & | & | & | & | & | & | & | \\ -12 & -11 & -10 & -9 & -8 & -7 & -6 & -5 & -4 & -3 & -2 & -1 & 0 \end{array}$

Start at -9. Then, add 2, a jump of **2 to the right** to reach -7.

$-9 + 2 = -7$

 Move to the right when adding a positive integer. Move to the left when adding a negative integer.

$-7 + (-3) = -10$ Continue from -7

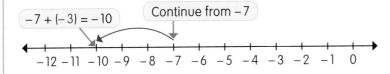
$\begin{array}{ccccccccccccc} & | & | & | & | & | & | & | & | & | & | & | & | \\ -12 & -11 & -10 & -9 & -8 & -7 & -6 & -5 & -4 & -3 & -2 & -1 & 0 \end{array}$

Next, add -3, a jump of **3 to the left** to reach -10.

$-7 + (-3) = -10$

So, $-9 + 2 + (-3) = -7 + (-3)$
$\qquad\qquad\qquad\quad = -10$

 You can also add 2 and -3 first. Then, add -9 to the result.
$-9 + 2 + (-3) = -9 + (-1)$
$\qquad\qquad\qquad = -10$

📌 **Math Note**

Associative Property of Addition:
If a, b, and c are integers, then $(a + b) + c = a + (b + c)$.

▶ **Method 2**

Add using absolute values.

First, group integers with the same sign.

$-9 + 2 + (-3) = -9 + (-3) + 2$ ⠀⠀Commutative property of addition

Next, add -9 and -3.

> Add their absolute values because the integers have the same sign.

$|-9| + |-3| = 9 + 3$ ⠀⠀Add the absolute values.
⠀⠀⠀⠀⠀⠀⠀⠀$= 12$ ⠀⠀Simplify.
⠀⠀$-9 + (-3) = -12$ ⠀⠀Use the common sign, a negative sign, for the sum.

Then, continue by adding 2 to -12.

> Subtract their absolute values because the integers have different signs.

$|-12| - |2| = 12 - 2$ ⠀⠀Subtract the lesser absolute value from the greater one.
⠀⠀⠀⠀⠀⠀⠀⠀$= 10$ ⠀⠀Simplify.

⠀⠀$-12 + 2 = -10$ ⠀⠀Use the sign of the addend with the greater absolute value, the negative sign of -12.

$-9 + 2 + (-3) = -9 + (-3) + 2$
⠀⠀⠀⠀⠀⠀⠀⠀$= -12 + 2$
⠀⠀⠀⠀⠀⠀⠀⠀$= -10$

TRY **Practice adding more than two integers with different signs**

Evaluate each sum.

1 ⠀$10 + (-3) + 6$

2 ⠀$-7 + (-23) + 15$

The temperature of a glass of water rose 4oF, fell 7°F, and then rose 2°F.

a If the water was originally at 68°F, what was the final temperature? Draw a number line to explain your thinking.

b If the final temperature of the water was 72°F, what was the original temperature?

LEARN Add integers with different signs in a real-world situation

① The water level in a large tank rises 5 feet, falls 9 feet, and then rises 3 feet.
Overall, how far does the water level rise or fall?

rises 5 ft

falls 9 ft   rises 3 ft

> Think of the water level rising as adding a positive integer and the water level falling as adding a negative integer. You can translate the verbal description to 5 + (− 9) + 3.

Evaluate 5 + (− 9) +3.

▶ **Method 1**

Add using a number line.

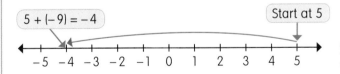

$5 + (− 9) = − 4$ Start at 5

Start at 5. Then, add − 9, a jump of 9 to the left to reach − 4.

$5 + (− 9) = − 4$

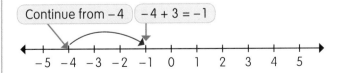

Continue from − 4 $− 4 + 3 = −1$

Next, add 3, a jump of 3 to the right to reach − 1.

$− 4 + 3 = −1$

$$5 + (− 9) + 3 = − 4 + 3$$
$$= −1$$

Overall, the water level falls 1 foot.

▶ Method 2

Add using absolute values.

First, add 5 and (− 9).

$|-9| - |5| = 9 - 5$ Subtract the lesser absolute value from the greater one.
$\qquad\quad = 4$ Simplify.

$5 + (-9) = -4$ Use the sign of the addend with the greater
absolute value, the negative sign of − 9.

Then, add 3 to − 4.

$|-4| - |3| = 4 - 3$ Subtract the lesser absolute value from the greater one.
$\qquad\quad = 1$ Simplify.

$(-4) + 3 = -1$ Use the sign of the addend with the greater absolute value,
the negative sign of − 4.

$5 + (-9) + 3 = -4 + 3$
$\qquad\qquad\quad = -1$

> You can evaluate
> 5 + (− 9) + 3 by adding
> from left to right. First,
> add 5 and (− 9). Then,
> add 3 to the result.

Overall, the water level falls 1 foot.

TRY Practice adding integers with different signs in a real-world situation

Solve.

1. A submarine is at 400 feet below sea level. If it ascends 150 feet and then descends 320 feet, how far is it above or below sea level?

> Think of the submarine ascending as adding a positive integer, and descending as adding a negative integer. You can translate the written description as − 400 + 150 + (− 320).

LET'S EXPLORE

The sum of three integers is 0. Each integer is nonzero. What could the integers be?

[⬚] + [⬚] + [⬚] = 0

INDEPENDENT PRACTICE

Evaluate each sum using a number line.

1 − 3 + (− 9)

2 − 8 + (− 4)

3 7 + (− 7)

4 − 9 + 9

5 − 10 + 6

6 − 17 + 9

Evaluate each sum using the absolute values.

7 − 23 + (− 9)

8 − 11 + (− 34)

9 − 15 + (− 7)

10 12 + (− 18)

11 − 40 + 26

12 − 75 + 19

Evaluate each sum.

13 − 8 + 4 + 5

14 5 + (− 10) + (− 6)

15 − 6 + (− 8) + (− 12)

16 − 13 + (− 17) + 7

17 − 20 + 16 + (− 7)

18 − 11 + (− 8) + 14

Solve.

19 The temperature is − 4°F. What will the temperature be if the temperature rises 20°F?

20 Mr. Clark parked his car in a parking garage 33 feet below street level. He then got in an elevator and went up 88 feet to his office. How far above street level is his office?

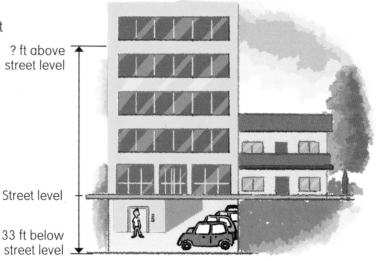

? ft above street level

Street level

33 ft below street level

21 A hiker starts hiking in Death Valley at an elevation of 143 feet below sea level. He climbs up 400 feet in elevation. What is his new elevation relative to sea level?

22 Emma was playing a board game with her friends. On her first turn, she moved 6 spaces forward. On her second turn, she moved another 5 spaces forward. On her third turn, she moved 4 spaces backward. How many squares forward or backward from her starting point was she after her third turn?

23 **Mathematical Habit 2** **Use mathematical reasoning**
In a game, all scores with even numbers are recorded as positive numbers. Odd numbers are recorded as negative numbers. Explain how to find Diego's total score in a game if his individual scores during the game are 9, 12, 7, 18, and 19.

Subtracting Integers

Learning Objectives:
• Subtract integers by adding their opposites.
• Find the distance between two integers.

THINK

a   Will the difference between two integers be always positive? Why do you think so?

b   What are the possible patterns you can observe when subtracting two integers? Give examples to justify your observations.

ENGAGE

Brianna went to a school fair. She played a game that cost 4 tickets. She won 1 ticket. Did she end up losing or winning tickets? Use ⚪🔵 to explain your reasoning.

LEARN   Subtract integers by adding their opposites

Activity   Exploring subtraction of integers

Work in pairs.

⚪ represents + 1 and 🔵 represents – 1.

⚪ + 🔵 represent a zero pair.

① Use counters to work out and complete the subtraction of a positive integer.

a Evaluate 5 – (+ 2) and compare with 5 + (– 2).

$$5 - (+ 2) \qquad = \qquad \underline{\hspace{2cm}}$$

Start with 5 ⚪ and remove 2 ⚪   becomes _____ ⚪

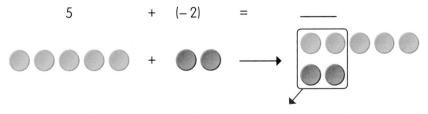

$$5 \qquad + \quad (- 2) \quad = \quad \underline{\hspace{2cm}}$$

Start with 5 ⚪   add 2 🔵   becomes _____ ⚪ after removing two zero pairs.

b Evaluate $-5 - (+2)$ and compare with $-5 + (-2)$.

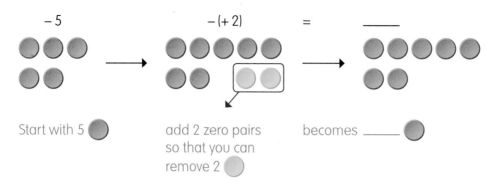

−5

Start with 5 ●

−(+2)

add 2 zero pairs so that you can remove 2 ●

= _____

becomes _____ ●

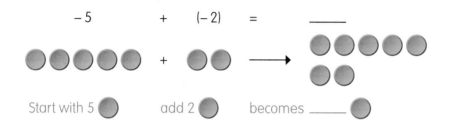

−5 + (−2) = _____

Start with 5 ●   add 2 ●   becomes _____ ●

② Use counters to evaluate each expression.

    a $6 - 4$ and $6 + (-4)$ **b** $-6 - 4$ and $-6 + (-4)$

③ Use counters to work out and complete the subtraction of a negative integer.

    a Evaluate $5 - (-2)$ and compare with $5 + 2$.

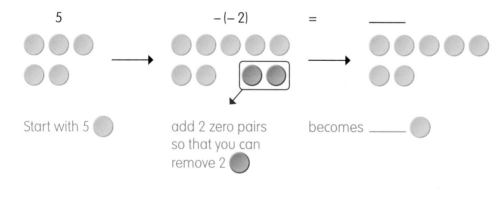

5

Start with 5 ●

−(−2)

add 2 zero pairs so that you can remove 2 ●

= _____

becomes _____ ●

5 + 2 = _____

Start with 5 ●   add 2 ●   becomes _____ ●

b Find $-5 - (-2)$ and compare with $-5 + 2$.

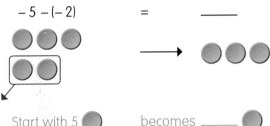

Start with 5 ● and remove 2 ● becomes _____ ●

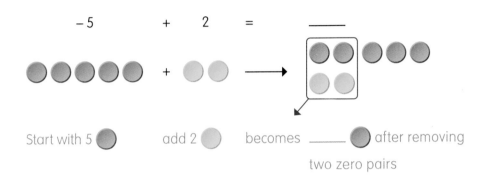

Start with 5 ● add 2 ● becomes _____ ● after removing two zero pairs

④ Use counters to evaluate each expression.

a $7 - (-3)$ and $7 + 3$

b $-7 - (-3)$ and $-7 + 3$

⑤ **Mathematical Habit 7** **Make use of structure**

Based on your results in ① to ④, explain how you can subtract integers.

1 Pedro scored 3 points in the first round of a game show
and lost 5 points in the second round. Find Pedro's final score.

You can translate the written description as 3 − 5.
Instead of subtracting 5 from 3, we can add its opposite,
which is − 5.

$$3 - 5 = 3 + \underbrace{(- 5)}_{\text{opposite of 5}}$$

> **Math Note**
>
> Addition and subtraction
> are inverse operations.
> When you subtract an
> integer, you are adding
> its additive inverse
> or opposite.

Evaluate 3 + (− 5).

▶ **Method 1**

Add using counters.

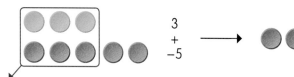

Remove three zero pairs.

$$3 - 5 = 3 + (- 5)$$
$$= - 2$$

Pedro's final score is − 2.

▶ **Method 2**

Add using a number line.

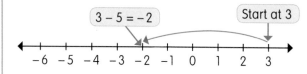

Start at 3. Then, add − 5, a jump of
5 to the left to reach − 2.

Pedro's final score is − 2.

2 You can use opposites to subtract negative integers.

For example, find $3 - (-5)$.

The opposite of -5 is 5. Instead of subtracting -5 from 3, you can add its opposite, which is 5.

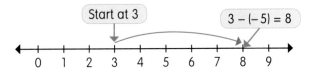

$3 - (-5) = 3 \underbrace{+ 5}_{\text{opposite of } -5}$

$\qquad\quad = 8$

So, $3 - (-5)$ can be rewritten as $3 + 5$ to give an answer of 8.

Instead of subtracting an integer, you can add its additive inverse or opposite as follows:

- Subtracting a positive integer, b, is the same as adding its opposite, $-b$.
  So, $a - b = a + (-b)$.

- Subtracting a negative integer, $-b$, is the same as adding its opposite, b.
  So, $a - (-b) = a + b$.

When you subtract integers on a horizontal number line,
- move to the left to subtract a positive integer.
- move to the right to subtract a negative integer.

3 A diver went 24 feet below the surface of the ocean, and then 47 feet farther down. What is the diver's new position relative to the surface?

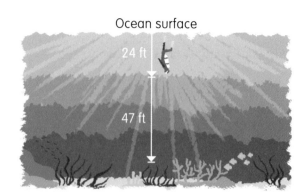

Ocean surface

24 ft

47 ft

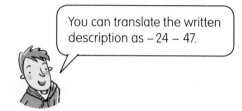

You can translate the written description as − 24 − 47.

Evaluate − 24 − 47.

$-24 - 47 = -24 + (-47)$ Rewrite subtraction as adding the opposite.

Using absolute values,
$|-24| + |-47| = 24 + 47$ Add the absolute values, because the addends have the same sign.
$\qquad\qquad\quad = 71$ Simplify.

$-24 - 47 = -24 + (-47)$
$\qquad\quad\ = -71$ Use the common sign, a negative sign, for the sum.

The diver's new position is 71 feet below the surface of the ocean.

4 Evaluate − 15 − (− 21).

$-15 - (-21) = -15 + 21$ Rewrite subtraction as adding the opposite.

Using absolute values,
$|21| - |-15| = 21 - 15$ Subtract the absolute values, because the addends have different signs.
$\qquad\qquad\quad = 6$ Simplify.

$-15 - (-21) = -15 + 21$
$\qquad\qquad\ = 6$ Use a positive sign, because 21 has a greater absolute value.

5 Evaluate − 11 − (− 5) − (− 20).

5 is the additive inverse of − 5.
20 is the additive inverse of − 20.

$-11 - (-5) - (-20) = -11 + 5 + 20$ Rewrite subtraction as adding the opposite.
$\qquad\qquad\qquad\quad = -6 + 20$ Add from left to right.
$\qquad\qquad\qquad\quad = 14$ Simplify.

TRY Practice subtracting integers by adding their opposites

Evaluate each expression.

1 21 – 30

2 17 – (– 4)

Solve.

3 A fishing boat drags its net 35 feet below the ocean's surface. Then, it lowers the net by an additional 12 feet. Find the fishing net's new position relative to the ocean's surface.

4 A submarine was 1,200 feet below sea level. It then moved to 1,683 feet below sea level. How many feet did the submarine descend?

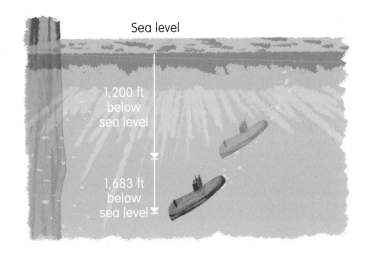

Evaluate each expression.

5 – 25 – (– 9)

6 – 19 – (– 7) – (– 6)

ENGAGE

1 The change in temperature recorded in November was between 2°F and 5°F. Draw a number line to find the change in temperature.
The change in temperature recorded in December was between –2°F and 5°F. Now, find the change in the temperature. What do you notice? Share your observations.

2 The lowest temperature recorded last month was below 0°F. This month, the lowest temperature recorded is above 0°F. If the difference between the two temperatures is 9°F, what could the temperatures be? List three possible sets of answers. Draw number lines to explain your thinking.

LEARN Find the distance between two integers

1 You can find the distance between two integers. First, plot the two integers on a number line. Then, count the units between them.

For example, find the distance between 3 and 7.

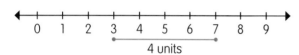

4 units

> First, plot the integers 3 and 7 on the number line. Then, count the units from 3 to 7 or from 7 to 3. Since you are finding the distance, and distance is always positive, it does not matter which integer you start counting from.

You can use absolute value to find the distance between two integers. It does not matter in which order you count, from 3 to 7, or from 7 to 3.

Distance between 3 and 7 can be represented as: $|7 - 3| = |3 - 7|$
$$= 4 \text{ units}$$

> For any two integers a and b, the distance between a and b is the absolute value of their difference, $|a - b|$. It does not matter which integer you decide to call a and which you decide to call b.

2 Find the distance between 2 and -6.

▶ **Method 1**

Use a number line to plot the points and count the units.

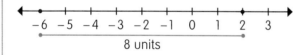

8 units

The distance between 2 and -6 is 8 units.

▶ **Method 2**

Use absolute value to find the distance between integers with different signs.

Distance between 2 and -6:

$|2 - (-6)| = |2 + 6|$ Rewrite subtraction as adding the opposite.
$\qquad = 8$ Add.

The distance between 2 and -6 is 8 units.

> You can also find the distance between 2 and -6 using $|-6 - 2|$.

Find the distance between each pair of integers.

① 3 and −2

② −5 and 4

ENGAGE

① The wind-chill temperature at 10 p.m. was −8°F. One hour later, the wind-chill temperature had fallen to −28°F. How do you find the change in temperature? Draw a number line to explain your reasoning.

② The highest temperature recorded in California was 134°F. The lowest temperature was −43°F. How can you find the difference between the two temperatures? Draw a number line to explain your reasoning.

LEARN Find the distance between two integers in a real-world situation

① The elevation of Death Valley in Eastern California is 86 meters below sea level. The elevation of the tallest mountain in California, Mount Whitney, is 4,421 meters above sea level. Find the difference in elevation between Death Valley and Mount Whitney.

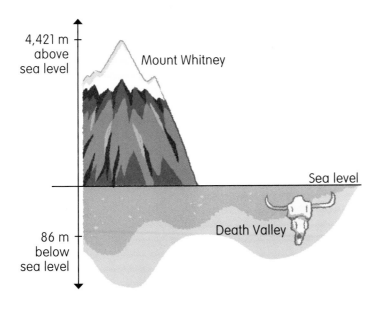

Elevation of Death Valley: − 86 m

Elevation of Mount Whitney: 4,421 m

Difference between the two elevations:

$|4,421 - (-86)| = |4,421 + 86|$ Rewrite subtraction as adding the opposite.
$ = 4,507$ m   Add.

The difference in elevation is 4,507 meters.

TRY Practice finding the distance between two integers in a real-world situation

Solve.

1. A particular town has an elevation of 8 feet below sea level. Another town on top of a mountain has an elevation of 2,421 feet above sea level. What is the difference in the elevations between the two towns?

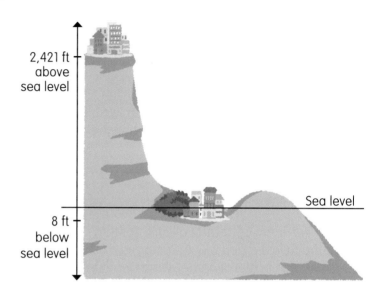

Name: _____   Date: _____

Evaluate each expression.

1 7 – 18

2 20 – 30

3 53 – 109

4 45 – (– 16)

5 –7 – (– 5)

6 – 94 – (– 68)

7 – 6 – 8 – 12

8 – 23 – 17 – 7

9 – 8 – (– 4) – 5

10 – 5 – (– 10) – 6

11 – 20 – (– 16) – (– 7)

12 – 11 – (– 8) – (– 14)

Evaluate the distance between each pair of integers.

13 4 and 20

14 16 and 52

15 – 15 and 36

16 – 7 and 41

17 – 28 and – 3

18 – 19 and – 8

Solve.

19 Ryan leaves to go skiing in Burlington, Vermont, when the temperature is – 4°C. The temperature drops 10°C when a cold front moves in. What is the new temperature?

20 The water level of the Dead Sea dropped from 390 meters below sea level in 1930 to 423 meters below sea level in 2010. By how much did the water level drop from 1930 to 2010?

21 **Mathematical Habit 6** **Use precise mathematical language**
Ms. Davis has only $420 in her bank account. Describe how to find the amount in her account after she writes a check for $590.

22 **Mathematical Habit 6** **Use precise mathematical language**
Kevin has trouble simplifying 15 – (– 36). Write an explanation to help him.

23 The lowest point in North America is in Death Valley, California, which is 86 meters below sea level at its lowest point. The highest point is Denali, a mountain in Alaska, with an elevation of 6,198 meters above sea level. What is the difference between their elevations?

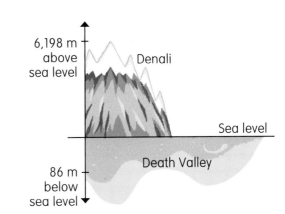

24 Ms. Scott has two freezers. Freezer A keeps frozen foods at a temperature of − 20°F, while Freezer B keeps frozen foods at a temperature of − 4°F. She transferred a package of frozen food from one freezer to the other.

   a What is the temperature difference between the two freezers?

   b If the temperature of the package rises after the transfer, from which freezer was the package taken?

25 You and a friend are playing a video game. Your score so far is 340 points and your friend's score is − 220 points. What is the difference between your scores?

26 Two record low monthly temperatures for Anchorage, Alaska, are − 34°F in January and 31°F in August. Find the difference between these two temperatures.

27 Town X is 120 feet above sea level, Town Y is 25 feet below sea level, and Town Z is 30 feet below sea level. How high is

   a Town X above Town Y ?   **b** Town Y above Town Z?   **c** Town X above Town Z?

28 **Mathematical Habit 3** Construct viable arguments

   a Find $|8 - 12|$ and $|8| - |12|$. Is $|8 - 12|$ equal to $|8| - |12|$?

   b Find $|12 - 8|$ and $|12| - |8|$. Is $|12 - 8|$ equal to $|12| - |8|$?

   c Jake thinks that to find the distance between two integers m and n, he can write $|m| - |n|$ or $|n| - |m|$. Use your answer in **a** and **b** to explain why you agree or disagree.

29 **Mathematical Habit 2** Use mathematical reasoning
   Use the data in the following table. Which two gases have boiling points that are closest in value? Explain.

Gas	Temperature (°F)
Oxygen	− 297
Hydrogen	− 423
Nitrogen	− 321

8 Multiplying and Dividing Integers

Learning Objective:
• Multiply and divide integers.

THINK

a Does the product or quotient of two integers with the same sign result in an answer with the same sign? Why do you think so?

b What are the possible patterns you can observe when multiplying or dividing two integers? Give examples to justify your observations.

ENGAGE

Show 2 × 4 using ⚪⚫ How do you show 2 × (−4)? Create a real-world problem to model each situation. Share your real-world problems.

LEARN Multiply two or more integers

Activity Exploring multiplication rules using repeated addition

Work in pairs.

You can think of multiplying integers as repeated addition.

① Use counters and a number line to model and complete the multiplication of integers as repeated addition.

a Evaluate 3 · 2.

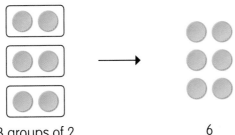

3 groups of 2   6

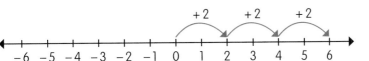

$3 \cdot 2 = 2 \cdot 3$
$\quad\quad = 2 + 2 + 2$
$\quad\quad = \underline{\quad\quad}$

> Commutative property of multiplication:
> Two or more numbers can be multiplied in any order.

b Evaluate 3 · (− 2).

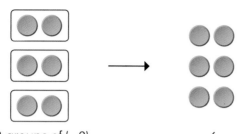

3 groups of (− 2)   − 6

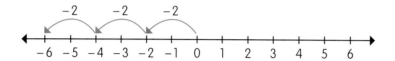

$3 \cdot (-2) = (-2) \cdot 3$
$\qquad = -2 + (-2) + (-2)$

$\qquad = \underline{\hspace{2cm}}$

The expression 3 · (− 2) can also be written as 3(− 2).
The expression (− 2) · 3 can also be written as − 2(3).

② Use repeated addition to fill in the table.

Product	Equivalent Sum	Answer	Sign
3(2)	2 + 2 + 2	6	+
3(− 2)	− 2 + (− 2) + (− 2)		
2(5)	5 + 5		
2(− 5)	− 5 + (− 5)		
4(3)			
4(− 3)			

③ Use a number line to model and complete the multiplication as addition of the opposite.

a Evaluate −3 · 2.

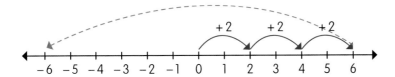

You can say that −3 · 2 is the opposite of 3 groups of 2.

−3 · 2 = −(3)(2)

= _____

b Evaluate −3 · (−2).

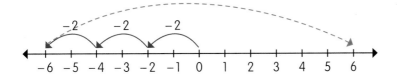

You can say that −3 · (−2) is the opposite of 3 groups of −2.

−3 · (−2) = −(3)(−2)

= −(_____)

= _____

④ Use addition of the opposite and your results from ② to fill in the table.

Product	Use Addition of Opposite	Use Results from ②	Answer	Sign
−3(−2)	−(3)(−2)	−(−6)	6	+
−2(−5)	−(2)(−5)	−(−10)		
−4(−3)				

⑤ **Mathematical Habit 8** **Look for patterns**

Based on your observations in ① to ④,

a what do you observe about the sign of the product of two integers with the same sign?

b what do you observe about the sign of the product of integers with different signs?

1 Evaluate − 5(4).

  − 5(4) = − 20   Product of two integers with different signs is negative.

2 Evaluate − 3 · (− 9).

  − 3 · (− 9) = 27   Product of two integers with the same sign is positive.

3 Evaluate 2(− 3)(− 7).

  ▶ **Method 1**

  2(− 3) (− 7) = **− 6**(− 7)   Product of two integers with different signs is negative.
            = 42   Product of two integers with the same sign is positive.

  ▶ **Method 2**

  2(− 3) (− 7) = 2 **(21)**   Product of two integers with the same sign is positive.
            = 42   Product of two integers with the same sign is positive.

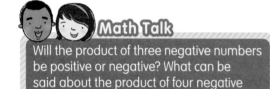

Math Talk

Will the product of three negative numbers be positive or negative? What can be said about the product of four negative numbers? Explain your answers.

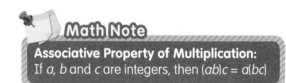

Math Note

Associative Property of Multiplication:
If a, b and c are integers, then $(ab)c = a(bc)$

TRY Practice multiplying two or more integers

Evaluate each product.

1   9(− 8)

2   − 6(9)

3   − 7 · (− 5)

4   4 · (− 10)

5   3(− 4)(6)

6   − 5(9)(− 2)

ENGAGE

Water leaks out of a tank at 2 liters each day for 9 days. How do you find the total change in the amount of water in the tank during this time? Share your method.

LEARN Multiply two or more integers in a real-world situation

1. A helicopter's altitude changes at a rate of – 17 feet per second. Find the change in the helicopter's altitude after 4 seconds.

Change in altitude
= Rate · Time
= – 17 · 4   Substitute – 17 for rate and 4 for time.
= – 68 ft   Multiply. Product of two integers with different signs is negative.

The change in the helicopter's altitude is – 68 feet.

TRY Practice multiplying two or more integers in a real-world situation

Solve.

1. Samuel plays four rounds in a golf championship. The score for a round is recorded as positive (over par) or negative (under par). If Sam scores 6 points under par for all four rounds, what is his total score for his game?

2. A shop owner sells 3 television sets at a loss. If the loss for each television set is $25, what is the shop owner's total loss?

ENGAGE

Divide 18 by 6. Now, divide – 18 by – 6. How does your knowledge of multiplying integers help you with dividing? Explain.

If the quotient of two numbers is 5, what possible numbers can they be?
If the quotient of two numbers is – 5, what possible numbers can they be?
List a few possible pairs of answers. How are they similar? How are they different? Explain.

LEARN Divide two integers

1. Division is the inverse (or reverse) of multiplication.

Multiplication	Division
3(5) = **15**	**15** ÷ 5 = **3**
3(– 5) = **– 15**	**– 15** ÷ (– 5) = **3**
(– 3)5 = **– 15**	**– 15** ÷ 5 = **– 3**
(– 3)(– 5) = **15**	**15** ÷ (– 5) = **– 3**

For the relationship between multiplication and division, you can conclude the following:

- When you divide two integers with the same sign, the quotient is positive.

  For example, $2 \div 3 = \frac{2}{3}$ and $-2 \div (-3) = \frac{2}{3}$.

- When you divide two integers with different signs, the quotient is negative.

  For example, $-2 \div 3 = -\frac{2}{3}$ and $2 \div (-3) = -\frac{2}{3}$.

Math Note

For negative fractions, the negative integer may be placed in either the numerator or the denominator:
$-\frac{m}{n} = \frac{-m}{n} = \frac{m}{-n}$, where m and n are integers with $n \neq 0$. So,

$$-2 \div 3 = \frac{-2}{3} \quad \text{and} \quad 2 \div (-3) = \frac{2}{-3}$$
$$= -\frac{2}{3} \qquad\qquad\qquad = -\frac{2}{3}$$

2 Evaluate $-25 \div (-5)$.

$-25 \div (-5) = 5$ Divide. Quotient of two integers with the same sign is positive.

3 Evaluate $-81 \div 3$.

$-81 \div 3 = -27$ Divide. Quotient of two integers with different signs is negative.

4 Evaluate $96 \div (-4)$.

$96 \div (-4) = -24$ Divide. Quotient of two integers with different signs is negative.

TRY **Practice dividing two integers**

Evaluate each quotient.

1 $-36 \div (-4)$

2 $-35 \div 5$

3 $45 \div (-3)$

ENGAGE

If an elevator in a skyscraper descends 1,500 feet in 60 seconds, how can you find the change in height per second? Discuss.

LEARN **Divide two integers in a real-world situation**

1 A submarine descends 720 feet in 6 minutes.
Find the submarine's change in elevation per minute.

Change in elevation per minute: $-\frac{720}{6} = -120$ ft/min

The submarine's change in elevation per minute is -120 feet per minute.

> A descent is in the negative direction. So, we translate the change in elevation as -720 feet.

TRY **Practice dividing two integers in a real-world situation**

Solve.

1 Find the change in elevation per minute of a hiker who descended 320 feet in 40 minutes.

© 2020 Marshall Cavendish Education Pte Ltd

INDEPENDENT PRACTICE

Evaluate each product.

① $5 \cdot (-7)$

② $12 \cdot (-9)$

③ $-6 \cdot 8$

④ $-3 \cdot 15$

⑤ $-4 \cdot (-12)$

⑥ $-8 \cdot (-20)$

⑦ $-14 \cdot 0$

⑧ $0 \cdot (-50)$

⑨ $-3 \cdot 12 \cdot 7$

⑩ $8 \cdot (-4) \cdot 2$

⑪ $20 \cdot 5 \cdot (-5)$

⑫ $-4 \cdot 10 \cdot (-6)$

⑬ $-7 \cdot (-2) \cdot 10$

⑭ $9 \cdot (-6) \cdot (-4)$

⑮ $-2 \cdot (-8) \cdot (-7)$

⑯ $-5 \cdot (-12) \cdot (-3)$

⑰ $14 \cdot 0 \cdot (-15)$

⑱ $-30 \cdot (-2) \cdot 0$

⑲ $-6 \cdot (-7) \cdot 2 \cdot 5$

⑳ $-8 \cdot (-2) \cdot (-4) \cdot 12$

㉑ $-9 \cdot (-5) \cdot (-4) \cdot (-3)$

Evaluate each quotient.

㉒ $125 \div (-25)$

㉓ $300 \div (-15)$

㉔ $-100 \div 25$

㉕ − 32 ÷ 4

㉖ − 480 ÷ (− 12)

㉗ − 144 ÷ (− 24)

㉘ 0 ÷ (− 8)

㉙ 0 ÷ (− 111)

Solve.

㉚ While returning to the glider port, Susan descended at a rate of 380 feet per minute for 3 minutes. Calculate her change in altitude.

㉛ A scuba diver took 6 minutes to rise to the surface at a rate of 20 feet per minute. How far was he below sea level?

㉜ A scientist measures the change in height per second of a diving osprey as − 198 feet per second. Find the change in the osprey's position after 2 seconds.

㉝ **Mathematical Habit 2** Use mathematical reasoning

Nicole wrote $-25 \div (-100) = \dfrac{-25}{-100} = -\left(\dfrac{1}{4}\right)$ and $-2 \cdot (-2) = -4$.

Discuss and correct her mistakes.

㉞ **Mathematical Habit 2** Use mathematical reasoning

Ian has trouble solving $-12 \div 3 \cdot 2 \div (-4)$. Write an explanation to help him.

 # Order of Operations with Integers

Learning Objective:
• Use addition, subtraction, multiplication, and division with integers.

THINK

Ravi thinks he can evaluate $8 \div (3 - 1) \cdot 2 + 4$ and $-8 \div (3 - 1) \cdot 2 + 4$ the same way.
Do you agree? Explain your reasoning.

ENGAGE

Use the order of operations to evaluate $8 \div 2 - 3 + 4(-5)$.
List the steps you would follow.

Create a mathematical expression involving the use of the order of operations.
Trade your expression with a partner and solve it.

Apply the order of operations with integers

The order of operations for integers is the same as the order of operations for whole numbers, fractions, and decimals.

 STEP 1 For expressions involving parentheses, evaluate expressions within parentheses first.

 STEP 2 Evaluate exponents.

 STEP 3 Working from left to right, perform multiplication and division.

 STEP 4 Working from left to right, perform addition and subtraction.

For expressions with parentheses, there may be more than one way of solving.
For example, evaluate $-13 + (-4) \cdot (2 - 10) + 8$.

▶ **Method 1**

Follow the order of operations.

$-13 + (-4) \cdot \underbrace{(2 - 10)} + 8$ Subtract within the parentheses.

$= -13 + \underbrace{(-4) \cdot (-8)} + 8$ Multiply.

$= -13 + \underbrace{\mathbf{32}} + 8$ Use the associative property of addition.

$= -13 + \underbrace{\qquad \mathbf{40}}$ Add.

$= \qquad 27$ Add.

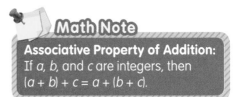

Math Note

Associative Property of Addition:
If a, b, and c are integers, then
$(a + b) + c = a + (b + c)$.

▶ **Method 2**

Use the distributive property first.

Caution

$(-4)(2 - 10) \neq (-4)(2) + (-4)(10)$

$-13 + (-4) \cdot (2 - 10) + 8$
$= -13 + (-4) \cdot (2) - (-4) \cdot (10) + 8$ Use the distributive property.
$= -13 + (-8) - (-40) + 8$ Multiply.
$= -13 + (-8) + 40 + 8$ Rewrite subtraction as adding the opposite.
$= -13 + 40 + (-8) + 8$ Use the commutative property of addition.
$= 27$ Add.

② Evaluate $-9 - 32 \div 4 - 21$.

$-9 - \mathbf{32 \div 4} - 21$
$= -9 - \mathbf{8} - 21$ Divide.
$= -9 + (-8) + (-21)$ Rewrite subtraction as adding the opposite.
$= \mathbf{-9 + (-21)} + (-8)$ Use the commutative property of addition.
$= \mathbf{-30} + (-8)$ Add.
$= -38$ Add.

Evaluate from left to right.
First, multiply and divide.
Then, add and subtract.

③ Evaluate $-5 + (8 - 12) \cdot (-4)$.

$-5 + \underbrace{\mathbf{(8 - 12)}} \cdot (-4)$

$= -5 + \underbrace{\mathbf{(-4)} \cdot (-4)}$ Simplify within the parentheses.

$= -5 + \underbrace{\qquad \mathbf{16}}$ Multiply.

$= \qquad 11$ Add.

Evaluate from left to right. First, evaluate
within the parentheses. Next, multiply
and divide. Then, add and subtract.

Evaluate each expression.

1. $14 + 8 - 9 \cdot 6$

2. $(-25 - 5) \div 6 - 21$

3. $-14 - (3 + 3) \cdot 2$

4. $48 \div (-8 + 6) + 2 \cdot 28$

ENGAGE

A game show awards 30 points for each correct answer and deducts 50 points for each incorrect answer. A contestant answers 2 questions incorrectly and 3 questions correctly. How do you write an expression to find the contestant's final score? Discuss.

LEARN Apply the order of operations with integers in a real-world situation

1. Ana uses a piece of rectangular paper to make a paper box. The paper's dimensions are 12 inches by 9 inches. To make the paper box, Ana cuts 4 identical rectangles from the corners of the paper. These cut-off rectangles are shown in the diagram on the right. What is the area of the piece of paper that remains?

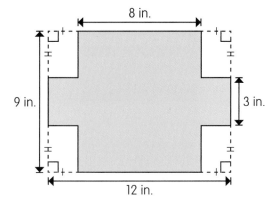

Length of 1 cut-off rectangle: $\left(\dfrac{9-3}{2}\right) = 3$ in.

Width of 1 cut-off rectangle: $\left(\dfrac{12-8}{2}\right) = 2$ in.

Area of remaining paper:

Area of original paper − Area of 4 cut-off rectangles
$= 12 \cdot 9 - 4(3 \cdot 2)$ Write an expression.
$= 108 - 24$ Multiply.
$= 84$ in.^{2} Subtract.

The area of the remaining paper is 84 square inches.

TRY Practice applying the order of operations with integers in a real-world situation

Solve.

1. Luis drew a hexagon on a 3-inch piece of square paper. He cut 4 identical right triangles from the corners of the paper.

   The height of each triangle was $\frac{1}{2}$ the length of the paper.

   The base of each triangle was $\frac{1}{3}$ the length of the paper.

   What was the area of the piece of paper that remained after these triangles were cut off?

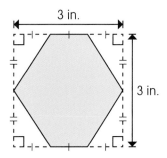

INDEPENDENT PRACTICE

Evaluate each expression.

1 $-3 \cdot 5 + 7$

2 $50 \div (-5) + (-4)$

3 $4 \cdot (-6) + (-3) \cdot 5$

4 $11 - 2 \cdot 8 - (-9)$

5 $-64 \div 4 \cdot 5 - 37$

6 $-28 - 350 \div 7 + 8$

7 $100 - (8 - 15) \cdot 9$

8 $70 \div (-4 - 3) + 60$

9 $(4 + 2) \cdot 3 - 8 \cdot (2 + 3)$

10 $-20 + 4 \cdot (2 + 7) - 35$

11 $15 \div (4 + 1) - 8 \cdot 3$

12 $24 \div 4 - (-13 + 3) \cdot 2$

13 $-12 + 50 \div (-2 - 3) + 72 \div (4 + 2)$

14 $180 \div (4 + 16) - 8 \cdot 3 + 7 \cdot (2 + 3)$

Solve.

15 Ella made a sketch of an octagonal window on a 27-inch square piece of paper. First, she cut 4 identical isosceles triangles from the corners of the paper. Then, she cut a square from the center of the octagon. Each leg of a cut-off triangle is $\frac{1}{3}$ the length of the paper. The side length of the cut-out square is also $\frac{1}{3}$ the length of the paper. What is the area of the sketch after she removed the triangles and the square?

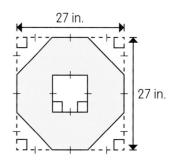

27 in.

27 in.

16 **Mathematical Habit 2** Use mathematical reasoning

Suppose that Lillian shows you some of her homework:

$$-2(6 - 8) = -2(6) - 2(8)$$
$$= -12 - 16$$
$$= -28$$

Lillian made a common error when she used the distributive property to evaluate the expression $-2(6 - 8)$. Evaluate the expression using the order of operations. Then, explain how Lillian can correctly use the distributive property to evaluate the expression.

17 Sarah took three turns in a video game. She scored -120 points during her first turn, 320 points during her second turn, and -80 points during her third turn. What was her average score for the three turns?

18 **Mathematical Habit 6** Use precise mathematical language

Benjamin wrote: $-20 + 4 \cdot 2 + 7 - 35 = -19$. Where can he place the parentheses so that the equation will be a true statement?

© 2020 Marshall Cavendish Education Pte Ltd

Operations with Fractions and Mixed Numbers

Learning Objectives:
- Add and subtract fractions and mixed numbers.
- Multiply and divide fractions and mixed numbers.

> **New Vocabulary**
> least common denominator
> complex fraction

THINK

Gracie thinks that when she adds the mixed number $-3\frac{1}{2}$ and the fraction $\frac{1}{4}$, the answer is negative. She also thinks that their difference, product, and quotient are negative. Do you agree? Explain your reasoning.

ENGAGE

Add $\frac{1}{5}$ and $\frac{2}{3}$. Now, add $\frac{1}{5}$ and $-\frac{2}{3}$. How does having a negative addend change the sum? Explain.

LEARN Add rational numbers

1. A rational number is a number that can be written as $\frac{m}{n}$, where m and n are integers with $n \neq 0$. If $\frac{m}{n}$ is negative, either m or n can be negative but not both m and n.

   You may rewrite rational numbers with a common denominator before you add them.

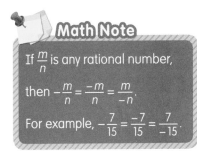

> **Math Note**
> If $\frac{m}{n}$ is any rational number,
> then $-\frac{m}{n} = \frac{-m}{n} = \frac{m}{-n}$.
> For example, $-\frac{7}{15} = \frac{-7}{15} = \frac{7}{-15}$.

The sum of two rational numbers with the same denominator:

Let $\frac{a}{b}$ and $\frac{c}{b}$ be any rational numbers.

$$\frac{a}{b} + \frac{c}{b} = \frac{a+c}{b}$$

The sum of two rational numbers with different denominators:

Let $\frac{a}{b}$ and $\frac{c}{d}$ be any rational numbers.

$$\frac{a}{b} + \frac{c}{d} = \frac{ad+bc}{bd}$$

To add two rational numbers such as $\frac{1}{5}$ and $\frac{-2}{3}$, you can apply the rules you know for adding integers.

First, find the **least common denominator** (LCD) of $\frac{1}{5}$ and $\frac{-2}{3}$, which is 15. Then, use the LCD to write equivalent fractions and evaluate.

$$\frac{1}{5} + \frac{-2}{3} = \frac{1 \cdot \mathbf{3}}{5 \cdot \mathbf{3}} + \frac{-2 \cdot \mathbf{5}}{3 \cdot \mathbf{5}} \qquad \text{Write equivalent fractions using the LCD.}$$

$$= \frac{3}{15} + \frac{-10}{15} \qquad \text{Multiply all products.}$$

$$= \frac{3 + (-10)}{15} \qquad \text{Simplify using a single denominator.}$$

$$= \frac{-7}{15} \qquad \text{Add.}$$

2 Evaluate $\frac{-2}{7} + \frac{3}{-5}$.

$$\frac{-2}{7} + \frac{3}{-5} = \frac{-2 \cdot (\mathbf{-5})}{7 \cdot (\mathbf{-5})} + \frac{3 \cdot \mathbf{7}}{-5 \cdot \mathbf{7}} \qquad \text{Write equivalent fractions using the LCD.}$$

$$= \frac{10}{-35} + \frac{21}{-35} \qquad \text{Multiply all products.}$$

$$= \frac{10 + 21}{-35} \qquad \text{Simplify using a single denominator.}$$

$$= \frac{31}{-35} \qquad \text{Add.}$$

$$= -\frac{31}{35} \qquad \text{Write an equivalent fraction.}$$

3 Evaluate $1\frac{2}{3} + \left(-2\frac{1}{6}\right)$.

$$1\frac{2}{3} + \left(-2\frac{1}{6}\right) = 1\frac{2 \cdot 2}{3 \cdot 2} + \left(-2\frac{1}{6}\right) \qquad \text{Rewrite the fraction part of each mixed number using the LCD.}$$

$$= 1\frac{4}{6} + \left(-2\frac{1}{6}\right) \qquad \text{Multiply all products.}$$

$$= 1 + \frac{4}{6} + (-2) + \left(-\frac{1}{6}\right) \qquad \text{Rewrite the sum.}$$

$$= 1 + (-2) + \frac{4}{6} + \left(-\frac{1}{6}\right) \qquad \text{Use the commutative property of addition.}$$

$$= -1 + \left(\frac{3}{6}\right) \qquad \text{Add the integers and the fractions.}$$

$$= \frac{-6}{6} + \frac{3}{6} \qquad \text{Write an equivalent fraction for the integer part using the same LCD.}$$

$$= -\frac{3}{6} \qquad \text{Add the like fractions.}$$

$$= -\frac{1}{2} \qquad \text{Write in simplest form.}$$

⚠️ **Caution**

$-2\frac{1}{6}$ is the sum of -2 and $-\frac{1}{6}$. Both the fraction part and the integer part of the mixed number are negative.

$$-2\frac{1}{6} = -2 + \left(-\frac{1}{6}\right)$$
$$= -2 - \frac{1}{6}$$
$$-2\frac{1}{6} \neq -2 + \frac{1}{6}$$

4 Evaluate $\frac{2}{5} + \left(\frac{-4}{15}\right) + \frac{1}{10}$.

▶ **Method 1**

Add two rational numbers at a time, working from left to right.

$$\frac{2}{5} + \left(\frac{-4}{15}\right) + \frac{1}{10} = \frac{2 \cdot 3}{5 \cdot 3} + \left(\frac{-4}{15}\right) + \frac{1}{10}$$ Write equivalent fractions for the first two fractions using the LCD.

$$= \frac{6}{15} + \left(\frac{-4}{15}\right) + \frac{1}{10}$$ Multiply all products.

$$= \frac{6 + (-4)}{15} + \frac{1}{10}$$ Write the first two fractions using a single denominator.

$$= \frac{2}{15} + \frac{1}{10}$$ Add.

$$= \frac{2 \cdot 2}{15 \cdot 2} + \frac{1 \cdot 3}{10 \cdot 3}$$ Write equivalent fractions using the LCD of the fractions in the new sum.

$$= \frac{4}{30} + \frac{3}{30}$$ Multiply all products.

$$= \frac{7}{30}$$ Add the like fractions.

▶ **Method 2**

Use a common denominator for all three fractions.

> Finding the LCD of $\frac{2}{5}$, $\frac{-4}{15}$, and $\frac{1}{10}$ is the same as finding the least common multiple (LCM) of 5, 15, and 10.
>
> $5 \,|\, \underline{5, \ 10, \ 15}$ Divide by the common prime factor 5.
> $ 1, \ \ 2, \ \ 3$ Stop dividing because 1, 2, and 3 have no common factor other than 1.
>
> $5 \cdot 1 \cdot 2 \cdot 3 = 30$ Multiply the factors.
> The LCM of 5, 10, and 15 is 30.

$$\frac{2}{5} + \left(\frac{-4}{15}\right) + \frac{1}{10} = \frac{2 \cdot 6}{5 \cdot 6} + \frac{-4 \cdot 2}{15 \cdot 2} + \frac{1 \cdot 3}{10 \cdot 3}$$ Write equivalent fractions using the LCD of all three fractions.

$$= \frac{12}{30} + \left(\frac{-8}{30}\right) + \frac{3}{30}$$ Multiply.

$$= \frac{12 + (-8) + 3}{30}$$ Rewrite using a single denominator.

$$= \frac{7}{30}$$ Add.

Evaluate each expression.

1 $\dfrac{-1}{9} + \dfrac{2}{-5}$

2 $-1\dfrac{1}{6} + 3\dfrac{4}{9}$

3 $\dfrac{1}{6} + \left(\dfrac{-5}{9}\right) + \left(\dfrac{-1}{3}\right)$

ENGAGE

Subtract $\dfrac{1}{4}$ from $\dfrac{1}{2}$. Now, subtract $\dfrac{1}{2}$ from $\dfrac{1}{4}$. How does changing the order of the numbers affect the result? Explain.

LEARN Subtract rational numbers

1 As with fractions, you may need to rewrite rational numbers so that they have a common denominator before you subtract.

> **The difference between two rational numbers with the same denominator:**
>
> Let $\dfrac{a}{b}$ and $\dfrac{c}{b}$ be any rational numbers. $\dfrac{a}{b} - \dfrac{c}{b} = \dfrac{a-c}{b}$
>
> **The difference between two rational numbers with different denominators:**
>
> Let $\dfrac{a}{b}$ and $\dfrac{c}{d}$ be any rational numbers. $\dfrac{a}{b} - \dfrac{c}{d} = \dfrac{ad-bc}{bd}$

For example, subtract $\dfrac{1}{2}$ from $\dfrac{2}{5}$.

$\dfrac{2}{5} - \dfrac{1}{2} = \dfrac{2 \cdot 2}{5 \cdot 2} - \dfrac{1 \cdot 5}{2 \cdot 5}$ Write equivalent fractions using the LCD.

$= \dfrac{4}{10} - \dfrac{5}{10}$ Multiply.

$= \dfrac{4-5}{10}$ Rewrite using a single denominator.

$= \dfrac{-1}{10}$ Subtract.

$= -\dfrac{1}{10}$ Write an equivalent fraction.

> Remember that subtracting a number is the same as adding its opposite.
> For example, $4 - 5 = 4 + (-5)$
> $= -1$

⚠️ **Caution**

The phrase "subtract a from b" does not mean $a - b$. It means $b - a$.

So, the phrase "subtract $\dfrac{1}{2}$ from $\dfrac{3}{5}$" means $\dfrac{3}{5} - \dfrac{1}{2}$.

2 Evaluate $\frac{1}{6} - \frac{3}{4}$.

$\frac{1}{6} - \frac{3}{4} = \frac{1 \cdot \mathbf{2}}{6 \cdot \mathbf{2}} - \frac{3 \cdot \mathbf{3}}{4 \cdot \mathbf{3}}$ Write equivalent fractions using the LCD.

$= \frac{2}{12} - \frac{9}{12}$ Multiply.

$= \frac{2 - 9}{12}$ Rewrite using a single denominator.

$= \frac{-7}{12}$ Subtract.

$= -\frac{7}{12}$ Rewrite an equivalent fraction.

3 Evaluate $2\frac{1}{4} - 4\frac{2}{3}$.

$2\frac{1}{4} - 4\frac{2}{3} = 2\frac{1 \cdot \mathbf{3}}{4 \cdot \mathbf{3}} - 4\frac{2 \cdot \mathbf{4}}{3 \cdot \mathbf{4}}$ Write equivalent fractions for the fraction part of each mixed number using the LCD.

$= 2\frac{3}{12} - 4\frac{8}{12}$ Multiply.

$= 2 + \frac{3}{12} - 4 - \frac{8}{12}$ Rewrite.

$= 2 - 4 + \left(\frac{3}{12} - \frac{8}{12} \right)$ Use the commutative property of addition.

$= -2 + \left(-\frac{5}{12} \right)$ Subtract the integers and the fractions.

$= -2\frac{5}{12}$ Simplify.

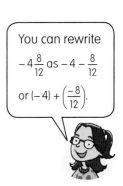

You can rewrite

$-4\frac{8}{12}$ as $-4 - \frac{8}{12}$

or $(-4) + \left(\frac{-8}{12} \right)$.

4 Evaluate $\frac{1}{3} - \frac{11}{12} - \frac{1}{2}$.

▶ **Method 1**

Subtract two rational numbers at a time, working from left to right.

$\frac{1}{3} - \frac{11}{12} - \frac{1}{2} = \frac{1 \cdot \mathbf{4}}{3 \cdot \mathbf{4}} - \frac{11}{12} - \frac{1}{2}$ Write equivalent fractions for the first two fractions using their LCD.

$= \frac{4}{12} - \frac{11}{12} - \frac{1}{2}$ Multiply.

$= \frac{4 - 11}{12} - \frac{1}{2}$ Rewrite the first two fractions using a single denominator.

$= \frac{-7}{12} - \frac{1}{2}$ Subtract.

$= \frac{-7}{12} - \frac{1 \cdot \mathbf{6}}{2 \cdot \mathbf{6}}$ Write equivalent fractions using the LCD.

$= \frac{-7}{12} - \frac{6}{12}$ Multiply.

$= \frac{-7 - 6}{12}$ Rewrite using a single denominator.

$= \frac{-13}{12}$ Subtract.

$= -1\frac{1}{12}$ Rewrite the improper fraction as a mixed number.

▶ Method 2

Use a common denominator for all three fractions.

$$\frac{1}{3} - \frac{11}{12} - \frac{1}{2} = \frac{1 \cdot 4}{3 \cdot 4} - \frac{11}{12} - \frac{1 \cdot 6}{2 \cdot 6}$$ Write equivalent fractions using the LCD for all three fractions.

$$= \frac{4}{12} - \frac{11}{12} - \frac{6}{12}$$ Multiply.

$$= \frac{4 - 11 - 6}{12}$$ Rewrite using a single denominator.

$$= \frac{-13}{12}$$ Subtract.

$$= -1\frac{1}{12}$$ Rewrite the improper fraction as a mixed number.

TRY Practice subtracting rational numbers

Evaluate each expression.

1 $\frac{7}{8} - \frac{9}{10}$

2 $3\frac{1}{4} - 7\frac{5}{6}$

3 $\frac{3}{7} - \frac{27}{28} - \frac{3}{14}$

ENGAGE

What is $\frac{1}{2}$ of $\frac{1}{3}$? What is $\frac{1}{2}$ of $-\frac{1}{3}$? Draw a sketch to show your thinking.

LEARN Multiply rational numbers

1 You have learned how to multiply positive fractions and how to multiply positive and negative integers. So, you can multiply both positive and negative rational numbers using the same rules for the signs of the products.

Multiply rational numbers with the same sign.

Examples:

$$\frac{1}{2} \cdot \frac{3}{4} = \frac{1 \cdot 3}{2 \cdot 4} = \frac{3}{8}, \text{ and } \left(-\frac{1}{2}\right) \cdot \left(-\frac{3}{4}\right) = \frac{1 \cdot 3}{2 \cdot 4} = \frac{3}{8}.$$

Multiply rational numbers with different signs.

Examples:

$$\frac{1}{2} \cdot \left(-\frac{3}{4}\right) = -\frac{1 \cdot 3}{2 \cdot 4} = -\frac{3}{8}, \text{ and } \left(-\frac{1}{2}\right) \cdot \frac{3}{4} = -\frac{1 \cdot 3}{2 \cdot 4} = -\frac{3}{8}.$$

> **Math Note**
>
> **Multiplying Positive and Negative Rational Numbers:**
>
> Two signs are the same:
> $(+) \cdot (+) = (+)$
> $(-) \cdot (-) = (+)$
> The product is positive.
>
> Two signs are different:
> $(+) \cdot (-) = (-)$
> $(-) \cdot (+) = (-)$
> The product is negative.

2 Evaluate $-\frac{3}{7} \cdot \frac{8}{15}$.

$-\frac{3}{7} \cdot \frac{8}{15} = \frac{-3 \cdot 8}{7 \cdot 15}$ Multiply the numerators, and multiply the denominators.

$= \frac{-1}{7 \cdot \cancel{15}_5}$ Divide the numerator and denominator by their greatest common factor (GCF), 3.

$= -\frac{8}{35}$ Simplify.

3 Evaluate $-2\frac{3}{5} \cdot \left(-1\frac{1}{4}\right)$.

$-2\frac{3}{5} \cdot \left(-1\frac{1}{4}\right) = -\frac{13}{5} \cdot \left(-\frac{5}{4}\right)$ Write as improper fractions.

$= \frac{13 \cdot \cancel{5}^1}{\cancel{5} \cdot 4}$ Divide the numerator and denominator by their GCF, 5.

$= \frac{13}{4}$ Simplify.

$= 3\frac{1}{4}$ Write as a mixed number.

TRY Practice multiplying rational numbers

Evaluate each product.

1 $-\frac{4}{5} \cdot \frac{20}{21}$

2 $-3\frac{1}{4} \cdot \left(-2\frac{2}{3}\right)$

ENGAGE

Do the rules for multiplying negative fractions apply to dividing negative fractions? How do you know? Explain your reasoning by providing specific examples.

LEARN Divide rational numbers

1 You have learned that dividing by a fraction is the same as multiplying by the reciprocal of the fraction.

You can use this same method to divide rational numbers, but you need to apply what you know about dividing numbers with the same or different signs.

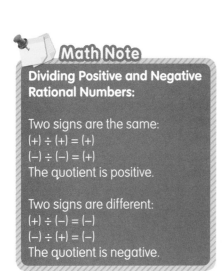

Math Note

Dividing Positive and Negative Rational Numbers:

Two signs are the same:
$(+) \div (+) = (+)$
$(-) \div (-) = (+)$
The quotient is positive.

Two signs are different:
$(+) \div (-) = (-)$
$(-) \div (+) = (-)$
The quotient is negative.

Two numbers are reciprocals if their product is 1.

3 and − 3 are not reciprocals because their product is − 9, not 1.

− 5 and $-\frac{1}{5}$ are reciprocals because their product is 1.

So, $3 \div \frac{1}{5} = 3 \cdot 5$.

The quotient of two rational numbers may be written as a complex fraction. A complex fraction is a fraction in which the numerator, the denominator, or both the numerator and denominator contain a fraction.

An example of a complex fraction whose numerator and denominator contain a fraction is

$\left(\frac{1}{3}\right)$ ⟶ **Numerator**
$\left(\frac{5}{6}\right)$ ⟶ **Denominator**

Other examples of complex fractions include $\dfrac{\left(\frac{2}{7}\right)}{8}$, $\dfrac{3}{\left(-\frac{5}{2}\right)}$, and $\dfrac{\left(-4\frac{1}{2}\right)}{\left(-1\frac{5}{16}\right)}$.

To simplify a complex fraction, rewrite the fraction using a division symbol '÷'.

$\dfrac{\left(\frac{1}{3}\right)}{\left(\frac{5}{6}\right)} = \dfrac{1}{3} \div \dfrac{5}{6}$ Rewrite as a division expression.

$= \dfrac{1}{3} \cdot \dfrac{6}{5}$ Multiply $\frac{1}{3}$ by the reciprocal of $\frac{5}{6}$.

$= \dfrac{1 \cdot 6}{3 \cdot 5}$ Multiply the numerators and denominators.

$= \dfrac{1 \cdot \overset{2}{\cancel{6}}}{\underset{1}{\cancel{3}} \cdot 5}$ Divide the numerator and the denominator by the GCF, 3.

$= \dfrac{2}{5}$ Simplify.

② Evaluate $-\dfrac{5}{6} \div \dfrac{1}{24}$.

$-\dfrac{5}{6} \div \dfrac{1}{24} = -\dfrac{5}{6} \cdot \dfrac{24}{1}$ Multiply $-\frac{5}{6}$ by the reciprocal of $\frac{1}{24}$.

$= \dfrac{-5 \cdot 24}{6 \cdot 1}$ Multiply the numerators and denominators.

$= \dfrac{-5 \cdot \overset{4}{\cancel{24}}}{\underset{1}{\cancel{6}} \cdot 1}$ Divide the numerator and denominator by the GCF, 6.

$= \dfrac{-20}{1}$ Simplify.

$= -20$ Write as a negative integer.

③ Evaluate $-5\frac{1}{3} \div \left(-2\frac{2}{5}\right)$.

$$-5\frac{1}{3} \div \left(-2\frac{2}{5}\right) = \frac{-16}{3} \div \frac{-12}{5} \qquad \text{Write as improper fractions.}$$

$$= \frac{-16}{3} \cdot \frac{5}{-12} \qquad \text{Multiply } \frac{-16}{3} \text{ by the reciprocal of } \frac{-12}{5}.$$

$$= \frac{^{4}\cancel{16} \cdot 5}{3 \cdot \cancel{12}_{3}} \qquad \begin{array}{l}\text{Multiply the numerators and denominators.} \\ \text{Divide the numerators and denominators by the GCF, 4.}\end{array}$$

$$= \frac{20}{9} \qquad \text{Simplify.}$$

$$= 2\frac{2}{9} \qquad \text{Write as a mixed number.}$$

④ Evaluate $\dfrac{\left(-\frac{1}{4}\right)}{\left(\frac{1}{2}\right)}$.

$$\frac{\left(-\frac{1}{4}\right)}{\left(\frac{1}{2}\right)} = -\frac{1}{4} \div \frac{1}{2} \qquad \text{Rewrite as a division expression.}$$

$$= -\frac{1}{4} \cdot \frac{2}{1} \qquad \text{Multiply } -\frac{1}{4} \text{ by the reciprocal of } \frac{1}{2}.$$

$$= -\frac{2}{4} \qquad \text{Multiply numerators and denominators.}$$

$$= -\frac{1}{2} \qquad \text{Write in simplest form.}$$

> $\frac{a}{b}$ means the same as $a \div b$. So, $\dfrac{\left(-\frac{1}{4}\right)}{\left(\frac{1}{2}\right)}$ is the same as $-\frac{1}{4} \div \frac{1}{2}$.

TRY **Practice dividing rational numbers**

Evaluate each quotient.

① $\dfrac{3}{20} \div \left(-\dfrac{6}{35}\right)$

② $-3\dfrac{1}{3} \div \left(-1\dfrac{1}{4}\right)$

③ $\dfrac{\left(\frac{1}{4}\right)}{\left(-\frac{3}{8}\right)}$

ENGAGE

A clock's battery is running low. Every 6 hours, the clock slows down by $\frac{1}{2}$ hour. How do you find out how much time the clock slows down by in 1 hour? Share your method.

LEARN Add, subtract, multiply, and divide rational numbers in a real-world situation

1 Mr. Turner has a partial roll of wire $18\frac{1}{4}$ feet long.

He needs $25\frac{1}{2}$ feet of wire for a remodeling project.

How much wire is he short of?

$18\frac{1}{4} - 25\frac{1}{2}$	Write an expression for this situation.
$= 18\frac{1}{4} - 25\frac{1 \cdot 2}{2 \cdot 2}$	Write equivalent fractions for the fraction parts using the LCD, 4.
$= 18\frac{1}{4} - 25\frac{2}{4}$	Multiply.
$= 18 + \frac{1}{4} - 25 - \frac{2}{4}$	Rewrite.
$= 18 - 25 + \left(\frac{1}{4} - \frac{2}{4}\right)$	Use the commutative property of addition to group the integers, and then the fractions.
$= -7 + \left(-\frac{1}{4}\right)$	Subtract the integers and then the fractions.
$= -7\frac{1}{4}$	Subtract.

He is short of $7\frac{1}{4}$ feet of wire.

TRY Practice adding, subtracting, multiplying, and dividing rational numbers in a real-world situation

Solve.

1 Philadelphia suffered a severe snowstorm in 1996 that left $30\frac{7}{10}$ inches of snow on the ground. Another severe snowstorm occurred in 2010, when $28\frac{1}{2}$ inches of snow fell.

a Write a subtraction expression for the difference in depth of these two record snowfalls.

b Rewrite the expression as an addition expression.

c Find the difference between the two record snowfalls.

2 A pancake recipe requires $1\frac{2}{3}$ cups of flour to make 20 pancakes and you have 9 cups of flour.

a How many pancakes can you make with 1 cup of flour?

b How many pancakes can you make with 9 cups of flour?

INDEPENDENT PRACTICE

Evaluate each expression. Give your answer in simplest form.

1 $\frac{1}{2} + \left(-\frac{5}{6}\right)$

2 $\frac{-6}{7} + \frac{3}{14}$

3 $-\frac{1}{7} + \frac{-3}{5}$

4 $\frac{1}{2} + \left(-\frac{2}{5}\right) + \frac{1}{4}$

5 $\frac{-1}{7} + \frac{-5}{6} + \frac{-1}{3}$

6 $\frac{3}{5} - \frac{2}{3}$

7 $\frac{-1}{7} - \frac{3}{14}$

8 $-\frac{1}{5} - \frac{-2}{7}$

9 $\frac{1}{3} - \left(-\frac{2}{5}\right) - \frac{3}{4}$

Evaluate each product. Give your answer in simplest form.

10 $-\frac{7}{25} \cdot \frac{5}{14}$

11 $\frac{5}{8} \cdot \left(-\frac{4}{15}\right)$

12 $\frac{7}{30} \cdot \left(-\frac{6}{7}\right)$

13 $-\frac{8}{27} \cdot \left(-\frac{9}{40}\right)$

14 $-\frac{11}{16} \cdot \left(-\frac{4}{33}\right)$

15 $\frac{5}{8} \cdot \left(-2\frac{4}{5}\right)$

16 $-\frac{3}{22} \cdot 1\frac{5}{6}$

17 $3\frac{1}{8} \cdot \left(-\frac{3}{10}\right)$

18 $-4\frac{1}{2} \cdot \left(-1\frac{8}{9}\right)$

Evaluate each quotient. Give your answer in simplest form.

19 $\frac{9}{25} \div (-18)$

20 $-\frac{3}{8} \div \left(-\frac{1}{8}\right)$

21 $-\frac{1}{4} \div \frac{3}{8}$

22 $\frac{5}{12} \div \left(-\frac{1}{6}\right)$

23 $-1\frac{1}{4} \div \frac{3}{4}$

24 $\frac{8}{15} \div \left(-2\frac{2}{3}\right)$

25 $2\frac{1}{2} \div \left(-1\frac{2}{3}\right)$

26 $-2\frac{2}{7} \div \left(-1\frac{3}{7}\right)$

27 $\frac{-7}{\left(-\frac{7}{3}\right)}$

28 $\frac{\left(-\frac{2}{3}\right)}{4}$

29 $\frac{\left(-\frac{3}{4}\right)}{\left(-\frac{5}{8}\right)}$

30 $\frac{\left(-\frac{1}{5}\right)}{\left(1\frac{2}{15}\right)}$

Solve.

31 Daniel biked $15\frac{9}{10}$ miles on Saturday and $6\frac{7}{10}$ miles on Sunday. How much farther did Daniel bike on Saturday than on Sunday?

32 A recipe calls for $\frac{3}{4}$ cup of flour, but David has only $\frac{1}{3}$ cup of flour. How much more flour does he need?

33 A weather report showed that the rainfall in Janesville was $2\frac{2}{3}$ inches during the first half of January. At the end of January, the total rainfall was $3\frac{1}{4}$ inches. How much did it rain in the second half of January?

34 The sum of two rational numbers is $5\frac{1}{2}$. If one of the numbers is $6\frac{3}{14}$, find the other number.

35 **Mathematical Habit 3** **Construct viable arguments**
Melanie adds $\frac{1}{a} + \left(-\frac{1}{b}\right)$ and says the answer is $\frac{1}{a-b}$. Give an example to show that Melanie is wrong.

36 **Mathematical Habit 6** **Use precise mathematical language**
Juan multiplies two mixed numbers, $-4\frac{3}{5}$ and $1\frac{2}{7}$, as shown. Describe Juan's mistakes. What is the correct answer?

$$-4\frac{3}{5} \cdot 1\frac{2}{7} = -4 \cdot 1 \cdot \frac{3}{5} \cdot \frac{2}{7}$$
$$= -4 \cdot \frac{3 \cdot 2}{5 \cdot 7}$$
$$= -4\frac{6}{35}$$

37 Package A weighs $5\frac{1}{2}$ pounds and Package B weighs $1\frac{1}{4}$ pounds. Find the average weight of the two packages.

38 A scientist measured the weight of some damp soil. After exposing the soil to the air for $4\frac{1}{2}$ weeks, the scientist found that the weight had decreased by $5\frac{5}{8}$ ounces. Find the soil's average weight loss per week.

39 A plank measures $4\frac{3}{4}$ feet. Rachel cuts off $\frac{2}{5}$ of the plank. How long is the plank now?

11 Operations with Decimals

Learning Objectives:
• Add and subtract decimals.
• Multiply and divide numbers in decimal or percent form.

THINK

Sofia evaluated the expression as shown.

$$-3.2 \cdot (-2.5 + 0.3) \div 0.4 = -3.2 \cdot (-2.2) \div 0.4$$
$$= -5.4 \div 0.4$$
$$= -13.5$$

Do you agree with Sofia's solution? Explain your reasoning.

ENGAGE

A company made a profit of $1.65 million in January but a loss of $2.8 million in February. How do you find how much the company lost in total within these two months? Share your method.

LEARN Add and subtract decimals

1. The table shows the monthly profits and losses in dollars of a company for the first three months of one year.

January	February	March
– $2.14 million	– $1.5 million	$2.17 million

From the table, the negative decimals mean that the company lost money doing business in January and February. It made a profit in March.

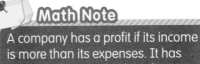

Math Note

A company has a profit if its income is more than its expenses. It has a loss if the income is less than its expenses.

Income and expenses are always positive, but business losses can be represented by negative numbers.

You can find the company's combined loss for January and February, as well as the net profit or loss the company made at the end of the three months.

To find the combined loss for January and February, evaluate the sum of -2.14 and -1.5. In this case, you are adding two negative decimals, -2.14 and -1.5.

Using absolute values,

$|-2.14| + |-1.5| = 2.14 + 1.5$ Add the absolute values.
$= 3.64$ Simplify.

Add the absolute values because you are adding two negative decimals.

Align decimal points
↓

   2 . 1 4
$+$ 1 . 5 0 ← Insert zero
   3 . 6 4

$-2.14 + (-1.5) = -3.64$ Use the common sign, a negative sign.

The combined loss for January and February was $3.64 million.

To find the net profit or loss of the company at the end of the three months, evaluate the sum of -2.14, -1.5, and 2.17. Since $-2.14 + (-1.5) = -3.64$, you only need to find $-3.64 + 2.17$. In this case, you are adding two decimals with different signs.

Using absolute values,

$|-3.64| - |2.17| = 3.64 - 2.17$ Subtract the lesser absolute value from the greater one.
$= 1.47$ Simplify.

Subtract the absolute values because you are adding two decimals with different signs.

Align decimal points
↓

      5 14
   3 . 6̶ 4̶
$-$ 2 . 1 7
   1 . 4 7

$-3.64 + 2.17 = -1.47$ Use a negative sign because -3.64 has a greater absolute value.

Since -1.47 is negative, you know that the company had a net loss at the end of the three months. The company had a net loss of $1.47 million.

2 Evaluate − 4.52 + 3.26.

Using absolute values,

| −4.52| − |3.26| = 4.52 − 3.26   Subtract the lesser absolute value from the greater one.
                 = 1.26   Simplify.

− 4.52 + 3.26 = − 1.26   Use a negative sign because − 4.52 has a greater absolute value.

3 Evaluate − 7.4 − 5.18.

− 7.4 − 5.18 = − 7.4 + (− 5.18)   Rewrite subtraction as adding the opposite.

Using absolute values,

|− 7.4| + | − 5.18| = 7.4 + 5.18   Add the absolute values.
                = 12.58   Simplify.

− 7.4 − 5.18 = − 12.58   Use the common sign, a negative sign.

TRY Practice adding and subtracting decimals

Evaluate each expression.

1 2.35 + (− 6.13)

2 − 8.6 − 3.27

3 3.38 + (− 5.6)

ENGAGE

a How can you multiply 3.2 by 0.5 in different ways?

b What happens to the product when one of the numbers is negative? What happens when both the numbers are negative? Explain your reasoning.

c How can you multiply 0.75 by a fraction? How can you multiply 0.75 by an integer? How can you multiply 0.75 by another decimal? How does each multiplication differ?

LEARN Multiply numbers in decimal or percent form

1 The rules for multiplying integers also apply to multiplying numbers in decimal form. For example, evaluate the product of − 2.05 and 1.2.

First, multiply the two decimals without their signs. Then, apply what you know about multiplying numbers with the same or different signs.

The product of − 2.05 and 1.2 has a negative sign because the two decimals have different signs. So, the product of − 2.05 and 1.2 is − 2.46.

− 2.05 · 1.2 = − 2.46

$$
\begin{array}{r}
{}^{1} \\
2.0\,5 \leftarrow \text{2 decimal places} \\
\times \quad 1.2 \leftarrow +\text{1 decimal place} \\
\hline
4\,1\,0 \\
2\,0\,5 \\
\hline
2.4\,6\,0 \leftarrow \text{3 decimal places}
\end{array}
$$

2 Evaluate $6.72 \cdot (-0.4)$.

$$
\begin{array}{r}
\overset{2}{6.7\,2} \leftarrow \text{2 decimal places} \\
\times \quad 0.4 \leftarrow +\text{1 decimal place} \\
\hline
2\,6\,8\,8 \\
0\,0\,0 \\
\hline
2.6\,8\,8 \leftarrow \text{3 decimal places}
\end{array}
$$

Multiply the numbers without their signs.

Add.

$6.72 \cdot (-0.4) = -2.688$ Product of two decimals with different signs is negative.

3 Evaluate $-51 \cdot (-8.5)$.

$$
\begin{array}{r}
5\,1 \leftarrow \text{0 decimal place} \\
\times \quad 8.5 \leftarrow +\text{1 decimal place} \\
\hline
2\,5\,5 \\
4\,0\,8 \\
\hline
4\,3\,3.5 \leftarrow \text{1 decimal place}
\end{array}
$$

Multiply the numbers without their signs.

Add.

$-51 \cdot (-8.5) = 433.5$ Product of two decimals with the same sign is positive.

4 Evaluate 6% of 530.

$$
\begin{array}{r}
\overset{1}{5\,3\,0} \leftarrow \text{0 decimal place} \\
\times \quad 0.0\,6 \leftarrow +\text{2 decimal places} \\
\hline
3\,1\,8\,0 \\
0\,0\,0 \\
0\,0\,0 \\
\hline
0\,3\,1.8\,0 \leftarrow \text{2 decimal places}
\end{array}
$$

Multiply the numbers without their signs.

Add.

$6\% \cdot 530 = 31.8$ Product of two numbers with the same sign is positive.

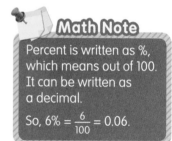

Math Note

Percent is written as %, which means out of 100. It can be written as a decimal.

So, $6\% = \frac{6}{100} = 0.06$.

TRY **Practice multiplying numbers in decimal or percent form**

Evaluate each product.

1 $-7.2 \cdot 4.6$

2 $-37 \cdot (-9.2)$

3 8% of $230

a   How can you divide 0.28 by −0.4 in different ways?

b   What happens to the quotient when one of the numbers is negative? What happens when both the numbers are negative? Explain your reasoning.

c   How can you divide 0.56 by a fraction? How can you divide 0.56 by an integer? How can you divide 0.56 by another decimal? How does each division differ?

LEARN Divide numbers in decimal form

①   The rules for dividing integers also apply to dividing numbers in decimal form.

For example, evaluate − 24.18 ÷ 2.6.

First, divide the two decimals without their signs. Then, use what you know about dividing numbers with the same or different signs.

$$2.6\overline{)24.18}$$ ⟶

Make the divisor a whole number by multiplying both the divisor and the dividend by 10.

```
        9.3
26 )241.8
    234
     78
     78
      0
```

Place the decimal point in the quotient above the decimal point in the dividend

> Use a negative sign because the two decimals have different signs.

− 24.18 ÷ 2.6 = − 9.3

②   Evaluate 13.14 ÷ (− 1.8).

$$1.8\overline{)13.14}$$ ⟶

Make the divisor a whole number by multiplying both the divisor and the dividend by 10.

```
        7.3
18 )131.4
    126
     54
     54
      0
```

Place the decimal point in the quotient above the decimal point in the dividend.

13.14 ÷ (− 1.8) = − 7.3

TRY Practice dividing numbers in decimal form

State whether each quotient is positive or negative. Then, evaluate the quotient.

①   − 21.7 ÷ 0.7

②   − 31.92 ÷ (− 4.2)

Tiana buys 4 boxes of paper clips. She pays with a $10 bill and receives $6.08 in change. How do you write an expression to find the price of 1 box of paper clips? Explain your reasoning.

LEARN Apply the order of operations to decimals in a real-world situation

1. A diver went 30.65 feet below the surface of the ocean, and then 46.5 feet further down. He then rose 52.45 feet. Find the diver's new depth.

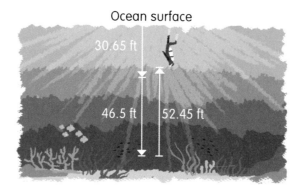

Ocean surface

30.65 ft

46.5 ft   52.45 ft

$-30.65 - 46.5 + 52.45$ Write an expression.
$= -30.65 + (-46.5) + 52.45$ Rewrite subtraction as adding the opposite.

Use absolute values to add the first two numbers.

$|-30.65| + |-46.5| = 30.65 + 46.5$ Add the absolute values of the first two numbers.
$= 77.15$ Simplify.

$-30.65 - 46.5 = -77.15$ Use the common sign, a negative sign.

Use absolute values to add the sum of the first two numbers to the third.

$|-77.15| - |52.45| = 77.15 - 52.45$ Subtract the lesser absolute value.
$= 24.7$ Simplify.

$-77.15 + 52.45 = -24.7$ Use a negative sign because -77.15 has a greater absolute value.

$-30.65 - 46.5 + 52.45 = -24.7$

The diver's new depth is 24.7 feet below the surface of the ocean.

2 A hot air balloon ascended at 0.7 meter per second for 8 seconds. It then descended at 0.5 meter per second for 6 seconds. Find the overall change in altitude.

$$0.7 \cdot 8 - 0.5 \cdot 6 = 5.6 - 3.0 \quad \text{Multiply.}$$
$$= 2.6 \quad \text{Subtract.}$$

The overall change in altitude is 2.6 meters.

3 An electronic game system costs $399 plus a 4% sales tax. What is the total cost of the game system?

▶ **Method 1**

$$\$399 + 0.04 \cdot \$399 = \$399 + \$15.96 \quad \text{Multiply.}$$
$$= \$414.96 \quad \text{Add.}$$

The total cost of the game system is $414.96.

The total cost is more than $399 because the customer must pay a 4% sales tax.

▶ **Method 2**

$$\$399 \cdot 1.04 = \$414.96 \quad \text{Multiply.}$$

The total cost of the game system is $414.96.

TRY **Practice applying the order of operations to decimals in a real-world situation**

Solve.

1. A town's temperature drops by 1.6°F per hour for 1.2 hours. It then drops by 0.8°F per hour for 2.5 hours. Find the total change in temperature.

You can use a negative number to represent the hourly drop in temperature.

2. A baker usually uses 0.5 cup of sugar to bake a raisin cake. To bake a healthier raisin cake, he decreases the amount of sugar by 20%. What is the amount of sugar that the baker uses for baking the healthier raisin cake?

3. Stratosphere Tower in Las Vegas, Nevada, is the tallest freestanding observation tower in the United States. Its height is 350.2 meters. The Eiffel Tower in Paris, France, is the country's tallest building. Its height is 324 meters. Find the difference in the structures' heights.

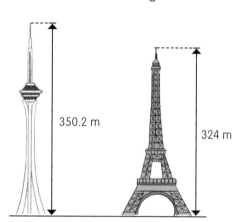

350.2 m

324 m

INDEPENDENT PRACTICE

Evaluate each sum or difference.

1 $-6.25 + 3.9$

2 $-2.074 + 1.8$

3 $-11.52 - 6.3$

4 $-29.4 - (-7.21)$

5 $-8.106 - 0.98$

6 $-3.502 - (-16.8)$

Evaluate each product.

7 $0.3 \cdot (-4.8)$

8 $-1.6 \cdot 2.9$

9 $-3.25 \cdot (-1.7)$

10 $2.03 \cdot (-5.4)$

11 $-0.08 \cdot 3.2$

12 $-0.45 \cdot (-0.82)$

Evaluate each quotient.

13 $-29.52 \div 3.6$

14 $107.64 \div (-2.3)$

15 $-40.56 \div (-5.2)$

Evaluate each expression.

16 $-0.59 - 1.2 - 3.4$

17 $-2.38 + 15.6 - 140.05$

18 $38.92 - 6.7 - (-12.04)$

19 $712.14 - 356.8 - (-9.03)$

20 $11.3 - 5.1 + 3.1 \cdot 0.2 - 1.1$

21 $(29.3 + 4) \div 3 + 0.5 \cdot 2$

Solve.

22 In Arizona, a minimum temperature of $-40.0°C$ was recorded at Hawley Lake in 1971. A maximum recorded temperature of $53.3°C$ was recorded at Lake Havasu City in 1994. Find the difference between these maximum and minimum temperatures.

23 A shop owner buys 5 handbags to sell in his shop. The owner pays $39.75 for each handbag. Later, the owner has to sell the handbags at a loss. If he charges $27.79 for each handbag, what is his total loss for the 5 handbags?

24 A state sales tax is 4.25%. Amy spends $208 at a department store, but only half of the merchandise she purchases is taxed. What is her total bill?

25 Kylie bought some T-shirts and a pair of shorts for $66.30. The pair of shorts costs $15.90, and each T-shirt costs $5.60. How many T-shirts did Kylie buy?

26 Ms. Parker wants to buy 10 books. Six of them cost $12.50 each, and the rest cost $26.35 each. If she only has $150, how much more does Ms. Parker need to buy all 10 books?

27 The recommended calcium intake for men and women is about 1.2 grams per day. A glass of milk contains about 0.27 gram of calcium. If a man drinks 3 glasses of milk, how much additional calcium does he need from other food sources?

28 **Mathematical Habit 2** Use mathematical reasoning
Maya evaluated an expression as follows:

$$48 \div 2 \cdot (0.9 + 0.3) = 48 \div 2 \cdot 1.2$$
$$= 48 \div 2.4$$
$$= 20$$

She made a common mistake when applying the order of operations. Explain her mistake and help her solve the problem correctly.

29 One day in February, the temperature at 9 A.M. was $-6.8°$F. At 3 P.M. on the same day, the temperature was $1.72°$F.

a Find the change in temperature.

b Find the average hourly rate of change in temperature.

30 A submarine was cruising at 1,328.4 feet below sea level. It then rose at a rate of 14.76 feet per minute for 15 minutes.

a Find the submarine's depth after it rose for 15 minutes.

b If the submarine continued to rise at this same rate, find the time it took to reach the surface from the depth you found in a.

31 José is climbing a mountain. Using a rope, José climbs down from the top of a steep cliff for 4 minutes at a rate of 12.2 feet per minute. He then climbs back up for 10 minutes at a rate of 3.6 feet per minute. How far from the top of the cliff is he after 14 minutes?

32 Ms. Nelson owns 120 shares in a shipping company. On Monday, the value of each share dropped by $0.38. On Tuesday, the value of each share rose by $0.16. Find the total change in the value of Ms. Nelson's 120 shares.

33 A company suffered a loss of $5.4 million in its first year. It lost another $3.1 million in the second year. It made a profit of $4.9 million in the third year.

a Find the average profit or loss for the first three years.

b After its fourth year of business, the company's combined profit for all four years was $0. Find the company's profit or loss during the fourth year.

© 2020 Marshall Cavendish Education Pte Ltd

Name: _____ Date: _____

Mathematical Habit 3 Construct viable arguments
Katherine evaluated the following expression incorrectly.
Explain the mistake to Katherine and show her the correct solution.

Katherine's solution:
$-9 + 15 \div (-3) + 24 \div (3 + 5)$
$= 6 \div (-3) + 24 \div 3 + 5$
$= (-2) + 8 + 5$
$= 11$

Explanation:

Correct solution:

How do you check your answer?

Problem Solving with Heuristics

1 **Mathematical Habit 7** **Make use of structure**

The **4** key on your calculator is not working. Show how you can use the calculator to find
$321 \cdot 64$.

2 **Mathematical Habit 2** **Use mathematical reasoning**

Isabella finds a way to use mental math to find the average of these numbers:

15, 19, 18, 12, 20

She guesses that the mean is about 17, and uses mental math to find out how far above or
below this value each data item is:

$-2, 2, 1, -5, 3$

She uses mental math to add these amounts:

$-2 + 2 + 1 + (-5) + 3 = -1$

Isabella then divides -1 by 5 to get an average of -0.2. She says this means that
the average of the numbers is 0.2 less than 17, the number she estimated. Check that
Isabella's method gives the correct average. Then, use the same method to find the
average of these four numbers:

32, 35, 38, 36

CHAPTER WRAP-UP

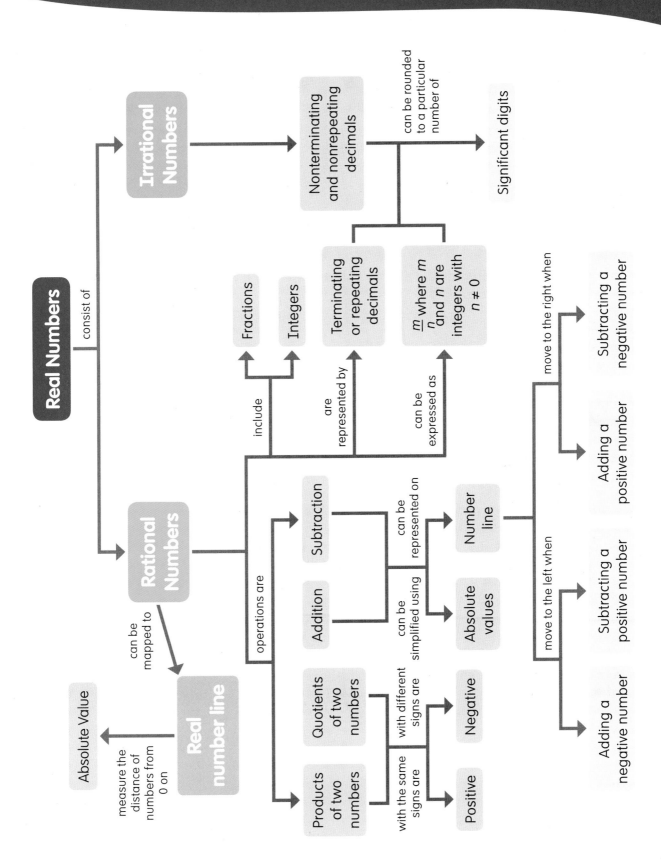

KEY CONCEPTS

- Rational numbers are found in every segment on the number line.

- Rational numbers can be expressed in the form $\frac{m}{n}$ where m and n are integers with $n \neq 0$.

- The decimal form of a rational number is either terminating or repeating.

- An irrational number is a number that cannot be written as $\frac{m}{n}$, where m and n are integers with $n \neq 0$.

- When written in decimal form, an irrational number is nonterminating and nonrepeating.

- You can make use of areas of squares to approximate the values of irrational numbers and estimate their locations on the number line. You can locate irrational numbers more precisely on a number line by using a calculator.

- The real number system is a combination of the set of rational numbers and the set of irrational numbers.

- To compare different forms of real numbers, it can be easier if you convert any non-decimal to decimal form before comparing.

- You use five rules to determine the number of significant digits in a given number.

- You can use a number line or absolute values to add or subtract integers, rational numbers, and decimal numbers. The sum of positive numbers is positive. The sum of negative numbers is negative.

- Subtracting a number is the same as adding its opposite, or additive inverse.
  Example:
  $3 - (-2) = 3 + 2$

- To evaluate the sum or difference of rational numbers with the same denominators, add or subtract their numerators.
  Examples:
  $\frac{1}{5} + \frac{2}{5} = \frac{1+2}{5} = \frac{3}{5}$ and $\frac{2}{3} - \frac{1}{3} = \frac{2-1}{3} = \frac{1}{3}$

- To evaluate the sum or difference of rational numbers with different denominators, rewrite the rational numbers using a common denominator, and then add or subtract.
  Example:
  $\frac{1}{2} - \frac{2}{3} = \frac{3}{6} - \frac{4}{6} = \frac{3-4}{6} = -\frac{1}{6}$

- The product or quotient of two numbers with the same sign is positive. The product or quotient of two numbers with different signs is negative.
  Examples:
  $-3(-2) = 6$ and $3(-2) = -6$

Name: _____ Date: _____

Write each number in $\frac{m}{n}$ form where m and n are integers with $n \neq 0$. Simplify your answers.

1 20.75

2 −0.48

3 $4\frac{6}{13}$

4 $-\frac{39}{56}$

5 1.34

6 60%

For each pair of numbers, find the absolute value of each number. Then, determine which number is farther from 0 on the number line.

7 −16 and −18

8 $-\frac{15}{4}$ and $\frac{18}{7}$

9 2.36 and −2.7

10 $\frac{31}{3}$ and $\frac{40}{6}$

Use long division to write each rational number as a decimal. Use the bar notation if the rational number is a repeating decimal.

11 $\frac{7}{56}$

12 $9\frac{13}{20}$

13 $\frac{100}{11}$

14 $-\frac{5}{12}$

15 $-2\frac{9}{55}$

16 47%

 Draw a number line. Then, locate each irrational number on the number line.

17 $\sqrt{46}$

18 $-\sqrt{133}$

19 $\sqrt[3]{170}$

20 $-\frac{2}{7}\pi^3$

 Locate each set of real numbers on a number line, and order the real numbers from greatest to least using the symbol >.

21 −1.2675 $3\sqrt{2}$ $\frac{22}{7}$ $6.\overline{67}$

22) $-\pi$ $5.\overline{3}$ $\sqrt[3]{90}$ $1\frac{3}{17}$ $-\sqrt{28}$

Find the number of significant digits in each number.

23) 4.23

24) 0.07009

25) 8657

26) 5.600

Round each number to the given number of significant digits.

27) 0.060984
(2 significant digits)

28) 0.060984
(3 significant digits)

29) 27,345
(1 significant digit)

30) 27,345
(3 significant digits)

Evaluate each sum or difference.

31) $-6 + 14$

32) $-25 + (-9)$

33) $52 + (-52)$

34) $46 + (-17) + 38$

35) $35 - 140$

36) $-61 - 28$

37) $-8 - (-50)$

38) $\frac{1}{4} - \frac{7}{8}$

39) $-6\frac{1}{7} + 3\frac{5}{14}$

Evaluate each product or quotient.

40) $-5 \cdot 11$

41) $-30 \cdot (-4)$

42) $144 \div (-6)$

43) $-48 \div (-3)$

44) $-126 \div 9$

45) $\frac{-5}{8} \cdot \frac{8}{15}$

46) $-\frac{3}{4} \cdot \left(-1\frac{2}{3}\right)$

47) $5\frac{1}{4} \div \left(-\frac{7}{12}\right)$

48) $\dfrac{\left(-\frac{2}{3}\right)}{\left(-\frac{8}{15}\right)}$

Evaluate each expression.

49) $12.3 - 8.1 + 2\frac{1}{10} \cdot 0.4 - 1.6$

50) $(25.7 + 4) \div 3 + 0.8 \cdot 2$

51 $10 - 32.86 \div 5.3 + 7\left(\dfrac{81}{100}\right)$

52 $3.25(0.9 - 0.74) + 6.3$

53 $\dfrac{\dfrac{1}{3} - \dfrac{1}{4}}{\dfrac{1}{8} + \dfrac{1}{2}}$

54 $8.5 - \dfrac{\left(-\dfrac{1}{6}\right)}{\left(-\dfrac{5}{18}\right)}$

Solve.

 55 Evaluate $\dfrac{38.14}{\sqrt{21} - \pi}$. Give your answer to 3 significant digits.

$ 8,299

 56 The price of a used car was $8,299 in April. The price of the used car was reduced by 20% one month later in May. Find the price of the used car in May. Give your answer to 3 significant digits.

57 A metal cube has a mass of 0.2531 kilograms. Express this mass in grams to 2 significant digits.

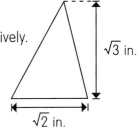

$\sqrt{3}$ in.

$\sqrt{2}$ in.

58 The base and height of a triangle are $\sqrt{2}$ inches and $\sqrt{3}$ inches respectively. Find the area of the triangle to 4 significant digits.

59 Gavin dug a hole that was $16\frac{1}{2}$ inches deep. He left a pile of dirt next to the hole that was $8\frac{3}{4}$ inches high. Show how you could use subtraction to find the distance from the top of the pile of dirt to the bottom of the hole.

60 A hiker descended 320 feet in 40 minutes. Find the hiker's average change in elevation per minute.

61 A hot air balloon descends 305 feet per minute for 4 minutes and then ascends at a rate of 215 feet per minute for another 2 minutes. Find the total change in the balloon's altitude.

62 Suppose you deposit $12.50 into your savings account each week for 4 weeks and then withdraw $4.80 each week for the next two weeks. Find the total change in the amount of money in your account.

63 A game show awards 30 points for each correct answer and deducts 50 points for each incorrect answer. A contestant answers 2 questions incorrectly and 3 questions correctly. What is his final score?

64 The price of a stock falls $1.50 each day for 7 days.

a Find the total change in the price of the stock.

b If the value of the stock was $36 before the price of the stock started falling for 7 days, find the price of the stock after those 7 days.

65 Matthew uses 24 boards that are each $5\frac{3}{4}$ feet long to build a tree house. The wood costs $1.65 per foot. Find the total cost of the wood.

Assessment Prep
Answer each question.

66 Which number is less than 3.142?

Ⓐ $\frac{22}{7}$　　　Ⓑ π　　　Ⓒ $3.14\overline{2}$　　　Ⓓ $3.1\overline{42}$

67 Which expressions are equivalent to $-3\frac{2}{5}-\left(-\frac{3}{4}\right)$? Choose all that apply.

Ⓐ $-3\frac{2}{5}+\left(\frac{3}{4}\right)$　　　Ⓑ $3\frac{2}{5}+\left(\frac{3}{4}\right)$

Ⓒ $-3\frac{2}{5}+\left(+\frac{3}{4}\right)$　　　Ⓓ $3\frac{2}{5}+\left(-\frac{3}{4}\right)$

Ⓔ $-3\frac{2}{5}-\left(\frac{3}{4}\right)$

68 Which expressions have products that are negative? Choose all that apply.

Ⓐ $\left(\frac{3}{4}\right)(-2)\left(-\frac{1}{5}\right)$　　　Ⓑ $(-5)(-0.3)\left(-\frac{1}{2}\right)$

Ⓒ $\left(2\frac{3}{5}\right)(2)\left(\frac{4}{5}\right)$　　　Ⓓ $(6)(-2)(-5)(3)$

Ⓔ $(-0.4)(-2.5)(-1.2)(0.6)$　　　Ⓕ $\left(-1\frac{2}{3}\right)(-10)\left(\frac{1}{5}\right)(-0.2)$

69 At midnight, the temperature was $-3.8°F$. It rose $5.7°F$ by noon, and dropped $4.8°F$ by the following midnight. Find the final temperature. Write your answer and your work or explanation in the space below.

Lighting for Ferris Wheel

1 Kevin, an electrician, was asked to install a rope light cable around the circular rim of a Ferris wheel. He had to estimate the cost of purchasing the total length of the cable based on the following information.

> Diameter of rim of Ferris wheel: 150 meters
> Cost of cable: $50 per meter
> Distance around rim of Ferris wheel: $\pi \times$ diameter

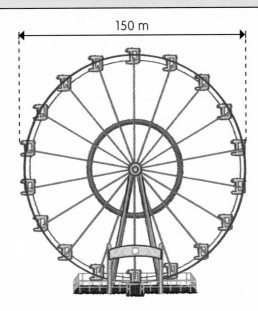

150 m

a Kevin calculated the cost using $\frac{22}{7}$ as an approximation for π. Find the cost obtained.

b Based on a suggestion, Kevin worked out the cost again using the calculator value of π. Find the cost obtained.

c Find the difference between the costs obtained. Which was more accurate? Explain.

2 How are $\frac{22}{7}$ and π classified in the real number system? Justify your answer.

Rubric

Point(s)	Level	My Performance
7–8	4	• Most of my answers are correct. • I showed complete understanding of the concepts. • I used effective and efficient strategies to solve the problems. • I explained my answers and mathematical thinking clearly and completely.
5–6	3	• Some of my answers are correct. • I showed adequate understanding of the concepts. • I used effective strategies to solve the problems. • I explained my answers and mathematical thinking clearly.
3–4	2	• A few of my answers are correct. • I showed some understanding of the concepts. • I used some effective strategies to solve the problems. • I explained some of my answers and mathematical thinking clearly.
0–2	1	• A few of my answers are correct. • I showed little understanding of the concepts. • I used limited effective strategies to solve the problems. • I did not explain my answers and mathematical thinking clearly.

Teacher's Comments

STEAM

Extreme Temperatures

Weather describes day-by-day outdoor conditions. Climate, however, describes decades of weather patterns. Over recent decades, the planet has experienced increasingly higher average temperatures.

No part of the globe can escape the effects of increased average temperatures, or global warming. Around the world, global warming leads to more extreme weather.

Task

Work in pairs or small groups to create an extreme weather infographic for your state.

1 The National Oceanic and Atmospheric Administration (NOAA), provides online access to U.S. climate and weather information through the National Centers for Environmental Information (NCEI). Use the site to search for data.

2 Collect and display data from the year you were born to the current year.

3 Use number lines and equations to show yearly ranges in temperature and precipitation.

4 Gather and illustrate economic data associated with extreme weather in your state, such as agricultural losses, transportation challenges, and property damages.

5 Use art materials or digital tools to create an infographic, or visual display, of your research. Share your work.

Chapter 2 Algebraic Expressions

How much does it cost?

When is the last time you went on a school field trip? Where did you go? Perhaps you visited a local museum, an aquarium, or a national monument such as the Statue of Liberty National Monument. Or perhaps you visited one of the locations on the National Register of Historic Places. Those include places as small as a one-room schoolhouse in Iowa and as large as the Grand Canyon in Arizona.

Most field trips come with expenses. After all, you probably traveled by bus, paid for an entrance ticket, and took time for lunch. Before leaving, your teacher planned ahead, using algebraic expressions to calculate the costs for a given number of students.

In this chapter, you will learn how to write algebraic expressions and to use algebraic reasoning to solve real-world problems, such as how much does it cost to go on a field trip.

How do you simplify, expand or factor algebraic expressions?

Name: _____ Date: _____

Recognizing parts of an algebraic expression

A variable can be used to represent an unknown value or quantity. An algebraic expression is a mathematical phrase that includes variables, numbers, and operation symbols.

Operation symbol

Constant term ↘   ↓   ↙ Coefficient

$7 + 2x$ ← Variable

Numerical term   Algebraic term

▶ Quick Check

Consider the algebraic expression $3x + 4$. Then, answer each question.

① How many terms are there?

② What is the coefficient of the algebraic term?

③ What is the constant term?

④ What is the operation symbol?

Evaluating algebraic expressions

Evaluate an algebraic expression by replacing all its variables with their assigned values.

Given that $a = 5$ in the expression $2a - 3$, find the value of the expression.

$$2a - 3 = (2 \cdot 5) - 3$$
$$= 10 - 3$$
$$= 7$$

▶ Quick Check

⑤ Fill in the table.

x	$x + 9$	$7x$	$5x - 2$
0	$0 + 9 = 9$		
2			
−1			
7			

Simplifying algebraic expressions

Simplify expressions by adding or subtracting the coefficients of like terms (terms that have the same variables with the same corresponding exponents). Algebraic terms cannot be added to or subtracted from constant terms.

Can be Simplified	Cannot be Simplified
• $4a + 3 + 6 = 4a + 9$	• $4x + 3y + 7$ has no like terms.
• $6x - 2x + 5 = 4x + 5$	• $2a - b + 3$ has no like terms.

▶ **Quick Check**

State whether each expression can be simplified. Explain your reasoning.

6 $2k - 3 + k$

7 $7x + 3 - 3y$

8 $6u + 5w - 1$

9 $4g - 3g - g$

Simplify each expression.

10 $4t + 1 + 6$

11 $5p - 5p$

12 $4y + 5y + 3$

13 $4m - 3m - 3$

Expanding algebraic expressions

Expand algebraic expressions by applying the distributive property to remove the parentheses.

$$3(p + 2) = 3(p) + 3(2)$$
$$= 3p + 6$$

$$6(w - 4) = 6(w) - 6(4)$$
$$= 6w - 24$$

▶ **Quick Check**

Expand each expression.

14 $4(h + 2)$

15 $5(4 + 5c)$

16 $3(4x - 11)$

17 $7(3 - 5p)$

Factoring algebraic expressions

Factoring is the inverse of expansion. Factor an algebraic expression by writing it as a product of its factors. Use the distributive property to factor expressions whose terms have a common factor.

$2x + 10 = 2(x) + 2(5)$ The common factor of $2x$ and 10 is 2.
$\quad\quad\quad\;\; = 2(x + 5)$

▶ **Quick Check**

Factor each expression.

18 $6m + 3$

19 $4v + 14$

20 $10p - 2$

21 $6 - 18c$

Recognizing equivalent expressions

Equivalent expressions are expressions that are equal for any values of the variables. Use an equal sign to relate equivalent expressions.

$4(x + 3)$ and $4x + 12$ are equivalent expressions because they are equal for all values of x. So, you can write $4x + 12 = 4(x + 3)$.

▶ **Quick Check**

Choose an equivalent expression.

22 $6y - 3$ is equivalent to

   a $3(3y - 1)$ b $3(2y - 1)$ c $3(2y - 3)$ d $6(3y - 1)$

Writing algebraic expressions to represent unknown quantities

Mason is 2 years older than his brother Evan.

• When Evan is 12 years old, Mason will be $(12 + 2) = 14$ years old.

• When Evan is x years old, Mason will be $(x + 2)$ years old.

▶ **Quick Check**

x is an unknown number. Write an expression for each of the following.

23 7 more than the number

24 Product of 8 and the number

25 5 less than twice the number

26 3 more than half the number

© 2020 Marshall Cavendish Education Pte Ltd

Adding Algebraic Terms

Learning Objective:
• Simplify algebraic expressions with integral, decimal, and fractional coefficients by adding like terms.

THINK

The perimeter of a triangle is $2x$ centimeters long. What are the possible lengths of each of its three sides?

ENGAGE

Use to represent x and ▮ to represent $-x$. How do you find $3x + 3x$? How about $3x + (-3x)$?

How is this similar to what you know about $3 + (-3)$? Explain.

Now, show three different expressions to represent $2x$ using algebra tiles. Include the use of negative terms. Draw a sketch of your methods to record your thinking.

LEARN Simplify algebraic expressions with integral coefficients by adding like terms

1. You have learned how to simplify an algebraic expression like $2x + 4x$, where x is a variable, by adding the like terms.

▮ represents $+x$.

$$2x + 4x \rightarrow 6x$$

So, $2x + 4x = 6x$.

> **Math Note**
> In the algebraic term, $2x$, the number that is multiplied by the variable x is called the coefficient.

2. You can also add algebraic expressions involving negative terms.

▮ represents $+x$ and ▮ represents $-x$.

a Simplify $2x + (-4x)$.

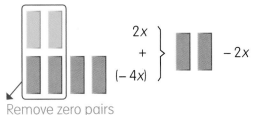

Remove zero pairs

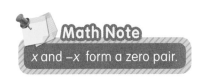

> **Math Note**
> x and $-x$ form a zero pair.

So, $2x + (-4x) = -2x$.

b Simplify $-2x + 4x$.

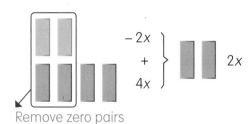

Remove zero pairs

So, $-2x + 4x = 2x$.

Caution

$-2x + 4x \neq -6x$

c Simplify $-2x + (-4x)$.

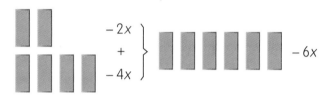

So, $-2x + (-4x) = -6x$.

TRY Practice simplifying algebraic expressions with integral coefficients by adding like terms

Simplify each expression.

1 $4x + (-2x)$

2 $7x + (-9x)$

3 $-4y + 6y$

4 $-10y + 3y$

5 $-5m + (-2m)$

6 $-3m + (-3m)$

ENGAGE

Show how you use a bar model to represent $0.7p + 0.4p$. Will the sum be greater than p? How do you know?

LEARN Simplify algebraic expressions with decimal or fractional coefficients by adding like terms

1 Simplify the expression $0.9p + 0.7p$.

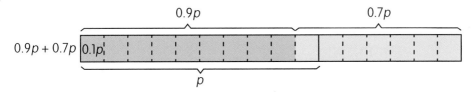

Represent the term $0.9p$ with nine $0.1p$ sections and the term $0.7p$ with seven $0.1p$ sections.

From the bar model, $0.9p + 0.7p = 1.6p$

The sum is the total number of colored sections in the model.

2 Simplify $m + \frac{2}{3}m$.

▶ **Method 1**

Use a bar model.

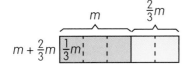

Represent the term m using a bar divided into three $\frac{1}{3}m$ sections.

From the bar model, $m + \frac{2}{3}m = \frac{5}{3}m$

▶ **Method 2**

Use a common denominator for both coefficients.

$m + \frac{2}{3}m = \frac{3}{3}m + \frac{2}{3}m$ Rewrite m as a fraction with denominator 3.

$= \frac{5}{3}m$ Simplify.

Math Note

In algebraic expressions, fractional coefficients that are greater than 1 are left as improper fractions.

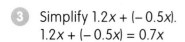 Simplify algebraic expressions with
decimal or fractional coefficients by
adding like terms

3 Simplify $1.2x + (-0.5x)$.
$1.2x + (-0.5x) = 0.7x$

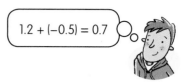
$1.2 + (-0.5) = 0.7$

4 Simplify $\frac{1}{4}y + \left(-\frac{1}{6}y\right)$.

$\frac{1}{4}y + \left(-\frac{1}{6}y\right) = \frac{3}{12}y + \left(-\frac{2}{12}\right)y$

$= \frac{1}{12}y$

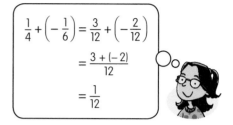
$\frac{1}{4} + \left(-\frac{1}{6}\right) = \frac{3}{12} + \left(-\frac{2}{12}\right)$

$= \frac{3 + (-2)}{12}$

$= \frac{1}{12}$

Math Note

The procedure for simplifying algebraic expressions
with decimal or fractional coefficients is similar to
that of simplifying decimals or fractions.

TRY Practice simplifying algebraic expressions with decimal and
fractional coefficients by adding like terms

Simplify each expression.

1 $0.8p + 0.5p$

2 $\frac{1}{2}p + \frac{2}{5}p$

3 $-0.2y + 0.7y$

4 $1.3g + (-0.9g)$

5 $-m + \frac{5}{6}m$

6 $\frac{1}{4}x + \left(-\frac{2}{3}x\right)$

 **Math Talk**

In **2** and **6**, you can multiply the two denominators
to get the LCD. Does this always work? Explain.

© 2020 Marshall Cavendish Education Pte Ltd

INDEPENDENT PRACTICE

Simplify each expression.

1. $15p + (-3p)$

2. $-8r + 2r$

3. $-7x + (-9x)$

Simplify each expression with decimal coefficients.

4. $0.2x + 0.8x$

5. $x + 0.6x$

6. $0.7b + 0.9b$

7. $0.5k + 1.6k$

8. $2.6p + (-0.3p)$

9. $-0.9r + 1.3r$

Simplify each expression with fractional coefficients.

10. $\frac{5}{8}m + \frac{7}{8}m$

11. $\frac{2}{3}b + \left(-\frac{1}{3}b\right)$

12. $-\frac{1}{9}h + \frac{5}{9}h$

Simplify each expression with fractional coefficients by rewriting the fractions.

13. $\frac{1}{6}a + \frac{1}{3}a$

14. $\frac{2}{5}p + \frac{7}{10}p$

15. $\frac{1}{4}b + \frac{1}{3}b$

16. $\frac{3}{5}x + \frac{3}{4}x$

17. $\frac{1}{2}k + \left(-\frac{1}{6}k\right)$

18. $-\frac{2}{3}m + \frac{3}{4}m$

Solve.

19. The figures show Rectangle A and Rectangle B. Write and simplify an algebraic expression for each of the following.

    a. The perimeter of Rectangle A.

    b. The perimeter of rectangle B.

    c. The sum of the perimeters of the two rectangles.

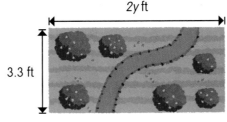

20. The length and width of two rectangular gardens are shown. Find the sum of the areas of the two gardens in simplest form.

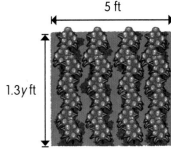

21 **Mathematical Habit 3** Construct viable arguments

Jacob and Evan simplified the same algebraic expression. Their work is shown.

Jacob's Work
$\frac{1}{5}x + 0.3x = \frac{1}{2}x$

Evan's Work
$\frac{1}{5}x + 0.3x = 0.5x$

Describe a method each person might have used to get his answer. Which method do you prefer? Why?

22 **Mathematical Habit 2** Use mathematical reasoning

Which of the following expressions has a greater value if y is a positive number? Explain your reasoning.

$$1.4y + \frac{2}{5}y \quad \text{or} \quad \frac{1}{3}y + \frac{3}{4}y$$

23 Each day, a restaurant serves x meals that consist of $\frac{1}{4}$ of a chicken each. It also makes soup using $\frac{1}{2}$ of a chicken each day. The chef expresses the number of chickens she uses each day as $\frac{1}{4}x + \frac{1}{2}$. How many chickens does she use in three days?

24 **Mathematical Habit 2** Use mathematical reasoning

Maria simplified the algebraic expression $\frac{2}{3}x + \frac{1}{4}x$ as shown below.

$$\frac{2}{3}x + \frac{1}{4}x = \frac{3}{7}x$$

Describe and correct the error Maria made.

Subtracting Algebraic Terms

Learning Objective:
• Simplify algebraic expressions with integral, decimal, and fractional coefficients by subtracting like terms.

THINK

The perimeter of a triangle is $5\frac{1}{2}x$ centimeters. The length of one of its sides is $0.7x$ centimeters. Find the possible lengths of each of the other two sides.

ENGAGE

Use to represent $+x$ and to represent $-x$. How do you find $2x - x$? How about $2x - (-x)$?

How is this similar to what you know about $2 - (-1)$? Explain.

Create as many subtraction equations as you can with the numbers 2, 1, -2, and -1. Repeat with $2x$, x, $-2x$, and $-x$. What do you notice? Share your observations.

LEARN Simplify algebraic expressions with integral coefficients by subtracting like terms

1. You can simplify an algebraic expression like $5x - 3x$, where x is a variable, by subtracting the like terms.

represents $+x$.

So, $5x - 3x = 2x$.

2 You can also subtract algebraic expressions involving negative terms.

 represents $+x$ and ▌ represents $-x$.

a Simplify $5x - (-3x)$.

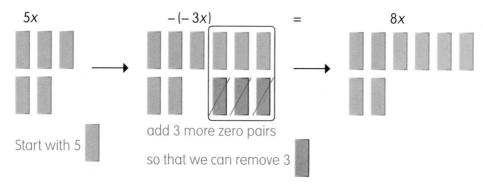

Start with 5 ▌

add 3 more zero pairs

so that we can remove 3 ▌

So, $5x - (-3x) = 8x$.

b Simplify $-5x - 3x$.

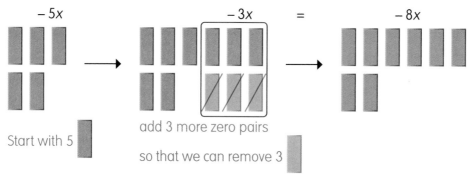

Start with 5 ▌

add 3 more zero pairs

so that we can remove 3 ▌

So, $-5x - 3x = -8x$.

c Simplify $-5x - (-3x)$.

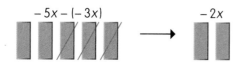

$-5x - (-3x)$ $-2x$

So, $-5x - (-3x) = -2x$.

Math Talk

What is another method to workout the answers to **a** and **b**?

Practice simplifying algebraic expressions with integral coefficients by subtracting like terms

Simplify each expression.

1. $3y - (-4y)$

2. $-6t - 6t$

3. $-5p - (-2p)$

4. $-3a - (-6a)$

ENGAGE

Draw a bar model to show how you can subtract 0.7y from 1.2y.
Share your method.

LEARN Simplify algebraic expressions with decimal or fractional coefficients by subtracting like terms

1. Simplify the expression $1.8y - 0.9y$.

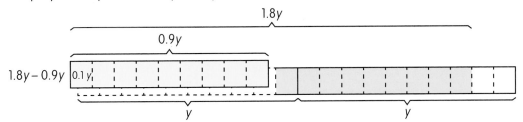

From the bar model, $1.8y - 0.9y = 0.9y$

> The difference is represented by the shaded part that remain.

2. Simplify the expression $\frac{2}{3}b - \frac{1}{4}b$.

▶ **Method 1**

$\frac{2}{3}b = \frac{8}{12}b$

$\frac{1}{4}b = \frac{3}{12}b$

$\frac{2}{3}b - \frac{1}{4}b$ — $\frac{1}{12}b$ ... b

The LCD of $\frac{2}{3}$ and $\frac{1}{4}$ is 12.
So, divide b into twelve $\frac{1}{12}b$ sections.

From the bar model,

$\frac{2}{3}b - \frac{1}{4}b = \frac{5}{12}b$.

▶ **Method 2**

$\frac{2}{3}b - \frac{1}{4}b = \frac{8}{12}b - \frac{3}{12}b$

$= \frac{5}{12}b$

The LCD of $\frac{2}{3}$ and $\frac{1}{4}$ is 12. Rewrite the coefficients as fractions with denominator 12.
Subtract.

3 Simplify the expression $4.6m - (-1.2m)$.

$4.6m - (-1.2m) = 4.6m + 1.2m = 5.8m$

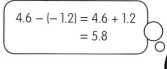

$4.6 - (-1.2) = 4.6 + 1.2$
$= 5.8$

Math Note

Subtracting a negative number, $-b$, is the same as adding its opposite, b.

4 Simplify the expression $\frac{3}{4}n - \left(-\frac{5}{8}n\right)$.

$\frac{3}{4}n - \left(-\frac{5}{8}n\right) = \frac{3}{4}n + \frac{5}{8}n$

$\qquad = \frac{6}{8}n + \frac{5}{8}n$

$\qquad = \frac{11}{8}n$

$\frac{3}{4} - \left(-\frac{5}{8}\right) = \frac{3}{4} + \frac{5}{8}$

$\qquad = \frac{6}{8} + \frac{5}{8}$

$\qquad = \frac{11}{8}$

TRY **Practice simplifying algebraic expressions with decimal and fractional coefficients by subtracting like terms**

Simplify each expression.

1 $1.1a - 0.2a$

2 $-\frac{5}{6}a - \frac{1}{3}a$

3 $0.7g - (-0.4)g$

4 $\frac{3}{4}p - \left(-\frac{1}{6}p\right)$

INDEPENDENT PRACTICE

Simplify each expression.

1 $12y - 8y$

2 $7p - (-6p)$

3 $-11x - 3x$

4 $-9k - (-12k)$

Simplify each expression with decimal coefficients.

5 $1.7p - 0.4p$

6 $2.3a - (-0.4a)$

7 $-0.2b - 1.4b$

8 $-4.2x - (-2.5x)$

Simplify each expression with fractional coefficients.

9 $\frac{7}{8}x - \frac{5}{8}x$

10 $\frac{9}{5}y - \frac{1}{5}y$

11 $-\frac{1}{3}m - \frac{2}{3}m$

12 $-\frac{3}{11}n - \left(-\frac{6}{11}n\right)$

Simplify each expression with fractional coefficients by rewriting the fractions.

13 $\frac{1}{4}a - \frac{1}{8}a$

14 $\frac{5}{6}m - \frac{2}{3}m$

15 $\frac{1}{2}h - \left(-\frac{3}{4}h\right)$

16 $\frac{4}{5}p - \frac{1}{3}p$

17 $\frac{3}{4}r - \frac{2}{3}r$

18 $-\frac{2}{3}y - \frac{2}{5}y$

19 $-\frac{3}{5}x - \left(-\frac{1}{4}x\right)$

20 $-\frac{1}{3}f - \left(-\frac{5}{7}f\right)$

Solve.

Mathematical Habit 2 Use mathematical reasoning

Luke simplified the algebraic expression $\frac{3}{2}x - \frac{1}{3}x$ as shown below.

$$\frac{3}{2}x - \frac{1}{3}x = \frac{18}{12}x - \frac{4}{12}x$$
$$= \frac{14}{12}x$$

Is Luke's simplification correct? Why or why not?

22 Rectangle A, shown below, is larger than Rectangle B. Write and simplify an algebraic expression that represents the difference in the areas of the two rectangles.

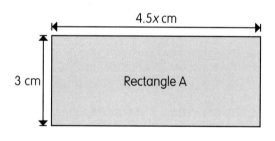

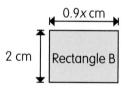

© 2020 Marshall Cavendish Education Pte Ltd

 **Simplifying Algebraic Expressions**

Learning Objectives:
• Simplify algebraic expressions with more than two terms.
• Simplify algebraic expressions by using the commutative property of addition.
• Simplify algebraic expressions with two variables.

THINK

Explain how you would simplify the expression $\frac{2}{3}x - \frac{1}{3}y + (-0.2x) + 0.6y$.

ENGAGE

Use ▌ to represent $+x$, ▌ to represent $-x$, and ▪ to represent $+1$. Simplify the expression

$2x + 3x + 4x$. What steps did you take? How does your method change when simplifying

$2x - 3x + 4$? Explain your reasoning.

LEARN Simplify algebraic expressions with more than two terms and involving negative coefficients

1 Algebraic expressions may contain more than two terms. Not all the terms may be like terms. To simplify such expressions, first identify the like terms. Then, add or subtract the like terms.

$3x - 5x + 2$ can be simplified as shown.

$3x - 5x + 2 = 3x + (-5x) + 2$

> Instead of subtracting $5x$ from $3x$, you can add its opposite, which is $-5x$.

▌ represents $+x$, ▌ represents $-x$, and ▪ represents $+1$.

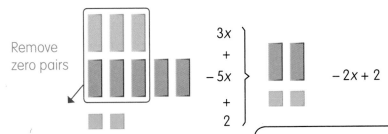

Remove zero pairs

$\left.\begin{array}{c}3x \\ + \\ -5x \\ + \\ 2\end{array}\right\}$ $-2x + 2$

So, $3x - 5x + 2 = -2x + 2$.

> $-2x$ and 2 are not like terms, so $-2x + 2$ cannot be simplified further.

2 Simplify $-3x + 2x - 3 + 1$.

■ represents $+x$, ▮ represents $-x$, ■ represents $+1$, and ■ represents -1.

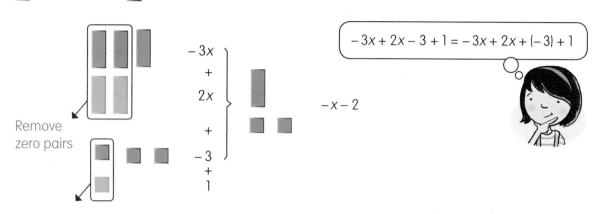

$$-3x + 2x - 3 + 1 = -3x + 2x + (-3) + 1$$

Remove zero pairs

$-x - 2$

$\begin{matrix} -3x \\ + \\ 2x \\ + \\ -3 \\ + \\ 1 \end{matrix}$

So, $-3x + 2x - 3 + 1 = -x - 2$.

TRY **Practice simplifying algebraic expressions with more than two terms and involving negative coefficients**

Simplify each expression.

1 $5 + (-2) + 4y$

2 $5 - 2 - 6x + x$

3 $-2k - 5k - 3 - 4$

ENGAGE

Draw a bar model to show how you simplify $0.3 + 0.2 + 2$. Now, show how you simplify $0.3x + 0.2x + 2$. Is there a value for x where the expressions will be equivalent? Explain.

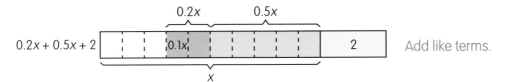

LEARN Simplify algebraic expressions with more than two terms and involving decimal and fractional coefficients

1. A bar model can help simplify expressions such as $0.2x + 0.5x + 2$.

$0.2x + 0.5x + 2$ Add like terms.

The like terms are $0.2x$ and $0.5x$.

From the bar model,

$0.2x + 0.5x + 2 = 0.7x + 2$.

> $0.7x$ and 2 are not like terms, so $0.7x + 2$ cannot be simplified further.

2. You can simplify algebraic expressions such as $\frac{1}{2}x - \frac{1}{4}x + 5 + 2$ by writing like terms with a common denominator.

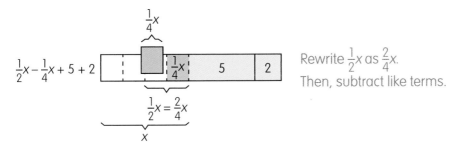

$\frac{1}{2}x - \frac{1}{4}x + 5 + 2$ Rewrite $\frac{1}{2}x$ as $\frac{2}{4}x$.
Then, subtract like terms.

From the bar model, $\frac{1}{2}x - \frac{1}{4}x + 5 + 2 = \frac{1}{4}x + 7$.

3. Simplify the expression $\frac{2}{5}x + \frac{3}{10}x - 1 - 2$.

$\frac{2}{5}x + \frac{3}{10}x - 1 - 2 = \frac{4}{10}x + \frac{3}{10}x - 1 - 2$ Rewrite the coefficients as fractions with denominator 10. Two like terms are $\frac{4}{10}x$ and $\frac{3}{10}x$. Two other like terms are -1 and -2.

$\qquad\qquad\qquad = \frac{7}{10}x - 3$ Simplify.

> Remember that
> $-1 - 2 = -1 + (-2)$
> $\qquad\quad = -3$

© 2020 Marshall Cavendish Education Pte Ltd

3 Simplifying Algebraic Expressions **135**

4 Simplify the expression $5m - 7 - (-3m) + 2$.

$$5m - 7 - (-3m) + 2 = 5m - 7 + 3m + 2 \quad \text{Rewrite subtraction as adding the opposite.}$$
$$= 5m + 3m - 7 + 2 \quad \text{Use commutative property to group like terms.}$$
$$= 8m - 5 \quad \text{Simplify.}$$

5 Simplify the expression $\frac{3}{8}b + \frac{2}{3} + \left(-\frac{1}{8}b\right) - \frac{1}{3}$.

$$\frac{3}{8}b + \frac{2}{3} + \left(-\frac{1}{8}b\right) - \frac{1}{3} = \frac{3}{8}b + \frac{2}{3} - \frac{1}{8}b - \frac{1}{3} \quad \text{Rewrite addition of a negative coefficient as subtraction.}$$
$$= \frac{3}{8}b - \frac{1}{8}b + \frac{2}{3} - \frac{1}{3} \quad \text{Group like terms.}$$
$$= \frac{2}{8}b + \frac{1}{3} \quad \text{Simplify.}$$
$$= \frac{1}{4}b + \frac{1}{3} \quad \text{Write fractions in simplest form.}$$

TRY Practice simplifying algebraic expressions with more than two terms and involving decimal and fractional coefficients

Simplify each expression.

1 $1.8m - 0.9m + 2$

2 $\frac{1}{3}d + \frac{7}{12}d - 5 - 1$

3 $3.4a + 5 + (-0.2a) - 3$

4 $\frac{1}{2}k - 8 - \left(-\frac{2}{5}k\right) + 2$

Use ▮ to represent +x and ▮ represents +y. Represent the stories given using algebra tiles.

Then, write an expression for the total number of pieces of fruit in each story.

a Logan has two bags of x apples. He buys one more bag of x apples.

b Molly has one bag of x apples. She buys one bag of y pears, and then another two bags of x apples.

How are the expressions different? Explain.

LEARN Simplify algebraic expressions with two variables

1. You have learned how to simplify expressions with one variable. Some expressions like x + y + 2x contain two variables, each representing a different unknown quantity.

To simplify x + y + 2x, you can add the like terms as shown below.

▮ represents +x and ▮ represents +y

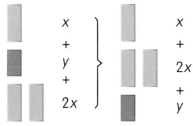

x + y + 2x = x + 2x + y   Group like terms.

= 3x + y   Simplify.

2. Simplify algebraic expressions such as 4x + 3y − x − 2y by first grouping the like terms. Then, add or subtract the like terms.

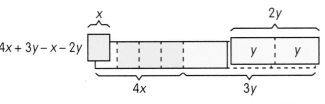

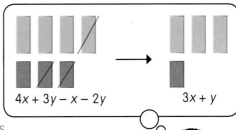

4x + 3y − x − 2y = (4x − x) + (3y − 2y)   Group like terms.

= 3x + y   Simplify.

3 Simplify the expression $5y + 3x + 2y + 2x$.

$$5y + 3x + 2y + 2x = (5y + 2y) + (3x + 2x)$$ Group like terms.
$$= 7y + 5x$$ Add like terms.

⚠ **Caution**

$7y + 5x \neq 12xy$

4 Simplify the expression $6c + 5d - c - 8d$.

$$6c + 5d - c - 8d = (6c - c) + (5d - 8d)$$ Group like terms.
$$= 5c - 3d$$ Simplify.

**Math Talk**

When adding or subtracting algebraic expressions,
how do you identify the like terms?

TRY **Practice simplifying algebraic expressions with two variables**

Simplify each expression.

1 $6a + 9b + a + b$

2 $3x + 2y - 2x - 3y$

3 $2.5x + 1.8z + 1.6x - 0.9z$

4 $\frac{2}{3}a - \frac{1}{6}a + \frac{3}{5}b - \frac{3}{10}b$

4 Expanding Algebraic Expressions

Learning Objective:
• Expand algebraic expressions with fractional, decimal, and negative factors.

THINK

Megan wants to insert two pairs of parentheses into the expression on the right side of the equation, so that it is equivalent to the expression on the left side.

$$-5(x - y) + 6(2 - 0.5x) = 5y - 6x - 14 - 2 + 2x$$

Identify where the pairs of parentheses should be inserted. Explain your answer.
(Hint: Take note of the change in signs after inserting the parentheses.)

ENGAGE

Use ▯ to represent $+x$ and ▮ to represent $+1$. Show how you expand $2(2x + 6)$.

Now, show how you simplify $\frac{1}{2}(2x + 6)$. Share your method.

LEARN Expand algebraic expressions with fractional and decimal factors

1 You have learned how to expand algebraic expressions involving integers, such as $3(2x + 4)$ and $2(5x - 1)$. Use the distributive property to expand such expressions.

▯ represents $+x$ and ▮ represents $+1$.

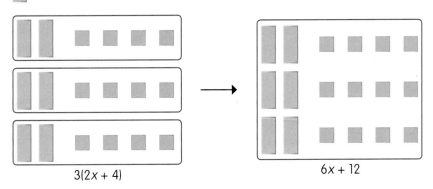

$$3(2x + 4)$$

$$6x + 12$$

$$3(2x + 4) = 3(2x) + 3(4) \qquad 2(5x - 1) = 2(5x) - 2(1) \quad \text{Use the distributive property.}$$
$$= 6x + 12 \qquad\qquad\qquad = 10x - 2 \quad\quad \text{Multiply.}$$

You will obtain an expression equivalent to the original expression after expanding. $3(2x + 4)$ and $6x + 12$ are equivalent expressions because the value of both expressions remains the same for all values of x. In the same way, $2(5x - 1)$ and $10x - 2$ are also equivalent expressions.

② Expand algebraic expressions like $\frac{1}{2}(2x + 4)$ using either bar models or the distributive property. This will produce an equivalent expression, just as expanding an expression with a whole number factor did.

▶ **Method 1**

Rearrange the bar model into two equal groups.

$2x + 4$ | x | x | 2 | 2 | ⟶ $2x + 4$ | x | 2 | x | |
$\underbrace{\qquad\qquad}_{\frac{1}{2}(2x + 4)}$

From the bar model,

$\frac{1}{2}(2x + 4) = x + 2$

Rearrange the bar model into 2 equal groups to find one half of $(2x + 4)$.

▶ **Method 2**

Use the distributive property to expand $\frac{1}{2}(2x + 4)$.

$\frac{1}{2}(2x + 4) = \frac{1}{2}(2x) + \frac{1}{2}(4)$ Use the distributive property.

$\qquad = x + 2$ Multiply.

$\frac{1}{2}(2x + 4)$ and $x + 2$ are equivalent expressions.

③ Expand the expression $\frac{1}{3}(3x + 15)$.

▶ **Method 1**

Use a bar model.

$3x + 15$ | x | 5 | x | 5 | x | 5 |
$\underbrace{\qquad}_{\frac{1}{3}(3x + 15)}$

Arrange the bar model for $3x + 15$ into 3 equal groups to find one third of $(3x + 15)$.

From the bar model, $\frac{1}{3}(3x + 15) = x + 5$

▶ **Method 2**

Use the distributive property.

$\frac{1}{3}(3x + 15) = \frac{1}{3}(3x) + \frac{1}{3}(15)$ Use the distributive property.

$\qquad = x + 5$ Multiply.

④ You can also use the distributive property to expand expressions involving decimals.

$$0.7(0.2t - 3) = 0.7[0.2t + (-3)]$$ Rewrite subtraction as adding the opposite.
$$= 0.7(0.2t) + 0.7(-3)$$ Use the distributive property.
$$= 0.14t + (-2.1)$$ Multiply.
$$= 0.14t - 2.1$$ Rewrite the expression.

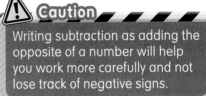

Caution

Writing subtraction as adding the opposite of a number will help you work more carefully and not lose track of negative signs.

TRY Practice expanding algebraic expressions with fractional and decimal factors

Expand each expression.

① $\frac{1}{4}(8x + 12)$

② $\frac{1}{3}(9x + 6)$

③ $\frac{1}{5}(25x + 15)$

Expand each expression.

④ $0.3(2x + 5)$

⑤ $0.5(1.4y - 2.1)$

⑥ $0.2(4x - 3.1)$

ENGAGE

Recall and show two different ways to expand $2(x + 1)$.
Explain how you would expand $-2(x + 1)$ using the distributive property.

LEARN Expand algebraic expressions with negative factors

1. When expanding algebraic expressions with negative factors, such as $-3(x + 2)$ and $-5(y - 2)$, use the distributive property and apply the rules for multiplying integers.

$$-3(x + 2) = -3(x) + (-3)(2) \quad \text{Use the distributive property.}$$
$$= -3x + (-6) \quad \text{Multiply.}$$
$$= -3x - 6 \quad \text{Rewrite the expression.}$$

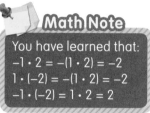
Math Note
You have learned that:
$-1 \cdot 2 = -(1 \cdot 2) = -2$
$1 \cdot (-2) = -(1 \cdot 2) = -2$
$-1 \cdot (-2) = 1 \cdot 2 = 2$

$$-5(y - 2) = -5[y + (-2)] \quad \text{Rewrite subtraction as adding the opposite.}$$
$$= -5(y) + (-5)(-2) \quad \text{Use the distributive property.}$$
$$= -5y + 10 \quad \text{Multiply.}$$

2. Expand the expression $-3\left(-\dfrac{2}{3}a + \dfrac{1}{5}\right)$.

$$-3\left(-\frac{2}{3}a + \frac{1}{5}\right) = -3\left(-\frac{2}{3}a\right) + (-3)\left(\frac{1}{5}\right) \quad \text{Use the distributive property.}$$
$$= 2a - \frac{3}{5} \quad \text{Multiply.}$$

3. Expand the expression $-(-0.4k - 2.5)$.

$$-(-0.4k - 2.5) = -1[-0.4k + (-2.5)] \quad \text{Rewrite the expression.}$$
$$= -1(-0.4k) + (-1)(-2.5) \quad \text{Use the distributive property.}$$
$$= 0.4k + 2.5 \quad \text{Multiply.}$$

4. Expand the expression $-\dfrac{1}{3}(p + 2q)$.

$$-\frac{1}{3}(p + 2q) = -\frac{1}{3}(p) + \left(-\frac{1}{3}\right)(2q) \quad \text{Use the distributive property.}$$
$$= -\frac{1}{3}p - \frac{2}{3}q \quad \text{Multiply.}$$

Expand each expression.

1 $-4(3d - 2)$

2 $-7(5k + e)$

3 $-4(0.6x - 4)$

4 $-\frac{1}{4}\left(-3y + \frac{1}{2}\right)$

ENGAGE

Show how you use bar models to simplify each expression.

a $2p + 5p$

b $2(p + 5p)$

c $2(p + 5q)$

d $2(p + 5q) - q$

What changes each time? Are there any rules you can develop based on what you noticed? Discuss.

LEARN Expand and simplify algebraic expressions

1 When you simplify an algebraic expression, you may need to expand it first before adding or subtracting the like terms.

To simplify an expression like $4(p + 5q) - 3q$, you need to expand $4(p + 5q)$ first.

$$4(p + 5q) - 3q = 4(p) + 4(5q) - 3q \qquad \text{Use the distributive property.}$$
$$= 4p + 20q - 3q \qquad \text{Multiply.}$$
$$= 4p + 17q \qquad \text{Simplify.}$$

2 Expand and simplify the expression $-2(0.5y - 3) + y$.

$$-2(0.5y - 3) + y = -2[0.5y + (-3)] + y \qquad \text{Rewrite the expression.}$$
$$= (-2)(0.5y) + (-2)(-3) + y \qquad \text{Use the distributive property.}$$
$$= -y + 6 + y \qquad \text{Multiply.}$$
$$= -y + y + 6 \qquad \text{Group like terms.}$$
$$= 6 \qquad \text{Simplify.}$$

3 Expand and simplify the expression $4(2n + 5) - (m - 1)$.

$$4(2n + 5) - (m - 1) = 4(2n + 5) + (-1)[m + (-1)] \qquad \text{Rewrite the expression.}$$
$$= 4(2n) + 4(5) + (-1)(m) + (-1)(-1) \qquad \text{Use the distributive property.}$$
$$= 8n + 20 + (-m) + 1 \qquad \text{Multiply.}$$
$$= 8n + (-m) + 20 + 1 \qquad \text{Group like terms.}$$
$$= 8n - m + 21 \qquad \text{Remove parentheses and simplify.}$$

Caution

$8n - m \neq 7nm$

TRY Practice expanding and simplifying algebraic expressions

Expand and simplify each expression.

1 $2(2a + 3b) + 5b$

2 $-3\left(\frac{1}{2}k - 4\right) - 2k$

3 $5(2h - 3) - (2k - 1)$

4 $3(2w + 3) - 2(0.5w - 1)$

5 $4p - 2(0.1p - 4)$

INDEPENDENT PRACTICE

Expand each expression.

1 $\frac{1}{4}(4x + 8)$

2 $\frac{1}{3}(6b + 9)$

3 $\frac{1}{5}(4a + 3)$

4 $\frac{1}{2}(4k - 6)$

5 $\frac{1}{3}(16a - 8)$

6 $\frac{1}{3}(5b - 1)$

7 $\frac{2}{5}(k - 10)$

8 $3(4x + 0.2)$

9 $4(0.1y + 5)$

10 $0.2(3x + 4)$

11 $0.6(3h + 5)$

12 $0.2(m - 3)$

13 $0.3(p - 3)$

14 $0.4(1.5d + 0.5)$

15 $1.2(0.3x - 1.4)$

Expand each expression with a negative factor.

16 $-3(2x + 5)$

17 $-3(4a + 9b)$

18 $-7(2k - h)$

19 $-4\left(p + \frac{1}{2}\right)$

20 $-\frac{1}{2}\left(6x - \frac{1}{3}\right)$

21 $-2(5k + 1.7)$

22 $-3(0.2m + 5)$

23 $-5(q - 0.3)$

24 $-0.6(0.4y - 1)$

Expand and simplify each expression.

25 $3(2y + 1) + 4$

26 $3(2a + 5) - 8$

27 $2(x + 2) + 3x$

28 $6(b + 3) - 2b$

29 $5\left(\frac{1}{6}a + 1\right) + 3$

30 $4\left(\frac{1}{8}a - 3\right) - \frac{1}{2}a$

31 $0.2(x + 1) + 0.7x$

32 $0.5(y + 2) - 0.3y$

33 $-2(4m + 1) - m$

34 $10 - 3(2n - 1)$

35 $-0.8(r + 3) + 2.2r$

36 $-(1.2x + 7) + 1.5x$

Expand and simplify each expression with two variables.

37 $4x + 6(3y + x)$

38 $7a + 5(3a - b)$

39 $4q + 6(p - 2q)$

40 $2(a + 2b) + (a + 3b)$

41 $3(m - 2n) + 6(n - 2m)$

42 $4(d + e) - 3(d - 2e)$

43 $3(3q - p) - (q - 6p)$

44 $-4(x + 3y) + 3(2x - 5y)$

45 $-7(y + 2t) - 3(y - t)$

Write an expression for the missing dimension of each shaded figure and a multiplication expression for its area. Then, expand and simplify the multiplication expression.

46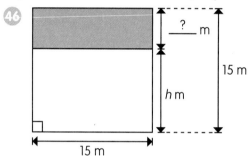

47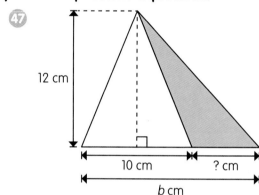

Write an expression for the area of the figure. Expand and simplify.

48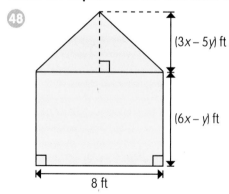

Factoring Algebraic Expressions

Learning Objectives:
- Factor algebraic expressions with two variables.
- Factor algebraic expressions with negative terms.

THINK

Cole wants to insert two terms to the expression on the right side of the equation, so that it is equivalent to the expression on the left side.

$-3 - 12x - 21y = -3(4x - y)$

Identify the terms and where they should be inserted. Explain how you arrived at your answer in two different ways.

ENGAGE

Use to represent $+x$, ▮ to represent $+y$, and ▪ to represent $+1$. Show how you factor $3x + 6$.

Now, show $3x + 6y$. How do you factor $3x + 6y$ using algebra tiles? Draw a sketch of your method to record your thinking.

LEARN Factor algebraic expressions with two variables

① You have learned how to factor an algebraic expression, such as $2x + 2$. You can factor the expression by using counters and tiles, or the greatest common factor (GCF).

▶ **Method 1**
Factoring $2x - 4$ results in an equivalent expression $2(x - 2)$.

▮ represents $+x$ and ▪ represents -1.

$$2x - 4 \longrightarrow 2(x - 2)$$

So, $2x - 4 = 2(x - 2)$.

You can check whether you have factored correctly by expanding $2(x - 2)$.

▶ **Method 2**
$2x - 4 = 2x + (-4)$	Rewrite the expression.
$= 2(x) + 2(-2)$	The GCF of $2x$ and -4 is 2.
$= 2(x - 2)$	Use the distributive property to factor 2 from each term.

2 You can also factor expressions with two variables, like $3a + 6b$, using models or the GCF.

▶ **Method 1**

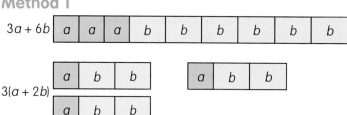

$3a + 6b$ | a | a | a | b | b | b | b | b | b

Draw a group of three a sections and six b sections.

$3(a + 2b)$

a	b	b
a	b	b
a	b	b

Rearrange into three identical groups. Each group has one a section and two b sections to represent $(a + 2b)$.

▶ **Method 2**

$$3a + 6b = 3(a) + 3(2b)$$ The GCF of $3a$ and $6b$ is 3.
$$= 3(a + 2b)$$ Factor 3 from each term.

Check

Expand the expression $3(a + 2b)$ to check the factoring.

$$3(a + 2b) = 3(a) + 3(2b)$$
$$= 3a + 6b$$

$3a + 6b$ is factored correctly.

3 Factor the expression $3x - 9y$.

▶ **Method 1**

Use a bar model.

$3x - 9y$ | x | x | x | −y | −y | −y | −y | −y | −y | −y | −y | −y

Draw a group of three x sections and nine $-y$ sections.

$3(x - 3y)$

x	−y	−y	−y
x	−y	−y	−y
x	−y	−y	−y

Rearrange into three identical groups. Each group has one x section and three $-y$ sections to represent $(x - 3y)$.

From the bar model,
$$3x - 9y = 3(x - 3y)$$

▶ **Method 2**

Use the distributive property.

$3x - 9y = 3x + (-9y)$ Rewrite the expression.

        $= 3(x) + 3(-3y)$ The GCF of $3x$ and $-9y$ is 3.

        $= 3(x - 3y)$ Factor 3 from each term.

The factors of 3 are 3 and 1.
3 is also a factor of -9
because $3(-3) = -9$.
So, the GCF of 3 and -9 is 3.

Check

Expand the expression $3(x - 3y)$ to check the factoring.

$3(x - 3y) = 3(x) + 3(-3y)$
           $= 3x - 9y$

$3x - 9y$ is factored correctly.

TRY Practice factoring algebraic expressions with two variables

Factor each expression.

1   $2j - 10k$

2   $6a - 18b$

3   $8p - 12q$

ENGAGE

Decide if each expression given is completely factored. Explain why or why not.

a $3x + 2$

b $2x - 3y$

c $-4x + 8y$

d $-10x - 5$

If -6 is is a factor of an algebraic expression involving the terms $2x$ and $3y$, what are the possible algebraic expressions? Explain your thinking.

LEARN Factor algebraic expressions with negative terms

1 An expression such as $-2x - 3$ is not factored completely because you can factor out -1 from the expression.

$$
\begin{aligned}
-2x - 3 &= -2x + (-3) &&\text{Rewrite the expression.}\\
&= (-1)(2x) + (-1)(3) &&\text{The GCF of } -2x \text{ and } -3 \text{ is } (-1).\\
&= -1(2x + 3) &&\text{Factor } (-1) \text{ from each term.}\\
&= -(2x + 3) &&\text{Simplify.}
\end{aligned}
$$

Check

Expand the expression $-(2x + 3)$ to check the factoring.

$$
\begin{aligned}
-(2x + 3) &= (-1)(2x + 3)\\
&= (-1)(2x) + (-1)(3)\\
&= -2x - 3
\end{aligned}
$$

$-2x - 3$ is factored correctly.

> The expression $-(2x + 3)$ is factored completely because the terms inside the parentheses have no common factors.

2 Factor the expression $-4a - 8$.

$$
\begin{aligned}
-4a - 8 &= -4a + (-8) &&\text{Rewrite the expression.}\\
&= (-4)(a) + (-4)(2) &&\text{The GCF of } -4a \text{ and } -8 \text{ is } (-4).\\
&= -4(a + 2) &&\text{Factor } (-4) \text{ from each term and simplify.}
\end{aligned}
$$

Check

Expand the expression $-4(a + 2)$ to check the factoring.

$$
\begin{aligned}
-4(a + 2) &= (-4)(a) + (-4)(2)\\
&= -4a - 8
\end{aligned}
$$

$-4a - 8$ is factored correctly.

TRY Practice factoring algebraic expressions with negative terms

Factor each expression.

1 $-5x - 3$

2 $-3f - 6$

3 $-8p - 10q$

INDEPENDENT PRACTICE

Factor each expression with two terms.

1. $2x + 8$

2. $5a + 5$

3. $3x - 12$

4. $4x - 16$

5. $2x + 8y$

6. $7a + 7b$

7. $5p + 15q$

8. $14w + 49m$

9. $4j - 16k$

10. $8t - 32u$

11. $2a - 10p$

12. $9h - 45f$

Factor each expression with negative terms.

13. $-p - 2$

14. $-x - 5$

15. $-2d - 7$

16. $-4y - 11$

17. $-3a - 6$

18. $-4x - 20$

19 $-5k - 25$

20 $-7u - 49$

21 $-1 - 4n$

22 $-3 - 6a$

23 $-12x - 16y$

24 $-25m - 10n$

Factor each expression with three terms.

25 $4x + 4y + 8$

26 $2a + 6b + 4$

27 $5p + 10q + 10$

28 $12d + 6e + 18$

29 $3s - 9t - 15$

30 $4a - 6b - 12$

31 $12a - 9b - 6$

32 $24g - 12h - 36$

Solve.

33 A rectangle has an area of $(12m - 30n)$ square units. Its width is 6 units. Factor the expression for the area to find an expression for the length of the rectangle.

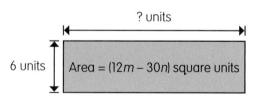

? units

6 units

Area = $(12m - 30n)$ square units

6 Writing Algebraic Expressions

Learning Objectives:
- Translate verbal descriptions into algebraic expressions with one or more variables.
- Translate verbal descriptions into algebraic expressions involving the distributive property.

THINK

Ava has x magnets. Leah has 25% fewer magnets than Ava. Katie has $\frac{1}{2}y$ magnets more than Leah. The three of them then share their magnets equally. How many magnets does each of them have after sharing the magnets? Simplify the expression, if necessary. Show two different methods the three girls can share the magnets among themselves, so that each of them has the same number of magnets.

ENGAGE

A wooden plank is x feet long. Draw a bar model and write an expression to represent the total length of two such planks.

Now, use the bar model to represent the length of $\frac{1}{3}$ of the total length of the two planks. How do you write an expression to show it? Explain your reasoning.

 LEARN Translate verbal descriptions into algebraic expressions with one variable

1. You have learned to translate verbal descriptions into algebraic expressions.

   You can translate verbal descriptions with variable terms that have decimal, fractional, and negative coefficients as in the following problem.

   Amy used two-thirds of a ribbon that is y-inches long to tie her hair. Write an algebraic expression for the length of the ribbon she used.

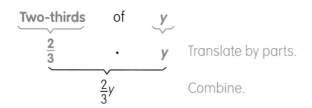

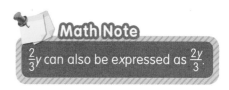

The length of the piece of ribbon is $\frac{2}{3}y$ inches.

2 You can translate verbal descriptions into algebraic expressions using more than one operation. Simplify algebraic expressions when you can.

Seven sticks of clay are shared equally among 28 students. Each stick of clay weighs c grams. Write an algebraic expression for the weight of the clay that each student receives.

Product of 7 and c	divided by	**28**
$7 \cdot c$	$\div$	**28**

Translate by parts.

$$\frac{7c}{28}$$

Combine and simplify.

$$= \frac{c}{4}$$

You can translate verbal descriptions into algebraic expressions by parts before you combine them into an expression.

Each student receives $\frac{c}{4}$ grams of clay.

3 Charles usually makes 7 quarts of fruit punch using r quarts of orange juice. This time, he uses 30% less orange juice. Write an expression for the number of quarts of fruit punch Charles makes this time.

7	adds to	-0.3	times	r
		-0.3	$\cdot$	r

Translate by parts.

7	$+$	$-0.3r$

Combine.

$7 + (-0.3r) = 7 - 0.3r$

Charles makes $(7 - 0.3r)$ quarts of fruit punch this time.

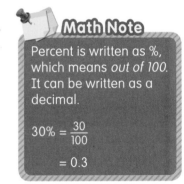

Math Note

Percent is written as %, which means *out of 100*. It can be written as a decimal.

$30\% = \frac{30}{100}$

$= 0.3$

4   Seven watermelons each weigh w pounds. A basket can hold 11 pounds less than two-fifths of the weight of the watermelons. What weight can the basket hold?

Since w represents the weight of one watermelon, $7 \cdot w$ represents the weight of seven watermelons.

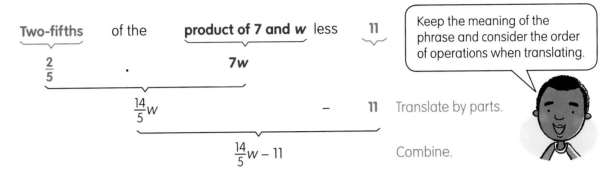

| Two-fifths | of the | product of 7 and w | less | 11 | Keep the meaning of the phrase and consider the order of operations when translating. |

$$\frac{2}{5} \qquad \cdot \qquad 7w$$

$$\frac{14}{5}w \qquad\qquad - \qquad 11 \qquad \text{Translate by parts.}$$

$$\frac{14}{5}w - 11 \qquad\qquad \text{Combine.}$$

The basket can hold $\left(\frac{14}{5}w - 11\right)$ pounds.

TRY Practice translating verbal descriptions into algebraic expressions with one variable

Solve.

1   The price of a ring was w dollars. Claire bought the ring at a price that was 25% cheaper than the usual price. Write an algebraic expression for the discounted price of the ring.

2   $6n$ lumps of clay are shared among 14 students. Write an algebraic expression for the number of lumps of clay that each student will get.

3   Tyler has w marbles and Megan has $\frac{1}{2}w$ marbles. Tyler gives one-tenth of his marbles and Megan gives two-fifth of her marbles to their cousin Joseph. Write an expression for the number of marbles Joseph receives.

4   After baking some bread, Zoe has $\frac{2}{3}b$ pounds of butter left. Then, she uses $\frac{3}{4}$ pound for some white sauce. Write an algebraic expression for the amount of butter left in the end.

Ms. Miller has a back yard that is in the shape of a rectangle as shown.

She wants to fence her back yard using wire. Write an algebraic expression with one variable to find the perimeter of her back yard.

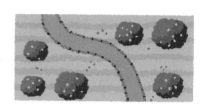

Ms. Miller decides to fence off a small rectangular section from a corner of her rectangular back yard as shown.

Will she need more or less wire? Explain your reasoning.

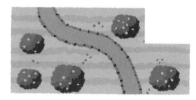

LEARN Translate real-world problems into algebraic expressions with one variable

1 You can use diagrams, models, or tables to visualize the information in a real-world problem. These visual aids help you to solve problems involving algebraic expressions.

Mr. Kim has a farm that is in the shape of a rectangle. Its width is x yards. Its length is 6 yards more than one-third of the width. Write an algebraic expression for the perimeter of Mr. Kim's farm.

$\left(\frac{1}{3}x + 6\right)$ yd

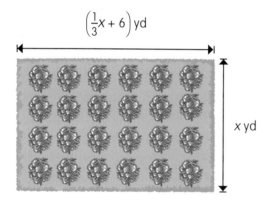

x yd

Draw a diagram to visualize the problem.

Perimeter of Mr. Kim's farm:

$x + \left(\frac{1}{3}x + 6\right) + x + \left(\frac{1}{3}x + 6\right) = \frac{8}{3}x + 12$ Add the like terms.

The perimeter of Mr. Kim's farm is $\left(\frac{8}{3}x + 12\right)$ yards.

TRY Practice translating real-world problems into algebraic expressions with one variable

Complete

1 Mr. Martin's garden is in the shape of an isosceles triangle with a base of length $2y$ feet and sides of length $\left(\frac{2}{5}y + 3\right)$ feet each.

Write an algebraic expression for the perimeter of Mr. Martin's garden.

Rafael has 6 apps on his phone. Emily has x more apps on her phone than Rafael. Draw a bar model and write an expression to show how many apps Emily has.

If Rafael has $2y$ apps on his phone, how many apps does Emily have? Explain your answer.

LEARN Translate verbal descriptions into algebraic expressions with more than one variable

1. Some situations may require you to use more than one variable.

   Adam has m coins. Rachel has $\frac{1}{2}r$ coins. Assuming Adam has more coins than Rachel, how many more does Adam have?

m	minus	$\frac{1}{2}r$	Translate by parts. Combine.
m	$-$	$\frac{1}{2}r$	

   Adam has $\left(m - \frac{1}{2}r \right)$ coins more than Rachel.

2. Eric made t dollars and his sister Lily made u dollars while working at a restaurant during their summer break. They gave 12% of their earnings to charity. Find the total amount they gave to the charity.

12%	of the	sum of t and u	
0.12	$\cdot$	$t + u$	Translate by parts.

   $0.12(t + u)$ Combine.

   Eric and Lily gave $[0.12(t + u)]$ dollars to the charity.

TRY Practice translating verbal descriptions into algebraic expressions with more than one variable

Solve.

1. There are $\frac{2}{3}x$ red balloons and y blue balloons. How many more blue balloons are there?

2. The price of a bag is p dollars and the price of a pair of shoes is $5q$ dollars. Ms. Scott bought them at a total discount of 20%. Write an algebraic expression for the total discounted price of the items.

A bowl cost x dollars and a cup cost $\frac{1}{2}x$ dollars. Mr. Perez bought 3 bowls and 6 cups. Draw a bar model to find the total cost of the items.

Then, Mr. Perez bought 5 plates and each plate cost y dollars. How do you find the total amount of money he spent? Share your method.

LEARN Translate real-world problems into algebraic expressions with more than one variable

1. Grapes, papayas, and strawberries are sold in a supermarket at the following prices:

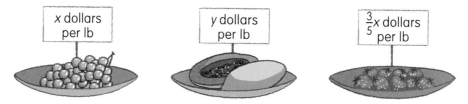

| x dollars per lb | y dollars per lb | $\frac{3}{5}x$ dollars per lb |

Julia bought 4.5 pounds of grapes, 2.65 pounds of papayas, and 6 pounds of strawberries. What is the total cost of the fruit she bought?

Fruit	Price Per Pound	Total Weight	Cost
Grapes	x dollars	4.5	4.5x dollars
Papayas	y dollars	2.65	2.65y dollars
Strawberries	$\frac{3}{5}x$ dollars	6	3.6x dollars

Use a table to organize the information.

Total cost of fruit:

$4.5x + 2.65y + 3.6x = 4.5x + 3.6x + 2.65y$ Group the like terms.
$ = 8.1x + 2.65y$ Add the like terms.

The total cost of the fruit that she bought is $(8.1x + 2.65y)$ dollars.

TRY Practice translating real-world problems into algebraic expressions with more than one variable

Solve.

1. The price of a buffet lunch is $14.80 per adult and $12 per child. For a group of m adults and n children, how much does the lunch cost before tax and tips?

2. Lucas had m quarters in his pocket. He also had one dime and n nickels. What was the total value of his coins?

Owen had *k* markers. He lost 6 markers. Draw a bar model and write an algebraic expression to show the number of markers he has left.

Owen then divided the markers he had left equally among 3 friends. How do you write an algebraic expression for the number of markers each friend received? Share your method.

LEARN Translate real-world problems into algebraic expressions involving the distributive property

1 Anya had *n* baseball cards that she wanted to give away. She gave 12 baseball cards to her brother and divided the rest of them equally among 4 friends. How many baseball cards did each friend receive?

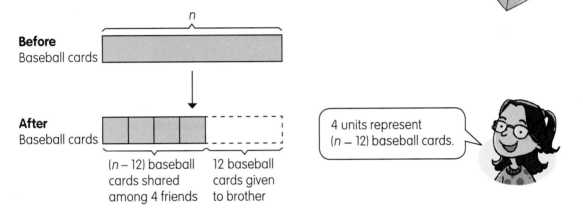

Before
Baseball cards

After
Baseball cards

$(n - 12)$ baseball cards shared among 4 friends

12 baseball cards given to brother

4 units represent $(n - 12)$ baseball cards.

From the bar model, the number of baseball cards each friend received is:

$\frac{1}{4}(n - 12) = \frac{1}{4}n - 3$ Use the distributive property.

Each friend received $\left(\frac{1}{4}n - 3\right)$ baseball cards.

Activity Using algebraic expressions in real-world situations

Work in groups.

Translate verbal descriptions into algebraic expressions.

Kayla used her cell phone for four days. Her average calling time was 130 minutes each day. Suppose that Kayla used the phone for *m* minutes on the fifth day.

1 Write an algebraic expression for the average number of minutes she spent on the phone over five days.

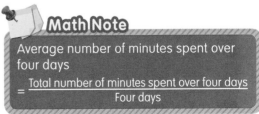

Math Note

Average number of minutes spent over four days

$= \dfrac{\text{Total number of minutes spent over four days}}{\text{Four days}}$

(2) Use a spreadsheet to solve real-world problem involving algebraic expressions.

a Label your spreadsheet and enter the values in column A as shown.

Enter the formula = 130*4+A2 in cell B2 to find the total number of minutes Kayla spent on her phone over five days. What is the value in cell B2 after you have entered the formula?

	A	B	C
	Number of Minutes Spent on Fifth Day (m)	Total Number of Minutes Spent over Five Days	Average Number of Minutes Spent over Five Days
1			
2	0	=130*4+A2	
3	50	570	
4	100	620	
5	150	670	
6	200	720	

b Complete cell C2 with a formula to find the average number of minutes Kayla spent on her phone over five days.

	A	B	C
	Number of Minutes Spent on Fifth Day (m)	Total Number of Minutes Spent over Five Days	Average Number of Minutes Spent over Five Days
1			
2	0	520	?
3	50	570	114
4	100	620	124
5	150	670	134
6	200	720	144

(3) Kayla would like to have an average number of minutes she spent on her cell phone over five days to be 150 minutes. Determine the number of minutes she can spend on the fifth day by repeating with different values in column A.

(4) **Mathematical Habit 4** Use mathematical models

Based on your activity, what is the relationship between the algebraic expressions of (1) and the formula used in the spreadsheet cell of (2)? Explain how you can use technology to solve real-world problems.

TRY Practice translating real-world problems into algebraic expressions involving the distributive property

Solve.

(1) Alan had b tennis balls. He gave 30 to his sister and divided the rest of the tennis balls equally among 5 friends. How many tennis balls did each friend receive?

INDEPENDENT PRACTICE

Translate each verbal description into an algebraic expression.
Simplify the expression when you can.

1 Sum of one-sixth of x and 2.8

2 One-half u subtracted from 3 times u

3 4.5 times q divided by 9

4 60% of one-half x

5 $5x$ increased by 120%

6 7 times z reduced by a third of the product

7 24% of w plus 50% of y

8 Three-fourths of v subtracted from 6 times two-ninths y

9 One-fourth of the sum of $2p$ and 11

10 Sum of $2x$, $\left(\frac{2}{3}x + 5\right)$, and $(11 - x)$

Solve. You may use a diagram, model, or table.

11 The length of $\frac{2}{3}$ of a rope is $(4u - 5)$ inches. Express the total length of the rope

12 If 50 lb = 22.68 kg, what is $\frac{15}{8}y$ pounds in kilograms?

13 The minute hand of a clock makes one complete round every 60 minutes. How many rounds does the minute hand make in $650x$ minutes?

14 Fifteen cards are added to n cards. 6 people then share the cards equally. Express the number of cards for each person in terms of n.

15 The pump price was g dollars per gallon of gasoline yesterday. The price increases by 10 cents per gallon today. If a driver pumps 12.4 gallons of gasoline today, how much does he have to pay?

16 Each algebraic expression contains an error. Fill in the table.

Verbal Description	Expression with Error	Description of Error	Correct Expression
35% of s plus 65% of t	$s + t$		
$\frac{1}{6}x$ subtracted from $\frac{1}{6}y$	$\frac{1}{6}x - \frac{1}{6}y$		
One more than half of n	$1\frac{1}{2}n$		
$\frac{2}{3}x$ divided by $\frac{1}{5}$	$\frac{2}{15}x$		

17 The ratio of red counters to blue counters is 9 : 11. There are y blue counters. Express the number of red counters in terms of y.

18 When 18 boys joined a group of y students, the ratio of boys to girls in the group became 4 : 5. Write an algebraic expression for the number of girls in terms of y.

19 Andrew is x years old. Brian is 7 years younger than Andrew. In 5 years' time, Brian will be twice the age of Carla. How old is Carla now in terms of x?

20 A group has an equal number of adults and children. When n oranges are given to the group, each adult gets two oranges while each child gets one orange and there are still 5 oranges left. Write an algebraic expression for the number of oranges given to the adults.

21 The list price of a camera was w dollars. Dylan bought the camera for $35 less than the list price. If the sales tax was 8%, how much did Dylan pay for the camera including the sales tax?

22 There were m visitors in an exhibition on the first day and 1,200 fewer visitors on the second day. On the third day, the number of visitors was 30% greater than the number of visitors on the second day. What was the average number of visitors over the three days?

23 A man drove x miles per hour for 3 hours and $(2x - 60)$ miles per hour for the next 4.75 hours.
  a Express the total distance he traveled in terms of x.

  b If $x = 64$, what is the total distance he traveled?

7 Real-World Problems: Algebraic Reasoning

Learning Objective:
• Solve real-world problems using algebraic reasoning.

THINK

A piece of string is $(w + 5)$ feet long. Ms. Reyes kept 60% of the piece of the string and used the rest to tie two boxes.

a If one of the pieces of string used to tie the box was at least $\frac{1}{3}$ as long as the other piece, find a possible length of the other piece of string.

b If one of the pieces of string was not more than $\frac{1}{3}$ of the length of the other piece, find a possible length of the other piece of string.

ENGAGE

Zachary bought 3 cartons of x eggs. He used 6 eggs to make a cake. He then used the remaining eggs equally to make 2 pies. Draw a bar model to show how many eggs were used in each pie. Now, write an expression to explain your reasoning.

LEARN Solve real-world problems using algebraic reasoning

① After Seth gives Elena 6 pears, Elena has $(x + 6)$ pears. If she gives one-third of her pears to Dae, how many pears, in terms of x, does Dae have?

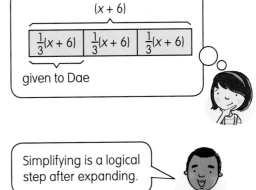

given to Dae

Number of pears that Dae has:

$\frac{1}{3}(x + 6)$ Translate verbal descriptions into algebraic expression.

$= \frac{1}{3} \cdot x + \frac{1}{3} \cdot 6$ Use the distributive property.

$= \frac{1}{3}x + 2$ Simplify.

Dae has $\left(\frac{1}{3}x + 2\right)$ pears.

Simplifying is a logical step after expanding.

② There are n apples in a box. 5 apples are green and the rest are red. Jade and Kyle share the red apples in the ratio 2 : 3. How many red apples does Kyle get?

STEP 1 Understand the problem.

How many apples are there in total? How many of the apples are red? How do Jade and Kyle share the red apples? What fraction of the red apples does Kyle get? What do I need to find?

STEP 2 Think of a plan.
I can draw a bar model or use algebraic reasoning.

STEP 3 Carry out the plan.

▶ **Method 1**
Draw a bar model.

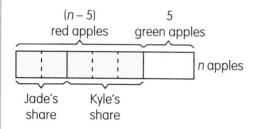

From the bar model, the number of red apples Kyle gets is:

$$\frac{3}{5}(n - 5) = \frac{3}{5}(n) - \frac{3}{5}(5)$$ Use the distributive property.

$$= \frac{3}{5}n - 3$$

Kyle gets $\left(\frac{3}{5}n - 3\right)$ red apples.

▶ **Method 2**
Use algebraic reasoning.

Only red apples are shared. So, subtract 5 green apples from *n* apples.

Jade's apples : Kyle's apples
          2 : 3

So, Kyle gets 3 out of every 5 red apples.

Number of red apples: $n - 5$

Number of red apples Kyle gets:

$$\frac{3}{5}(n - 5) = \frac{3}{5}(n) - \frac{3}{5}(5)$$ Use the distributive property.

$$= \frac{3}{5}n - 3$$

Kyle gets $\left(\frac{3}{5}n - 3\right)$ red apples.

STEP 4 Check the answer.

I can work backwards to check my answer.

Jade's apples : Kyle's apples

2 : 3

$\frac{2}{5}(n-5) : \frac{3}{5}(n-5)$

Number of red apples : $\frac{2}{5}(n-5) + \frac{3}{5}(n-5) = n-5$

Total number of apples = Number of red apples + Number of green apples

$= n - 5 + 5$

$= n$

My answer is correct.

TRY Practice solving real-world problems using algebraic reasoning

Solve.

1. The area of a triangle is $(u + 10)$ square centimeters. The ratio of the area of the unshaded region to the area of the shaded region is $1 : 3$. Using algebraic reasoning, express the area of the shaded region in terms of u.

2. There are 25 nickels and quarters. w coins are nickels and the rest are quarters.

   a Write an algebraic expression for the number of coins that are quarters.

   b Find the total value of the quarters.

ENGAGE

Luke thinks of three consecutive even numbers. Using x to represent one of the even numbers, write an expression for each of the other two even numbers. How do you find the sum of the three even numbers? Share and explain your method.

LEARN Solve a word problem involving algebraic expressions

1. One number is n and a second number is $\left(\frac{2n}{3} + 2\right)$. A third number is $\frac{n}{6}$ less than the second number. Express the sum of the three numbers in terms of n.

First Number   Second Number   Third Number

Sum of three numbers: $n + \left(\frac{2n}{3} + 2\right) + \left(\frac{2n}{3} + 2 - \frac{n}{6}\right)$ Write the addition expression.

$= n + \frac{2}{3}n + 2 + \frac{2}{3}n + 2 - \frac{1}{6}n$ Rewrite the expression.

$= n + \frac{2}{3}n + \frac{2}{3}n - \frac{1}{6}n + 2 + 2$ Group like terms.

$= \frac{6}{6}n + \frac{4}{6}n + \frac{4}{6}n - \frac{1}{6}n + 2 + 2$ LCM of 3 and 6 is 6.

$= \frac{13}{6}n + 4$ Simplify.

The sum of the three numbers is $\left(\frac{13}{6}n + 4\right)$.

TRY Practice solving a word problem involving algebraic expressions

Solve.

1. Hana has x comic books, Mario has $\left(\frac{2x}{5} + 1\right)$ comic books, and John has $\frac{x}{10}$ fewer comic books than Mario. Express the total number of comic books that Hana, Mario, and John have in terms of x.

ENGAGE

Ms. Evans bought a total of 60 pens and pencils. There was an equal number of pens and pencils. She gave x percent of the pens and y percent of the pencils to her students. Use algebraic reasoning to write an algebraic expression for the number of pens and pencils that she gave to her students. Share your reasoning.

LEARN Solve a percent problem involving algebraic expressions using algebraic reasoning

1. There is an equal number of boys and girls in a group of 80 children. Within the group, p percent of the boys and q percent of the girls wear glasses. Write an algebraic expression for the number of children who wear glasses. Factor any terms with a common factor.

$80 \div 2 = 40$

There are 40 boys and 40 girls.

Number of boys who wear glasses = $0.01p \cdot 40$
$= 0.4p$

Number of girls who wear glasses = $0.01q \cdot 40$
$= 0.4q$

Number of children who wear glasses = $0.4p + 0.4q$
$= 0.4(p + q)$

The number of children who wear glasses is $0.4(p + q)$.

p percent = $\frac{p}{100}$ q percent = $\frac{q}{100}$
$= 0.01p$ $= 0.01q$

TRY Practice solving a percent problem involving algebraic expressions using algebraic reasoning

Solve.

1. A store stocks x pairs of sneakers and y pairs of sandals. During a promotion, a pair of sneakers is priced at $50 and a pair of sandals at $36. The shop manages to sell half the sneakers and 80% of the sandals. Write an expression for the total dollar amount the store makes.

Name: _____ Date: _____

Solve each question using algebraic reasoning.

1 40% of *k* liters of acid are added to 60% of *w* liters of water. Write an algebraic expression for the total volume of the solution.

2 Write an algebraic expression for the perimeter of the quadrilateral shown.

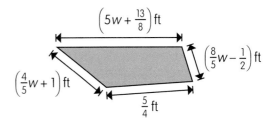

$\left(5w + \frac{13}{8}\right)$ ft

$\left(\frac{8}{5}w - \frac{1}{2}\right)$ ft

$\left(\frac{4}{5}w + 1\right)$ ft

$\frac{5}{4}$ ft

3 If the average daily sales amount for the past 5 days was (2.3*q* + 1.4) dollars, write an algebraic expression for the total sales amount for the past 5 days.

4 The weight of 2 science fiction books and 1 autobiography is $\frac{5}{6}w$ pounds. What is the total weight of 4 of these science fiction books and 2 of these autobiographies?

5 On her way to work, Ms. Lee waited 20 minutes at a subway station. The train ride took her (*x* + 30) minutes to reach Grand Central Station. Then, she walked for another $\frac{1}{3}x$ minutes before reaching her office. How much time, in minutes, did Ms. Lee take to travel to her office?

6 A piece of ribbon measuring (*v* + 4) feet in length was cut into two smaller pieces in the ratio 3 : 7. What was the length of the longer piece?

7 When one-fifth of the boys left, there were still *b* boys and *g* girls who stayed to see a musical performance. What was the total number of boys and girls at the beginning of the performance?

8 Mr. Gomez is paid at an hourly-rate of $15 and overtime hourly-rate of 1.5 times his hourly-rate for his work. If Mr. Gomez puts in w regular hours and y overtime hours in a week, what is his total wage for the week?

9 Jaden is p years old now. In 10 years' time, he will be 3 times as old as Cody. Express Cody's age 10 years from now in terms of p.

10 Ms. Walker bought a computer for 15% off from the list price of p dollars. If the sales tax was 8%, how much did she pay for the computer including sales tax?

11 A farmer collected some eggs from his farm and found b eggs broken. He packed the remaining eggs in c egg cartons. Each egg carton can hold a dozen eggs and no eggs were leftover. Write an algebraic expression for the number of eggs he collected initially in terms of b and c.

12 A teacher from Anderson Middle School printed k nametags in preparation for a science fair. Half of the nametags were given out to students and 100 nametags were given out to parents. Three-fifths of the remaining nametags were given out to teachers and contest judges. How many nametags were not given out?

13 At the beginning of a journey, the fuel tank of a car was $\frac{3}{4}$ full. When the car reached its destination, it had consumed 60% of the gasoline in the tank. The full capacity of the fuel tank was w gallons.

a Write an algebraic expression for the amount of gasoline left in the fuel tank.

b If $w = 15.5$, how much gasoline was left at the end of the journey?

Name: _____ Date: _____

Mathematical Habit 3 Construct viable arguments

Briella expanded and simplified the expression $6(x + 3) - 2(x + 1) + 5$ as follows:

$$6(x + 3) - 2(x + 1) + 5 = 6x + 3 - 2x + 1 + 5$$
$$= 6x - 2x + 3 + 1 + 5$$
$$= 4x + 9$$

Explain to Briella her mistake and show the correct solution.

Explanation:

Correct solution:

How do you check your answer?

Problem Solving with Heuristics

1 **Mathematical Habit 2** **Use mathematical reasoning**

A planner was drawing up a floorplan of a children's playground for a neighborhood. The playground was in the shape of a rectangle with length $(x + 5)$ meters and width $(x - 3)$ meters. It was then decided that the length needed to be reduced to $\frac{4}{5}$ of the original length, and the width needed to be increased to 1.2 times the original width.

a Find an expression for the perimeter of the new playground. Was there any change to the perimeter?

b If the shape of the playground were a square instead, do you think the decrease in length by 20% and the increase in width by 20% would affect the perimeter of the playground? Explain your answer.

2 **Mathematical Habit 4** **Use mathematical models**

Steven and his father are from Singapore, where the temperature is measured in degrees Celsius. While visiting downtown Los Angeles, Steven saw a temperature sign that read 72°F. He asked his father what the equivalent temperature was in °C.

His father could not recall the

Fahrenheit-to-Celsius conversion formula,

$C = \frac{5}{9}(F - 32)$. However, he remembered

that water freezes at 0°C or 32°F and boils

at 100°C or 212°F.

Using these two pieces of information, would you be able to help Steven figure out the above conversion formula? Explain.

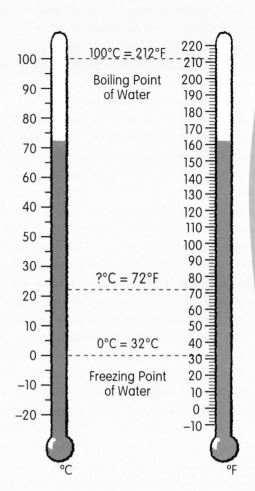

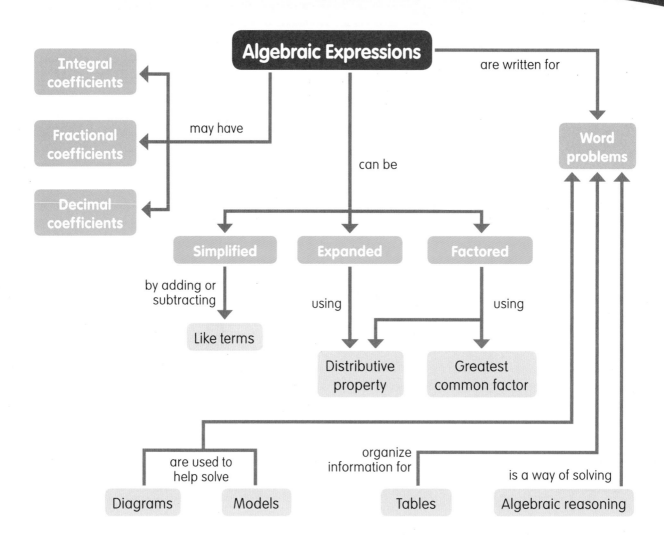

KEY CONCEPTS

- Algebraic expressions may contain more than one variable with rational coefficients and rational constants.
  Example: $\frac{1}{2}x + 1.2v - 3$.
- Algebraic expressions are written in simplest form by adding and subtracting the coefficients of the like terms.
- Algebraic expressions may be simplified using the commutative property of addition.
- Algebraic expressions are expanded using the distributive property.
- Algebraic expressions are factored using the greatest common factor (GCF) of the terms and the distributive property.
- You can use diagrams, models, or tables to help solve real-world problems algebraically.

Name: _____ Date: _____

Simplify each expression.

1) $1.4w - 0.6w$

2) $\frac{3}{4}m + \frac{4}{5}m$

3) $\frac{1}{6}y + \frac{1}{2}y + \frac{1}{3}y$

4) $1.8m + (-0.2m) - 7m$

5) $1.3a - 0.8b + 2.2b - a$

6) $1 + \frac{1}{5}a + \frac{3}{5}b - \left(-\frac{4}{5}a\right)$

Expand each expression. Then, simplify when you can.

7) $1.2(2p - 3)$

8) $\frac{1}{3}(12p + 9q)$

9) $\frac{1}{5}\left(\frac{t}{3} + \frac{1}{2}\right)$

10) $-4(-2q + 2.5)$

11) $-\frac{2}{3}(6x + 3)$

12) $-0.5(2m - 4n)$

13) $4(2p - 3) - 3(p + 2)$

14) $2.5(m - 2) + 5.6m$

15) $4(0.6n - 3) - 0.2(2n - 3)$

Factor each expression.

16) $4t - 20s$

17) $-6p - 21q$

18) $8i + 12 + 4j$

19) $6a + 10b - 20$

20) $-9m - 3n - 6$

21) $-15x - 6 - 12y$

Translate each verbal description into an algebraic expression. Then, simplify when you can.

22. One-fourth x less than the sum of 7 and $2x$.

23. 4 times $5y$ divided by 18.

24. Five-ninths of $(3p + 1)$ subtracted from one-third of $(q + p)$.

Solve.

25. After 14 boys leave a concert, the ratio of boys to girls is 3 : 10. If there are p girls at the concert, write an algebraic expression for the number of boys at the beginning of the concert in terms of p.

26. 40% of the fish in a pond are goldfish and the rest are Koi. The number of goldfish is g. The farmer then increases the number of Koi by 10%. How many Koi are there in the pond, in terms of g, now?

27. Three-fourths of the weight of a bunch of grapes is equivalent to three-fifths of the weight of a papaya. If the grapes weigh $(x + 28)$ pounds, what is the weight of a papaya in terms of x?

28. Mr. Lee ordered some pizzas to be delivered. The bill for the pizza was m dollars. Mr. Lee tipped the deliverer 15% of the bill.

    a Write an expression for the total amount of money Mr. Lee paid.

    b The bill for the pizza was $30. Find the amount of money Mr. Lee paid.

© 2020 Marshall Cavendish Education Pte Ltd

29 A box contains n quarters and some dimes. The ratio of quarters to dimes is $1 : 2$.

 a Write an expression for the total amount of money in the box.

 b If there are 12 quarters, find the total amount of money in the box.

30 Ms. Smith is considering two cell phone plans that charge for each call made. The charges are shown below.

Cell Phone Plan	Monthly Subscription	Cost Per Minute
A	$10	21.4¢/min
B	$14	18.5¢/min

On average, Ms. Smith uses n minutes of calling time each month.

 a Write an expression for the total charges for Ms. Smith's usage based on each cell phone plan.

 b If $n = 100$, find the total cost for each cell phone plan. Which cell phone plan should Ms. Smith choose? Justify your choice.

31 The admission fee to a museum is $12.50 per nonsenior adult, $8 per child, and $6.50 per senior citizen. A tour group consists of m nonsenior adults, $\left(\frac{5}{4}m + 6\right)$ children, and $8n$ senior citizens.

 a What is the total admission fee of the group?

 b Write an expression for the admission fees of the children in the group subtracted from the combined admission fees of the nonsenior adults and senior citizens in the group.

 c Evaluate your expression from b, when $m = 24$ and $n = 4$.

Assessment Prep
Answer each question.

32 Which expression is equivalent to $(4x + 3) + (-2x + 4)$?

   Ⓐ $-2x + 12$

   Ⓑ $-8x + 12$

   Ⓒ $6x + 7$

   Ⓓ $2x + 7$

33 Which expressions are equivalent to $-3.75 + 2(-4y + 6.1) - 3.25y$? Choose all that apply.

   Ⓐ $7y - 2y + 8.1$

   Ⓑ $8.45 - 8y - 3.25y$

   Ⓒ $-1.75 - 7.25y + 6.1$

   Ⓓ $-11.25y + 12.2 - 3.75$

34 What is the value of k when the expression $21.2x + k$ is equivalent to $5.3(4x + 2.6)$?
Write your answer and your work or explanation in the space below.

35 A printer takes 2.4 seconds longer to print a page in color than a page in black and white. A page in black and white can be printed in 4 seconds. There are $\left(\frac{5}{8}w + 6\right)$ color pages and $(1.2w + 5)$ black and white pages to print. How long does it take to print all the pages? Write your answer and your work or explanation in the space below.

Name: _____   Date: _____

School Trip to National Park

1 A survey was conducted with x students. 10% of those surveyed said that they have been to a national park. Of the students who had never been to a national park, 50 of them planned to eventually visit a national park. Write an algebraic expression that represents the students who did not plan on visiting a national park.

2 y students went on a school trip to a national park. $\frac{1}{3}$ of the students had a parent accompanying them. 6 teachers also joined the trip. The cost of the trip was 9 dollars per person. Write an algebraic expression, in simplest form, to represent the total cost.

3 Of the total number of students who went for the school trip, 4 less than $\frac{1}{4}$ of them were girls. Do you agree or disagree that the expression $y - 4$, represents 4 times the number of students who were girls? Justify your reasoning with precise mathematical language. You can make use of expressions, equations, bar models or counters.

Rubric

Point(s)	Level	My Performance
7–8	4	• Most of my answers are correct. • I showed complete understanding of the concepts. • I used effective and efficient strategies to solve the problems. • I explained my answers and mathematical thinking clearly and completely.
5–6	3	• Some of my answers are correct. • I showed adequate understanding of the concepts. • I used effective strategies to solve the problems. • I explained my answers and mathematical thinking clearly.
3–4	2	• A few of my answers are correct. • I showed some understanding of the concepts. • I used some effective strategies to solve the problems. • I explained some of my answers and mathematical thinking clearly.
0–2	1	• A few of my answers are correct. • I showed little understanding of the concepts. • I used limited effective strategies to solve the problems. • I did not explain my answers and mathematical thinking clearly.

Teacher's Comments

STEAM

A Field Trip

Seventh-graders across the United States often take a special field trip as a class. Many students visit their state's capital or a state history museum. Where do seventh-graders at your school go on a class field trip? Where do you think they would like to go?

Task

Work in small groups to plan a class field trip.

1 Use the internet to learn more about field-trip possibilities in your community or state.

2 Select a destination. Then examine the costs associated with the trip. Remember to consider the cost of transportation to and from your destination. Also investigate the cost of entrance tickets, food, and special venues or activities at the site.

3 Calculate costs by hand, or use a digital tool. Write and solve equations identifying the total per-student cost and the total amount your teacher will need to collect before the day of the trip.

4 To help students make the most of a new experience, prepare an activity guide. Draw or use digital tools to prepare a brochure. You can also plan something more original, like a scavenger hunt. Use your research to make a map of your destination. Then provide clues that students must follow to locate specific objects, places, or information. Have students take photographs to record their discoveries.

5 Share your work with other teams.

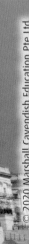

Algebraic Equations and Inequalities

How much can you raise?

There are many good causes that you can walk, run, or swim to support. Participating in a sport for charity is good for you, and good for the organizations that receive the money you raise.

The first step is to find a charity you want to support. Perhaps you see a sign or receive an online notice. You register, and the organization sends you volunteer materials, including a fundraising form. You explain the purpose of the event to friends and family members, and you invite them to donate money. Some supporters donate a specific amount. Others donate an amount for every mile you walk, run, or swim. You can use algebraic equations to calculate how much you will need to collect from each supporter after the event.

In this chapter, you will learn how to use algebraic equations and inequalities to represent and solve a variety of real-world problems similar to this one.

How do you solve algebraic equations and inequalities?

Name: _____ Date: _____

Solving algebraic equations by balancing

You can use inverse operations to solve an equation. When you do, keep the equation balanced by performing addition, subtraction, multiplication, or division by the same nonzero number on both sides.

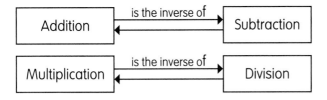

Solve each equation.

a $x + 2 = 9$

$$x + 2 = 9$$
$$x + 2 - 2 = 9 - 2 \quad \text{Subtract 2 from both sides.}$$
$$x = 7 \quad \text{Simplify.}$$

b $\frac{2}{3}x = 2$

$$\frac{2}{3}x = 2$$

$$\frac{2}{3}x \div \frac{2}{3} = 2 \div \frac{2}{3} \quad \text{Divide both sides by } \frac{2}{3}.$$

$$\frac{2}{3}x \cdot \frac{3}{2} = 2 \cdot \frac{3}{2} \quad \text{Rewrite division as multiplication by the reciprocal of } \frac{2}{3}.$$

$$x = 3 \quad \text{Simplify.}$$

▶ **Quick Check**

Solve each equation.

1 $x + 4 = 10$

2 $x - \frac{1}{2} = 2$

3 $\frac{1}{5}x = 3$

4 $1.2x = 2.4$

Solving algebraic equations by substitution

You can use substitution to solve an algebraic equation.

Solve $x + 6 = 8$.

If $x = 1$,　　$x + 6 = 1 + 6$　　Substitute 1 for x.
　　　　　　　　　$= 7$　$(\neq 8)$　1 is not the solution.

If $x = 2$,　　$x + 6 = 2 + 6$　　Substitute 2 for x.
　　　　　　　　　$= 8$　　　2 is the solution.

The equation $x + 6 = 8$ is true when $x = 2$.
$x = 2$ gives the solution of the equation $x + 6 = 8$.

▶ **Quick Check**

State whether each statement is True or False.

⑤　$x = 1$ gives the solution of the algebraic equation $3x + 5 = 8$.

⑥　$y = 2$ gives the solution of the algebraic equation $6y - 3 = 8$.

⑦　$z = 6$ gives the solution of the algebraic equation $\frac{z}{3} = 3$.

⑧　$w = 3$ gives the solution of the algebraic equation $2w = 6$.

Graphing inequalities on a number line

You can represent an inequality on a number line using circles and arrows.

$p > 5.5$

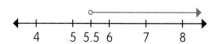

Use an empty circle to show that
5.5 is not a solution of the inequality.

$q \leq 11$

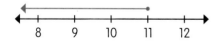

Use a shaded circle to show that
11 is a solution of the inequality.

▶ **Quick Check**

Draw a number line to represent each inequality.

⑨　$x \geq 3.5$　　　　　　　　　　　⑩　$y < \frac{1}{2}$

Writing algebraic inequalities

Use >, <, ≥, ≤, or ≠ to compare unequal quantities or quantities that may not be equal.

Verbal Descriptions	Algebraic Inequality
The cost of an apple, *a*, is not $3.	$a \neq 3$
The cost of a greeting card, *c*, is less than $6.	$c < 6$
The mass of the strawberries, *s*, is more than 500 grams.	$s > 500$
The width of the pond, *w*, is at most 5 meters. OR The width of the pond, *w*, is no more than 5 meters. OR The width of the pond, *w*, is less than or equal to 5 meters.	$w \leq 5$
The length of the ribbon, *r*, is at least 10 inches. OR The length of the ribbon, *r*, is no less than 10 inches. OR The length of the ribbon, *r*, is greater than or equal to 10 inches.	$r \geq 10$

▶ **Quick Check**

Compare each pair of numbers or expressions using <, >, or =.

⑪ $11 \bigcirc -12$

⑫ $-9 \bigcirc -7$

⑬ $25 \cdot (-1) \bigcirc (-1) \cdot 25$

⑭ $3 \div (-1) \bigcirc (-1) \div 3$

Use *x* to represent the unknown quantity. Write an algebraic inequality for each statement.

⑮ The box can hold less than 70 pounds.

⑯ You have to be at least 17 years old to qualify for the contest.

⑰ The width of luggage that you can carry onto the plane is at most 17 inches.

⑱ There are more than 120 people standing in line for the roller coaster.

Identifying Equivalent Equations

Learning Objective:
• Identify equivalent equations.

> **New Vocabulary**
> equivalent equations

THINK

The width of a rectangle is 5 inches shorter than its length. Its perimeter is $39\frac{1}{2}$ inches. Chloe wrote "$l + (l - 5) + l + (l - 5) = 39\frac{1}{2}$" and David wrote "$2(l + l - 5) = 39\frac{1}{2}$" to represent the situation. Explain whether they are correct. What equation can you write to represent the situation? Explain.

ENGAGE

Consider the following equations:

a $7 + 3 - 1 = 10 - 1$

b $7 + 3 + 2 = 10 + 2$

c $(7 + 3) \cdot 3 = (7 \times 3) + (3 \times 3)$

d $(7 + 3) \div 5 = 10 \div 5$

What do you notice? Is there a pattern?
Share your observations.

LEARN Identify equivalent equations

① You have learned that factoring, simplifying, or expanding an expression produces an equivalent expression. Equivalent expressions have the same value for any given value of the variable.

Examples of equivalent expressions:

$4x + 3 + 3x = 7x + 3$ Group like terms.

$4x + 6 = 2(2x + 3)$ Factor. The common factor of $4x$ and 6 is 2.

$2(x - 5) = 2x - 10$ Use the distributive property to expand.

Equivalent equations are equations that have the same solution. Given an equation, use the operations of addition, subtraction, multiplication, or division to produce an equivalent equation. For example, you can subtract 2 from both sides of the equation $x - 1 = 7$ as shown.

Balance	Algebraic Equation
■ represents 1 counter. ▬ represents x counters. $x - 1 \{$ [balance diagram] Subtract 2 counters from both sides. $x - 1 \{$ [balance diagram]	Left side = Right side ↓ ↓ $x - 1 = 7$ $x - 1 - 2 = 7 - 2$ Subtract both sides by 2. $x - 3 = 5$ Simplify.

Compare the solutions of the original equation and the new equation:
$x = 8$ gives the solution of the equation $x - 1 = 7$.
$x = 8$ gives the solution of the equation $x - 3 = 5$.

Now suppose you add 3 to both sides of the equation $x - 3 = 5$.

Balance	Algebraic Equation
[balance diagram] $x - 3 \{$	$x - 3 + 3 = 5 + 3$ Add 3 to both sides. $x = 8$ Simplify.

Compare the solutions of the original equation and the new equation:
$x = 8$ gives the solution of the equation $x - 3 = 5$.
$x = 8$ gives the solution of the equation $x = 8$.

Then, suppose you multiply both sides of the equation $x = 8$ by 2.

Balance	Algebraic Equation
Multiply both sides by 2.	$x \cdot \mathbf{2} = 8 \cdot \mathbf{2}$ Multiply both sides by 2. $2x = 16$ Simplify.

Compare the solutions of the original equation and the new equation:
$x = 8$ gives the solution of the equation $x = 8$.
$x = 8$ gives the solution of the equation $2x = 16$.

Finally, suppose you divide both sides of the equation $2x = 16$ by 4.

Balance	Algebraic Equation
Divide into four equal groups.	$2x \div \mathbf{4} = 16 \div \mathbf{4}$ Divide both sides by 4. $\frac{1}{2}x = 4$ Simplify.

Compare the solutions of the original equation and the new equation:

$x = 8$ gives the solution of the equation $2x = 16$.

$x = 8$ gives the solution of the equation $\frac{1}{2}x = 4$.

So, performing the same operation on both sides of an equation may produce an equivalent equation with the same solution. You can use the fact that equivalent equations have the same solution to decide whether two equations are equivalent.

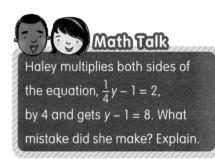

Math Talk

Haley multiplies both sides of the equation, $\frac{1}{4}y - 1 = 2$, by 4 and gets $y - 1 = 8$. What mistake did she make? Explain.

2 Determine whether $x + 3 + 6x = 13$ and $7x + 3 = 13$ are equivalent equations. Explain your answer.

$x + 3 + 6x = 13$
$x + 6x + 3 = 13$ Use commutative property to group like terms.
$7x + 3 = 13$ Add like terms.

$x + 3 + 6x = 13$ can be rewritten as $7x + 3 = 13$ using familiar number properties.
So, the equations have the same solution and are equivalent.

3 Determine whether $5x - 4 = 6$ and $5x = 20$ are equivalent equations. Explain your answer.

Check if both equations have the same solution.
First, solve $5x = 20$.

$5x \div \mathbf{5} = 20 \div \mathbf{5}$ Divide both sides by 5.
$\qquad x = 4$ Simplify.

Then, check if $x = 4$ is the solution for the equation, $5x - 4 = 6$.

If $x = 4$, $5x - 4 = 5 \cdot 4 - 4$ Substitute 4 for x.
$\qquad\qquad\qquad = 16$ $(\neq 6)$ 4 is not a solution.

Since the equations have different solutions, they are not equivalent equations.
So, $5x - 4 = 6$ and $5x = 20$ are not equivalent equations.

4 Determine whether $\frac{2}{3}x = 4$ and $x = 6$ are equivalent equations. Explain your answer.

Check if both equations have the same solution.

If $x = 6$, $\frac{2}{3}x = \frac{2}{3} \cdot 6$ Substitute 6 for x.
$\qquad\qquad\quad = 4$ 6 is a solution.

Since the equations have the same solution, 6, they are equivalent equations.
So, $\frac{2}{3}x = 4$ and $x = 6$ are equivalent equations.

TRY **Practice identifying equivalent equations**

Determine whether each pair of equations are equivalent. Explain your answer.

1 $x + 7 = 12$ and $2x = 10$

2 $1.2x = 2.4$ and $x - 6 = 8$

3 $0.2x = 0.6$ and $3x + 1 = 10$

4 $\frac{2}{5}x = 4$ and $x = 10$

INDEPENDENT PRACTICE

Determine whether each pair of equations are equivalent. Explain your answer.

1 $2x = 4$ and $4x + 5 = 13$

2 $-2x + 9 = 7$ and $-2x = 2$

3 $5x - 4 + 3x = 8$ and $8x = 12$

4 $\frac{3}{4}x - 7 = 2$ and $x = 12$

Match each equation with an equivalent equation.

5 $0.5x + 1 = 1.5$

a $6x = 9$

6 $9 + 3.5x = 16$

b $\frac{3}{5}x = \frac{1}{15}$

7 $\frac{4}{5}x = 4$

c $\frac{3}{2}x = 3$

8 $2x + \frac{1}{2} = \frac{7}{2}$

d $\frac{2}{3}x = \frac{2}{3}$

9 $x - 8.3 = 1.3$

e $2x = 10$

10 $13.9 = 2.5x$

f $1.2 + x = 6.76$

11 $4x = \frac{4}{9}$

g $\frac{1}{2}x = 4.8$

Solve.

12 **Mathematical Habit 3** **Construct viable arguments**

Chris was asked to write an equation equivalent to $\frac{2}{3}x = 3 - x$. He wrote the following:

$$\frac{2}{3}x = 3 - x$$

$$\frac{2}{3}x \cdot 3 = 3 \cdot 3 - x$$

$$2x = 9 - x$$

Chris concluded that $\frac{2}{3}x = 3 - x$ and $2x = 9 - x$ are equivalent equations.

Do you agree with his conclusion? Give a reason for your answer.

Solving Algebraic Equations

Learning Objectives:
• Solve algebraic equations with variables on the same side of the equation.
• Solve algebraic equations in factored form.

THINK

Fill in the blank in the equation, $2x + 2(2x - \underline{\hspace{1cm}}) = 8$, so that $x < 2$.
Show how you find the answer.

ENGAGE

Use and the idea of balance to find the value of x in the equation $2x + 6 = 12$.

Share your method.

Now, consider this problem.
At the bowling alley, the total cost of bowling is $6 per game plus $3 for shoes. On one visit, Eric spent $21 altogether. How many games did Eric bowl? Explain your thinking.

LEARN Solve algebraic equations

1. To solve an equation means to find the value of the variable that makes the equation true. You can add, subtract, multiply, or divide both sides of the equation by the same nonzero number to solve an equation. Our goal is to produce an equivalent equation in which the variable is alone, or "isolated" on one side of the equation.

For example, to solve $2x + 6 = 9$,

Balance	Algebraic Equation
■ represents 1 counter. ⊠ represents x counters.	Solve the equation by isolating the variable, x. Left side Equals Right side $2x + 6$ $=$ 9

Remove 6 counters from both sides.

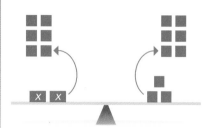

First, isolate the algebraic term, 2x, on one side of the equation.

Decide which operation to use. Subtraction is the inverse of addition. To undo the addition of 6 to 2x, subtract 6 from both sides of the equation.

$$2x + 6 - \mathbf{6} = 9 - \mathbf{6}$$ Subtract 6 from both sides.
$$2x = 3$$ Simplify.

Divide each into two equal groups.

The counters on both sides are equal.

Then, isolate the variable, x. In other words, x will have a coefficient of 1.

Decide which operation to use. Division is the inverse of multiplication. To undo the multiplication of 2 and x, divide both sides of the equation by 2.

$$2x \div \mathbf{2} = 3 \div \mathbf{2}$$ Divide both sides by 2.
$$x = 1.5$$ Simplify.

$x = 1.5$ gives the solution of the equation $2x + 6 = 9$.

Remember to keep an equation "balanced" by performing the same operation on both sides.

To check if $x = 1.5$ is the solution, substitute the value of $x = 1.5$ into the original equation.
$$2x + 6 = 2 \cdot (1.5) + 6$$
$$= 9$$

When $x = 1.5$, the equation $2x + 6 = 9$ is true.

When an expression in an algebraic equation involves more than one operation, you can use the order of operations "in reverse" to undo the operations and isolate the variable.

Steps for solving an equation:

 "Undo" addition or subtraction using inverse operations.

 "Undo" multiplication or division using inverse operations.

© 2020 Marshall Cavendish Education Pte Ltd

2 Solve $3x + 7 = 28$.

$$3x + 7 = 28$$
$$3x + 7 - \mathbf{7} = 28 - \mathbf{7} \quad \text{Subtract 7 from both sides to undo addition.}$$
$$3x = 21 \quad \text{Simplify.}$$
$$3x \div \mathbf{3} = 21 \div \mathbf{3} \quad \text{Divide both sides by 3 to undo multiplication.}$$
$$x = 7 \quad \text{Simplify.}$$

$x = 7$ gives the solution of the equation $3x + 7 = 28$.

Check

Substitute the value of $x = 7$ into the original equation.

$$3x + 7 = 3 \cdot 7 + 7$$
$$= 28$$

When $x = 7$, the equation $3x + 7 = 28$ is true.
$x = 7$ gives the solution.

3 Solve $0.5x + 1.5 = 4.5$.

$$0.5x + 1.5 = 4.5$$
$$0.5x + 1.5 - \mathbf{1.5} = 4.5 - \mathbf{1.5} \quad \text{Subtract 1.5 from both sides.}$$
$$0.5x = 3 \quad \text{Simplify.}$$
$$0.5x \cdot \mathbf{2} = 3 \cdot \mathbf{2} \quad \text{Multiply both sides by 2 to undo.}$$
$$x = 6 \quad \text{Simplify.}$$

$x = 6$ gives the solution of the equation $0.5x + 1.5 = 4.5$.

$$0.5 = \frac{1}{2}$$
$$\frac{1}{2} \cdot 2 = 1$$

Check

Substitute the value of $x = 6$ into the original equation.

$$0.5x + 1.5 = 0.5 \cdot 6 + 1.5$$
$$= 4.5$$

When $x = 6$, the equation $0.5x + 1.5 = 4.5$ is true.
$x = 6$ gives the solution.

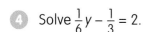

④ Solve $\frac{1}{6}y - \frac{1}{3} = 2$.

▶ **Method 1**
Solve by balancing the equation.

$$\frac{y}{6} - \frac{1}{3} = 2$$

$$\frac{y}{6} - \frac{1}{3} + \frac{1}{3} = 2 + \frac{1}{3} \qquad \text{Add } \frac{1}{3} \text{ to both sides.}$$

$$\frac{y}{6} = \frac{7}{3} \qquad \text{Simplify.}$$

$$6 \cdot \left(\frac{y}{6}\right) = 6 \cdot \left(\frac{7}{3}\right) \qquad \text{Multiply both sides by 6, which is the reciprocal}$$
$$\text{of the coefficient, } \frac{1}{6}.$$

$$y = 14 \qquad \text{Simplify.}$$

> The term $\frac{1}{6}y$ can be written as $\frac{y}{6}$. There are two operations to undo: The subtraction of $\frac{1}{3}$ and the division by 6.

▶ **Method 2**
Solve by multiplying the equation by the least common denominator (LCD).

$$6 \cdot \left(\frac{y}{6} - \frac{1}{3}\right) = 6 \cdot 2 \qquad \text{Multiply both sides by 6, the LCD of } \frac{1}{6} \text{ and } \frac{1}{3}.$$

$$6 \cdot \frac{y}{6} - 6 \cdot \frac{1}{3} = 6 \cdot 2 \qquad \text{Use the distributive property.}$$

$$y - 2 = 12 \qquad \text{Simplify.}$$

$$y - 2 + 2 = 12 + 2 \qquad \text{Add 2 to both sides.}$$

$$y = 14 \qquad \text{Simplify.}$$

When $y = 14$, the equation $\frac{1}{6}y - \frac{1}{3} = 2$ is true.

$y = 14$ gives the solution of the equation $\frac{1}{6}y - \frac{1}{3} = 2$.

 Math Note
When you multiply equations involving fractional coefficients by the LCD, the two sides of the equation will remain equal. This will result in equivalent equations that do not contain fractions.

Math Note

Multiplying and dividing rational numbers:

Two signs are the same:		Two signs are different:	
Multiplication	**Division**	**Multiplication**	**Division**
$(+) \cdot (+) = (+)$	$(+) \div (+) = (+)$	$(+) \cdot (-) = (-)$	$(+) \div (-) = (-)$
$(-) \cdot (-) = (+)$	$(-) \div (-) = (+)$	$(-) \cdot (+) = (-)$	$(-) \div (+) = (-)$
For example, $(-1) \cdot (-2) = 2$ and $1 \cdot 2 = 2$.		For example, $(-1) \cdot 2 = -2$, and $1 \cdot (-2) = -2$.	

Solve.

1. $6x + 2 = 8$

2. $3 - 7x = 10$

3. $5 - 3x = 20$

4. $4x - 3 + 0.5x = 1.5$

5. $\frac{9}{10}x - \frac{4}{5} = 1$

6. $\frac{9}{10} - \frac{4}{5}x = 1$

ENGAGE

Look at these expressions.

a $2(x - 1)$ b $\frac{1}{2}(x + 1)$ c $3x + 4(x - 1)$

How do you expand the expressions? What do you get? Discuss.
Riley says using the above results, she can solve the following equations.

a $2(x - 1) = 5$ b $\frac{1}{2}(x + 1) = 3$ c $3x + 4(x - 1) = 10$

Do you agree or disagree? Explain your thinking.

LEARN Solve algebraic equations in factored form

1 Solve $2(3x + 1) = 11$.

▶ **Method 1**
Use the distributive property and inverse operations.

First, use the distributive property to expand the expression.

$2(3x + 1) = 11$
$2 \cdot 3x + 2 \cdot 1 = 11$ Use the distributive property.
$6x + 2 = 11$ Simplify.

Then, isolate the algebraic term.

$6x + 2 - \mathbf{2} = 11 - \mathbf{2}$ Subtract 2 from both sides.
$6x = 9$ Simplify.

Finally, isolate the variable.

$6x \div \mathbf{6} = 9 \div \mathbf{6}$ Divide both sides by 6.
$x = 1.5$ Simplify. Express in simplest form.

▶ **Method 2**
Use inverse operations.

First, divide both sides by 2 to "undo" the multiplication.

$2(3x + 1) = 11$
$\dfrac{2(3x + 1)}{\mathbf{2}} = \dfrac{11}{\mathbf{2}}$ Divide both sides by 2.
$3x + 1 = 5.5$ Simplify.

Then, isolate the algebraic term.

$3x + 1 - \mathbf{1} = 5.5 - \mathbf{1}$ Subtract 1 from both sides.
$3x = 4.5$ Simplify.

Finally, isolate the variable.

$3x \div \mathbf{3} = 4.5 \div \mathbf{3}$ Divide both sides by 3.
$x = 1.5$ Simplify. Express in simplest form.

> To simplify $\dfrac{2(3x + 1)}{2}$, think of $(3x + 1)$ as a single number. Just as $\dfrac{2x}{2} = x$, so does $\dfrac{2(3x + 1)}{2} = 3x + 1$.

2 Solve $\frac{1}{6}(z + 1) = 6$.

▶ **Method 1**
Use the distributive property and inverse operations.

$$\frac{1}{6}(z + 1) = 6$$

$$\frac{1}{6} \cdot z + \frac{1}{6} \cdot 1 = 6 \qquad \text{Use the distributive property.}$$

$$\frac{1}{6}z + \frac{1}{6} = 6 \qquad \text{Simplify.}$$

$$\frac{1}{6}z + \frac{1}{6} - \frac{1}{6} = \frac{36}{6} - \frac{1}{6} \qquad \text{Subtract } \frac{1}{6} \text{ from both sides. Rewrite 6 as } \frac{36}{6}.$$

$$\frac{1}{6}z = \frac{35}{6} \qquad \text{Simplify.}$$

$$6 \cdot \frac{1}{6}z = 6 \cdot \frac{35}{6} \qquad \text{Multiply both sides by 6.}$$

$$z = 35 \qquad \text{Simplify.}$$

▶ **Method 2**
Use inverse operations.

$$\frac{1}{6}(z + 1) = 6$$

$$6 \cdot \frac{1}{6}(z + 1) = 6 \cdot 6 \qquad \text{Multiply both sides by 6.}$$

$$z + 1 = 36 \qquad \text{Simplify.}$$

$$z + 1 - 1 = 36 - 1 \qquad \text{Subtract 1 from both sides.}$$

$$z = 35 \qquad \text{Simplify.}$$

3 Solve $1.5(w + 2) + 2 = 8$.

$$1.5(w + 2) + 2 = 8$$
$$1.5 \cdot w + 1.5 \cdot 2 + 2 = 8 \qquad \text{Use the distributive property.}$$
$$1.5w + 5 = 8 \qquad \text{Simplify.}$$
$$1.5w + 5 - 5 = 8 - 5 \qquad \text{Subtract 5 from both sides.}$$
$$1.5w = 3 \qquad \text{Simplify.}$$
$$1.5w \div 1.5 = 3 \div 1.5 \qquad \text{Divide both sides by 1.5.}$$
$$w = 2 \qquad \text{Simplify.}$$

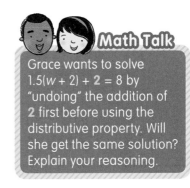

Math Talk

Grace wants to solve $1.5(w + 2) + 2 = 8$ by "undoing" the addition of 2 first before using the distributive property. Will she get the same solution? Explain your reasoning.

4 Solve $2x + 5(2 - x) = 40$.

> There is more than one way to solve this equation. Suppose you first divide each term by 5:
>
> $2x \div 5 + 5(2 - x) \div 5 = 40 \div 5$
>
> $$\frac{2}{5}x + (2 - x) = 8$$
>
> $$\frac{2}{5}x + 2 - x = 8$$
>
> $$-\frac{3}{5}x + 2 = 8$$
>
> Then, you have to solve an equation involving a variable with a negative fractional coefficient. A better method is to use the distributive property first.

$$2x + 5(2 - x) = 40$$
$$2x + 5 \cdot 2 - 5 \cdot x = 40 \qquad \text{Use the distributive property.}$$
$$2x + 10 - 5x = 40 \qquad \text{Simplify.}$$
$$10 - 3x = 40 \qquad \text{Subtract the like terms.}$$
$$10 - 3x - 10 = 40 - 10 \qquad \text{Subtract 10 from both sides.}$$
$$-3x = 30 \qquad \text{Simplify.}$$
$$-\frac{3x}{-3} = \frac{30}{-3} \qquad \text{Divide both sides by } -3.$$
$$x = -10 \qquad \text{Simplify.}$$

 Practice solving algebraic equations in factored form

Solve each equation. Check your solutions.

1 $1.5(p + 3) = 18$

2 $\frac{1}{4}(q + 1) = 9$

3 $2(x - 3) + 2 = 14$

4 $3(y - 1) + y = 1$

3 Real-World Problems: Algebraic Equations

Learning Objective:
• Solve real-world problems algebraically.

THINK

Ethan ran at an average speed of 12 km/h for 15 minutes, and then continued to walk for half an hour at a certain average speed. If his average speed for the entire journey is 6 km/h, how can you find his average walking speed algebraically? How do you check your answer? Explain.

ENGAGE

A photo frame has a border of x inches. It surrounds a photograph that is placed within it. A photograph measuring 5 inches by 7 inches can fit in neatly without any white space. What are the dimensions of the frame? Draw a sketch to show your thinking.

If the outer perimeter of the frame is 28 inches, use an equation to model the situation. Share and explain how you find the width of the frame border.

LEARN Solve real-world problems algebraically

1 Evelyn framed a drawing as shown. The border of the frame is x inches wide. The dimensions of the drawing are 12 inches by 5 inches. If the outer perimeter of the frame is 58 inches, find the width of the frame border.

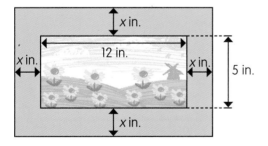

STEP 1 Understand the problem.

What are the dimensions of the drawing?
What are the dimensions of the frame?
What is the outer perimeter of the frame?
What do I need to find?

STEP 2 Think of a plan.
I can use algebraic reasoning to translate the problem into algebraic expressions.

 STEP 3 Carry out the plan.
Using the diagram, write algebraic expressions for the dimensions of the frame.

Length of the frame: $12 + 2x$
Width of the frame: $5 + 2x$

Then, write an algebraic equation.

$$2(\ell + w) = \text{Perimeter}$$ Write a perimeter formula.
$$2(12 + 2x + 5 + 2x) = 58$$ Substitute.
$$2(17 + 4x) = 58$$ Add like terms.

Finally, solve the equation.

$$2 \cdot 17 + 2 \cdot 4x = 58$$ Use the distributive property.
$$34 + 8x = 58$$ Simplify.
$$34 + 8x - 34 = 58 - 34$$ Subtract 34 from both sides.
$$8x = 24$$ Simplify.
$$\frac{8x}{8} = \frac{24}{8}$$ Divide both sides by 8.
$$x = 3$$ Simplify.

The border of the frame is 3 inches wide.

 STEP 4 Check the answer.
I can substitute $x = 3$ into the dimensions of the frame to check my answer.

Length of frame = $12 + 2x$ Width of frame = $5 + 2x$
                = $12 + 2(3)$ = $5 + 2(3)$
                = 18 in.   = 11 in.

$2(18) + 2(11)$ = $36 + 22$
                = 58 in.
                = Outer perimeter of frame

My answer is correct.

2 Luis wrote a riddle: A positive number is $\frac{1}{3}$ of another positive number. If their difference is 48, find the two positive numbers.

Solve using algebraic reasoning.

Let one of the numbers be x. Define the variable.

Then, the other number is $\frac{1}{3}x$. Write the other number in terms of the variable.

Since $x > \frac{1}{3}x$ and their difference is 48, I can write $x - \frac{1}{3}x = 48$.

Find one of the numbers, x:

$x - \frac{1}{3}x = 48$ Write an equation.

$\frac{3}{3}x - \frac{1}{3}x = 48$ Rewrite x as $\frac{3}{3}x$.

$\frac{2}{3}x = 48$ Simplify.

$\frac{2}{3}x \cdot \frac{3}{2} = 48 \cdot \frac{3}{2}$ Multiply both sides by the reciprocal of $\frac{2}{3}$.

$x = 72$ Simplify.

Find the other number: $\frac{1}{3}x = \frac{1}{3} \cdot 72$ Evaluate $\frac{1}{3}x$ when $x = 72$.

$\qquad\qquad\qquad = 24$

The two positive numbers are 72 and 24.

Check:

$\frac{72}{3} = 24$

24 is $\frac{1}{3}$ of 72. ✓

$72 - 24 = 48$ ✓

The difference between the two numbers is 48.

The two positive numbers, 72 and 24, are correct.

③ A theater is divided into a red section and a blue section. The red section has 350 seats, and the rest of the seats are in the blue section. A ticket for a red section seat costs $75, and a ticket for a blue section seat costs $50.

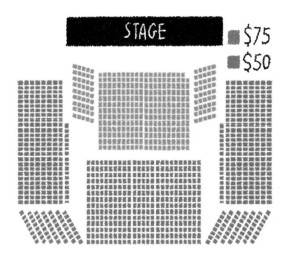

a Write an expression for the total amount collected from the sale of tickets for all the seats in the two sections.

Let *x* represent the number of blue section tickets.   Define the variable.

Total sales from 350 red section tickets: 75 · 350 = 26,250
Total sales from *x* blue section tickets: 50 · x = 50x
Total sales equal sales of red section tickets plus sales of blue section tickets.

The total sales are (26,250 + 50t) dollars.

b The total sales when all the tickets are sold are $68,750.
How many seats are in the blue section?

$$26,250 + 50x = 68,750$$ Write an equation.
$$26,250 + 50x - \mathbf{26,250} = 68,750 - \mathbf{26,250}$$ Subtract 26,250 from both sides.
$$50x = 42,500$$ Simplify.

$$\frac{50x}{50} = \frac{42,500}{50}$$ Divide both sides by 50.

$$x = 850$$ Simplify.

There are 850 seats in the blue section.

4 Ivan has 12 more comic books than Hana. If they have 28 comic books altogether, how many comic books does Ivan have?

Hana has **some** comic books. Ivan has **12 more than** Hana.
?   (? + 12)
They have **28 books altogether**.
? + (? + 12) = **28**

Let the number of comic books that Hana has be x.   Define the variable.
Then, the number of comic books that Ivan has is $x + 12$.

Because they have 28 comic books altogether,

$x + (x + 12) = 28$ Write an equation.
$2x + 12 = 28$ Simplify.
$2x + 12 - 12 = 28 - 12$ Subtract 12 from both sides.
$2x = 16$ Simplify.
$\dfrac{2x}{2} = \dfrac{16}{2}$ Divide both sides by 2.
$x = 8$ Simplify.

Number of books that Ivan has: $x + 12 = 8 + 12$ Evaluate $x + 12$ when $x = 8$.
$= 20$

Ivan has 20 comic books.

TRY Practice solving real-world problems algebraically

Solve.

1. Matthew wrote a riddle: A negative number is $\frac{2}{5}$ of another negative number. If the sum of the two negative numbers is -35, find the two negative numbers.

2. At an auditorium, tickets are sold for "circle seats" and "row seats." There are 220 circle seats, and the rest of the seats are row seats. Each circle seat ticket costs $100 and each row seat ticket costs $60.

   a Write an expression for the total amount collected from the sale of all the seats at the auditorium.

   b The total amount collected when all the tickets are sold is $68,800. How many row seat tickets are sold?

3. Ethan has 16 more game cards than Sofia. If they have 48 game cards altogether, find the number of game cards Ethan has.

4. A bike shop charges x dollars to rent a bike for half a day. It charges $(x + 40)$ dollars to rent a bike for a full day. The table shows the shop's bike rentals for one day. On that day, the shop made a total of $600 from bike rentals.

Time Period	Amount ($)	Number of Bikes
Half day	x	5
Full day	$x + 40$	3

   How much does it cost to rent a bike for a full day?

5. An artist is weaving a rectangular wall hanging. The wall hanging is already 18 inches long, and the artist plans to weave an additional 2 inches each day. The finished wall hanging will be 60 inches long. How many days will it take the artist to finish the wall hanging?

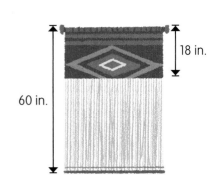

18 in.

60 in.

6. Ms. Lopez plans to buy a laptop for $1,345 in 12 weeks. She has already saved $145. How much should she save each week so she can buy the laptop?

Equations

Algebraic Equations and Inequalities

Solving Algebraic Inequalities

Learning Objectives:
• Solve algebraic inequalities.
• Graph the solution set of an inequality on a number line.
• Solve multi-step algebraic inequalities.

> **New Vocabulary**
> solution set
> equivalent inequalities

THINK

Which of the following inequalities is equivalent to $8 + 2(1 - 4y) < 8$?
$8 - 4y > 7$ or $4y + 3 > 4$

ENGAGE

Draw a balance scale to represent $x > 2$.

What are the possible values of x? Draw a number line to support your answer.

What happens if you add 1 to both sides of the balance scale? What happens if you take away 1 from both sides of the balance scale? Explain your thinking.

If $x < -2$, what are the possible values of x? What operations could you carry out on both sides of the inequality so that it remains true? Substitute possible values of x to justify your answers.

 Solve and graph the solution sets of algebraic inequalities using addition and subtraction

1. An inequality is a mathematical statement that compares two numbers or expressions that are not equal or may not be equal. An inequality symbol such as $>$, $<$, $\geq$, $\leq$, or $\neq$ is used to make the comparison.

   Examples: $-3 < 5$, $-0.5 > -2$, $x < 6$, $3x \geq 12$, $x \neq 0$

   The solutions of an inequality are all of the values of the variable that make the inequality true. These values are also called the solution set of an inequality.

   Consider the inequality $x + 3 > 4$

   ▶ **Method 1**
   Solve by substitution.

   When $x = 0$, $x + 3 = 0 + 3$
   $\qquad\qquad\qquad = 3$
   The inequality $x + 3 > 4$ is false.

When $x = 1$, $x + 3 = 1 + 3$
                  $= 4$
The inequality $x + 3 > 4$ is false.

When $x = 1.1$, $x + 3 = 1.1 + 3$
                   $= 4.1$
$x + 3 > 4$ is true.

When $x = 2$, $x + 3 = 2 + 3$
                  $= 5$
$x + 3 > 4$ is true.

> The solutions of an inequality such as $x + 3 > 4$ always form a set of values. It is not just one value, unlike most equations.

When $x = 3$, $x + 3 = 3 + 3$
                  $= 6$
$x + 3 > 4$ is true, and so on.

So, when $x > 1$, the inequality $x + 3 > 4$ is true. The solution set is $x > 1$.

▶ **Method 2**
Solve by using inverse operations.

When you perform addition or subtraction on both sides of an inequality, the solution set of the inequality is still the same. You can use inverse operations to solve inequalities.

Solve the inequality $x + 3 > 4$.

Balance	Algebraic Equation
■ represents 1 counter. ▣ represents x counter. 	$x + 3 > 4$ Solve the inequality by using inverse operations to isolate the variable. Decide which operation to use. To undo the addition of 3 to x, you subtract 3 from both sides. $x + 3 - \mathbf{3} > 4 - \mathbf{3}$ Subtract 3 from both sides. $x > 1$ Simplify.

The solution set is $x > 1$. The inequalities $x + 3 > 4$ and $x > 1$ are ==equivalent inequalities== because the same set of values make both inequalities true.

2 When you solve an inequality such as $0 \geq y - 3$, you are finding the solution set that makes the inequality true. You can graph the solution set of the inequality on a number line after you have solved it.

$$0 \geq y - 3$$
$$0 + 3 \geq y - 3 + 3 \quad \text{Add 3 to both sides.}$$
$$3 \geq y \quad \text{Solution set.}$$

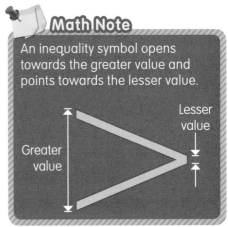

Math Note

An inequality symbol opens towards the greater value and points towards the lesser value.

The solution set $3 \geq y$ means that the value of y is less than or equal to 3. You can rewrite $3 \geq y$ as $y \leq 3$. The inequality symbol still opens towards 3 and points to y. So, $y \leq 3$ and $3 \geq y$ are equivalent inequalities.

You can change the direction of the inequality symbol in the solution set $3 \geq y$ to help you graph the solution of the original inequality $0 \geq y - 3$.

$y \leq 3$ Switch sides and change direction.

The solution set is $y \leq 3$ and it can be represented on a number line as follows:

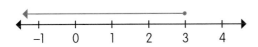

Use a shaded circle above 3 to indicate that 3 is a solution of the inequality, $0 \geq y - 3$.

To check the solution of an equation, you can substitute one value into the original equation to see if it is true. But you cannot check all the solutions of an inequality.

Instead, you can check the solution set by choosing some convenient values from the solution set, $y \geq 3$. You can substitute these values into the original inequality, $0 \geq y - 3$.

Check
When $y = 2.8$,

$$y - 3 = 2.8 - 3 \quad \text{Evaluate } y - 3 \text{ when } y = 2.8.$$
$$= -0.2 \quad (\leq 0) \quad 2.8 \text{ is in the solution set.}$$

When $y = 3$,

If you substitute a value greater than 3, then the inequality $y - 3 \leq 0$ is not true. For example, if $y = 4$, then $4 - 3 = 1$.
Since 1 is not less than or equal to 0, $y = 4$ is not in the solution set.

$$y - 3 = 3 - 3 \quad \text{Evaluate } y - 3 \text{ when } y = 3.$$
$$= 0 \quad (\leq 0) \quad 3 \text{ is also in the solution set.}$$

The original inequality, $0 \geq y - 3$, is true for any value of $y \leq 3$.

$y \leq 3$ is the correct solution set.

3 Solve the inequality $12 - y > 3$ and graph the solution set on a number line.

$$12 - y > 3$$
$$12 - y + y > 3 + y \qquad \text{Add } y \text{ on both sides.}$$
$$12 > 3 + y \qquad \text{Simplify.}$$
$$12 - 3 > 3 + y - 3 \qquad \text{Subtract 3 on both sides.}$$
$$9 > y \qquad \text{Simplify.}$$
$$y < 9 \qquad \text{Rewrite.}$$

The solution set is $y < 9$ and it can be represented on a number line as follows:

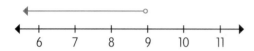

Since $y < 9$, we use an empty circle above 9 to indicate that 9 is not a solution of the inequality. To check the solution set, substitute any value less than 9 into the original inequality. For example, you can choose $y = 0$, the most convenient number.

Check

Substitute the value of $y = 0$ into the original inequality.

$$12 - y = 12 - 0 \qquad \text{Evaluate } 12 - y \text{ when } y = 0.$$
$$= 12 \ (> 3) \qquad \text{0 is in the solution set.}$$

The original inequality, $12 - y > 3$, is true for any value of $y < 9$.

$y < 9$ is the solution set.

TRY Practice solving and graphing the solution sets of algebraic inequalities using addition and subtraction

Solve each inequality and graph the solution set on a number line.

1 $x - 8 \geq 15$

2 $m + 11 < 26$

3 $6 + y \leq 2$

4 $13 < p - 5$

ENGAGE

Consider the inequality 6 > 4.

What happens if you multiply both sides of the inequality by 2? What happens if you divide both sides of the inequality by 2? Explain your thinking.

Now, what happens if you multiply or divide both sides of the inequality by −2? Explain your thinking.

Write another inequality involving two numbers. Do the conclusions that you have drawn above apply to your inequality? Discuss.

LEARN Solve and graph the solution sets of algebraic inequalities using multiplication and division

Activity Exploring division and multiplication properties of an inequality

Work in pairs.

1 Fill in the table. Use the symbols > or <.

Mathematical Operation	Number	Inequality Symbol	Number
You know that	16	>	8
Divide by −2	$\frac{16}{-2} = -8$		$\frac{8}{-2} = -4$
Divide by 2	$\frac{16}{2} = 8$		$\frac{8}{2} = 4$
Divide by −4	$\frac{16}{-4} = -4$		$\frac{8}{-4} = -2$
Divide by 4	$\frac{16}{4} = 4$		$\frac{8}{4} = 2$
Divide by −8	$\frac{16}{-8} = -2$		$\frac{8}{-8} = -1$
Divide by 8	$\frac{16}{8} = 2$		$\frac{8}{8} = 4$

a **Mathematical Habit 8 Look for patterns**
What happens to the direction of the inequality symbol when you divide by a positive number? Based on your observation, write a rule for dividing both sides of an inequality by a positive number.

b **Mathematical Habit 8 Look for patterns**
What happens to the direction of the inequality symbol when you divide by a negative number? Based on your observation, write a rule for dividing both sides of an inequality by a negative number.

(2) Fill in the table. Use the symbols > or <.

Mathematical Operation	Number	Inequality Symbol	Number
You know that	4	<	7
Multiply by −2	$4 \cdot (-2) = -8$		$7 \cdot (-2) = -14$
Multiply by 2	$4 \cdot 2 = 8$		$7 \cdot 2 = 14$
Multiply by −3	$4 \cdot (-3) = -12$		$7 \cdot (-3) = -21$
Multiply by 3	$4 \cdot 3 = 12$		$7 \cdot 3 = 21$
Multiply by −5	$4 \cdot (-5) = -20$		$7 \cdot (-5) = -35$
Multiply by 5	$4 \cdot 5 = 20$		$7 \cdot 5 = 35$

a **Mathematical Habit 8 Look for patterns**
What happens to the direction of the inequality symbol when you multiply by a positive number? Based on your observation, write a rule for multiplying both sides of an inequality by a positive number.

b **Mathematical Habit 8 Look for patterns**
What happens to the direction of the inequality symbol when you multiply by a negative number? Based on your observation, write a rule for multiplying both sides of an inequality by a negative number.

When you multiply or divide both sides of an inequality by the **same positive number**, the inequality symbol remains in the **same direction** for the inequality to be true. When you multiply or divide both sides of an inequality by the **same negative number**, you **reverse the direction** of the inequality symbol for the inequality to be true.

You can apply these rules when we solve an algebraic inequality such as $6x < -24$.

$6x < -24$

$\dfrac{6x}{6} < \dfrac{-24}{6}$ Divide both sides by 6.

$x < -4$ Simplify.

The solution set of the inequality $6x < -24$ can be represented on a number line as shown:

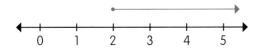

You can check that $x < -4$ is the solution by checking to see if values smaller than -4 make the original inequality $6x < -24$ true:
If $x = -5$, then $6 \cdot -5 < -24$ (true)
If $x = -6$, then $6 \cdot -6 < -24$ (true)

If you substitute a value more than or equal to -4, then the original inequality $6x < -24$ is not true. For example, if $x = -3$, then $6 \cdot -3 = -18$. -18 is greater than -24, not less than -24.

2 Solve the inequality $-5y \leq -10$ and graph the solution set on a number line.

$$-5y \leq -10$$

$$\frac{-5y}{-5} \geq \frac{-10}{-5} \quad \text{Divide both sides by } -5 \text{ and reverse the inequality symbol.}$$

$$y \geq 2 \quad \text{Simplify.}$$

The solution set of the inequality $-5y \leq -10$ can be represented on a number line as follows:

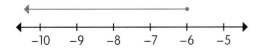

3 Solve the inequality $-\frac{1}{2}p \geq 3$ and graph the solution set on a number line.

$$-\frac{1}{2}p \geq 3$$

$$-\frac{1}{2}p \cdot (-2) \leq 3 \cdot (-2) \quad \text{Multiply both sides by } -2 \text{ and reverse the inequality symbol.}$$

$$p \leq -6 \quad \text{Simplify.}$$

The solution set can be represented on a number line as shown:

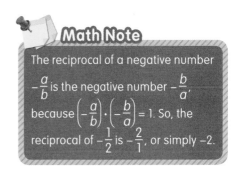

Math Note

The reciprocal of a negative number $-\frac{a}{b}$ is the negative number $-\frac{b}{a}$, because $\left(-\frac{a}{b}\right) \cdot \left(-\frac{b}{a}\right) = 1$. So, the reciprocal of $-\frac{1}{2}$ is $-\frac{2}{1}$, or simply -2.

TRY Practice solving and graphing the solution sets of algebraic inequalities using multiplication and division

Solve each inequality and graph the solution set on a number line.

1 $8a \leq 48$

2 $\frac{1}{5}w \geq 2$

3 $-7m > 21$

4 $6 > -0.3y$

Consider the inequality $5 + 2x < 17$.

Make a list of numbers less than 17 and work backward to find the possible values of x. Share your method.

How is solving the equation $5 + 2x = 17$ similar to solving $5 + 2x < 17$? How is it different? Discuss.

LEARN Solve multi-step algebraic inequalities

① You can use the same methods you use to solve multi-step equations to solve and then graph multi-step inequalities. Your goal is to isolate the variable on one side of the inequality.

Solve $3a - 7 > 26$ by using inverse operations.

First, isolate the algebraic term.

$$3a - 7 > 26 \qquad \text{Add 7 to both sides.}$$
$$3a - 7 + 7 > 26 + 7 \qquad \text{Simplify.}$$
$$3a > 33$$

Then, isolate the variable.

$$\frac{3a}{3} > \frac{33}{3} \qquad \begin{array}{l}\text{Divide both sides by 3.}\\[4pt]\text{Simplify.}\end{array}$$
$$a > 11$$

The solution set is $a > 11$.

The solution set can be represented on a number line as follows:

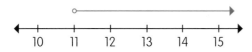

Solve the inequality $\frac{4}{5}x + 1 > 1\frac{3}{5}$ and graph the solution set on a number line.

$$\frac{4}{5}x + 1 > 1\frac{3}{5} \qquad \text{Subtract 1 from both sides.}$$
$$\frac{4}{5}x + 1 - 1 > 1\frac{3}{5} - 1 \qquad \text{Simplify.}$$
$$\frac{4}{5}x > \frac{3}{5} \qquad \text{Multiply both sides by } \frac{5}{4}, \text{ which is the reciprocal of } \frac{4}{5}.$$
$$\left(\frac{4}{5}x\right)\cdot\left(\frac{5}{4}\right) > \left(\frac{3}{5}\right)\cdot\left(\frac{5}{4}\right) \qquad \text{Simplify.}$$
$$x > \frac{3}{4}$$

The solution set can be represented on a number line as shown:

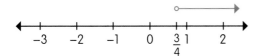

Remember to check your solution set. You can substitute any value within the solution set into the original inequality.

3 Solve the inequality $9 - 0.2a \geq 21$ and graph the solution set on a number line.

$$9 - 0.2a \geq 21$$

$9 - 0.2a - \mathbf{9} \geq 21 - \mathbf{9}$	Subtract 9 from both sides.
$-0.2a \geq 12$	Simplify.
$\dfrac{-0.2a}{-0.2} \leq \dfrac{12}{-0.2}$	Divide both sides by -0.2 and reverse the inequality symbol.
$a \leq -60$	Simplify.

Reverse the direction of the inequality symbol when you multiply or divide both sides of the inequality by the same negative number.

The solution set can be represented on a number line as shown:

$$
\begin{array}{ccccccc}
\longleftarrow & & & & \bullet & & \\
\hline
-64 & -63 & -62 & -61 & -60 & -59 &
\end{array}
$$

4 Solve the inequality $2(3 - x) \leq 8$ and graph the solution set on a number line.

▶ **Method 1**
Use the distributive property and inverse operations.

$2(3 - x) \leq 8$	
$2 \cdot 3 - 2 \cdot x \leq 8$	Use the distributive property.
$6 - 2x \leq 8$	Simplify.
$6 - 2x - \mathbf{6} \leq 8 - \mathbf{6}$	Subtract 6 from both sides.
$-2x \leq 2$	Simplify.
$\dfrac{-2x}{-2} \geq \dfrac{2}{-2}$	Divide both sides by -2 and reverse the inequality symbol.
$x \geq -1$	Simplify.

The solution set can be represented on a number line as shown:

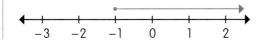

▶ **Method 2**
Use inverse operations.

$$2(3 - x) \leq 8$$
$2(3 - x) \div \mathbf{2} \leq 8 \div \mathbf{2}$ Divide both sides by 2.
$3 - x \leq 4$ Simplify.
$3 - x - \mathbf{3} \leq 4 - \mathbf{3}$ Subtract 3 from both sides.
$-x \leq 1$ Simplify.
$\dfrac{-x}{-1} \geq \dfrac{1}{-1}$ Divide both sides by −1 and reverse the inequality symbol.
$x \geq -1$ Simplify.

The solution set can be represented on a number line as shown:

TRY Practice solving multi-step algebraic inequalities

Solve each inequality and graph the solution set on a number line.

1 $4y + 7 < 27$

2 $-5x - 9 \leq 21$

3 $\dfrac{1}{2}r + \dfrac{3}{4} \geq 5$

4 $1.5 - 0.3p > 3.6$

5 $4(2 - m) \geq 20$

5 Real-World Problems: Algebraic Inequalities

Learning Objective:
• Solve real-world problems involving algebraic inequalities.

 THINK

Mr. Lee wants to rent a room for a private function. He approached two centers and here are the rates:

	Room Rental Per Hour	Set-Up Fee
Center A	$15	$40
Center B	$12	$80

Mr. Lee has $140 to spend. Which center should he rent from?

ENGAGE

Look at these values: 10, 5, 18, 11, and x.
Show how you find the average of these values. If the average of these values is at least 10, what inequality can you write to represent the situation? If the average of these values is more than 10, how would the inequality change? How would the possible values of x change? Explain your reasoning.

LEARN Solve real-world problems involving algebraic inequalities

1. Steven's scores for four math tests are 70, 75, 83, and 80. If he wants to get an average of at least 80 marks for 5 tests, what score should Steven get for his fifth test?

You can use algebraic reasoning to translate the problem into an algebraic inequality.

Let x be the score for the fifth test.   Define the variable.

$$\text{Average} \geq 80$$

$\dfrac{70 + 75 + 83 + 80 + x}{5} \geq 80$	Write an inequality.
$\dfrac{308 + x}{5} \geq 80$	Simplify.
$5 \cdot \left(\dfrac{308 + x}{5}\right) \geq 5 \cdot 80$	Multiply both sides by 5.
$308 + x \geq 400$	Simplify.
$308 + x - 308 \geq 400 - 308$	Subtract 308 from both sides.
$x \geq 92$	Simplify.

Steven should get 92 marks or more for his fifth test.

2 Kaylee goes to an amusement park with her friends. The admission fee to the amusement park is $4 and each ride costs $0.80. If Kaylee has only $25 to spend, how many rides can she go on?

Let x be the number of rides that Kaylee can go on.   Define the variable.

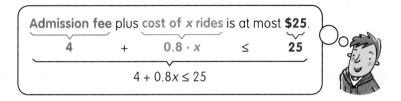

Admission fee plus cost of x rides is at most **$25**.

| 4 | + | $0.8 \cdot x$ | $\leq$ | **25** |

$$4 + 0.8x \leq 25$$

$4 + 0.8x \leq 25$	Write an inequality.
$4 + 0.8x - 4 \leq 25 - 4$	Subtract 4 from both sides.
$0.8x \leq 21$	Simplify.
$\dfrac{0.8x}{0.8} \leq \dfrac{21}{0.8}$	Divide both sides by 0.8.
$x \leq 26.25$	Simplify.

Kaylee can go for at most 26 rides.

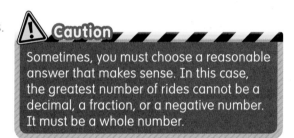

⚠ **Caution**

Sometimes, you must choose a reasonable answer that makes sense. In this case, the greatest number of rides cannot be a decimal, a fraction, or a negative number. It must be a whole number.

TRY **Practice solving real-world problems involving algebraic inequalities**

Solve.

1 The average length of four edges is at least 90 inches. The lengths of three of the edges are 87 inches, 90 inches, and 89 inches. Describe the length of the fourth edge.

2 Riley is at the bookstore with $75 to spend. She plans to buy a reference book that costs $18 and some novels that cost $12 each. Find how many novels Riley can buy along with the reference book.

3 Ms. Cooper pays $200 in advance on her account at a health club. Each time she visits the club, $8 is deducted from the account. If she needs to maintain a minimum amount of $50 in the account, how many visits can Ms. Cooper make before she needs to top up the account again?

4 Carlos has at most 7 hours to spend in an amusement park, in which he uses 1 hour for lunch and the rest of the time on park rides. What is the maximum number of rides Carlos can complete if each ride takes 15 minutes?

INDEPENDENT PRACTICE

Solve.

1 The perimeter of an equilateral triangle is at most 45 centimeters. Find the possible length of each side.

2 Robert scored 1,800 points in four rounds of a debate competition. His opponent, Audrey, scored 324 points in the first round, 530 points in the second round, and 619 points in the third round. How many points must Audrey score in the final round to surpass Robert's score?

3 Blake plans to sign up for a language class that will cost at least $195. His father gives him $75 and he earns $28 from mowing the lawn for his neighbors. Write and solve an inequality to find out how much more money he needs to save before he can sign up for the class.

4 In her last basketball game, Carla scored 46 points. In the current game, she has scored 24 points so far. How many more two-point baskets must she make if she wants her total score in her current game to be at least as great as her score in the last game?

5 At Middleton Middle School, Maya must score an average of at least 80 points on 4 tests before she can apply for a scholarship. If she scored 79, 81, and 77 for the first three tests, what must she score on her last test?

6 At the movies, a bag of popcorn costs $3.50 and a bottle of water costs $2.75. If Jessica has $18 and bought only 2 bottles of water, how many bags of popcorn can she buy at most?

7   Party favors are on sale for $2.40 each. You have $380 to spend on the decorations and gifts, and you have already spent $270 on decorations. Write and solve an inequality to find the number of party favors you can buy.

8   Evelyn can either take her lunch or buy it at school. It costs $1.95 to buy lunch. If she wants to spend no more than $30 each month, how many lunches can she buy at most?

9   Bryan always likes to have at least $150 in his savings account. Currently he has $800 in the account. If he withdraws $35 each week, after how many weeks will the amount in his savings account be less than $150?

10 A cab company charges $0.80 per mile plus $2 for tolls. Rachel has at most $16 to spend on her cab fare. Write and solve an inequality for the maximum distance she can travel. Can she afford to take a cab from her home to an airport that is 25 miles away?

11 Nine subtracted from four times a number is less than or equal to fifteen. Write an inequality and solve it.

Mathematical Habit 6 **Use precise mathematical language**

Compare the inequality $-5(x + 6) < 10$ with solving the equation $-5(x + 6) = 10$. Describe the similarities and differences between solving the inequality and solving the equation. How does the solution set of the inequality $-5(x + 6) < 10$ differ from the solution of the equation $-5(x + 6) = 10$?

Similarities:

Differences:

Problem Solving with Heuristics

1 **Mathematical Habit 1** **Persevere in solving problems**

A father said, "My son is five times as old as my daughter. My wife is five times as old as my son and I am twice as old as my wife. Grandmother here, who is as old as all of us put together, is celebrating her 81st birthday today." What is the age of the man's son?

2 **Mathematical Habit 4** **Use mathematical models**

Sara can buy 40 pens with a sum of money. She can buy 5 more pens if each pen costs $0.05 less.

a How much does each pen cost?

b If Sara wants to buy at least 10 more pens with the same amount of money, how much can each pen cost at most?

CHAPTER WRAP-UP

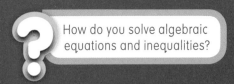
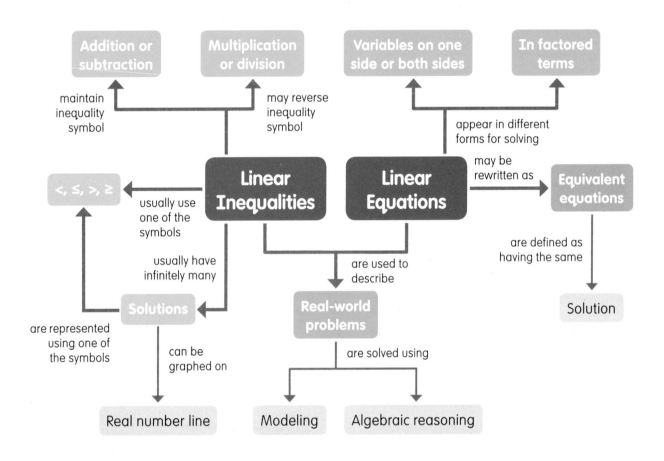

KEY CONCEPTS

- Equations with the same solution are called equivalent equations.
- Solving an equation involves isolating the variable on one side of the equation by writing a series of equivalent equations.
- An inequality symbol is used to compare two quantities that are not equal or may not be equal.
- The orientation of the inequality symbol must be reversed when both sides of an inequality are multiplied or divided by the same negative number.

Name: _____ Date: _____

Solve each equation.

1 $8x - 7 = 17$

2 $4 - 6x = 8$

3 $6 - \dfrac{y}{3} = 0$

4 $3 - 3.6x = 4.2$

5 $3.4y - 5.2 - 3y = 2$

6 $15y - 4(2y - 3) = -2$

7 $\dfrac{1}{4}(x + 3) + \dfrac{3}{8}x = \dfrac{13}{4}$

8 $0.4(x + 0.7) - 0.6x = -4.2$

Solve each inequality. Graph each solution set.

9 $4x - 3 > 1$

10 $6 \le 1 - 5x$

11 $\dfrac{2}{3} - \dfrac{x}{6} \ge -\dfrac{1}{2}$

12 $-6.9 < 8.1 - 1.5x$

13 $12.9 < 0.3(5.3 - x)$

14 $3(x + 1) - 5x > 7$

Write an equation for each question. Then, solve.

15 Mia is 6 years older than her sister Natalie. The sum of their ages is 48. How old is Natalie?

16 The sum of the page numbers of two facing pages in a book is 145. What are the page numbers?

17 The perimeter of an equilateral triangle is $6\dfrac{3}{4}$ inches. Find the length of each side of the equilateral triangle.

18 The sum of the interior angle measures of a quadrilateral is 360°. The measure of angle A is 3 times the measure of angle D. The measure of angle B is 4 times that of angle D. The measure of angle C is 24° more than angle B. Find the measure of each angle of the quadrilateral.

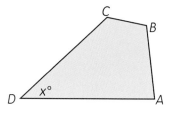

The diagram may not be drawn to scale.

Write an inequality for each question. Then, solve.

19 Julia wants the average amount of money she spends each day on her four-day vacation to be no more than $64. On the first three days, she spends $71, $62, and $59. What is the greatest amount of money she can spend on the fourth day?

20 Mr. Jones has found a job in a computer store. As shown below, he has two options for how he will be paid. The commission he makes for Option B is based on his weekly sales. For example, if his sales total $1,000 a week, he receives his base salary of $250 plus 8% of $1,000.
Mr. Jones is thinking about Option B. What would his weekly sales need to be for him to make at least as much as he would for Option A?

Option A	Option B
Fixed salary of $600 per week with no commission	Fixed salary of $250 per week plus commission of 8% of his weekly sales

21 The school events committee is planning to buy a banner and some helium balloons for graduation night. A store charges them $35 for the banner and $3.50 for each helium balloon. If the committee has at most $125 to spend, how many helium balloons can they buy?

 22 The coach of the field hockey team can spend at most $475 on new team uniforms. The coach will order the uniforms online and pay a mailing cost of $6.50. If each uniform costs $29, how many uniforms can the coach order?

Assessment Prep
Answer each question.

23 Solve the equation for y.
$5(3 - 2y) = 18$
Write your answer and your work or explanation.

24 The width of a rectangular wall panel is 3 feet shorter than its length. The perimeter of the panel is 54 feet.

Part A
Which equation can be used to determine x, the length of the panel, in feet?

(A) $x + x + 3 = 54$

(B) $x + 3x = 54$

(C) $2x + 2(x - 3) = 54$

(D) $2x + 2(x + 3) = 54$

Part B
What is the length of the panel, in feet? Write your answer and your work or explanation.

25 Which is the solution of the inequality, $-4a + 3 < -13$?

(A) $a > 4$ (B) $a < 4$ (C) $a > -4$ (D) $a < -4$

Name: _____ Date: _____

Walkathon

1 Alma, Brooklyn, Carla, and Diana had collected donations following a walkathon. Alma had collected 3 times as much as Jayla. Carla had collected $25 less than Alma. Diana had collected twice as much as Alma. Then, Diana received a check of $55 from her grandmother.

a Write an expression to represent the amount Alma collected in terms of the amount Brooklyn collected.

b Write an expression to represent the amount Carla collected in terms of the amount Brooklyn collected.

c Write an expression to represent the amount Diana collected in terms of the amount Brooklyn collected.

2 Their teacher also took part in the walkathon and collected $1,070. The amount that their teacher collected had the same combined total amount that Alma, Brooklyn, Carla, and Diana had collected.

a Find the amount that Brooklyn collected.

b How much in donations did Alma, Carla, and Diana each collect?

Rubric

Point(s)	Level	My Performance
7–8	4	• Most of my answers are correct. • I showed complete understanding of the concepts. • I used effective and efficient strategies to solve the problems. • I explained my answers and mathematical thinking clearly and completely.
5–6	3	• Some of my answers are correct. • I showed adequate understanding of the concepts. • I used effective strategies to solve the problems. • I explained my answers and mathematical thinking clearly.
3–4	2	• A few of my answers are correct. • I showed some understanding of the concepts. • I used some effective strategies to solve the problems. • I explained some of my answers and mathematical thinking clearly.
0–2	1	• A few of my answers are correct. • I showed little understanding of the concepts. • I used limited effective strategies to solve the problems. • I did not explain my answers and mathematical thinking clearly.

Teacher's Comments

Linear Equations and Inequalities

Who wants to go bowling?

You and three friends want to go bowling. The bowling alley charges $3.25 for each pair of shoes you rent and $4.75 per game. All four of you need to rent shoes and you are not sure yet how many games you will play. What will be your group's total cost? In this situation, there are two quantities that can vary: the number of games your group plays and the group's total cost. In this chapter, you will learn how to write linear equations to represent situations in which there are two variables.

How do you solve for a variable in a linear equation with two variables?

Name: _____   Date: _____

Recall Prior Knowledge

Identifying equivalent equations

Equivalent equations are equations that have the same solution. Performing the same operation on both sides of an equation produces an equivalent equation.

For example, $x = 8$ and $x - 2 = 6$ are equivalent equations. If you subtract 2 from both sides of $x = 8$, you obtain $x - 2 = 6$. The solution to both equations is $x = 8$.

▶ **Quick Check**

Determine whether each pair of equations is equivalent. Justify each answer.

① $x + 4 = 10$ and $x - 1 = 3$

② $\frac{1}{5}x = 4$ and $x = 20$

③ $0.5x + 1 = 1.5$ and $2x = 2$

④ $2(x + 9) = 14$ and $2(x - 7) = -18$

Expressing the relationship between two quantities with a linear equation

A wall has width w feet and length $2w$ feet. The perimeter, P feet, of the wall is $2w + 2w + w + w = 6w$ feet.

You can express the relationship between the perimeter and the width of the wall with the linear equation $P = 6w$. In the equation, w is the independent variable and P is the dependent variable because the value of P depends on the value of w.

▶ **Quick Check**

Write a linear equation for each situation. State the independent and dependent variables for each equation.

⑤ A manufacturer produces beverages in small and large bottles. Each small bottle contains s liters of beverages. Each large bottle contains t liters, which is 1 more liter than the quantity in the small bottle. Express t in terms of s.

⑥ Hunter is 4 years younger than Alex. Express Alex's age, a, in terms of Hunter's age, h.

⑦ A bouquet of lavender costs $12. Find the cost, C dollars, of n bouquets of lavender.

⑧ The distance traveled by a bus, d miles, is 40 times the time, t hours, of the journey. Find d in terms of t.

Solving algebraic equations

To solve an equation, you isolate the variable on one side of the equation. To do this, you add, subtract, multiply or divide both sides of the equation by the same nonzero number.

$$4x + 7 = 15$$
$$4x + 7 - 7 = 15 - 7 \qquad \text{Subtract 7 from both sides.}$$
$$4x = 8 \qquad \text{Simplify.}$$
$$\frac{4x}{4} = \frac{8}{4} \qquad \text{Divide both sides by 4.}$$
$$x = 2 \qquad \text{Simplify.}$$

> Remember to keep an equation balanced by performing the same operation on both sides.

When solving the equation $5x + 3(x - 2) = 50$, which includes an expression with parentheses, you need to use the distributive property.

$$5x + 3(x - 2) = 50$$
$$5x + 3x - 6 = 50 \qquad \text{Use the distributive property.}$$
$$8x - 6 = 50 \qquad \text{Combine like items.}$$
$$8x - 6 + 6 = 50 + 6 \qquad \text{Add 6 to both sides.}$$
$$8x = 56 \qquad \text{Simplify.}$$
$$\frac{8x}{8} = \frac{56}{8} \qquad \text{Divide both sides by 8.}$$
$$x = 7 \qquad \text{Simplify.}$$

▶ Quick Check

Solve each equation.

9 $4x - 2 = 14$

10 $\frac{1}{3}v + 9 = 2$

11 $c + 2(1 - c) = 10$

Representing fractions as repeating decimals

A repeating decimal has a group of one or more digits that repeat endlessly. You use bar notation to show the digits that repeat.

To write $\frac{40}{33}$ as a decimal:

```
        1.2121
  33√40.0000
     33
      7 0
      6 6
        40
        33
        70
        66
          40      Divide until the remainders start repeating.
          33
           7
```

So, $\frac{40}{33} = 1.2121\ldots = 1.\overline{21}$.

▶ **Quick Check**

Write the decimal for each fraction. Use bar notation.

⑫ $\dfrac{3}{18}$

⑬ $\dfrac{16}{99}$

Solving algebraic inequalities

The process of solving an algebraic inequality is the same as solving an algebraic equation, except that you have to reverse the direction of the inequality symbol when you multiply or divide both sides by a negative number.

$$3(3 - 4x) - 1 \leq 20$$

$9 - 12x - 1 \leq 20$	Use the distributive property.
$-12x + 8 \leq 20$	Simplify.
$-12x + 8 - \mathbf{8} \leq 20 - \mathbf{8}$	Subtract 8 from both sides.
$-12x \leq 12$	Simplify.
$\dfrac{-12x}{\mathbf{-12}} \geq \dfrac{12}{\mathbf{-12}}$	Divide both sides by −12 and reverse the inequality symbol.
$x \geq -1$	Simplify.

The solution set is represented on a number line as shown.

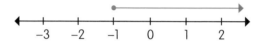

You use a shaded circle above −1 to indicate that −1 is a solution of the inequality $3(3 - 4x) - 1 \leq 20$.

The solution set $x > 4$ of another equality is represented on a number line as shown.

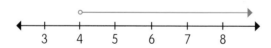

You use an empty circle above 4 to indicate that 4 is not a solution of the inequality.

▶ **Quick Check**

Solve each inequality and graph the solution set on a number line.

⑭ $x - 6 \leq 9$

⑮ $3 - 5(x - 1) < 18$

© 2020 Marshall Cavendish Education Pte Ltd

1 Solving Linear Equations With One Variable

Learning Objectives:
- Solve linear equations with one variable.
- Solve real-world problems involving linear equations with one variable.

THINK

Hailey was told that the length of a rectangle was 2.5 inches longer than its width, and that the perimeter of the rectangle was 75.4 inches. She found the length and width algebraically. How could she use estimation to check if her answers were reasonable?

ENGAGE

Draw a bar model to represent $5x - 2$. Now use that model to solve the equation $5x - 2 = 3x + 3$.

Discuss your methods with your partner and discuss if there is another way to solve this equation.

LEARN Solve linear equations with one variable

1. To solve an equation, you add, subtract, multiply or divide both sides of the equation by the same nonzero number. You keep the equation "balanced" by performing the same operation on both sides. This method is also used to solve an equation with variables on both sides.

2. Solve the equation $4x + 7 = x + 13$.

$$4x + 7 = x + 13$$
$$4x + 7 - x = x + 13 - x \quad \text{Subtract } x \text{ from both sides.}$$
$$3x + 7 = 13 \quad \text{Simplify.}$$
$$3x + 7 - 7 = 13 - 7 \quad \text{Subtract 7 from both sides.}$$
$$3x = 6 \quad \text{Simplify.}$$
$$\frac{3x}{3} = \frac{6}{3} \quad \text{Divide both sides by 3.}$$
$$x = 2 \quad \text{Simplify.}$$

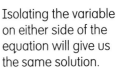

Isolating the variable on either side of the equation will give us the same solution.

3. Solve the equation $x = 44 - 0.1x$.

$$x = 44 - 0.1x$$
$$x + 0.1x = 44 - 0.1x + 0.1x \quad \text{Add } 0.1x \text{ to both sides.}$$
$$1.1x = 44 \quad \text{Simplify.}$$
$$\frac{1.1x}{1.1} = \frac{44}{1.1} \quad \text{Divide both sides by 1.1.}$$
$$x = 40 \quad \text{Simplify.}$$

4 Solve the equation $2(x + 11) = 8 - 5x$.

$2(x + 11) = 8 - 5x$	
$2x + 22 = 8 - 5x$	Use the distributive property.
$2x + 22 + \mathbf{5x} = 8 - 5x + \mathbf{5x}$	Add $5x$ to both sides.
$7x + 22 = 8$	Simplify.
$7x + 22 - \mathbf{22} = 8 - \mathbf{22}$	Subtract 22 from both sides.
$7x = -14$	Simplify.
$\dfrac{7x}{7} = \dfrac{-14}{7}$	Divide both sides by 7.
$x = -2$	Simplify.

5 Solve the equation $\dfrac{3x}{4} = \dfrac{2x+1}{4} - 1.5$.

$\dfrac{3x}{4} = \dfrac{2x+1}{4} - 1.5$	
$\dfrac{3x}{4} - \dfrac{\mathbf{2x+1}}{\mathbf{4}} = \dfrac{2x+1}{4} - 1.5 - \dfrac{\mathbf{2x+1}}{\mathbf{4}}$	Subtract $\dfrac{2x+1}{4}$ from both sides.
$\dfrac{3x}{4} - \dfrac{2x+1}{4} = -1.5$	Simplify.
$\dfrac{3x - (2x+1)}{4} = -1.5$	Rewrite the left side as a single fraction.
$\dfrac{3x - 2x - 1}{4} = -1.5$	Use the distributive property.
$\dfrac{x-1}{4} = -1.5$	Simplify the numerator.
$\dfrac{x-1}{4} \cdot \mathbf{4} = -1.5 \cdot \mathbf{4}$	Multiply both sides by 4.
$x - 1 = -6$	Simplify.
$x - 1 + \mathbf{1} = -6 + \mathbf{1}$	Add 1 to both sides.
$x = -5$	Simplify.

> **Math Note**
> Notice that $2x + 1$ is placed in parentheses, because the fraction bar acts as a grouping symbol. So, $-\dfrac{2x+1}{4}$ can be written as $\dfrac{-(2x+1)}{4}$.

 Practice solving linear equations with one variable

Solve each linear equation.

1 $x + 16 = 11 - 4x$

2 $0.6x + 11 = 0.6 + 0.2x$

3 $2(3x + 1) = 14 + 2x$

4 $\dfrac{3x}{5} = \dfrac{2}{15} - \dfrac{x-1}{3}$

ENGAGE

How do you write 0.83 as a fraction? What is $1 \cdot 0.8\overline{3}$? What is $10 \cdot 0.8\overline{3}$?
How does knowing the above help you find $9 \cdot 0.8\overline{3}$?
How do you write $0.8\overline{3}$ as a fraction? Discuss.

LEARN Write repeating decimals as fractions

1. Write the repeating decimal $0.1\overline{6}$ as a fraction.

   STEP 1 Assign a variable to the repeating decimal.

   Let $x = 0.1\overline{6}$.
   $$x = 0.166666\ldots$$
   $$10x = 1.666666\ldots$$

   Math Note

   When you multiply both sides of the equation $x = 0.1\overline{6}$ by 10, the infinite number of repeating digits does not change. So, you can subtract one equation from the other to eliminate the infinite string of digits.

   STEP 2 Subtract x from $10x$ to obtain a terminating decimal.

   $$10x - x = 1.666666\ldots - 0.166666\ldots$$
   $$9x = 1.5$$

   STEP 3 Solve for x.

   $$\frac{9x}{9} = \frac{1.5}{9} \qquad \text{Divide both sides by 9.}$$
   $$x = \frac{1}{6} \qquad \text{Simplify.}$$

   $$\frac{1.5}{9} = \frac{3}{18} = \frac{1}{6}$$

   Math Talk

   If a decimal has two digits that repeat instead of one, what number do you multiply the decimal by before subtracting? Explain.

   So, $0.1\overline{6} = \frac{1}{6}$.

TRY Practice writing repeating decimals as fractions

Write each repeating decimal as a fraction.

1. $0.\overline{09}$

2. $0.\overline{8}$

ENGAGE

A belt costs $30 less than a pair of jeans. The ratio of the cost of the jeans to the cost of a shirt is 2 : 1. The total cost of the three items is $75.50. You can represent the costs using a bar model as shown.

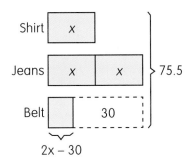

How much does a shirt cost? Solve using the bar model.
Now, write an algebraic equation to represent the bar model. Solve the equation.
What does the value of the variable represent?

LEARN Solve real-world problems involving linear equations with one variable

1 Juan's bathroom walls are $91\frac{1}{4}$ inches tall. He wants to mount a mirror with a height of $28\frac{1}{4}$ inches on the wall. The distance from the top of the mirror to the ceiling should be $\frac{1}{2}$ the distance from the bottom of the mirror to the floor. Find the distance of the mirror from the floor.

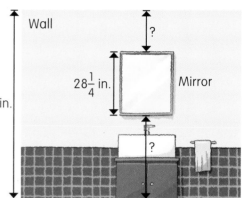

Wall

?

$28\frac{1}{4}$ in.   Mirror

$91\frac{1}{4}$ in.

?

Let the distance of the mirror from the floor be x inches.

So, the distance of the mirror from the ceiling is $\frac{1}{2}x$ inches.

$$x + 28\frac{1}{4} + \frac{1}{2}x = 91\frac{1}{4}$$ Write an equation.

$$\frac{3}{2}x + 28\frac{1}{4} = 91\frac{1}{4}$$ Add like terms.

$$\frac{3}{2}x + 28\frac{1}{4} - 28\frac{1}{4} = 91\frac{1}{4} - 28\frac{1}{4}$$ Subtract $28\frac{1}{4}$ from both sides.

$$\frac{3}{2}x = 63$$ Simplify.

$$\frac{3}{2}x \cdot \frac{2}{3} = 63 \cdot \frac{2}{3}$$ Multiply both sides by $\frac{2}{3}$.

$$x = 42$$ Simplify.

> The wall's height is about 90 inches and the mirror's height is about 30 inches. So, the total distance above and below the mirror is about 60 inches. $\frac{2}{3}$ of 60 inches is 40 inches. The answer is reasonable.

The distance of the mirror from the floor is 42 inches.

TRY Practice solving real-world problems involving linear equations with one variable

Solve the problem algebraically.

1 Jocelyn wants to add a circular pond to her backyard. The backyard is $20\frac{1}{2}$ yards long and the pond will be $6\frac{1}{4}$ yards across. The distance from the pond to the back fence will be half the distance from the pond to the back of the house. How far will the pond be from the back of the house?

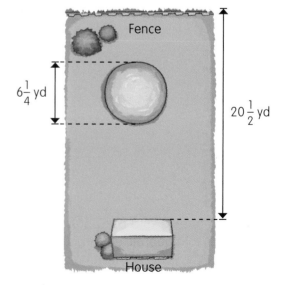

Fence

$6\frac{1}{4}$ yd

$20\frac{1}{2}$ yd

House

INDEPENDENT PRACTICE

Solve each linear equation.

1 $4x - 10 = 10 - x$

2 $3x - 2 = 5.6 - 0.8x$

3 $2(x - 1) - 6 = 10(1 - x) + 6$

4 $6 + \frac{1}{3}(x - 9) = \frac{1}{2}(2 - x)$

5 $\frac{3x - 2}{8} + \frac{1}{2} = -\frac{2 - x}{4}$

6 $\frac{4(2x + 3)}{5} = \frac{x + 1}{4} + \frac{31}{5}$

Write each repeating decimal as a fraction.

7 $0.8\overline{3}$

8 $0.0\overline{45}$

Solve each problem algebraically.

9 Diego saves $5.50 in dimes and quarters over a week. He has 20 more dimes than quarters. Find the number of dimes and quarters he saves.

10 Aiden earns $2\frac{1}{2}$ times as much as Evan in a day. Jake earns $18 more than Evan in a day. If the total daily salary of all three people is $306, find Aiden's daily salary.

Identifying the Number of Solutions to a Linear Equation

Learning Objective:
- Identify linear equations with no solution, one solution, or infinitely many solutions.

> **New Vocabulary**
> inconsistent equation
> consistent equation
> identity

THINK

Consider the following equations.

$$3x - 2 = -3\left(\frac{2}{3} - x\right)$$

$$3x + 6 = -2\left(\frac{3}{2} - x\right)$$

$$\frac{1}{4}(2x - 1) = \frac{1}{2}x + \frac{3}{8}$$

Identify the equation with one solution, the equation with no solution, and the equation with an infinite number of solutions. Explain your answer.

ENGAGE

Solve the equation $x + 3 = 5$. What is the solution?
Now, consider the equation $x + 3 = x$. What is the solution?
What do you notice? Share your observations. Discuss what the solution shows.

LEARN Identify a linear equation with no solution

① Not all linear equations have one solution.

Consider the equation $x + 4 = x$.

$$x + 4 = x$$
$$x + 4 - x = x - x \quad \text{Subtract } x \text{ from both sides.}$$
$$4 = 0 \quad \text{Simplify.}$$

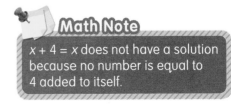

Math Note
$x + 4 = x$ does not have a solution because no number is equal to 4 added to itself.

The variable x has disappeared. 4 is not equal to 0.
Since the solution ends with a false statement,
the equation has no solution.

> An inconsistent equation is an equation with no solution.

2 Determine whether the equation $5(x + 3) = 5x + 3$ is an inconsistent equation.

$$5(x + 3) = 5x + 3$$
$$5x + 15 = 5x + 3 \qquad \text{Use the distributive property.}$$
$$5x + 15 - \mathbf{5x} = 5x + 3 - \mathbf{5x} \qquad \text{Subtract } 5x \text{ from both sides.}$$
$$15 = 3 \qquad \text{Simplify.}$$

Since 15 is not equal to 3, the equation has no solution.

The equation has no solution. The equation is an inconsistent equation.

3 Determine whether the equation $3(x - 4) = 2(x - 1)$ is an inconsistent equation.

$$3(x - 4) = 2(x - 1)$$
$$5x - 12 = 2x - 2 \qquad \text{Use the distributive property.}$$
$$3x - 12 - \mathbf{2x} = 2x - 2 - \mathbf{2x} \qquad \text{Subtract } 2x \text{ from both sides.}$$
$$x - 12 = -2 \qquad \text{Simplify.}$$
$$x - 12 + \mathbf{12} = -2 + \mathbf{12} \qquad \text{Add 12 to both sides.}$$
$$x = 10 \qquad \text{Simplify.}$$

The equation has one solution, that is $x = 10$.

The equation has one solution. The equation is a consistent equation.

TRY Practice identifying a linear equation with no solution

Determine whether each equation is a consistent equation or an inconsistent equation.

1 $5\left(x + \dfrac{1}{5}\right) = 5x + 3$

2 $x + \dfrac{1}{4} = -\dfrac{1}{4}(4x - 1)$

2 $x + \dfrac{1}{4} = -\dfrac{1}{4}(4x - 1)$

ENGAGE

Consider the equation $2x - 7 + 4 = 3x - 3 - x$. What could be a solution to the problem? Share your observations. Discuss what the solution shows.

Create another problem where your solution would be true. Discuss your work.

LEARN Identify a linear equation with infinitely many solutions

1. Try solving the equation $3x + 5 = x + 2x + 5$.

$$3x + 5 = x + 2x + 5$$
$$3x + 5 = 3x + 5 \quad \text{Combine like terms.}$$
$$3x + 5 - \mathbf{3x} = 3x + 5 - \mathbf{3x} \quad \text{Subtract } 3x \text{ from both sides.}$$
$$5 = 5 \quad \text{Simplify.}$$

⚠ **Caution**
$5 = 5$ does not mean that $x = 5$.

> An **identity** is an equation that is true for all values of the variable.

2. Determine whether the equation $7x - 10 = 3(x - 2) + 4(x - 1)$ is an identity.

$$7x - 10 = 3(x - 2) + 4(x - 1)$$
$$7x - 10 = 3x - 6 + 4x - 4 \quad \text{Use the distributive property.}$$
$$7x - 10 = 7x - 10 \quad \text{Combine like terms.}$$
$$7x - 10 - \mathbf{7x} = 7x - 10 - \mathbf{7x} \quad \text{Subtract } 7x \text{ from both sides.}$$
$$-10 = -10 \quad \text{Simplify.}$$

> Since $-10 = -10$ is always true no matter what the value of x is, the equation has infinitely many solutions.

The equation has infinitely many solutions. The equation is an identity.

3. Determine whether the equation $\frac{x}{3} + \frac{2(2x + 1)}{5} = \frac{1}{3}$ is an identity.

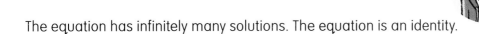

$$\frac{x}{3} + \frac{2(2x + 1)}{5} = \frac{1}{3}$$

$$\frac{5x}{15} + \frac{6(2x + 1)}{15} = \frac{1}{3} \quad \text{Write equivalent fractions using the LCD, 15.}$$

$$\frac{5x + 6(2x + 1)}{15} = \frac{1}{3} \quad \text{Rewrite the left side as a single fraction.}$$

$$\frac{5x + 12x + 6}{15} = \frac{1}{3} \quad \text{Use the distributive property.}$$

$$\frac{17x + 6}{15} = \frac{1}{3} \quad \text{Combine like terms.}$$

$$\frac{17x + 6}{15} \cdot \mathbf{15} = \frac{1}{3} \cdot \mathbf{15} \quad \text{Multiply both sides by 15.}$$

$$17x + 6 = 5 \qquad \text{Simplify.}$$
$$17x + 6 - 6 = 5 - 6 \qquad \text{Subtract 6 from both sides.}$$
$$17x = -1 \qquad \text{Simplify.}$$
$$\frac{17x}{17} = \frac{-1}{17} \qquad \text{Divide both sides by 17.}$$
$$x = \frac{-1}{17} \qquad \text{Simplify.}$$

> The equation has one solution, that is $x = -\dfrac{1}{17}$.

The equation has one solution. The equation is not an identity.

TRY Practice identifying a linear equation with infinitely many solutions

Determine whether each equation is an identity.

1 $2(x - 1) + 3 = 2x + 1$

2 $6(x + 5) - 10 = 3(2x - 3)$

> You can try substituting some values of x into each equation. If you find that the left side is always equal to the right side, the equation is an identity.

INDEPENDENT PRACTICE

Determine whether each equation is a consistent equation, an inconsistent equation or an identity.

1. $3x - 3 = -2\left(\frac{3}{2} - x\right)$

2. $2x + 5 = -4\left(\frac{3}{2} - x\right)$

3. $3x + 5 = 2x - 7$

4. $5y + (86 - y) = 86 + 4y$

5. $0.5(6x - 3) = 3(1 + x)$

6. $4(18a - 7) + 40 = 3(4 + 24a)$

7. $\frac{1}{7}(7x - 21) = 8x + 7x - 24$

8. $\frac{1}{6}(12x - 18) = 2\left(x - \frac{3}{2}\right)$

9. $7 - 0.75x = -7\left(\frac{3}{28}x + 1\right)$

10. $6 + 0.5y = -2\left(3 - \frac{1}{4}y\right)$

11. $\frac{x - 3}{4} = 0.25x - 0.75$

12. $\frac{1}{3}x + 5 = \frac{1}{6}(2x - 5)$

Solve.

13 Cabinet A is 5 inches taller than Cabinet B. Cabinet C is 3 inches taller than Cabinet B. The height of Cabinet B is x inches.

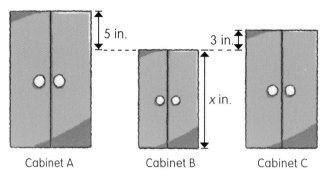

Cabinet A   Cabinet B   Cabinet C

a Write algebraic expressions for the heights of cabinets A and C.

b If the total height of the three cabinets is (3x + 8) inches, can you solve for the height of Cabinet B? Explain.

14 The floor of a room is y meters long. The width is 5 meters shorter. If the perimeter of the floor is (4y + 1) meters, can you solve for its length? Explain.

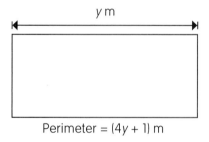

Perimeter = (4y + 1) m

15 | Mathematical Habit 2 | Use mathematical reasoning
Grace gave her sister the following riddle.
I have a number x. I add 15 to twice of x to obtain A. I subtract 4 from x to obtain B. I multiply B by 3 to obtain C. A is equal to C.

Grace's sister said the riddle cannot be solved but Grace thought otherwise. Who is right? Explain.

3 Understanding Linear Equations with Two Variables

Learning Objectives:
- Express a linear relationship between two variables.
- Represent a linear relationship using a table of values.

THINK

Owen sells blood pressure monitors. He earns a monthly salary that includes a basic amount of $750 and $4 for each monitor sold. Write a linear equation for his monthly salary, M dollars, in terms of the number, n, of monitors sold. Think about what kind of restrictions the variables should have, then deduce if it is possible for Owen to earn a monthly salary of $832.

ENGAGE

Michael is 5 years younger than Daniel. Create a table to show their possible ages. What are the variables involved? How are the variables related to each other? Explain your answer.

LEARN Express a linear relationship between two variables

1. The table shows the ages of Diana and Brian over five years.

	2008	2009	2010	2011	2012
Brian's Age	1	2	3	4	5
Diana's Age	4	5	6	7	8

Notice that Diana's age is always 3 years more than Brian's age. You can represent the relationship between their ages using a linear equation with two variables.

> Look for a pattern between the values for Brian's age and the values for Diana's age.

If Brian is x years old and Diana is y years old, the variables x and y are related by the linear equation $y = x + 3$.

 **Math Talk**

What expression can you write to express Brian's age in terms of Diana's age? What equation can you write using this expression? Is the equation equivalent to $y = x + 3$? Explain.

2 Write a linear equation for the relationship between hours, h, and minutes, m.

An hour has 60 minutes.

A linear equation for m in terms of h is $m = 60h$.

> You can also write the equation $h = \dfrac{m}{60}$ to represent the relationship between h and m. The equations $m = 60h$ and $h = \dfrac{m}{60}$ are equivalent.

3 Kaitlyn heated a liquid and measured its temperature. She recorded the results in the following table.

Time (*t* minute)	0	1	2	3	4
Temperature (*T* °C)	25	30	35	40	45

Write a linear equation for T in terms of t.

The initial temperature was 25°C. After that, the temperature rose by 5°C every minute.

t	T
0	$25 = 25 + 0\ = 25 + 5 \cdot \mathbf{0}$
1	$30 = 25 + 5\ = 25 + 5 \cdot \mathbf{1}$
2	$35 = 25 + 10 = 25 + 5 \cdot \mathbf{2}$
3	$40 = 25 + 15 = 25 + 5 \cdot \mathbf{3}$
4	$45 = 25 + 20 = 25 + 5 \cdot \mathbf{4}$

Observe that the expressions for T follow a pattern. They also contain a varying number that has the same value as t. You can replace the varying number by t to obtain the general expression $25 + 5t$ for T.

A linear equation for T in terms of t is $T = 25 + 5t$.

Practice expressing a linear relationship between two variables

Write a linear equation for the relationship between the given quantities.

① days, d, and weeks, w

Solve.

② Samuel rented a car from a company for a week. The table shows the rental charges.

Distance (d miles)	0	1	2	3	4
Rental Charge (C dollar)	100	100.10	100.20	100.30	100.40

Write a linear equation for C in terms of d.

ENGAGE

The sum of the measures of the angles in a polygon is related to the number of sides that a polygon has. Think of three shapes and the sum of the measure of their angles. How can you display this information? Share and discuss your answer with your partner.

LEARN Represent a linear relationship using a table of values

① Find the value of y when $x = 7$ in the equation $y = \frac{x-5}{2}$.

$y = \frac{7-5}{2}$ Substitute 7 for x.

$y = \frac{2}{2}$ Subtract.

$y = 1$ Simplify.

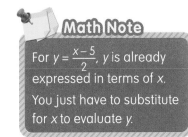

Math Note

For $y = \frac{x-5}{2}$, y is already expressed in terms of x. You just have to substitute for x to evaluate y.

② Find the value of y when $x = 7$ in the equation $3y + 4 = 2x$.

$3y + 4 = 2(7)$ Substitute 7 for x.

$3y + 4 - 4 = 14 - 4$ Subtract 4 from both sides.

$3y = 10$

$\frac{3y}{3} = \frac{10}{3}$ Divide both sides by 3.

$y = 3\frac{1}{3}$ Simplify.

③ Find the value of y when $x = 7$ in the equation $\frac{9}{2}y - x = 15.5$.

$\frac{9}{2}y - 7 = 15.5$ Substitute 7 for x.

$\frac{9}{2}y - 7 + 7 = 15.5 + 7$ Add 7 to both sides.

$\frac{9}{2}y = 22.5$ Simplify.

$\frac{9}{2}y \cdot 2 = 22.5 \cdot 2$ Multiply both sides by 2.

$9y = 45$ Simplify.

$9y \div 9 = 45 \div 9$ Divide both sides by 9.

$y = 5$ Simplify.

Math Note

For $3y + 4 = 2x$ and $\frac{9}{2}y - x = 15.5$, when you substitute a value for x, you obtain an equation with one variable y. You have to solve this one-variable equation to find the value of y.

Another way to find the value of y is to express y in terms of x before substituting the value of x into the expression for y. You will learn how to do this in the next lesson.

④ Create a table of x- and y-values for the equation $\frac{y}{2} = \frac{3}{2}x + 2$.

Use integer values of x from −1 to 1.

Substitute −1 for x into the equation.

$\frac{y}{2} = \frac{3}{2}(-1) + 2$

$\frac{y}{2} = \frac{1}{2}$ Simplify.

$\frac{y}{2} \cdot 2 = \frac{1}{2} \cdot 2$ Multiply both sides by 2.

$y = 1$ Simplify.

Substitute 0 for x into the equation.

$\frac{y}{2} = \frac{3}{2}(0) + 2$

$\frac{y}{2} = 2$ Simplify.

$\frac{y}{2} \cdot 2 = 2 \cdot 2$ Multiply both sides by 2.

$y = 4$ Simplify.

Substitute 1 for x into the equation.

$$\frac{y}{2} = \frac{3}{2}(1) + 2$$

$$\frac{y}{2} = \frac{7}{2} \qquad \text{Simplify.}$$

$$\frac{y}{2} \cdot 2 = \frac{7}{2} \cdot 2 \qquad \text{Multiply both sides by 2.}$$

$$y = 7 \qquad \text{Simplify.}$$

So, you have the following table of values.

x	−1	0	1
y	1	4	7

When solving a linear equation in two variables, you know that each x-value has a corresponding y-value. So, the equation has an infinite number of solutions. One way to represent some of these solutions is with a table of values.

5 Complete the table of values for the equation $8y = 5(x − 4)$.

x	2	?	6
y	?	0	?

Substitute 2 for x into the equation.

$$8y = 5(2 − 4)$$
$$8y = −10 \qquad \text{Simplify.}$$
$$8y \div 8 = −10 \div 8 \qquad \text{Divide both sides by 8.}$$
$$y = −1.25 \qquad \text{Simplify.}$$

Substitute 0 for y into the equation.

$$0 = 5(x − 4)$$
$$0 \div 5 = 5(x − 4) \div 5 \qquad \text{Divide both sides by 5.}$$
$$0 = x − 4 \qquad \text{Simplify.}$$
$$0 + 4 = x − 4 + 4 \qquad \text{Add 4 to both sides.}$$
$$4 = x \qquad \text{Simplify.}$$

To solve the equation $0 = 5(x − 4)$, you should be able to observe that $x − 4$ is 0 because any number multiplied by 0 equals 0.

Substitute 6 for x into the equation.

$$8y = 5(6 − 4)$$
$$8y = 10$$
$$8y \div 8 = 10 \div 8 \qquad \text{Divide both sides by 8.}$$
$$y = 1.25 \qquad \text{Simplify.}$$

So, you have the following table of values.

x	2	4	6
y	−1.25	0	1.25

Activity Using a graphing calculator to create tables of values for linear equations with two variables

Mathematical Habit 5 Use tools strategically

Work in pairs.

(1) Enter the equation $y = \frac{x}{\pi}$ using the equation screen of a graphing calculator.

(2) Set the table function to use values of x starting at 0, with increments of 1.

(3) Display the table. It will be in two columns as shown.

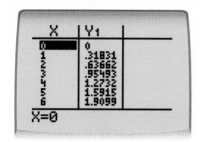

(4) Repeat (1) to (3) for the equation $y = -2x + \sqrt{2}$.

Caution

For (4), use the (–) key for the negative coefficient, –2.

TRY Practice representing a linear relationship using a table of values

Find the value of y when $x = -4$.

(1) $y = 7 + 3x$

(2) $\frac{1}{3}y = 2\left(x - \frac{1}{6}\right)$

(3) $-6x - y = 17.75$

Create a table of x- and y-values for each equation. Use integer values of x from 1 to 3.

(4) $2y = 1.2x + 1$

(5) $4y - 11x = 6$

Fill in the table of values for each equation.

(6) $\frac{y-2}{3} = x$

x		0	1
y	–1		

(7) $3(x + 1) - 2y = 0$

x			
y	9	$16\frac{1}{2}$	24

INDEPENDENT PRACTICE

Write a linear equation for the relationship between the given quantities.

1. meters, m, and centimeters, c

2. hours, h, and seconds, s

3. feet, f, and inches, i

4. dollars, d, and cents, c

Find the value of y when $x = 2$.

5. $2x - 1 = y + 4$

6. $y = \frac{1}{7}(x + 5)$

7. $3x - 11 = 2(y - 4)$

8. $4y = 5(x - 1)$

Find the value of x when $y = -7$.

9. $2(3x - 7) = 9y$

10. $\frac{2x - 1}{5} = 2(y + 7)$

11. $2x + y = 0.1(y + 3)$

12. $2y - 5x = 26$

Create a table of x- and y-values for each equation. Use integer values of x from 1 to 3.

13. $y = \frac{1}{4}(8 - x)$

14. $x + 7 = \frac{1}{2}(y - 5)$

15. $-4y = 2x + 5$

16. $\frac{1}{2}(x + 4) = \frac{1}{3}(y + 1)$

Fill in the table of values for each equation.

17 $y = 5(x + 3)$

x	0	1	2
y			

18 $\frac{x}{4} + y = 1$

x	2		
y		0	−0.5

19 $3x - 4y = \frac{5}{3}$

x	−3	−2	−1
y	$-2\frac{2}{3}$		

20 $5(y + 4) = 8x$

x			
y	−4	12	28

Solve.

21 A research student recorded the distance traveled by a car for every gallon of gasoline used. He recorded the results in the table. Write a linear equation for the distance, traveled, *d* miles in terms of the amount, of gasoline used, *g* gallons.

Amount of Gasoline Used (*g* gallons)	1	2	3	4
Distance Traveled (*d* miles)	40.5	81	121.5	162

4

Solving for a Variable in a Two-Variable Linear Equation

Learning Objective:
• Solve for a variable in a two-variable linear equation.

THINK

Leah's train will leave her local train station in 24 minutes. She is y miles from the station. To catch the train, she walks at a speed of 4 miles per hour and later runs at a speed of 8 miles per hour.
  a Write an equation in terms of y for the distance, w miles, Leah has to walk to reach the station in 24 minutes.
  b Solve for y in terms of w. How far is Leah from the station if she has to walk 1 mile to reach the station on time?
  c Why do the values of y have to be between 1.6 and 3.2?

ENGAGE

You can convert yards (y) to feet (t) using the formula $t = 3y$.
Write an equation to convert feet to yards.
Use three different values for feet to show that your equation is equivalent to the one given.

LEARN Solve for a variable in a two-variable linear equation

1. Given the formula $P = 4\ell$, you can use this formula to find the value of ℓ when you know the value of P. For example, if $P = 18$, you find the value of ℓ by substituting the value of P into the equation and solving for ℓ.

$$P = 4\ell$$
$$18 = 4\ell \qquad \text{Substitute 18 for } P.$$
$$\frac{18}{4} = \frac{4\ell}{4} \qquad \text{Divide both sides by 4.}$$
$$4.5 = \ell \qquad \text{Simplify.}$$

If you are given many values of P and asked to find the corresponding values of ℓ, you may want to solve the equation for ℓ first. That is, you express ℓ in terms of P before substituting values of P. To solve the equation for ℓ, you carry out the following steps.

$$P = 4\ell$$
$$\frac{P}{4} = \frac{4\ell}{4} \qquad \text{Divide both sides by 4.}$$
$$\frac{P}{4} = \ell \qquad \text{Simplify.}$$

Evaluate ℓ when $P = 18$ again.

$\ell = \dfrac{P}{4}$

$\ell = \dfrac{18}{4}$ Substitute 18 to P.

$\ell = 4.5$ Simplify.

> Using either method, you obtain the same value for ℓ.

2   Express F in terms of C for the equation $C = \dfrac{5}{9}(F - 32)$. Find the value of F when $C = 10$.

$C = \dfrac{5}{9}(F - 32)$

$C \cdot \dfrac{9}{5} = \dfrac{5}{9}(F - 32) \cdot \dfrac{9}{5}$ Multiply both sides by $\dfrac{9}{5}$.

$\dfrac{9}{5}C = F - 32$ Simplify.

$\dfrac{9}{5}C + 32 = F - 32 + 32$ Add 32 to both sides.

$\dfrac{9}{5}C + 32 = F$ Simplify.

> **Math Note**
>
> Notice that the equation of F in terms of C and the equation of C in terms of F are both linear. If an equation with two variables is linear, expressing either variable in terms of the other produces an equivalent linear equation.

> To solve the equation for F, you have to isolate F on one side of the equation.

Substitute 10 for C into the equation $F = \dfrac{9}{5}C + 32$.

$F = \dfrac{9}{5}(10) + 32$

$ = 50$

 **Math Talk**

> Do you think it is easier to find the value of F by expressing F in terms of C first? Why?

③ In a right isosceles triangle, the lengths of the sides can be expressed as s units, s units, and $s\sqrt{2}$ units. So, its perimeter, P units, is given by $P = s + s + s\sqrt{2}$.

Math Note

The expression $s\sqrt{2}$ means s times the square root of 2.

a Express s in terms of P.

$P = s + s + s\sqrt{2}$

$P = 2s + s\sqrt{2}$ Simplify.

$P = (2 + \sqrt{2})s$ Factor the right side.

$\dfrac{P}{2 + \sqrt{2}} = \dfrac{(2 + \sqrt{2})s}{2 + \sqrt{2}}$ Divide both sides by $2 + \sqrt{2}$.

$\dfrac{P}{2 + \sqrt{2}} = s$ Simplify.

> $\dfrac{P}{2 + \sqrt{2}} = s$ is a linear equation that is equivalent to $P = s + s + s\sqrt{2}$.

b Create a table of values for P and s when $P = 4, 6, 8,$ and 10. Round the values of s to 2 decimal places.

Substitute 4, 6, 8, and 10 for P into the equation $s = \dfrac{P}{2 + \sqrt{2}}$.

$s = \dfrac{4}{2 + \sqrt{2}} \approx 1.17$

$s = \dfrac{6}{2 + \sqrt{2}} \approx 1.76$

$s = \dfrac{8}{2 + \sqrt{2}} \approx 2.34$

$s = \dfrac{10}{2 + \sqrt{2}} \approx 2.93$

So, you have the following table of values.

P	4	6	8	10
s	1.17	1.76	2.34	2.93

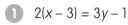 **Practice solving for a variable in a two-variable linear equation**

Express x in terms of y. Find the value of x when y = 3.

1 $2(x - 3) = 3y - 1$

To solve the equation for x, isolate x on one side of the equation.

Solve.

2 The formula for finding the mean, M, of the numbers x, $x\sqrt{3}$, and 2 is $M = \frac{x + x\sqrt{3} + 2}{3}$.

a Express x in terms of M.

b Create a table of values for M and x when $M = 0, 1, 2,$ and 3. Round each x-value to the nearest hundredth.

INDEPENDENT PRACTICE

Express *y* in terms of *x*. Find the value of *y* when *x* = –1.

1 $5 - y = 3x$

2 $-3(x + 2) = 5y$

3 $6(x - y) = 19$

4 $4x - 3 = 0.4x - 2y$

5 $\frac{1}{6}x + \frac{3}{4}y = 4$

6 $0.5y - 2 = 0.25x$

Express *x* in terms of *y*. Find the value of *x* when *y* = 5.

7 $5x - y = 3(x + y)$

8 $3(x + 2y) = 2x + 5y$

9 $1.5(x - y) = 1$

10 $2y + 8 = \frac{1}{4}x$

11 $\frac{2(x - 3)}{y} = 5$

12 $\frac{1}{3}(6x - 1) = \frac{6y}{5}$

Solve.

13 The perimeter, P inches, of a semicircle of diameter, d inches, is represented by $P = 0.5\pi d + d$.

 a Express d in terms of P.

 b Find the diameter if the perimeter is 36 inches. Use $\frac{22}{7}$ as an approximation for π.

14 The horizontal distance, X inches, and vertical distance, Y inches, of each step of a staircase are related by the linear equation $X = \frac{1}{2}(20 + Y)$.

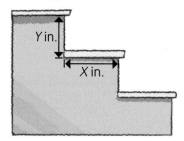

 a Express Y in terms of X.

 b Fill in the table.

X		16			19
Y	10		14	16	

 c Find the values of X and Y if $X = Y$.

15 A rectangle has a width of w units and a length of 5 units. Its perimeter, P units, is given by $P = 2(w + 5)$. Solve for w in terms of P. Create a table of values for $P = 12, 14, 16,$ and 18.

5

Solving Linear Inequalities With One Variable

Learning Objectives:
• Solve linear inequalities with one variable.
• Solve real-world problems involving linear inequalities with one variable.

THINK

Sarah is traveling overseas and wants to leave her dog at a pet hotel. Pet hotel A charges a monthly membership fee of $430 payment plus $20 per day if the dog is left at the hotel. Pet hotel B charges a monthly membership fee of $110 payment plus $30 per day if the dog is left at the hotel. Represent this as an inequality and solve it. Hence suggest whether Sarah should leave her dog at pet hotel A or hotel B, for lower rates.

ENGAGE

Solve $x - 4 = 6 - 3x$. Discuss with your partner how you can use the method for solving the equation to solve the inequality $x - 4 > 6 - 3x$. What are the similarities and the differences in the methods and the solutions?

LEARN Solve linear inequalities with one variable

1️⃣ You can apply the techniques of solving algebraic equations with variables on both sides to solve algebraic inequalities with variables on both sides.

2️⃣ Solve the inequality $x - 7 \leq 5 - 2x$ and graph the solution set on a number line.

$$x - 7 \leq 5 - 2x$$
$$x - 7 + 2x \leq 5 - 2x + 2x \quad \text{Add } 2x \text{ to both sides.}$$
$$3x - 7 \leq 5 \quad \text{Simplify.}$$
$$3x - 7 + 7 \leq 5 + 7 \quad \text{Add 7 to both sides.}$$
$$3x \leq 12 \quad \text{Simplify.}$$
$$\frac{3x}{3} \leq \frac{12}{3} \quad \text{Divide both sides by 3.}$$
$$x \leq 4 \quad \text{Simplify.}$$

The solution set is represented on a number line as shown.

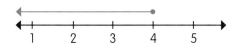

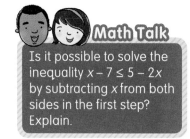

Math Talk

Is it possible to solve the inequality $x - 7 \leq 5 - 2x$ by subtracting x from both sides in the first step? Explain.

3️⃣ Solve the inequality $3.7x + 2.1 \geq 1.9x - 6.9$ and graph the solution set on a number line.

$$3.7x + 2.1 \geq 1.9x - 6.9$$
$$3.7x + 2.1 - 1.9x \geq 1.9x - 6.9 - 1.9x \quad \text{Subtract } 1.9x \text{ from both sides.}$$
$$1.8x + 2.1 \geq -6.9 \quad \text{Simplify.}$$

$$1.8x + 2.1 - \mathbf{2.1} \geq -6.9 - \mathbf{2.1} \quad \text{Subtract 2.1 from both sides.}$$
$$1.8x \geq -9 \qquad\qquad \text{Simplify.}$$
$$\frac{1.8x}{\mathbf{1.8}} \geq \frac{-9}{\mathbf{1.8}} \qquad\qquad \text{Divide both sides by 1.8.}$$
$$x \geq -5 \qquad\qquad \text{Simplify.}$$

The solution set is represented on a number line as shown.

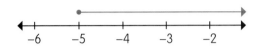

④ Solve the inequality $x - 6 > 2(12 + 2x)$ and graph the solution set on a number line.

$$x - 6 > 2(12 + 2x)$$
$$x - 6 > 24 + 4x \qquad\qquad \text{Use the distributive property.}$$
$$x - 6 - \mathbf{4x} > 24 + 4x - \mathbf{4x} \qquad \text{Subtract 4x from both sides.}$$
$$-3x - 6 > 24 \qquad\qquad \text{Simplify.}$$
$$-3x - 6 + \mathbf{6} > 24 + \mathbf{6} \qquad\qquad \text{Add 6 to both sides.}$$
$$-3x > 30 \qquad\qquad \text{Simplify.}$$
$$\frac{-3x}{-3} < \frac{30}{-3} \qquad\qquad \text{Divide both sides by } -3 \text{ and reverse the inequality symbol.}$$
$$x < -10 \qquad\qquad \text{Simplify.}$$

The solution set is represented on a number line as shown.

⑤ Solve the inequality $\frac{1}{3}x + 1 \leq \frac{1}{4}x + \frac{2}{3}$ and graph the solution set on a number line.

$$\frac{1}{3}x + 1 \leq \frac{1}{4}x + \frac{2}{3}$$
$$\frac{1}{3}x + 1 - \frac{1}{4}\mathbf{x} \leq \frac{1}{4}x + \frac{2}{3} - \frac{1}{4}\mathbf{x} \qquad \text{Subtract } \frac{1}{4}x \text{ from both sides.}$$
$$\frac{4}{12}x + 1 - \frac{3}{12}x \leq \frac{2}{3} \qquad \text{Write equivalent fractions using the LCD, 12.}$$
$$\frac{1}{12}x + 1 \leq \frac{2}{3} \qquad \text{Simplify.}$$
$$\frac{1}{12}x + 1 - \mathbf{1} \leq \frac{2}{3} - \mathbf{1} \qquad \text{Subtract 1 from both sides.}$$
$$\frac{1}{12}x \leq -\frac{1}{3} \qquad \text{Simplify.}$$
$$\frac{1}{12}x \cdot \mathbf{12} \leq -\frac{1}{3} \cdot \mathbf{12} \qquad \text{Multiply both sides by 12.}$$
$$x \leq -4 \qquad \text{Simplify.}$$

The solution set is represented on a number line as shown.

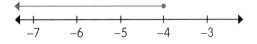

Solve each inequality and graph the solution set on a number line.

1 $x + 19 \leq 6x - 41$

2 $-0.3x + 2 \geq 14 + 0.5x$

3 $3(x - 1) > 7 + 4(x - 1)$

4 $\frac{1}{2}x - 1\frac{2}{3} < \frac{1}{3}x - 1$

ENGAGE

Antonia has a certain amount of game cards. The number of game cards Sarah has is 3 less than twice the amount Antonia has. Given that Sarah has lesser game cards than Antonia, how can you represent this information using an inequality? What are the possible number of game cards Antonia has? Explain your answer.

LEARN Solve real-world problems involving linear inequalities with one variable

① Kimberly is searching for a room to rent and found the payment plans shown offered by two landlords A and B. After how many months will renting with landlord A be cheaper than landlord B?

Landlord A	Landlord B
Initial charge: $300	Initial charge: $100
Monthly charge: $450	Monthly charge: $500

Let x be the number of months.   Define the variable.

Landlord A charges $300 + $450 \cdot x = $300 + $450x$.
Landlord B charges $100 + $500 \cdot x = $100 + $500x$.

$$300 + 450x < 100 + 500x$$ Write an inequality.
$$300 + 450x - 500x < 100 + 500x - 500x$$ Subtract 500x from both sides.
$$300 - 50x < 100$$ Simplify.
$$300 - 50x - 300 < 100 - 300$$ Subtract 300 from both sides.
$$-50x < -200$$ Simplify.
$$\frac{-50x}{-50} > \frac{-200}{-50}$$ Divide both sides by –50 and reverse the inequality symbol.
$$x > 4$$ Simplify.

Renting with landlord A will be cheaper than landlord B after 4 months.

TRY Practice solving real-world problems involving linear inequalities with one variable

Solve.

① Alexa and Jada each saves a portion of their allowances every day. The table shows the amounts.

Alexa	Jada
Initial amount of savings: $75	Initial amount of savings: $32
Daily savings: $0.50	Daily savings: $1

After how many days will Jada's savings be more than Alexa's savings?

INDEPENDENT PRACTICE

Solve each inequality and graph the solution set on a number line.

1 $2 - 3x > 8 - x$

2 $7.2 + 3.4x < 4.6x + 9.6$

3 $5(2x - 1) - 10 < 11 - 3(3x - 4)$

4 $6(3x + 4) \leq 22 + 8(2x + 1)$

5 $\frac{1}{4}x + 6 \leq \frac{3}{8}x - 2$

6 $\frac{3}{2} - \frac{2}{3}x \geq \frac{1}{6}x - \frac{1}{6}$

Solve.

7 Twenty-four minus three times an integer, x, is less than x minus four.

   a Write an inequality, in terms of x, to represent the information.

   b What is the smallest possible value of x?

8 Companies A and B provide housekeeping services. The charges are shown in the table.

Company A	Company B
First hour: $28	First hour: $20
Every subsequent half hour: $10	Every subsequent half hour: $12

After how many hours will Company A be cheaper than Company B?

Mathematical Habit 2 Use mathematical reasoning

Look at this "proof" that 2 = 0.

> When $a = 1$ and $b = 1$, then
> $(a - b)(a + b) = 0$
> $\quad\quad a + b = 0$ Divide both sides by $a - b$.
> $\quad\quad 1 + 1 = 0$ Substitute for a and b.
> $\quad\quad\quad\, 2 = 0$ Simplify.

What is wrong with this proof? How can a true statement lead to an inconsistent equation?

Problem Solving with Heuristics

① **Mathematical Habit 2** **Use mathematical reasoning**
Maria runs a private tutoring business. She rents a room for $500 a month, which is her only expense. She charges $50 an hour per student. She gives each student two lessons per month. Each lesson lasts 1.5 hours.

$$x^2 + x - 1 = 0$$

a Write an equation for her monthly profit, P dollars, in terms of the number of students, s, that Maria has.

b Find the monthly profit if Maria has 40 students.

c Find the minimum number of students that Maria needs if she wants to make a monthly profit of at least $4,600.

2 **Mathematical Habit 8** **Look for patterns**

A polygon has n sides. The sum of the measures of a polygon's interior angles is equal to the sum of the measures of r right angles. A table of r- and n values is shown below.

n	3	4	5	6
r	2	4	6	8

Explain how you would find a linear equation involving r and n.

CHAPTER WRAP-UP

How do you solve for a variable in a linear equation with two variables?

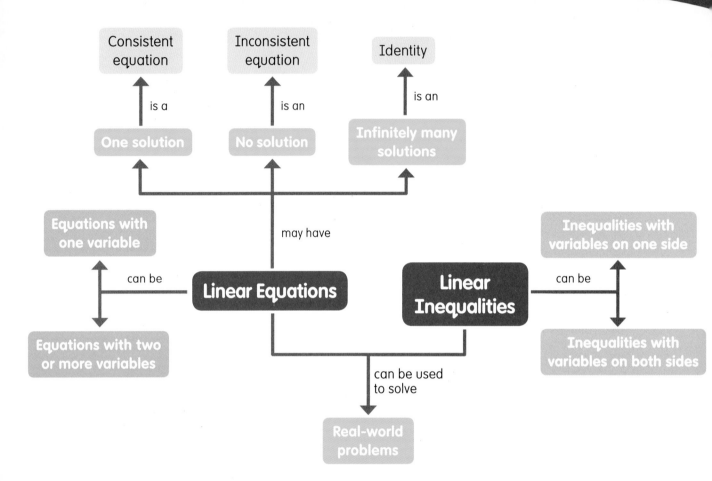

KEY CONCEPTS

- A linear equation can have one or more variables.
- A consistent equation in one variable is an equation that has one solution.
- An inconsistent equation is an equation that has no solution.
- An identity is an equation that is true for all values of the variable.
- A linear relationship between two variables can be represented with an equation or a table of values.
- Solving for a variable in a multi-variable linear equation means expressing the variable in terms of the other variable(s).
- A linear inequality can have a variable on one or both sides.
- Linear equations and inequalities can be used to represent and solve real-world problems.

Name: _____ Date: _____

Solve each linear equation.

① $2(x - 5) = 20x + 8$

② $4x = \frac{3}{5} + \frac{5 - 2x}{5}$

Write each repeating decimal as a fraction.

③ $0.\overline{2}$

④ $0.9\overline{3}$

⑤ $0.2\overline{6}$

⑥ $0.3\overline{16}$

Determine whether each equation is a consistent equation, on inconsistent equation or on identity.

⑦ $2x + 4 = 2\left(\frac{1}{2} + x\right)$

⑧ $6y + (16 - 2y) = 4(4 + y)$

⑨ $4x + 5 = 2x - 7$

⑩ $2x + 5 = -4\left(-\frac{5}{4} - \frac{1}{2}x\right)$

Write a linear equation for the relationship between the given quantities.

11 kilometers, k, and meters, m

12 days, d, and hours, h

Find the value of y when $x = 4$.

13 $x - 4y = 2$

14 $y - x = \frac{1}{3}(x + 14)$

15 $\frac{1}{7}(3x + y) = x$

16 $\frac{3y + 1}{4} = 2x$

Express x in terms of y. Find the value of x when $y = -2$.

17 $3(x - 2y) = 4x + 5y$

18 $\frac{0.5(x - 3)}{y} = 10$

Solve each inequality and graph the solution set on a number line.

19 $3(7 - 0.3x) < 0.1x - 3$

20 $11 + \frac{1}{4}x < 25 - \frac{3}{4}x$

Solve.

21 Some students painted a design on the wall of the cafeteria using the school colors. The middle section of the design is 4.2 feet tall, and is painted white. The top section is red, and the bottom section is blue. The ratio of the height of the blue section to the height of the red section is 1 : 2. The total height of the design is 10.5 feet. Find the height of the red section of the design.

22 The company Jaden uses for Internet service charges $25 each month plus $0.04 for each minute of usage time.

a Write a linear equation for the monthly charge, *M* dollars, in terms of the usage time, *t* minutes.

b Express *t* in terms of *M*.

c Calculate Jaden's usage time in hours if he paid $49 for his Internet bill in November.

23 Madeline plans to enrol in an online course. The course offers two payment options as shown.

Option A	Option B
One time registration fee: $100 Fee per module: $275	One time registration fee: $65 Fee per module: $280

After how many modules will Option A be less expensive than Option B?

Assessment Prep
Answer each question.

24 Julian was 32 years old when his son was born. Now Julian is three times as old as his son.

Part A

Which equation could be used to determine the age, *x* years, of Julian's son?

(A) $32 + 3x = x$

(B) $32 + x = 3x$

(C) $32 - 3x = x$

(D) $32 - x = 3x$

Part B

What is the age of Julian's son? Write your answer and your working or explanation in the space below.

25 Which is the solution to the inequality $3x \leq 4x + 9$?

(A) $x \geq 9$

(B) $x \geq -9$

(C) $x \leq 9$

(D) $x \leq -9$

Name: _____   Date: _____

Bowling

1 Joseph and two friends want to go bowling. The bowling alley charges $3.25 for each pair of shoes they rent and $4.75 per game. All three of them need to rent shoes, and they are not sure yet how many games they will play.

a Write a linear equation for the total cost, *C* dollars, if they play *g* games.

b Find the total cost for playing 0, 1, 2, and 3 games. Fill in the table to show the total cost.

Number of Games	Total Cost
0	$9.75
1	
2	
3	

c Can you triple the cost of playing 2 games to find the cost of playing 6 games? Justify your reasoning.

d Joseph and his friends decide to spend not more than a total of $30 for the games. By writing an inequality, find the maximum number of games they can play.

Rubric

Point(s)	Level	My Performance
7–8	4	• Most of my answers are correct. • I showed complete understanding of the concepts. • I used effective and efficient strategies to solve the problems. • I explained my answers and mathematical thinking clearly and completely.
5–6	3	• Some of my answers are correct. • I showed adequate understanding of the concepts. • I used effective strategies to solve the problems. • I explained my answers and mathematical thinking clearly.
3–4	2	• A few of my answers are correct. • I showed some understanding of the concepts. • I used some effective strategies to solve the problems. • I explained some of my answers and mathematical thinking clearly.
0–2	1	• A few of my answers are correct. • I showed little understanding of the concepts. • I used limited effective strategies to solve the problems. • I did not explain my answers and mathematical thinking clearly.

Teacher's Comments

Chapter 5

Lines and Linear Equations

How steep is that slope?

If you like to snowboard, you probably want to know how steep a mountain is before you try to go down it. You can describe how steep a mountain is by using a ratio to compare the change in elevation between two points to the horizontal distance between the two points. The greater that ratio, the steeper the mountain. In this chapter, you will learn how to find slopes of lines on coordinate planes.

How do you write an equation of a linear graph?

Name: ______________________ Date: ____________

RECALL PRIOR KNOWLEDGE

Identifying and plotting coordinates

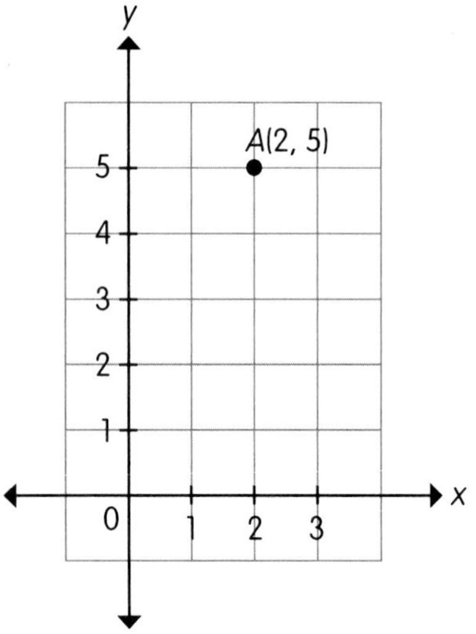

An ordered pair (*x*, *y*) is used to represent the location of a point on a graph.

Point *A* (2, 5) represents the location of a point that is 2 units to the right of the origin, and 5 units up from the origin. The *x*-coordinate of point *A* is 2 and the *y*-coordinate is 5.

The coordinates of the origin are (0, 0).

▶ Quick Check

Use the coordinate plane below.

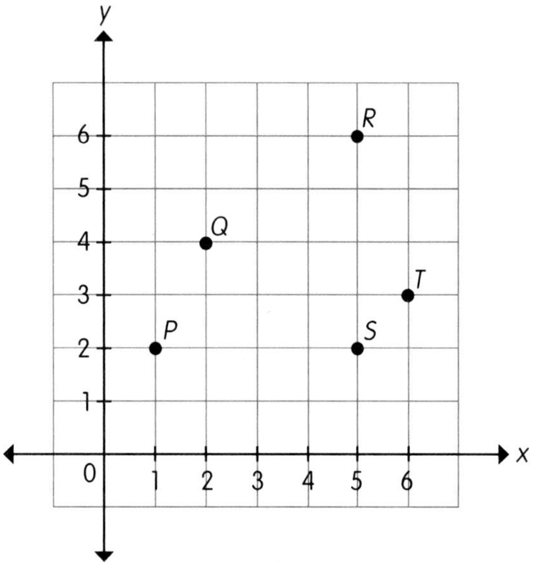

1. Give the coordinates of points *P*, *Q*, *R*, *S*, and *T*.

Finding and Interpreting Slopes of Lines

Learning Objective:
• Find slopes of lines.

> **New Vocabulary**
> slope
> rise
> run

THINK

Jason says that the line in Graph B has a greater slope than the line in Graph A because it is steeper. What error is Jason making? Justify your answer.

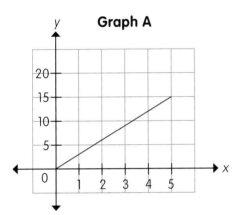

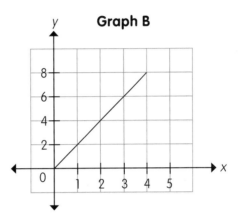

ENGAGE

The graph shows that y is directly proportional to x. The line passes through the points (2, 100) and (7, 350). A right triangle is drawn as shown. What are the lengths of the vertical and horizontal sides of the triangle? How do you find the constant of proportionality using the answers obtained? Discuss.

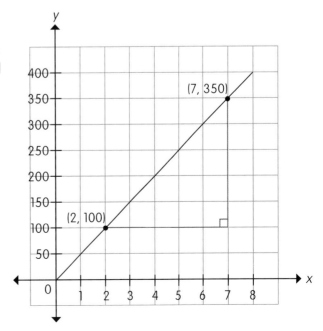

1 If you leave home and walk in a given direction at a steady pace, your distance, *d* feet, from home is directly proportional to the time, *x* minutes, you walk. You can use a table and a graph to represent this proportional relationship.

Time (x minutes)	1	2	3	4	5
Distance from Home (d feet)	250	500	760	1,000	1,250

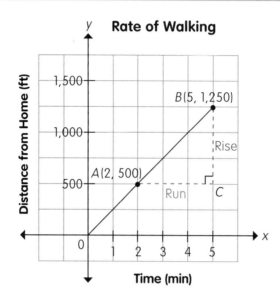

From the table, you see that the constant of proportionality is 250. You have learned that the point (1, *y*) on a direct proportion graph can be used to find the constant of proportionality. Another way to find the constant of proportionality is to find the slope of the line. You can find the slope by choosing two points and comparing the vertical change from the first point to the second, to the horizontal change from the first point to the second. The vertical change is called the **rise**. The horizontal change is called the **run**.

Suppose you choose the points *A* (2, 500) and *B* (5, 1,250) from the graph above.

Run = Horizontal change
    = 5 − 2
    = 3

Rise = Vertical change
    = 1,250 − 500
    = 750

$\dfrac{\text{Rise}}{\text{Run}} = \dfrac{750}{3}$
    = 250

As you can see, for this graph of a direct proportion, the slope of the line is 250, which is equal to the constant of proportionality.

© 2020 Marshall Cavendish Education Pte Ltd

2 The graphs give information about a penguin's number of heart beats, *b*, over time, *t* minutes, during normal resting and just before diving. When is the penguin's heart rate greater, during normal resting or just before diving?

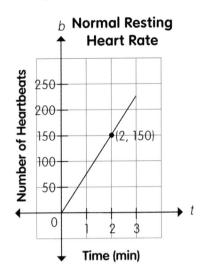

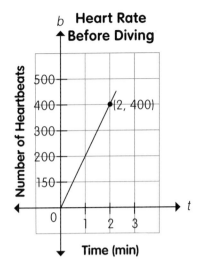

To find each heart rate, find the unit rate for each graph. To find the unit rate, you find the slope of the line. To find the slope, find the ratio $\frac{\text{Rise}}{\text{Run}}$ from the point (0, 0) to a convenient point on the graph.

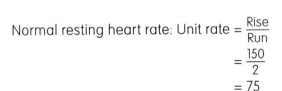

Normal resting heart rate: Unit rate $= \frac{\text{Rise}}{\text{Run}}$

$= \frac{150}{2}$

$= 75$

Heart rate before diving: Unit rate $= \frac{\text{Rise}}{\text{Run}}$

$= \frac{400}{2}$

$= 200$

Math Note

Because the graphs have different scales on their vertical axes, you may not be able to tell just by seeing that the slope of one line is greater than the slope of the other line. You need to calculate the slopes of the lines to see which is greater.

The slope for the normal resting heart rate graph is 75.
So, the unit rate is 75 beats per minute.

The slope for the heart rate before diving graph is 200.
So, the unit rate is 200 beats per minute.

A penguin's heart rate before diving is greater than its normal resting heart rate.

Practice using slopes to compare two unit rates

Solve.

1. The graphs give information about the distance, *d* miles, traveled over time, *t* hours, by cars and trucks on a highway. Which speed is lower?

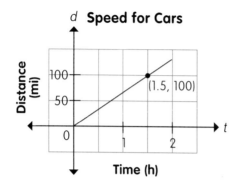

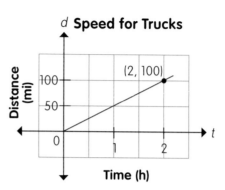

ENGAGE

Find the ratio $\frac{\text{Rise}}{\text{Run}}$, or the slope, of each line. How do the slopes compare?
Explain your thinking.

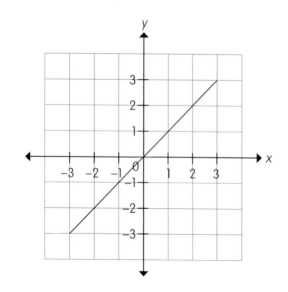

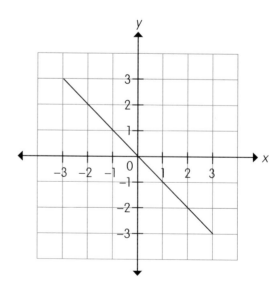

1 Consider a line graph that goes up from left to right.

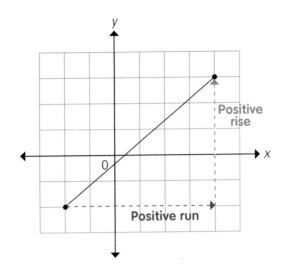

When the graph goes up from left to right, the run and the rise are both positive.

$$\text{Slope} = \frac{\text{Positive rise}}{\text{Positive run}}$$

So, the slope is positive.

Consider a line graph that goes down from left to right.

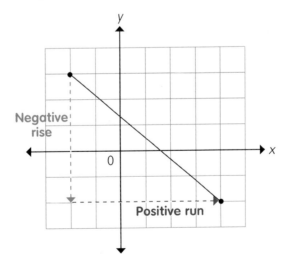

When the graph goes down from left to right, the run is positive, but the rise is negative.

$$\text{Slope} = \frac{\text{Negative rise}}{\text{Positive run}}$$

So, the slope is negative.

When you divide a negative number by a positive number, you obtain a negative quotient.

A line graph has a positive slope if it goes up from left to right. A line graph has a negative slope if it goes down from left to right.

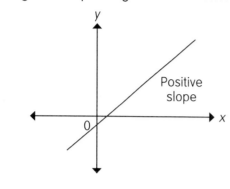

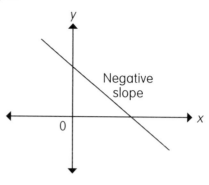

2 Find the slope of the line.

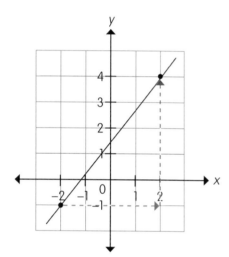

Move from (−2, −1) to (2, 4):
Vertical change = 4 − (−1)
= **5 units**

Horizontal change = 2 − (−2)
= **4 units**

So, the rise is 5 units, and the run is 4 units.

The graph passes through the points (−2, −1) and (2, 4).

$$\text{Slope} = \frac{\text{Rise}}{\text{Run}}$$
$$= \frac{4 - (-1)}{2 - (-2)}$$
$$= \frac{5}{4}$$

The slope is $\frac{5}{4}$.

Math Note

It is important to remember to subtract the coordinates in the same order in both the numerator and the denominator.

3 Find the slope of the line.

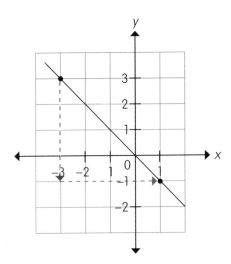

Move from (−3, 3) to (1, −1):
Vertical change = −1 − 3
= **−4 units**

Horizontal change = 1 − (−3)
= **4 units**

So, the rise is −4 units, and the run is 4 units.

The graph passes through the points (−3, 3) and (1, −1).

Slope = $\dfrac{\text{Rise}}{\text{Run}}$

$= \dfrac{-1 - 3}{1 - (-3)}$

$= \dfrac{-4}{4}$

$= -1$

The slope is −1.

TRY Practice finding the slope of a line given the graph

Find the slope of each line.

1

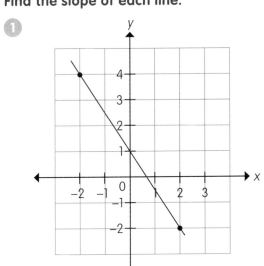

2

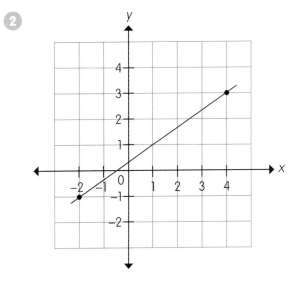

ENGAGE

Using the coordinate plane, draw two graphs to represent the given situations:
Carla is running at a constant speed of 5 miles per hour.
Hayden is running at a constant speed of 6 miles per hour.

What do you notice when comparing the graphs? Share your observations.

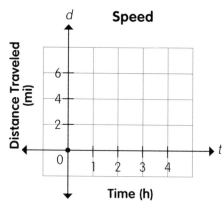

LEARN Compare two slopes to make a conclusion about real-world situations

1 A red car and a blue car leave the same garage at the same time. Each driver drives at a steady rate. The graph represents the distance, *d* miles, traveled by the red car over time, *t* hours. The blue car traveled 140 miles over the same length of time.

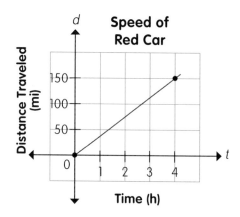

a At what speed is the red car traveling?

Find the slope of the graph and use the slope to find the rate, or speed, of the red car.

$$\text{Slope} = \frac{\text{Rise}}{\text{Run}}$$
$$= \frac{150}{4}$$
$$= 37.5 \text{ mi/h}$$

> The vertical axis shows distance in miles.
> The horizontal axis shows time in hours.
> So, the rate is in miles per hour.

The red car is traveling at a speed of 37.5 miles per hour.

b At what speed is the blue car traveling?

You are given that the blue car traveled 140 miles in 4 hours.

$$\text{Speed} = \frac{\text{Distance}}{\text{Time}}$$
$$= \frac{140}{4}$$
$$= 35 \text{ mi/h}$$

The blue car is traveling at a speed of 35 miles per hour.

c Suppose you graph a line showing the distance traveled by the blue car after t hours on the same coordinate plane as the one showing the distance traveled by the red car after t hours. Would the graph of the blue car be steeper than the graph of the red car?

The speed of the blue car is 35 miles per hour, which is less than the speed of the red car. The slope of its graph will be 35, which is less than the slope of the graph of the red car.

So, the graph of the blue car will be less steep.

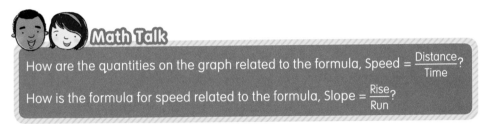

Math Talk

How are the quantities on the graph related to the formula, Speed = $\frac{\text{Distance}}{\text{Time}}$?

How is the formula for speed related to the formula, Slope = $\frac{\text{Rise}}{\text{Run}}$?

TRY Practice comparing two slopes to make a conclusion about real-world situations

Solve.

1 The graphs represent the amount of water, w gallons, in Pool A over time, t hours, and the amount of water, w gallons, left in Pool B over time, t hours.

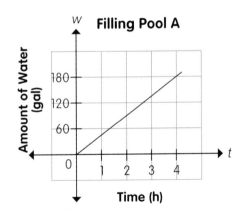

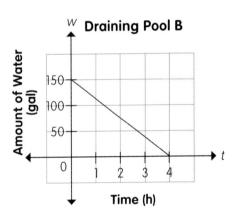

a Find the slope of the line graph for Pool A. What does it represent?

b Find the slope of the line graph for Pool B. What does it represent?

Consider a horizontal line graph and a vertical line graph.

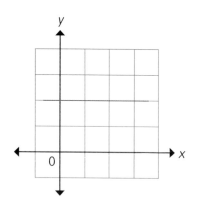
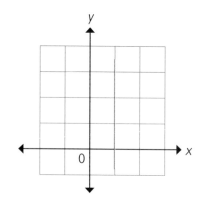

What do you think is the slope of each line? Explain your thinking.

Create a real-world situation for each line. Discuss your work.

LEARN Find slopes of horizontal and vertical lines

1   In a horizontal line graph, the run is positive.

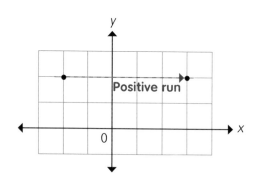

Positive run

The rise is zero since the *y*-coordinates of any two points are the same.

$$\text{Slope} = \frac{0}{\text{Positive run}}$$

So, the slope is always zero.

> For a horizontal line, the vertical change (rise) from one point to another is 0. So, $\dfrac{\text{Rise}}{\text{Run}} = \dfrac{0}{\text{Run}} = 0$.

In a vertical line graph, the rise is positive.

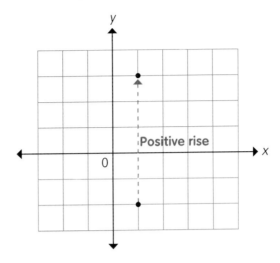

The run is zero since the *x*-coordinates of any two points on the line are the same.

Slope = $\dfrac{\text{Positive rise}}{0}$

So, the slope is undefined.

For a vertical line, the horizontal change (run) from one point to another is 0.
So, $\dfrac{\text{Rise}}{\text{Run}} = \dfrac{\text{Rise}}{0}$ = undefined. You cannot divide by zero.

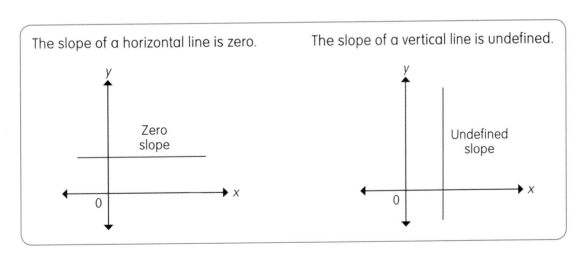

The slope of a horizontal line is zero.

Zero slope

The slope of a vertical line is undefined.

Undefined slope

2 Find the slope of the line.

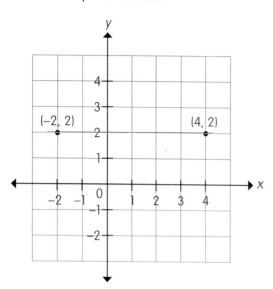

Use the points (–2, 2) and (4, 2).

$$\text{Slope} = \frac{\text{Rise}}{\text{Run}}$$
$$= \frac{2 - 2}{4 - (-2)}$$
$$= \frac{0}{6}$$
$$= 0$$

The slope is 0.

TRY **Practice finding slopes of horizontal and vertical lines**

Find the slope of the line.

1

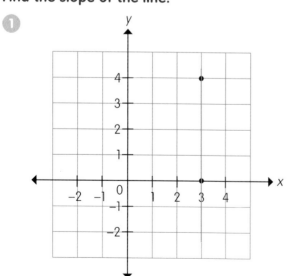

ENGAGE

A line passes through $(-2, -1)$ and $(2, 4)$. Draw the line on the coordinate plane below.

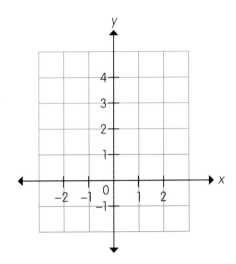

Using any two points on the line, find the rise and the run, and use them to find the slope of the line. Discuss with your partner if it is possible to be able to find the slope of the line without drawing the line. Explain your answer.

LEARN Find the slope of a line passing through two given points

1. When you want to find the slope of a line, you do not need to draw the line.

   Given any two points A (x_1, y_1) and B (x_2, y_2) on a line, you can find the rise and the run by subtracting the coordinates.

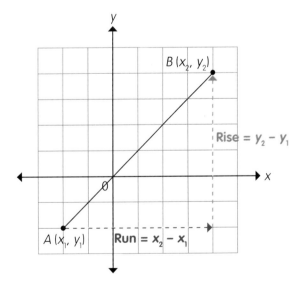

$$\text{Rise} = y_2 - y_1$$
$$\text{Run} = x_2 - x_1$$

So, slope $= \dfrac{\text{Rise}}{\text{Run}}$

$\qquad = \dfrac{y_2 - y_1}{x_2 - x_1}.$

Find the rise from point A to point B by subtracting the y-coordinate of point A from the y-coordinate of point B. Find the run from point A to point B by subtracting the x-coordinate of point A from the x-coordinate of point B.

When you find the rise or the run, it does not matter whether you subtract the coordinates of A from the coordinates of B, or the other way round. What matters is that you use the same order for both rise and run.

$$\text{Rise} = y_1 - y_2$$
$$\text{Run} = x_1 - x_2$$

So, slope $= \dfrac{\text{Rise}}{\text{Run}}$

$\qquad = \dfrac{y_1 - y_2}{x_1 - x_2}.$

Find the rise from point B to point A by subtracting the y-coordinate of point B from the y-coordinate of point A. Find the run from point B to point A by subtracting the x-coordinate of point B from the x-coordinate of point A.

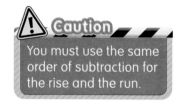

The slope of a line passing through two points (x_1, y_1) and (x_2, y_2) is equal to $\dfrac{y_2 - y_1}{x_2 - x_1}$ or $\dfrac{y_1 - y_2}{x_1 - x_2}$.

⚠ **Caution**

You must use the same order of subtraction for the rise and the run.

② Find the slope of the line passing through the points A (4, 8) and B (1, 4).

Let A (4, 8) be (x_1, y_1) and B (1, 4) be (x_2, y_2).

▶ **Method 1**

Subtract the coordinates of B from the coordinates of A.

Slope $= \dfrac{y_1 - y_2}{x_1 - x_2}$

$\qquad = \dfrac{8 - 4}{4 - 1}$

$\qquad = \dfrac{4}{3}$

The slope is $\dfrac{4}{3}$.

▶ Method 2

Subtract the coordinates of A from the coordinates of B.

$$\text{Slope} = \frac{y_2 - y_1}{x_2 - x_1}$$

$$= \frac{4 - 8}{1 - 4}$$

$$= \frac{-4}{-3}$$

$$= \frac{4}{3}$$

You can find the slope of the line by calculating the rise and the run either from point A to point B or from point B to point A.

The slope is $\frac{4}{3}$.

3 Find the slope of the line passing through the points P (2, 5) and Q (8, 2).

Let P (2, 5) be (x_1, y_1) and Q (8, 2) be (x_2, y_2).

▶ Method 1

Subtract the coordinates of Q from the coordinates of P.

$$\text{Slope} = \frac{y_1 - y_2}{x_1 - x_2}$$

$$= \frac{5 - 2}{2 - 8}$$

$$= \frac{3}{-6}$$

$$= -\frac{1}{2}$$

The slope is $-\frac{1}{2}$.

▶ Method 2

Subtract the coordinates of P from the coordinates of Q.

$$\text{Slope} = \frac{y_2 - y_1}{x_2 - x_1}$$

$$= \frac{2 - 5}{8 - 2}$$

$$= \frac{-3}{6}$$

$$= -\frac{1}{2}$$

The slope is $-\frac{1}{2}$.

Activity Exploring the slope of a line passing through two given points

Work in pairs.

① Using a geometry software, graph the line that passes through each pair of points and fill in the table.

	Coordinates of Points	Slope of Line	$y_2 - y_1$	$x_2 - x_1$
a	$P(2, 1)$ and $Q(4, 7)$	Positive	$7 - 1 =$	$4 - 2 =$
b	$R(7, 6)$ and $S(4, 9)$			
c	$T(1, 1)$ and $U(4, 1)$			
d	$V(-2, 3)$ and $W(-2, 6)$			

② When the signs of $y_2 - y_1$ and $x_2 - x_1$ are the same, what do you observe about the sign of the slope?

③ When the signs of $y_2 - y_1$ and $x_2 - x_1$ are different, what do you observe about the sign of the slope?

④ When the signs of $y_2 - y_1 = 0$, what do you observe about the slope?

⑤ When the signs of $x_2 - x_1 = 0$, what do you observe about the slope?

TRY Practice finding the slope of a line passing through two given points

Find the slope of the line passing through each pair of points.

❶ $M(-2, 0)$ and $N(0, 4)$

❷ $S(-5, 8)$ and $T(-2, 2)$

> You can use either $\dfrac{y_1 - y_2}{x_1 - x_2}$ or $\dfrac{y_2 - y_1}{x_2 - x_1}$ to find the slope.

INDEPENDENT PRACTICE

Find the slope of each line.

1

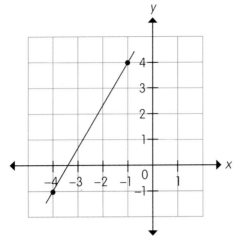

2

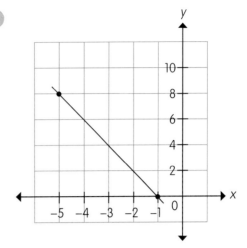

3

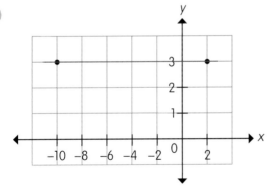

4

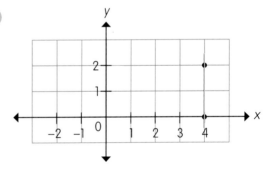

Solve.

5 **Mathematical Habit 6** Use precise mathematical language

Andrew graphs a vertical line through the points (5, 2) and (5, 5). He says the slope of the line is $\frac{3}{0}$. What error is he making?

Find the slope of the line passing through each pair of points.

6 A (–10, 3) and B (0, 3)

7 S (5, –2) and T (2, –5)

8 P (0, –7) and Q (–3, 5)

9 X (4, 4) and Y (4, –2)

Solve.

10 **Mathematical Habit 2** Use mathematical reasoning

Two points have the same x-coordinate but different y-coordinates. Make a prediction about the slope of a line drawn through the points. Justify your prediction.

11 **Mathematical Habit 2** Use mathematical reasoning

Two points have the same y-coordinate but different x-coordinates. Make a prediction about the slope of a line drawn through the points. Justify your prediction.

12 In the Fahrenheit system, water freezes at 32°F and boils at 212°F. In the Celsius system, water freezes at 0°C and boils at 100°C.

Freezes at 32°F or 0°C   Boils at 212°F or 100°C

a Translate the verbal description into a pair of points in the form (temperature in °C, temperature in °F).

b Find the slope of the line passing through the pair of points in a.

c Suppose the temperature in a room goes up by 5°C. By how much does the temperature go up in degrees Fahrenheit?

13. The table and the graph show the relationship between the cost, y dollars, of x gallons of gasoline purchased at each of the two stations, A and B, on a particular day.

Amount of Gasoline (x gallons)	Cost at Station A (y dollars)	Cost at Station B (y dollars)
1	3	4
3	11	10
5	19	16

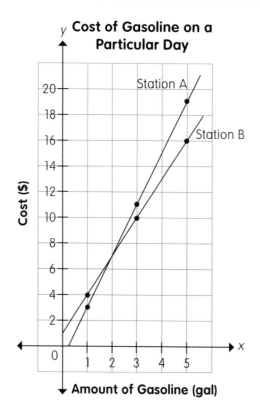

a At which station is each additional gallon of gasoline more expensive?

b Which graph is steeper?

2 Understanding Slope-Intercept Form

Learning Objective:
• Write an equation of a line in the form $y = mx$ or $y = mx + b$.

> **New Vocabulary**
> y-intercept
> x-intercept
> slope-intercept form

THINK

Line A passes through the origin and has a negative slope. Line B crosses the y-axis above the origin and has a positive slope. Line C crosses the y-axis below the origin and has a negative slope. Line D crosses the x-axis to the right of the origin and is parallel to the y-axis. Give a possible equation for each line. Justify your answer.

ENGAGE

Use the graph to find the slope of Line P. You can use the equation $y = 2x + 3$ to describe Line P. How does the equation relate to what you notice about the line? Line Q has the same slope as Line P. What might be the equation of Line Q?

Now draw a line that has the same slope as Line P but passes through −2 on the y-axis and label it as Line R. What might be the equation of Line R? Explain your thinking.

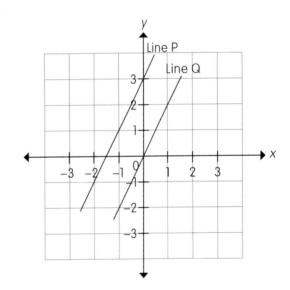

LEARN Write an equation of a line in the form $y = mx$ or $y = mx + b$

1. Jesse and his brother, Seth, walk from one end of a block to the other. Jesse starts at a curb. Seth starts 4 feet ahead of him. Both brothers walk at a rate of 4 feet per second.

   The table shows the times, x seconds, and the corresponding distances, y feet, from the curb.

Time (x seconds)	0	1	2	3	4	5	6
Jesse's distance from curb (y feet)	0	4	8	12	16	20	24
Seth's distance from curb (y feet)	4	8	12	16	20	24	28

The graph shows each brother's distance from the curb after x seconds.

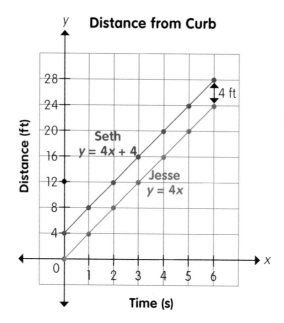

Jesse's graph represents a direct proportion. The rate, 4 feet per second, is also the slope of the red line. The equation of the red line is given by $y = 4x$. Seth is always 4 feet ahead of Jesse, but traveling at the same rate of 4 feet per second. So, for Seth's graph, the equation of the blue line is given by $y = 4x + 4$.

Jesse's graph and Seth's graph have the same slope because they walked at the same rate of 4 feet per second. So, their equations involve the same rate of change.

The graphs are different because they cross the y-axis at different points. Jesse's graph passes through the point (0, 0). Seth's graph crosses the y-axis at the point (0, 4).

The y-intercept of a line is the y-coordinate of the point where the line intersects the y-axis. The y-intercept of Jesse's graph is 0, hence, the equation is given by $y = 4x + 0$ or $y = 4x$. The y-intercept of Seth's graph is 4, hence, the equation is given by $y = 4x + 4$.

The x-intercept of a line is the x-coordinate of the point where the line intersects the x-axis.

A linear equation written in the form $y = mx + b$ is said to be written in slope-intercept form. The constant, m, represents the slope of the line. The constant, b, represents the y-intercept of the line.

> In the equation $y = 4x + 4$, m is 4 and b is 4.
> In the equation $y = 4x$, m is 4 and b is 0.

An equation of a line that passes through the origin, O (0, 0), is $y = mx$.

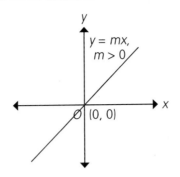

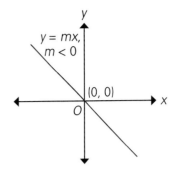

An equation of a line that intersects the y-axis at (0, b) is $y = mx + b$.

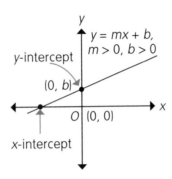

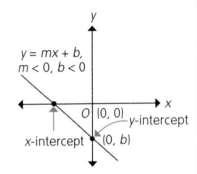

An equation of a straight line parallel to the x-axis and passing through the point (0, d) is $y = d$, where d is the y-intercept.

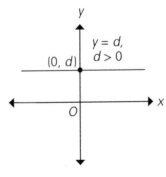

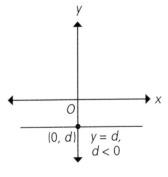

An equation of a straight line parallel to the y-axis and passing through the point (c, 0) is $x = c$, where c is the x-intercept.

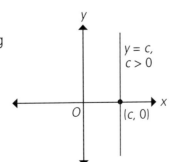

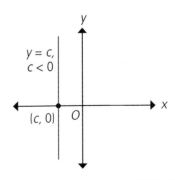

2 Write an equation in the form $y = mx$ or $y = mx + b$ for the line.

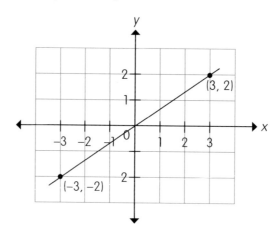

The line passes through the points $(-3, -2)$ and $(3, 2)$.

Slope, $m = \dfrac{2 - (-2)}{3 - (-3)}$

$\quad = \dfrac{4}{6}$

$\quad = \dfrac{2}{3}$

The line intersects the y-axis at the point $(0, 0)$. So, the y-intercept, b, is 0.

Slope-intercept form: $y = \dfrac{2}{3}x + 0$ Substitute the values of m and b.

$\qquad\qquad\qquad y = \dfrac{2}{3}x$ Simplify.

An equation of the line is $y = \dfrac{2}{3}x$.

3 Write an equation in the form $y = mx$ or $y = mx + b$ for the line.

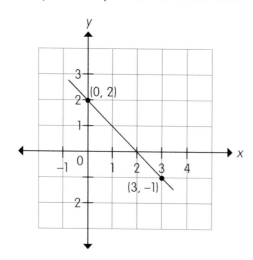

The line passes through the points (0, 2) and (3, −1).

Slope, $m = \dfrac{-1-2}{3-0}$

$= \dfrac{-3}{3}$

$= -1$

The line intersects the y-axis at the point (0, 2). So, the y-intercept, b, is 2.

Slope-intercept form: $y = (-1)x + 2$ Substitute the values of m and b.

$y = -x + 2$ Simplify.

The equation of the line is $y = -x + 2$.

Activity Exploring the relationship between $y = mx$ and $y = mx + b$

Work in pairs.

① Press [Y=] to display the Y = window. Enter an equation from the table below. Then press [GRAPH] to graph the function.

② Press [2ND] [TRACE] to select 6: dy/dx. The press [ENTER] to find the slope.

③ Press [2ND] [TRACE] to select 1: Value. Then press [0] to find the y-intercept.

④ Repeat ① to ④ to the other equations in the table. Record your results.

Equation	$y = 3x + 5$	$y = -2x + 1$	$y = 1.5x + 2$
m			
b			

⑤ **Mathematical Habit 8 Look for patterns**
The equation of another line is given by $2y = 5x - 4$. Predict the y-intercept. Use the graphing calculator to check your prediction.

Write an equation in the form $y = mx$ or $y = mx + b$ for each line.

1

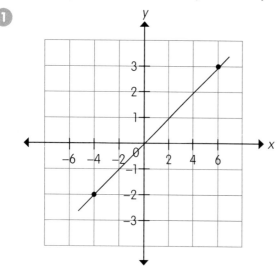

2

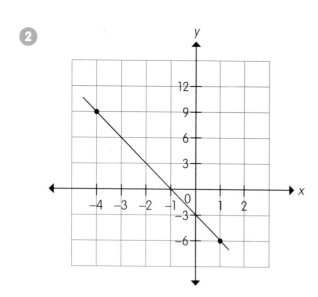

INDEPENDENT PRACTICE

Identify the *y*-intercept for each line. Then, write an equation in the form $y = mx$ or $y = mx + b$ for each line.

1

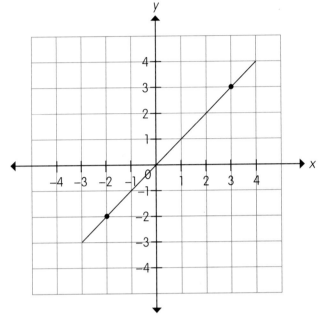

2

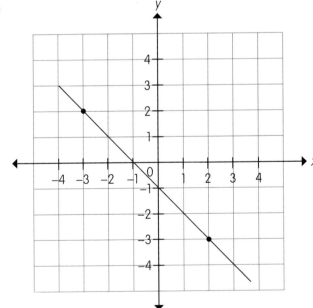

3

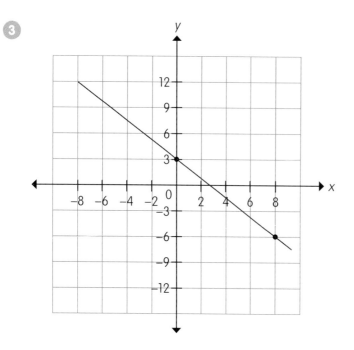

4

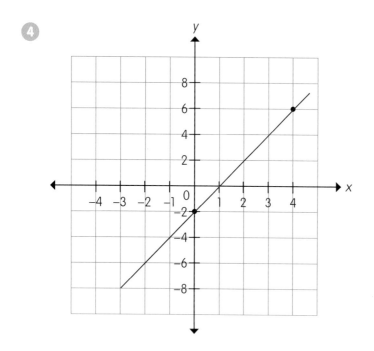

Write an equation in the form $y = mx$ or $y = mx + b$ for each line.

5

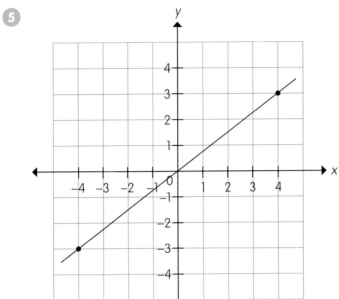

6

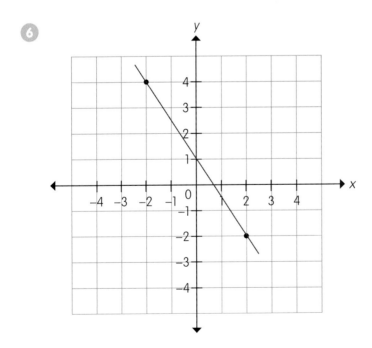

7

Graph each line. Use graph paper. Then, write the equation for each line.

8 The line passes through the points (−4, 3) and (−4, −2).

9 The line passes through the points (−3, 4) and (1, 4).

Writing Linear Equations

Learning Objectives:

- Use slope-intercept form to identify slopes and y-intercepts
- Write an equation of a line in slope-intercept form.
- Write an equation of a line parallel to another line.

THINK

The five items below describe part of a line. Form ten pairs of conditions using these five items. Then, for each pair, determine if the information is enough to find the equation of the line. If it is possible, describe the steps to find the equation; if it is not possible, explain why.

a   the slope of the line

b   the y-intercept

c   a point on the line

d   the slope of a line parallel to it

e   the y-intercept of a line parallel to it

ENGAGE

Kimberly says, "If the equation $y = 2x + 5$ has a slope of 2 and a y-intercept of 5, then the equation $y + 3x - 4 = 0$ must have a slope of 3 and a y-intercept of -4." Do you agree or disagree with her? Justify your answer.

LEARN Use slope-intercept form to identify slopes and y-intercepts

1   When given an equation, you can add, subtract, multiply, or divide both sides of the equation by the same number to write an equivalent equation in slope-intercept form.
To write an equation like $y + 2x - 6 = 0$ in slope-intercept form, you need to perform operations on both sides of the equation. What are the slope and y-intercept?

$$y + 2x - 6 = 0$$
$$y + 2x - 6 + 6 = 0 + 6 \quad \text{Add 6 to both sides.}$$
$$y + 2x = 6 \quad \text{Simplify.}$$
$$y + 2x - 2x = 6 - 2x \quad \text{Subtract } 2x \text{ from both sides.}$$
$$y = -2x + 6 \quad \text{Simplify.}$$

Compare $y = -2x + 6$ with $y = mx + b$.

Slope, $m = -2$
y-intercept, $b = 6$

Math Talk

Eve notices that the ordered pair (0, 6) is a solution of $y = -2x + 6$. Is this ordered pair also a solution of $y + 2x - 6 = 0$? Is any ordered pair (x, y) that is a solution of $y = -2x + 6$ also a solution of $y + 2x - 6 = 0$? Why or why not?

TRY Practice using slope-intercept form to identify slopes and y-intercepts

Find the slope and y-intercept of the line.

1. $5x + 4y = 8$

ENGAGE

The slope of a line is $\frac{1}{2}$ and the y-intercept is 2. Sketch a quick graph of the line.

How do you write the equation of the line? Explain your thinking.

LEARN Write an equation of a line given its slope and y-intercept

1. You have learned that the slope-intercept form of an equation of a line is given by $y = mx + b$. Given the slope, m, and y-intercept, b, of a line, you can substitute these values into $y = mx + b$ to write an equation of the line.

   Use the slope, $\frac{1}{4}$, and the y-intercept of a line, 3, to write the equation of the line in slope-intercept form.

   Slope, $m = \frac{1}{4}$

   y-intercept, $b = 3$

   $y = mx + b$

   $y = \frac{1}{4}x + 3$ Substitute the given values for m and b.

   The equation of the line is $y = \frac{1}{4}x + 3$.

2. Use the slope, −2, and the y-intercept, −5, of a line to write an equation of the line in slope-intercept form.

   Slope, $m = -2$

   y-intercept, $b = -5$

   $y = mx + b$
   $y = -2x + (-5)$ Substitute the given values for m and b.
   $y = -2x - 5$ Simplify.

   The equation of the line is $y = -2x - 5$.

Math Talk

If you graph the equations $y = \frac{1}{4}x + 3$ and $y = -2x - 5$, which line would go upward from left to right? Which line would go downward from left to right? Which line would be steeper? Explain.

© 2020 Marshall Cavendish Education Pte Ltd

Use the given slope and *y*-intercept of each line to write an equation in slope-intercept form.

① Slope, $m = -\dfrac{2}{3}$

    y-intercept, $b = 4$

② Slope, $m = 4$

    y-intercept, $b = -7$

ENGAGE

Draw two parallel lines on the coordinate plane.

Now, write the equation of each line. How do you justify that they are parallel? Explain your thinking.

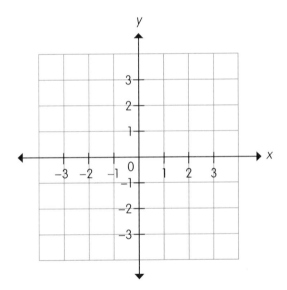

LEARN Write equations of parallel lines

① The lines shown are parallel.

Lines on the coordinate plane that have the same slope but different *y*-intercepts are always parallel.

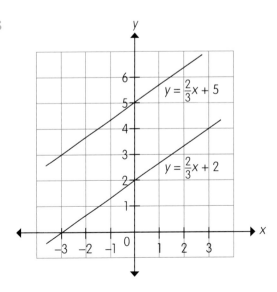

You can also use the equations of the lines to check whether the lines are parallel.

$y = \dfrac{2}{3}x + 2$

$y = \dfrac{2}{3}x + 5$

The two equations above have the same slope but different y-intercepts. So, they are parallel.

2 A line has the equation $2y = 6 - 3x$. Write an equation of a line parallel to the given line that has a y-intercept of 6.

Write the given equation in slope-intercept form.

$2y = 6 - 3x$

$\dfrac{2y}{2} = \dfrac{6 - 3x}{2}$ Divide both sides by 2.

$y = 3 - \dfrac{3}{2}x$ Simplify.

$y = -\dfrac{3}{2}x + 3$ Write in slope-intercept form.

The given line has slope $-\dfrac{3}{2}$ and y-intercept 3.

Write the equation for the parallel line with $m = -\dfrac{3}{2}$ and $b = 6$.

$y = mx + b$

$y = -\dfrac{3}{2}x + 6$ Substitute the values for m and b.

The equation of a line parallel to the given line that has a y-intercept of 6 is $y = -\dfrac{3}{2}x + 6$.

 **Math Talk**

Give an example of another equation for a line that is parallel to $2y = 6 - 3x$ and $y = -\dfrac{3}{2}x + 6$.

TRY Practice writing equations of parallel lines

Solve.

1 A line has the equation $3y + 6 = 10x$. Write the equation of a line parallel to the given line that has a y-intercept of 2.

You have learned to find the equation of a line by substituting the values of the given slope and y-intercept into $y = mx + b$. The line shown has a slope of $\frac{1}{6}$, but you can only estimate the y-intercept to be somewhere between 1 and 2. You also see that the line passes through the point (3, 2). How do you find the equation of the line? Discuss.

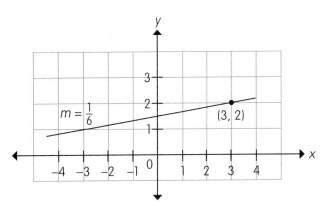

LEARN Write the equation of a line given its slope and a point on the line

1 The line shown has a slope of $\frac{2}{5}$ and passes through the point (2, 3).

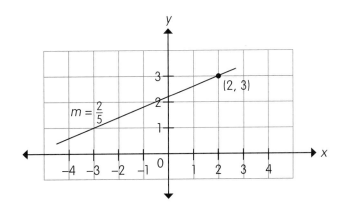

Use the given slope and the coordinates of the given point to find the y-intercept.

$$y = mx + b$$

$3 = \frac{2}{5}(2) + b$ Substitute the values for m, x, and y.

$3 = \frac{4}{5} + b$ Simplify.

$3 - \frac{4}{5} = \frac{4}{5} + b - \frac{4}{5}$ Subtract $\frac{4}{5}$ from both sides.

$\frac{11}{5} = b$ Simplify.

Use the given slope and the y-intercept to write an equation in slope-intercept form.

$$y = mx + b$$

$y = \frac{2}{5}x + \frac{11}{5}$ Substitute the values for m and b.

The equation of the line is $y = \frac{2}{5}x + \frac{11}{5}$.

2 A line has a slope of –5 and passes through the point (1, –8). Write the equation of the line.

Use the given slope and the coordinates of the given point to find the y-intercept.

$y = mx + b$
$-8 = -5(1) + b$ Substitute the values for m, x, and y.
$-8 = -5 + b$ Simplify.
$-8 + 5 = -5 + b + 5$ Add 5 to both sides.
$-3 = b$ Simplify.

Use the given slope and the y-intercept to write an equation in slope-intercept form.

$y = mx + b$
$y = -5x + (-3)$ Substitute the values for m and b.
$y = -5x - 3$ Simplify.

The equation of the line is $y = -5x - 3$.

TRY Practice writing the equation of a line given its slope and a point on the line

Solve.

1 A line has a slope of –3 and passes through the point (–6, 8). Write an equation of the line.

ENGAGE

The equation for the red line shown in the graph is $2y = 3x + 4$. What is the slope of the red line? The blue line is parallel to the red line and passes through the point (2, 7). How do you use the equation of the red line to find the equation of the blue line? Discuss.

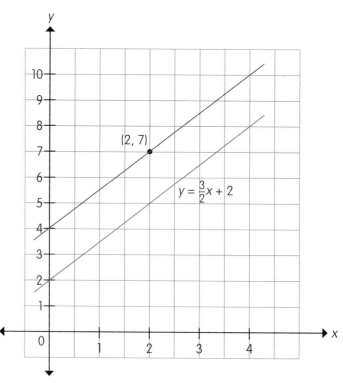

$(2, 7)$

$y = \frac{3}{2}x + 2$

1 Consider the following graph.

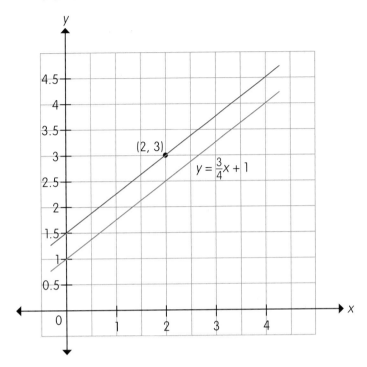

You can use the equation of the red line to find the equation of the blue line.

Since the blue line is parallel to the red line, you know the slope of the blue line. You also know that the blue line passes through the point (2, 3). You can use the slope and the given point to write and solve an equation to find the y-intercept of the line.

$y = mx + b$

$3 = \frac{3}{4}(2) + b$ Substitute the values for m, x, and y.

$3 = \frac{3}{2} + b$ Simplify.

$3 - \frac{3}{2} = \frac{3}{2} + b - \frac{3}{2}$ Subtract $\frac{3}{2}$ from both sides.

$\frac{3}{2} = b$ Simplify.

The equation of the blue line is $y = \frac{3}{4}x + \frac{3}{2}$.

2 Write the equation of the line that passes through the point $\left(\frac{1}{4}, 8\right)$ and is parallel to $y = 2 - 4x$. Write the equation $y = 2 - 4x$ in slope-intercept form.

$y = 2 - 4x$
$y = -4x + 2$

The line has slope -4. So, the line parallel to $y = 2 - 4x$ has a slope of -4.

Write the equation of a line given a
point on the line and the equation
of a parallel line

Write the equation of the line that passes through $\left(\frac{1}{4}, 8\right)$ and has a slope of -4.

$y = mx + b$
$8 = -4\left(\frac{1}{4}\right) + b$ Substitute the values for m, x, and y.
$8 = -1 + b$ Simplify.
$8 + 1 = -1 + b + 1$ Add 1 to both sides.
$9 = b$ Simplify.

The equation of the line is $y = -4x + 9$.

Math Talk

If you graph the parallel lines $y = 2 - 4x$ and $y = -4x + 9$ on the same coordinate plane, will the graph of $y = -4x + 9$ lie above or below the graph of $y = 2 - 4x$? Explain.

TRY Practice writing the equation of a line given a point on the line and the equation of a parallel line

Solve.

1. Write the equation of the line that passes through the point $(-2, 1)$ and is parallel to $y = 5 - 3x$.

ENGAGE

Recall how you can use the slope of a line and a point on the line to find the equation of that line. Explain how you can extend this knowledge to find the equation of a line that passes through $(4, -2)$ and $(0, 6)$. Draw a quick sketch of the line to verify your answer.

LEARN Write the equation of a line given two points

1. You can find an equation of a line if two points on the line are given. You first use the two given points to find the slope. Then, you use this slope and either one of the given points to find the equation.

2. Write an equation of the line that passes through the points $(1, 3)$ and $(2, -4)$.
Use the slope formula to find the slope.

Slope, $m = \frac{-4 - 3}{2 - 1}$
$= \frac{-7}{1}$
$= -7$

Use $m = -7$ and $(1, 3)$ to find the y-intercept, b.

$y = mx + b$
$3 = -7(1) + b$ Substitute the values for m, x, and y.
$3 + 7 = -7 + b + 7$ Simplify. Add 7 to both sides.
$10 = b$ Simplify.

You can also use $(2, -4)$ to find the y-intercept.

The equation of the line is $y = -7x + 10$.

TRY Practice writing the equation of a line given two points

Solve.

1. Write an equation of the line that passes through the points $(-2, -5)$ and $(2, -1)$.

INDEPENDENT PRACTICE

Find the slope and *y*-intercept of each line.

1 $y = -5x + 7$

2 $y = 2x + 3$

3 $5x + 2y = 6$

4 $2x - 7y = 10$

Use the given slope and *y*-intercept of each line to write an equation in slope-intercept form.

5 Slope, $m = \dfrac{1}{2}$

y-intercept, $b = 3$

6 Slope, $m = -2$

y-intercept, $b = 5$

Solve.

7 A line has the equation $4y = 3x - 8$. Write an equation of a line parallel to the given line that has a *y*-intercept of 2.

8 A line has the equation $3y = 3 - 2x$. Write an equation of a line parallel to the given line that has a *y*-intercept of 5.

9 **Mathematical Habit 3** **Construct viable arguments**
Anna says that the graphs of $y = -3x + 7$ and $y = 3x - 7$ are parallel lines. Do you agree? Explain.

10 A line has a slope of $-\dfrac{1}{3}$ and passes through the point (0, 4). Write the equation of the line.

11 A line has a slope of $-\dfrac{1}{2}$ and passes through the point (−4, −2). Write the equation of the line.

12 Write the equation of the line that passes through the point (−5, 7) and is parallel to $y = 4 - 3x$.

13 Write the equation of the line that passes through the point (0, 2) and is parallel to $6y = 5x - 24$.

14 Write the equation of the line that passes through the points (−5, −1) and (0, 4).

15 Write the equation of the line that passes through the points (−3, 2) and (−2, 5).

Sketching Graphs of Linear Equations

Learning Objective:
• Graph a linear equation by using two or more points.

THINK

Graph the equation $y = 2 - \frac{2}{3}x$. Now draw another line parallel to the first line that passes through the point (2, 4). Explain, without measuring other points on the graph, how you can determine the equation of this new line.

ENGAGE

Use the equation $y = 2x + 1$ to fill in the table.

x	1		6
y		5	

How do you graph the equation using these values? Discuss.
How will the graph look? Explain your thinking.

LEARN Graph a linear equation using a table of values

1. A linear equation has an infinite number of solutions and each of them lies on the graph of the equation. You will learn to draw graphs of linear equations in this lesson.

To graph the equation $y = \frac{1}{2}x + 1$, you use the following steps.

STEP 1 Construct a table of values. Choose three values for x and solve to find the corresponding values for y.

x	2	4	6
y	2	3	4

> Choose values of x that give integer values of y.
>
> When $x = 2$, $y = \frac{1}{2}(2) + 1 = 2$.
>
> When $x = 4$, $y = \frac{1}{2}(4) + 1 = 3$.
>
> When $x = 6$, $y = \frac{1}{2}(6) + 1 = 4$.

STEP 2 Graph the equation using the table of values.

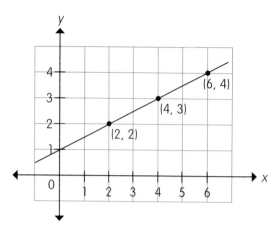

 Math Talk

Can you draw the graph with just two points? Why is it a good idea to include a third
point when you graph an equation?

2 Graph the equation $y = \frac{3}{4}x + 2$. Use 1 grid square on both axes to represent 1 unit for
the x interval from −4 to 4 and the y interval from −1 to 5.

STEP 1 Construct a table of values. Choose three values for x and solve to find the
corresponding values for y.

x	−4	0	4
y	−1	2	5

> You may evaluate values of x
> that give integer values of y.

STEP 2 Graph the equation using the table of values.

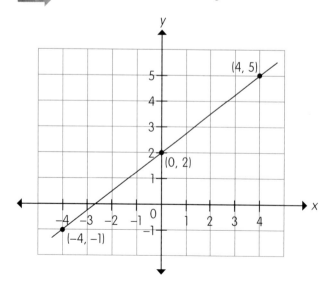

Graph the linear equation. Use graph paper. Use 1 grid square to represent 1 unit for the x interval from –2 to 2 and the y interval from –2 to 4.

1 $y = \frac{3}{2}x + 1$

ENGAGE

Consider the equation $y = 3x + 1$. Use the equation to determine two points on the line and graph the equation. Discuss with your partner if there is an easier way to graph the equation.

LEARN Graph a linear equation using m and b

1 One way to graph an equation in slope-intercept form is to use the y-intercept to plot a point on the x-axis. Then, use the slope of the line to find a second point on the line.

2 Graph the equation $y = x + 2$. Use 1 grid square on both axes to represent 1 unit for the x interval from 0 to 4 and the y interval from 0 to 6.

STEP 1 Plot a point on the y-axis. $y = x + 2$ has y-intercept, $b = 2$. So, it passes through the point (0, 2). Plot the point (0, 2) on the graph.

STEP 2 Use the slope to find another point on the graph. The slope of the line is 1. So, the ratio $\frac{\text{Rise}}{\text{Run}} = 1$. $\frac{\text{Rise}}{\text{Run}} = \frac{1}{1} = \frac{2}{2} = \frac{3}{3} = \frac{4}{4} \ldots$. Using $\frac{4}{4}$, you move up 4 units and then 4 units to the right to plot the point (4, 6).

> You can use convenient points, integer values, for the rise and the run as long as the ratio $\frac{\text{Rise}}{\text{Run}} = 1$. In this case, you use 4 for both the rise and the run.

STEP 3 Use a ruler and draw a line through the points. This line is the graph of the equation $y = x + 2$.

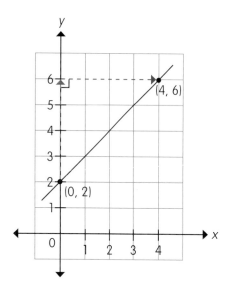

 Math Note

The line graph contains all the points (x, y) with the values of x and y that make the equation true. Only some of those points can be seen on this graph. So, you can choose any convenient points of integer values for x and y.

3 Graph the equation $y = -\frac{1}{2}x - 3$. Use 1 grid square on both axes to represent 1 unit for the x interval from 0 to 4 and the y interval from 0 to −5.

STEP 1 Plot a point on the *y*-axis. $y = -\frac{1}{2}x - 3$ has *y*-intercept, $b = -3$. So, it passes through the point (0, −3). Plot the point (0, −3) on the graph.

STEP 2 Use the slope to find another point on the graph. The slope of the line is $-\frac{1}{2}$. So,

the ratio $\frac{\text{Rise}}{\text{Run}} = -\frac{1}{2}$. $\frac{\text{Rise}}{\text{Run}} = \frac{-1}{2} = \frac{1}{-2} = \frac{-2}{4} = \frac{2}{-4} = \dots$. Using $\frac{-2}{4}$, you move down 2 units and then 4 units to the right to plot the point (4, −5).

You can use convenient points, integer values, for the rise and the run as long as the ratio $\frac{\text{Rise}}{\text{Run}} = -\frac{1}{2}$. In this case, you use −2 for the rise and 4 for the run.

STEP 3 Use a ruler and draw a line through the points. This line is the graph of the equation $y = -\frac{1}{2}x - 3$.

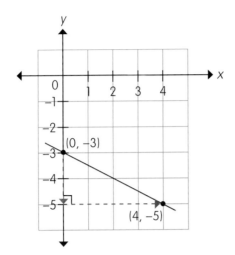

 Math Talk

Suppose that you are given the slope of a line and, instead of the y-intercept, a point on the line. For example, suppose you know a line passes through the point (4, 5) and has slope 3. Explain how you could graph the line.

TRY Practice graphing a linear equation using *m* and *b*

Graph each linear equation. Use graph paper. Use 1 grid square to represent 1 unit on both axes. Use suitable intervals for both axes.

1. $y = 2x + 1$

2. $y = -\frac{1}{3}x - 2$

ENGAGE

a A line has a slope of 2 and its *y*-intercept is 3. Find the equation of the line and draw its graph.

b Compare the method you used in **a** with your partner. Discuss how you would draw a line that has a slope of 2 and passes through (1, 5).

LEARN Graph a linear equation using *m* and a point

1 You can also graph a line using the information from a point on the line and the slope of the line, as shown in the following example.

2 Graph a line with slope 4 that passes through the point (3, 2). Use 1 grid square on both axes to represent 1 unit for the interval from 0 to 6.

STEP 1 Plot the given point (3, 2).

STEP 2 Use the slope to find another point on the graph. The slope of the line is 4. So, the ratio $\frac{\text{Rise}}{\text{Run}} = 4$. $\frac{\text{Rise}}{\text{Run}} = \frac{4}{1} = \frac{8}{2} = \frac{12}{3} = \frac{16}{4} = \ldots$. Using $\frac{4}{1}$, you can move up 4 units and then 1 unit to the right to plot the point (4, 6).

STEP 3 Use a ruler and draw a line through the points. This is the line with slope 4 that passes through the point (3, 2).

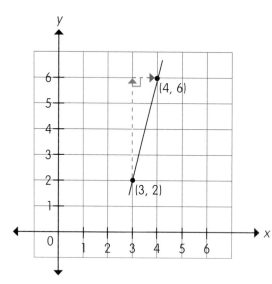

TRY Practice graphing a linear equation using *m* and a point

Graph each line. Use graph paper. Use 1 grid square on both axes to represent 1 unit for the *x* interval from − 2 to 2 and the *y* interval from 0 to 10.

1 A line with a slope of − 2 that passes through the point (2, 2).

2 A line with a slope of 2 that passes through the point (− 2, 1).

INDEPENDENT PRACTICE

Graph each linear equation. Use graph paper. Use 1 grid square to represent 1 unit on both axes. Use suitable intervals for both axes.

1 $y = \frac{1}{3}x + 1$

2 $y = \frac{1}{6}x + 3$

3 $y = \frac{1}{2}x + 2$

4 $y = \frac{2}{3}x - 1$

5 $y = -x + 5$

6 $y = 3 - \frac{1}{4}x$

7 $y = 1 - \frac{1}{2}x$

8 $y = -\frac{1}{5}x - 2$

Solve.

9 **Mathematical Habit 2** **Use mathematical reasoning**

Maria says that the point $(4, -2)$ lies on the graph of the equation $y = -\frac{1}{4}x - 1$. Explain how you can find out if she is right without actually graphing the equation.

Graph each line. Use graph paper. Use 1 grid square to represent 1 unit on both axes. Use suitable intervals for both axes.

10 A line with a slope of $\frac{2}{5}$ that passes through the point $(5, 4)$.

11 A line with a slope of $\frac{2}{3}$ that passes through the point $(6, 1)$.

12 A line with a slope of -3 that passes through the point $(1, 0)$.

13 A line with a slope of -2 that passes through the point $(-1, -2)$.

5 Real-World Problems: Linear Equations

Learning Objective:
• Explain slope and *y*-intercept in the context of real-world problems.

> **New Vocabulary**
> linear relationship

THINK

A scientist attaches a spring that is 11 inches long to the ceiling and hangs weights from the spring to see how far it will stretch. The scientist records the length of the spring, *y* inches, for different weights, *x* pounds.

Weight (x pounds)	0	1	2	3	4
Length of Spring (y inches)	11	13	15	17	19

Write an equation relating the spring length and the pounds of weights hung from the spring. Explain what information the vertical intercept and the slope of the graph of the equation give about the situation.

ENGAGE

A taxi service charges a $5 fixed fee plus $3 for every mile traveled. Use this information to construct a table of values comparing the distance traveled and the total charge. Then draw the graph using your table of values. What is the slope and the vertical intercept of the graph? How do they relate to the information given in the question? Will this always be the case for the slope and the vertical intercept?

LEARN Explain slope and *y*-intercept in the context of real-world problems

1. When there is a constant variation between two quantities, the relationship between the two quantities is a **linear relationship**. The relationship can be represented on a coordinate plane as a line. Consider the graph of the linear equation $y = 2x + 1$.

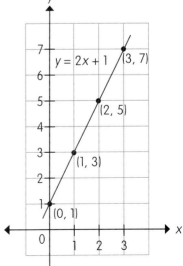

Find the rate of change for the points (0, 1) and (3, 7).

$$\frac{\text{Change in } y}{\text{Change in } x} = \frac{7-1}{3-0}$$
$$= \frac{6}{3}$$
$$= 2$$

Find the rate of change for the points (1, 3) and (2, 5).

$$\frac{\text{Change in } y}{\text{Change in } x} = \frac{5-3}{2-1}$$
$$= \frac{2}{1}$$
$$= 2$$

So, for any two points on the line, the unit rate of change, change in *y* per change in *x*, is the same as the slope of the equation.

For any linear relationship, the quantity on the horizontal axis of a graph of the relationship is the independent variable. The quantity on the vertical axis of the graph is the dependent variable.

When you graph a real-world linear relationship, the slope of the line is the rate of change in the dependent variable to the change in the independent variable.

2 A swimming pool when full holds a certain amount of water. When the drain is opened, the amount of water in the pool drains out at a constant rate. The graph shows the amount of water in the pool, *y* gallons, *x* hours after the drain is opened.

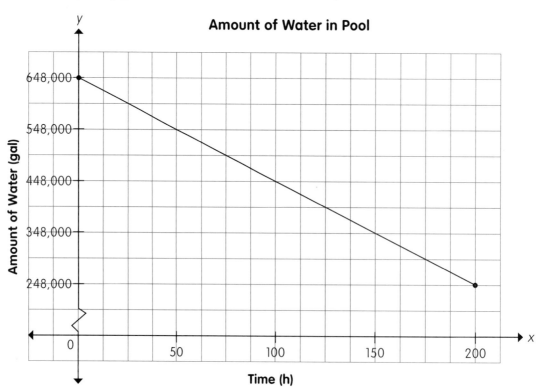

a Find the vertical intercept of the graph and explain what information it gives about the situation.

b Find the slope of the graph and explain what information it gives about the situation.

In this situation, the amount of water in the pool depends on the number of hours the pool has been draining. So, the amount of water is the dependent variable and the number of hours is the independent variable.

STEP 1 Understand the problem.

What information can I get from the graph? What do I need to find?

STEP 2 Think of a plan.

I can use the graph.

STEP 3 Carry out the plan.

a From the graph, the vertical intercept is 648,000. This is the number of gallons of water in the pool when it is full.

The vertical intercept or y-intercept corresponds to the initial number of gallons of water in the pool before it begins to drain.

b The graph passes through (200, 248,000) and (0, 648,000).

$$\text{Slope} = \frac{648,000 - 248,000}{0 - 200}$$
$$= \frac{400,000}{-200}$$
$$= -2,000$$

The negative slope means that as time increases, the amount of water decreases.

The graph has slope −2,000. The slope represents the rate, in gallons per hour, at which water is draining out of the pool. So, 2,000 gallons of water drains from the pool every hour.

STEP 4 Check the answer.

You can use another pair of points to check if your answer for the slope of the graph
is correct.

The graph passes through (50, 548,000) and (150, 348,000).

$$\text{Slope} = \frac{548,000 - 348,000}{50 - 150}$$

$$= \frac{200,000}{-100}$$

$$= 2,000$$

My answer is correct.

③ Lauren and Caleb are salespeople. Each of them earns a fixed monthly salary. They also earn
an additional percent of the amount from their sales. So, the total monthly earnings, *y* dollars,
depends on his or her sales, *x* dollars.

a Find the fixed monthly salary for each person.

From the graph, the vertical intercept for Lauren's graph is 2,500. So, Lauren's fixed monthly
salary is $2,500.

From the graph, the vertical intercept for Caleb's graph is 1,500. So, Caleb's fixed monthly
salary is $1,500.

b Both Lauren and Caleb earn a percent commission. Who earns a greater commission rate?

For each dollar a salesperson makes in sales, that person earns a certain amount of money as commission. The person's commission rate is usually expressed as a percent. The rate is also the slope of the line graph for that person. You can see that Caleb's line is steeper. So, Caleb earns a greater commission rate.

c Find each person's rate of commission.

Lauren's graph passes through (0, 2,500) and (5,000, 2,750).

$$\text{Slope} = \frac{2,750 - 2,500}{5,000 - 0}$$
$$= \frac{250}{5,000}$$
$$= \frac{1}{20}$$

$$\text{Commission rate} = \frac{1}{20} \cdot 100\%$$
$$= \frac{100}{20}\%$$
$$= 5\%$$

Lauren's commission rate is 5% of her sales.

Caleb's graph passes through (0, 1,500) and (2,500, 2,000).

$$\text{Slope} = \frac{2,000 - 1,500}{2,500 - 0}$$
$$= \frac{500}{2,500}$$
$$= \frac{1}{5}$$

$$\text{Commission rate} = \frac{1}{5} \cdot 100\%$$
$$= \frac{100}{5}\%$$
$$= 20\%$$

Caleb's commission rate is 20% of his sales.

 **Math Talk**

Because Lauren's base salary is greater, she assumes that she will earn more than Caleb in any given month. Is this true? Explain.

4 Brianna and Sierra each have a coin bank. Brianna starts with a certain amount of money
and adds money at regular intervals. Sierra starts with a different amount of money and
takes money out over time. The amount of money, y dollars, in Sierra's coin bank after
x weeks is given by the equation $y = -24x + 120$. The graph shows the amount of money in
Brianna's coin bank after x weeks.

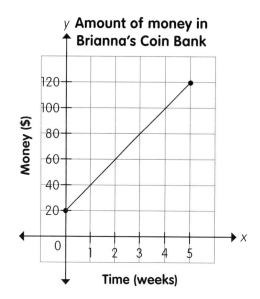

a Find the vertical intercept of Brianna's graph and explain what information it gives about
the situation.

From the graph, the vertical intercept is 20. This is the amount of money that Brianna
starts with.

b Find the slope of Brianna's graph and explain what information it gives about the situation.

The graph passes through (0, 20) and (5, 120).

$$\text{Slope} = \frac{120 - 20}{5 - 0}$$
$$= \frac{100}{5}$$
$$= 20$$

The graph has slope 20. The slope represents the rate at which Brianna is adding money.
So, Brianna adds $20 every week.

c Is Brianna adding money at a faster rate or is Sierra taking out money at a faster rate?
Explain.

From the equation $y = -24x + 120$, you see that each week Sierra takes out $24.

Because $24 > $20, she is taking out money at a faster rate than Brianna is adding money.

Solve.

1. Melanie rents a bike while visiting a city. She pays $7 per hour to rent the bike. She also pays
$8 to rent a baby seat for the bike. She pays this amount for the baby seat no matter how
many hours she rents the bike. The graph shows her total cost, *y* dollars, after *x* hours.

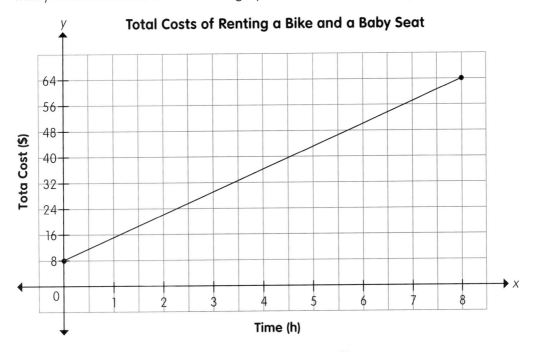

Total Costs of Renting a Bike and a Baby Seat

Tota Cost ($)

Time (h)

Bike $7 per hour
Baby Seat $8

a Find the vertical intercept of the graph and explain what information it gives about
the situation.

b Find the slope of the graph and explain what information it gives about the situation.

2 Both Xavier and Nicole are salespeople. Each of them earns a fixed weekly salary and a percent commission based on the total sales he or she makes in a week. The graphs show the total earnings, E dollars, each person can make in one week, based on the person's total sales of S dollars.

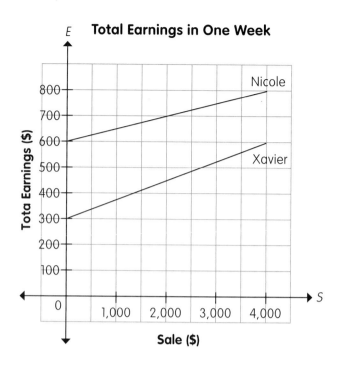

Total Earnings in One Week

a Find the fixed weekly salary for each person.

b Both Xavier and Nicole earn a percent commission. Who earns a greater percent in commission?

c Find each person's rate of commission.

3 Sean and Timothy are brothers who live at the same house but go to different cities for vacation. When the vacation is over, they begin driving back home at the same time but at different speeds. Sean's distance, D miles, from their house x hours after he starts driving is given by the equation $D = -50x + 150$. The graph shows Timothy's distance, D miles, from their house x hours after he starts driving home.

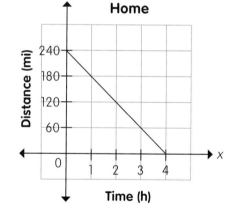

Timothy's Drive Home

a Find the vertical intercept of Timothy's graph and explain what information it gives about the situation.

b Find the slope of Timothy's graph and explain what information it gives about the situation.

c Which brother is driving faster? How do you know?

When comparing rates of change in c, you only look at the absolute value of the slope. The sign is not taken into consideration.

INDEPENDENT PRACTICE

Solve.

1   Ang pays a fixed amount each month to use his cell phone. He also pays for each minute that he makes calls on the phone. The graph shows the amount, C dollars, he pays in a given month based on x minutes of call time.

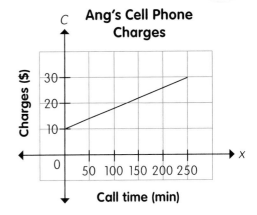

Ang's Cell Phone Charges

   a   Find the vertical intercept of the graph and explain what information it gives about the situation.

   b   Find the slope of the graph and explain what information it gives about the situation.

2   Ryan and Adam are brothers. Each of them has a coin bank. In January, the boys had different amounts of money in their coin banks. Then, for each month after that, each boy added the same amount of money to his coin bank. The graphs show the amount, S dollars, of savings in each coin bank after t months.

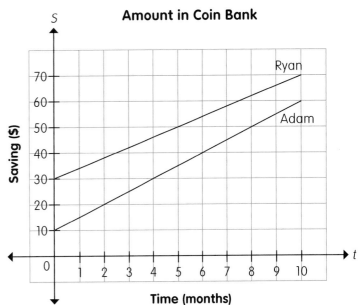

Amount in Coin Bank

   a   Find the initial amount of money in each coin bank.

   b   Who added a greater amount of money each month into his coin bank?

3 Patrick and Steven drive from Town A to Town B in separate cars. The initial amount of gasoline in each car is different. The graphs show the amount, y gallons, of gasoline in each person's car after x miles.

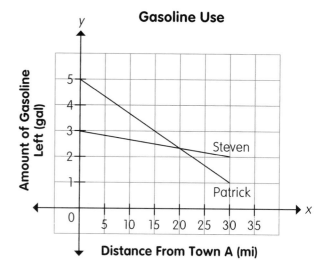
Gasoline Use

a Find the initial amount of gasoline in each car.

b Whose car uses more gasoline?

4 Mason and Zoe visit Star Café every day. They pay for the items there using a gift card. The amount, y dollars, on Zoe's gift card after x days is given by the equation $y = 100 - 19x$. The graph shows the amount on Mason's gift card over x days.

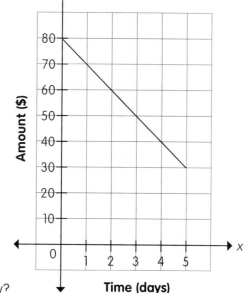
Amount Left on Mason's Gift Card

a Write an equation for the amount on Mason's gift card.

b Using your answer in a, whose gift card had a higher initial amount?

c Using your answer in a, who spends more each day?

Mathematical Habit 3 Construct viable arguments

Suppose Gabriella shows you her homework.

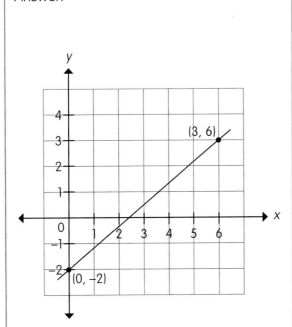

Graph the equation $y = -2x + \frac{1}{2}$

Answer:

Describe Gabriella's mistake. Graph the equation correctly.

Problem Solving with Heuristics

Mathematical Habit 4 **Use mathematical models**

1. Carter and Alexis are both students. Carter has $28 to spend for the whole week, and he decides to spend the same amount every day. Alexis currently does not have any savings. She is given a daily allowance, and she decides to save the same amount every day. After four days, both have the same amount of money. The graph shows the amount of money Carter has, *y* dollars, after *x* days during one week.

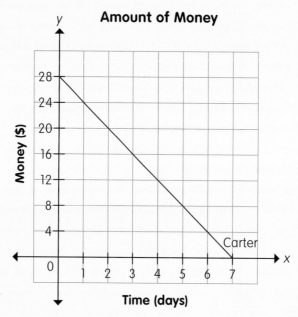

Amount of Money

a Draw a line on the graph to represent the amount of money Alexis has after *x* days.

b Find the slope of Carter's graph and explain what information it gives about the situation.

c Write an equation to represent the amount of money each person has during that week.

2 Gavin left Townsville at 12 P.M. and started biking to Kingston 50 miles away. One and a half hours later, Jonathan left Kingston and started biking toward Townsville at a speed of 20 miles per hour. The graph shows Gavin's distance, d miles, from Townsville after t hours.

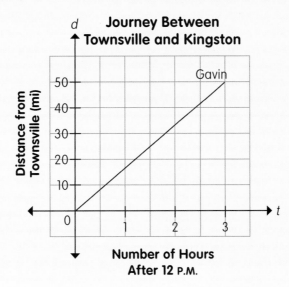

a Draw a line on the graph to represent Jonathan's distance from Kingston after t hours.

b Find the slope of Gavin's graph and explain what information it gives about this situation.

c Write an equation to represent each person's distance from Townsville after t hours.

CHAPTER WRAP-UP

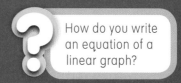

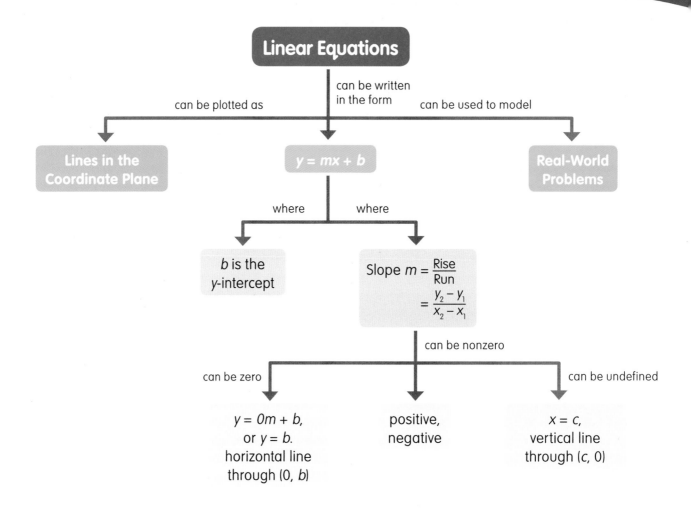

Linear Equations

can be plotted as → **Lines in the Coordinate Plane**

can be written in the form → $y = mx + b$

can be used to model → **Real-World Problems**

where → b is the y-intercept

where → Slope $m = \dfrac{\text{Rise}}{\text{Run}}$
$= \dfrac{y_2 - y_1}{x_2 - x_1}$

can be zero → $y = 0m + b$, or $y = b$. horizontal line through $(0, b)$

can be nonzero → positive, negative

can be undefined → $x = c$, vertical line through $(c, 0)$

KEY CONCEPTS

- The slope-intercept form of a linear equation is given by $y = mx + b$, where m represents the slope and b is the y-intercept of the graph of the equation.

- The slope of a line passing through two points (x_1, y_1) and (x_2, y_2) is equal to $\dfrac{y_2 - y_1}{x_2 - x_1}$ or $\dfrac{y_1 - y_2}{x_1 - x_2}$.

- The slope is always the same between any two distinct points on a line and can be positive, negative, zero or undefined.

- The equation of a horizontal line through the point (c, d) is $y = d$. The equation of a vertical line through the point (c, d) is $x = c$.

- You can write an equation of a line given the slope m and the y-intercept b, the slope m and a point, or the coordinates of two points.

- You can write an equation of a line parallel to a given line if you know the y-intercept of the line you want to draw or the coordinates of a point on the line you want to draw.

- You can use linear equations and graphs to model and solve real-world problems.

Find the slope of each line using the points indicated.

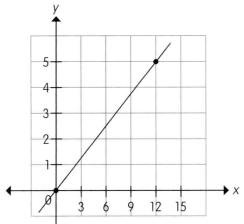

Write the equation of each line.

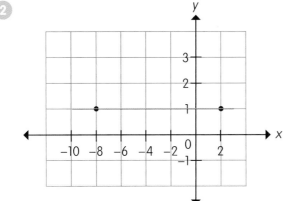

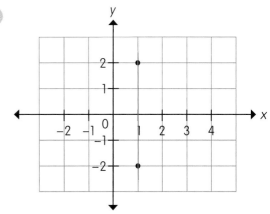

Find the slope and _y_-intercept of each line.

5 $y = \frac{1}{2}x - 3$

6 $y = -3x + 4$

Use the given slope and *y*-intercept of each line to write an equation.

7 Slope, $m = -4$

y-intercept, $b = -\dfrac{1}{3}$

8 Slope, $m = \dfrac{2}{5}$

y-intercept, $b = 3$

Solve.

9 A line has equation $5y = 3x + 12$. Write an equation of a line parallel to the given line that has a *y*-intercept of 2.

10 A line has slope $-\dfrac{1}{2}$ and passes through the point $(-4, 5)$. Write an equation of the line.

11 Write an equation of the line that passes through the point $(-4, -4)$ and is parallel to $2y - x = -6$.

12 Write an equation of the line that passes through the point $(-4, -3)$ and is parallel to $4y - x = -16$.

13 Write an equation of the line that passes through the points $(0, 0)$ and $(7, 7)$.

14 Write an equation of the line that passes through the points $(1, 2)$ and $(4, 8)$.

Graph each linear equation. Use graph paper. Use 1 grid square to represent 1 unit on both axes.

15 $4y = -3x - 8$

16 A line with slope $\dfrac{1}{3}$ that passes through the point $(0, -2)$.

© 2020 Marshall Cavendish Education Pte Ltd

17 Landscaping Company A and Company B each charges a certain amount, *C* dollars, as consultation fee, plus a fixed hourly charge. The graph shows the total charges for *x* hours.

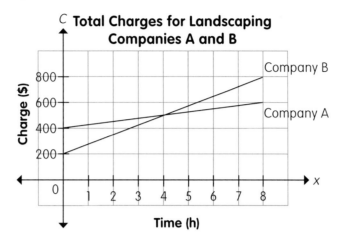

a Find the amount each landscaping company charges as its consultation fee.

b Which company charges a greater amount per hour?

18 The operator of a charter bus service charges a certain amount for a bus, plus per-passenger charge. The graph shows the total charge, *C* dollars, for carrying *x* passengers.

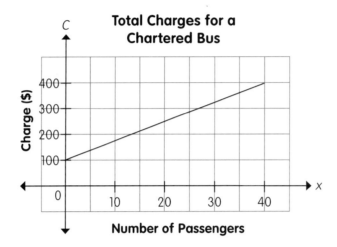

a Find the vertical intercept and explain what information it gives about the situation.

b Find the slope of the graph and explain what information it gives about the situation.

Assessment Prep
Answer the question.

19 This question has four parts.

Line P is shown on the coordinate plane.

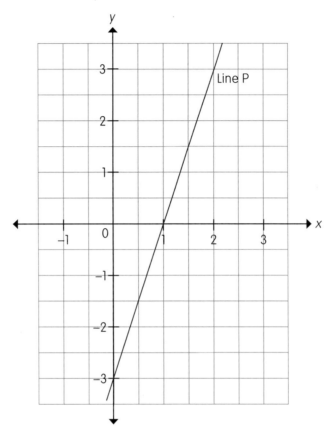

Part A

What is the slope of Line P?

Ⓐ $\dfrac{1}{3}$

Ⓑ 3

Ⓒ −3

Ⓓ $-\dfrac{1}{3}$

Part B

What is the *y*-intercept of Line P?

Ⓐ $-\dfrac{1}{3}$

Ⓑ 3

Ⓒ $-\dfrac{1}{3}$

Ⓓ −3

Part C

Line M (not shown) has the same slope and passes through the point (0, 2). Which table represents 4 points on line M?

Ⓐ

x	y
−2	−4
−1	−1
0	2
1	5

Ⓑ

x	y
−2	−5
−1	−2
0	2
1	4

Ⓒ

x	y
−2	12
−1	9
0	2
1	3

Ⓓ

x	y
−2	10
−1	8
0	2
1	1

Part D

Which equation could represent Line M?

Ⓐ $y = -3x + 2$

Ⓑ $y = 3x + 2$

Ⓒ $y = \dfrac{1}{3}x + 2$

Ⓓ $y = -\dfrac{1}{3}x + 2$

Name: _____   Date: _____

Snowboarding Trails

1 The table shows the slope profiles of two snowboarding trails, A and B.

Trail	Vertical Drop (meter)	Length (meter)
A	160	625
B	87	500

a Write a linear equation for the relationship between vertical drop, *y* meters, and length, *x* meters, for Trail A.

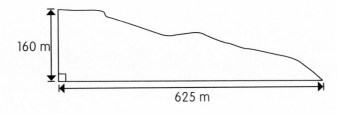

160 m   625 m

b Write a linear equation for the relationship between vertical drop, *y* meters, and length, *x* meters, for Trail B.

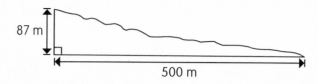

87 m

500 m

c By graphing the slope profiles of Trail A and Trail B on the same coordinate plane, state the trail that has a steeper slope.

d Using your graph, estimate the vertical drop of Trail A so that it has the same slope as Trail B with the length unchanged. Give your answer to the nearest meter.

e The difficulty level of a snowboarding trail can be measured by percent slope.

$$\text{Percent slope} = \frac{\text{Vertical drop}}{\text{Length}} \cdot 100\%$$

Level of Difficulty	Description
Easy	Percent slope ranging from 6% to 25%
Intermediate	Percent slope ranging from more than 25% to 40%
Advanced	Percent slope of more than 40%

Find the percent slopes of Trail A and Trail B. Hence, state the level of difficulty for each of the trails based on the description provided in the table.

Rubric

Point(s)	Level	My Performance
7–8	4	• Most of my answers are correct. • I showed complete understanding of the concepts. • I used effective and efficient strategies to solve the problems. • I explained my answers and mathematical thinking clearly and completely.
5–6	3	• Some of my answers are correct. • I showed adequate understanding of the concepts. • I used effective strategies to solve the problems. • I explained my answers and mathematical thinking clearly.
3–4	2	• A few of my answers are correct. • I showed some understanding of the concepts. • I used some effective strategies to solve the problems. • I explained some of my answers and mathematical thinking clearly.
0–2	1	• A few of my answers are correct. • I showed little understanding of the concepts. • I used limited effective strategies to solve the problems. • I did not explain my answers and mathematical thinking clearly.

Teacher's Comments

Chapter 6

Functions

How much can a food truck owner earn at a football game?

Inside a football stadium, two teams play to win the game. There is a different kind of competition outside the stadium. Food trucks line up side by side to sell delicious food to hungry spectators.

Imagine setting up a food truck at a football game. Your earnings will depend on a number of factors, such as the number of customers, or the number of food items you sell.

In other words, there is a relation between two quantities, such as "number of customers" and "earnings". In mathematics, certain types of relations between quantities are called functions. In this chapter, you will learn to represent functions using tables, equations and graphs.

How can you represent and interpret a function?

Name: _____   Date: _____

Writing algebraic expressions to represent unknown quantities

Sara buys 8 ribbons at x dollars each. She spends another $5. Write an algebraic expression for the total amount of money she spends.

Product of 8 and x	Plus	5	
$8 \cdot x$	$+$	5	Translate by parts.
$8x + 5$			Combine.

She spends $(8x + 5)$ dollars in total.

▶ **Quick Check**

Write an algebraic expression.

1. y highlighters are shared equally among 9 students. One of the students, María, buys another 3 highlighters. Write an algebraic expression for the number of highlighters that she has in total.

Graphing a linear equation using a table of values

Graph the equation $y = 0.5x + 2$.

Construct a table showing the coordinates of three points, then graph the equation.

x	−2	0	2
y	1	2	3

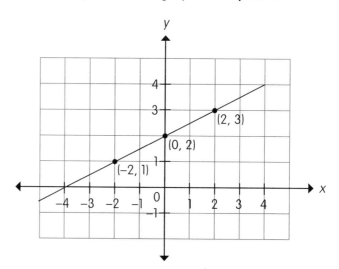

▶ **Quick Check**

Construct a table of values for each linear equation. Graph the equation on graph paper.

2. $y = -2x + 3$

3. $y = \dfrac{4}{3}x - 2$

Understanding Relations and Functions

Learning Objectives:
- Classify relations.
- Identify functions.

> **New Vocabulary**
>
> | | |
> |---|---|
> | relation | input |
> | output | mapping diagram |
> | map | one-to-one |
> | one-to-many | many-to-one |
> | many-to-many | function |
> | vertical line test | curve |

THINK

Given the following inputs and outputs of relations, how do you classify them? Which of these relations are functions?

a The inputs are the students in your Mathematics class. The outputs are the last names of the students.

b The inputs are the eighth graders in your school. The outputs are the student ID numbers of the eighth graders.

c The inputs are the movies showing in the movie theatres in your city. The outputs are the movie theatres in your city.

ENGAGE

Amy downloaded some songs that cost $2 each. Use a table to show how much it would cost if she bought 2 songs, 5 songs, 7 songs, or 10 songs. Explain and describe any pattern you can see between the number of songs purchased and the total amount of money she spends.

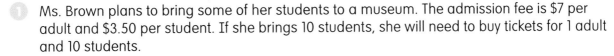 Understand and classify relations

1 Ms. Brown plans to bring some of her students to a museum. The admission fee is $7 per adult and $3.50 per student. If she brings 10 students, she will need to buy tickets for 1 adult and 10 students.

Total admission fee = Ticket cost for 1 adult + Ticket cost for 10 students
$$= \$7 + 10 \cdot \$3.50$$
$$= \$7 + \$35$$
$$= \$42$$

When you find the cost for Ms. Brown to bring a certain number of students to the museum, you pair two quantities: the number of students and the total admission fee.

Notice that the number of adults is fixed. The number of students determines the total admission fee. The number of students is called the independent variable or **input**, and the total admission fee is called the dependent variable or **output**.

If Ms. Brown brings 10 students with her, she will have to pay $42. So, an input of 10 results in an output of 42. You can represent this by the ordered pair (10, 42).

The pairing of the two quantities as an ordered pair (number of students, total admission fee) is called a relation.

(10, 42)

input   output

A relation pairs a set of inputs with a set of outputs

You often need to decide which quantity should be the input and which should be the output in a relation. If Ms. Brown has a certain amount of money to spend on the total admission fee, and she wants to find the number of students she can bring to the museum, then the input is the total admission fee while the output is the number of students.

2 You can use a mapping diagram to represent the relation between the inputs and the outputs. The mapping diagram below represents the relation which have the ordered pairs (0, 0), (0, 1), (0, 2), and (1, 2).

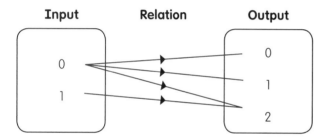

Input	Relation	Output
0		0
1		1
		2

An arrow is used to map each input to one or more outputs.

There are four different types of relations. You can represent each type by a mapping diagram as follows:

a One-to-one relation

Each input maps to only one output. Each output has only one input.

Input	Relation	Output
A		60
B		61
C		62
D		59

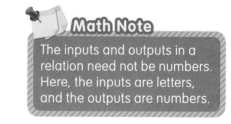

Math Note

The inputs and outputs in a relation need not be numbers. Here, the inputs are letters, and the outputs are numbers.

b One-to-many relation
One input maps to many outputs.

Input **Relation** **Output**

A
B

60
61
62
59

Math Note

You can also use a table to represent a relation. For the one-to-many relation:

Input	Output
	60
A	61
	62
B	59

c Many-to-one relation
Many inputs map to the same output.

Input **Relation** **Output**

A
B
C

60
70

d Many-to-many relation
One input maps to many outputs, and many inputs map to the same output.

Input **Relation** **Output**

A
B
C

60
61
62

A many-to-many relation has the properties of both the one-to-many relation and the many-to-one relation.

3 The table shows the test scores of five students.

Name of Student	Joseph	Hugo	Hana	Amber	Matthew
Test Score	60	59	62	60	61

Use a mapping diagram to show the relation between the students and their test scores. Identify the type of relation between the students and the test scores.

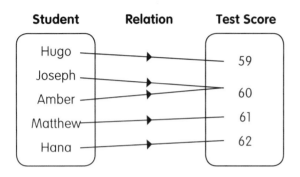

Two inputs, Joseph and Amber, have the same output, 60.

The relation between the students and the test scores is a many-to-one relation.

 **Math Talk**

If Joseph's score is 63 instead of 60, what type of relation would this become? Is it possible for a relation between students and test scores for one test to be one-to-many?

TRY Practice classifying relations

Identify the type of relation between the inputs and the outputs.

1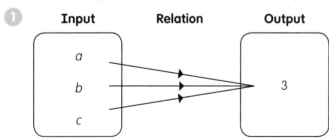

2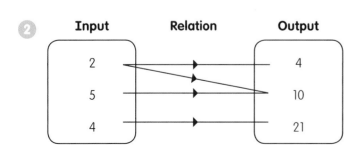

3

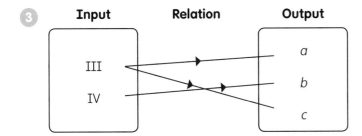

Input	Relation	Output
III		a
IV		b
		c

Use a mapping diagram. Describe the relation between the inputs and outputs.

4 The table shows the heights of five statues, A–E, and their weights.

Statues	A	B	C	D	E
Height (in.)	40	35	56	70	47
Weight (lb)	85	84	90	99	86

ENGAGE

In your own words, explain each of the relations below.

a One-to-one relation
b One-to-many relation
c Many-to-one relation
d Many-to-many relation

For each relation, think of a real-world example that suits it. Explain your thinking.

LEARN Understand and identify functions

1 A function is a special type of relation in which each input maps to only one output.

> All functions are either one-to-one relations or many-to-one relations.

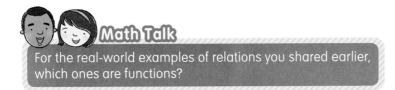

Math Talk

For the real-world examples of relations you shared earlier, which ones are functions?

2 The relation between pressing a key on the keyboard and the letter that appears on the monitor screen is a function. Each key you press on the keyboard will result in a specific letter appearing on the monitor screen. You see a one-to-one relation on the mapping diagram.

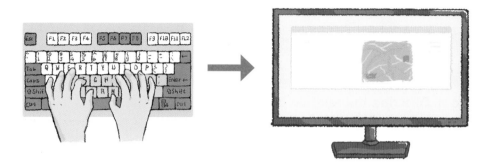

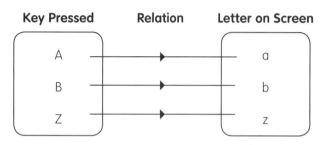

The function can be represented using a table.

Input	Output
A	a
B	b
Z	z

3 In a store that is selling every product for $2, the relation between a product and its price is a function. The mapping diagram shows a many-to-one relation.

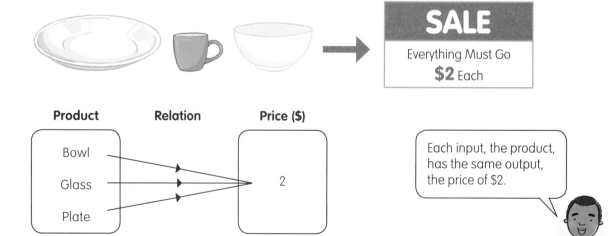

Each input, the product, has the same output, the price of $2.

4 The relation between a football player and his position is a function. Each player can play only one position at a time. The mapping diagram shows a many-to-one relation.

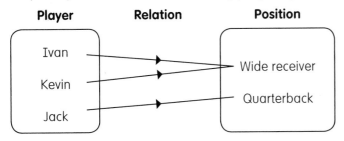

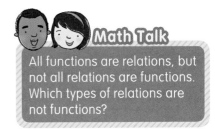

Math Talk

All functions are relations, but not all relations are functions. Which types of relations are not functions?

In all three examples **2**, **3**, and **4**, each input has only one output. So, they are functions.

5 When at least one input in a relation has more than one output, the relation is not a function.

For example, some libraries use the Dewey Decimal System to categorize books. In the example shown below, all books on philosophy and psychology have a number in the 100s. You can think of the numbers in the list as inputs. The outputs are types of books, by subject, that are matched to these numbers.

Dewey Decimal System
000 Computer Science and Information
100 Philosophy and Psychology
200 Religion and Mythology
300 Social Science
400 Language
500 Science and Mathematics
600 Technology
700 Arts and Recreation
800 Literature
900 History and Geography

A table can also be used to tell whether a relation is a function.

Input	Output
400	English
	German
500	Probability
	Zoology

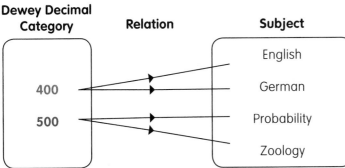

In the mapping diagram, you see that the Dewey Decimal Category 400 has two subjects, English and German. Likewise, the Dewey Decimal Category 500 has two subjects, Probability and Zoology. So, the relation is not a function because each input has more than one output.

This is a one-to-many relation.

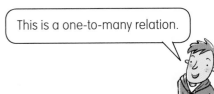

6 The athletes at a high jump event have numbers on their outfits. Each of the five athletes made one jump. The height cleared by each athlete is shown in the table.

Athlete Number	1	2	3	4	5
Height Cleared (cm)	145	143	139	151	151

> You can use ordered pairs to represent the relation.
> (1, 145), (2, 143), (3, 139), (4, 151), and (5, 151).

a Use a mapping diagram to represent the relation between the numbers of the athletes and the heights they cleared.

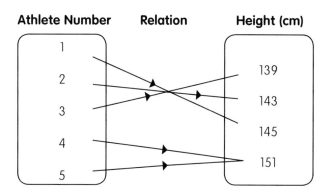

> Two inputs, 4 and 5, have the same output, 151. So, this is a many-to-one relation.

> It is impossible for each athlete to have two different recorded heights for one jump.

b Is this relation a function? Explain your answer.

This relation is a function because each input has only one output.

c Consider the reverse relation. Suppose the inputs are the heights cleared by the athletes, and the outputs are the numbers of the athletes. Draw a mapping diagram to represent the relation. Is this relation a function?

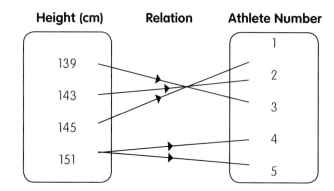

> The height of 151 centimeters was cleared by more than one athlete. So, this is a one-to-many relation.

This relation is not a function because one input, 151, has more than one output, 4 and 5.

Which of the following relations is a function? Explain.

1   **Input**   **Relation**   **Output**

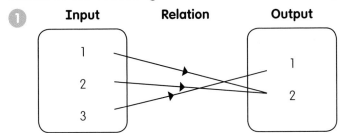

2   **Input**   **Relation**   **Output**

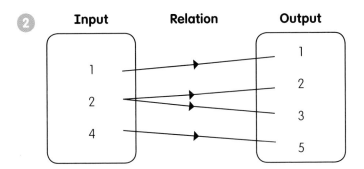

3

Input	Output
1	2
3	4
5	6
7	8

ENGAGE

Create a table of values for x(input) and y(output) such that the relation is a function. Ensure there are at least 5 pairs of values. Use these pairs of values to create ordered pairs (x, y) and plot these points on a graph paper. Compare your plots with your partner's. Are there any similarities that you can spot? Discuss with your partner to come up with an explanation for these similarities.

LEARN Identify functions represented by graphs

1 You used mapping diagrams and tables to identify functions. You can also use a graph.

The mapping diagram shows a one-to-one relation between x and y. So, this relation is a function.

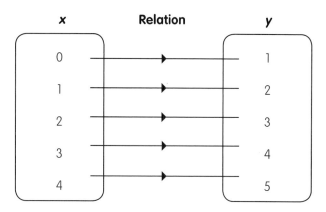

Writing each mapping as an ordered pair, you get (0, 1), (1, 2), (2, 3), (3, 4) and (4, 5).

You can also represent this function using a graph. Write each input and output as an ordered pair (x, y) and graph each point on a coordinate plane.

The graph for this relation is shown. A vertical line through each point is drawn. You see that each vertical line passes through only one point.

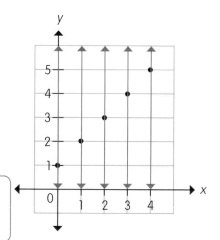

Vertical Line Test:
If a relation is a function, then any vertical line drawn through the graph of the relation will pass through only one point on the graph.

2 The mapping diagram shows a one-to-many relation between x and y. So, this relation is not a function.

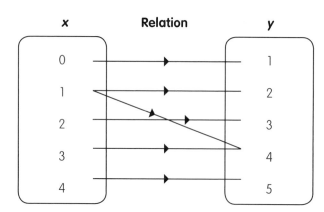

The ordered pairs are (0, 1), (1, 2), (1, 4), (2, 3), (3, 4) and (4, 5).

If you graph the ordered pairs (x, y), you get the graph shown. A vertical line through each point is drawn.

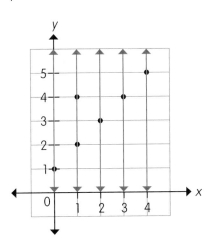

For the input $x = 1$, there are two outputs, $y = 2$ and $y = 4$.

You see that the vertical line $x = 1$ passes through two points, $(1, 2)$ and $(1, 4)$. So, the graph of this relation does not pass the vertical line test. This relation is not a function.

3 The graph shows the relation between the maximum heights eight students jump, y centimeters, and the students' heights, x centimeters. The relation is represented by the graph shown. Is the relation a function?

To answer this question, use the vertical line test. If you can draw a vertical line passing through more than one point on the graph, then the relation is not a function.

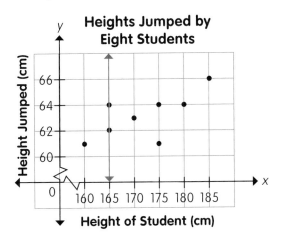

For $x = 165$, there are two points, where $y = 62$ and $y = 64$. This means that there are two students who are 165 centimeters tall. One student jumps 62 cm, the other student jumps 64 cm.

On the graph, you see that the vertical line, $x = 165$, passes through two points, $(165, 62)$ and $(165, 64)$. So, the relation represented by the graph is not a function.

Math Talk

Can you draw other vertical lines passing through more than one point on the graph? What are the coordinates of these points?

4 When a rocket is launched straight up in the air, it travels quickly at first and then slows down until it begins to fall back towards the ground. As the rocket falls, the pull of gravity causes it to fall faster and faster. The graph shows the distance, h meters, of a small rocket from the ground, t seconds after it was launched into the air. Is the relation between time and distance a function?

You can use the vertical line test. Draw a vertical line anywhere within the range of values of x between the origin and the end point of the graph. You will see that any vertical line you draw intersects the graph at only one point. So, the relation between time and distance is a function.

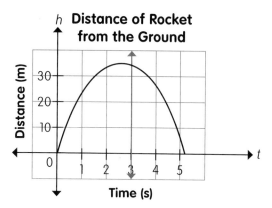

Math Note

The graph shows all the possible points representing ordered pairs of time and distance, which can be decimal values. The graph is a curve, not a straight line.

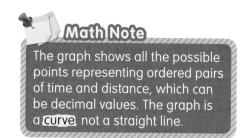

TRY Practice identifying functions represented by graphs

Which of these relations, each represented by a graph, is a function? Explain.

1

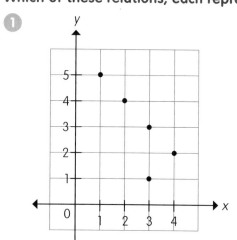

2

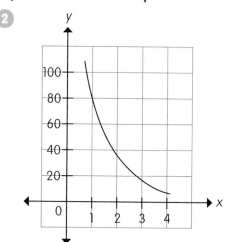

INDEPENDENT PRACTICE

Given the relation described, identify the input and the output.

1 Mr. Jones wants to find out the price of the same stereo speaker sold at different stores.

2 Five students, Julia, Sean, Brandon, Vijay, and Riley, have different heights. Their teacher wants to record their heights.

Solve.

3 The table shows the number of pieces of each type of fruit sold at a supermarket. Draw a mapping diagram to represent the relation between the type of fruit and how many pieces of fruit were sold. Identify the type of relation between the type of fruit and how many pieces of fruit were sold.

Input, Fruit	Apple	Apricot	Lemon	Orange	Papaya
Output, Number of Pieces Sold	256	187	256	256	93

Identify the type of relation represented by each mapping diagram. Determine whether the relation is a function. Explain.

4

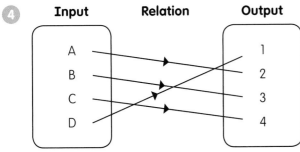

Input   Relation   Output

A, B, C, D → 1, 2, 3, 4

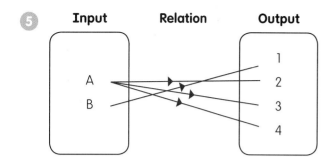

5 Input   Relation   Output

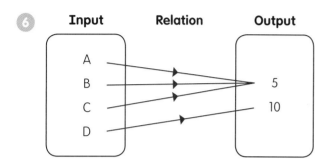

6 Input   Relation   Output

State whether each statement is True or False. Explain.

`Mathematical Habit 3` **Construct viable arguments**

7 In a relation, either the inputs or the outputs must be numbers.

8 A function is a type of relation.

9 All relations are functions.

10 A one-to-many relation is a function.

11 The only type of relation that is a function is a many-to-one relation.

Solve.

12 The table shows the number of books sold by each of six bookstores and the amount of money (sales) made by each store in one week.

Bookstore	A	B	C	D	E
Number of Books Sold	523	702	523	982	754
Sales	$2,569	$869	$2,317	$5,032	$869

a Draw a mapping diagram to represent the relation between each bookstore (input) and number of books sold (output). Which type of relation is this? Is the relation a function?

b Draw a mapping diagram to represent the relation between each bookstore (input) and sales (output). Which type of relation is this? Is the relation a function?

c The store owners want to know if the relation between number of books sold (input) and sales (output) is a function. Draw a mapping diagram to represent this relation. Which type of relation is this? Is the relation a function?

d **Mathematical Habit 3** **Construct viable arguments**
Bookstore A and Bookstore C sold the same number of books but Bookstore A made more sales than Bookstore C. Give a possible reason for this.

13 **Mathematical Habit 2** Use mathematical reasoning

Is the relation between the side length and the area of a square a function? Explain.

Mathematical Habit 6 Use precise mathematical language
Which of these graphs represents a function? Explain.

 14

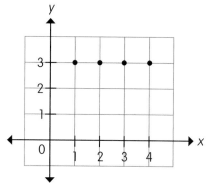

15

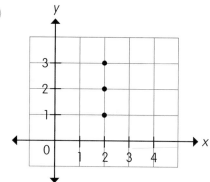

16

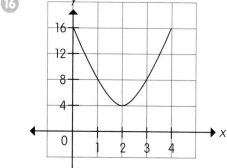

Representing Functions

Learning Objectives:
- Use functions to model relationships between quantities.
- Represent a function in different forms.

New Vocabulary
linear function

THINK

Find an equation which represents each of these tables of values. Which tables represent y as a function of x? Explain.

A

x	0	1	2	3
y	2	2	2	2

B

x	3	3	3	3
y	0	1	2	3

C

x	1	2	3	4
y	0	2	4	6

ENGAGE

Chris rented a car at $90 per day during his trip to New Orleans. Construct a table to show the rental costs for 1, 2, 3, and 4 days of rental. Is the relation between the number of days of rental and the rental cost a function? Discuss what are the various ways you can represent this relation. Explain your thinking.

LEARN Represent functions in different forms

1. Melissa plans to enroll in a Spanish class at a language school. She has to pay a registration fee of $100 plus $20 for each lesson she takes. The relation between the number of lessons that she takes and the total amount that she pays is a function.

A verbal description of the function is:

The **total amount of money Melissa pays** equals $100 registration fee plus $20 times the **number of lessons**.

You can translate this verbal description into an algebraic equation.
Let the number of lessons be x.
Let the total amount she pays be y.

$y = 100 + (20 \cdot x)$ Write an equation.
$y = 100 + 20x$ Simplify.
$y = 20x + 100$ Write the equation in slope-intercept form.

> x is the **input** and y is the **output** of the function.

In algebraic form, the function is $y = 20x + 100$.

You can also use a table of values to represent the function. Substitute 0, 1, 2, and 3 for x in the equation $y = 20x + 100$:

$y = 20(0) + 100$ $y = 20(1) + 100$ $y = 20(2) + 100$ $y = 20(3) + 100$
$\quad = 100$ $\quad = 120$ $\quad = 140$ $\quad = 160$

The table represents the function in numerical form:

Number of Lessons (x)	0	1	2	3
Total Amount of Money (y dollars)	100	120	140	160

So, the input values are the number of lessons Melissa takes:
0, 1, 2, 3, ...

The output values are the corresponding amounts she pays:
$100, $120, $140, $160, ...

To represent the function in graphical form, you can graph the table of values.

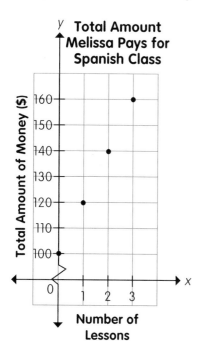

Math Note

The input and output values of this function are integers. They cannot be decimals. For example, the number of lessons cannot be 2.5. The amount she pays cannot be $120.50. So, the information is represented by points on the graph. Do not draw a line through the points.

The graph shows 4 points. Other points could be plotted to show the amounts Melissa pays for taking more than 3 lessons.

Because the points lie on the same line, the function $y = 20x + 100$ is called a linear function.

A function with input x and output y can be represented in four ways: numerically by constructing a table of x and y values, algebraically by using an equation, graphically by graphing the equation or the table of values, and by giving a verbal description of the function.

2 A fire sprinkler sprays water at the rate of 3 gallons per minute. The amount of water sprayed, y gallons, is a function of the number of minutes, x, that the sprinkler sprays water.

When you say "y is a function of x", it means the input is x and the output is y.

a Give a verbal description of the function. Then write an equation to represent the function.

The **amount of water sprayed** equals the rate of water sprayed times the **number of minutes**.

$y = 3 \cdot x$ Write an equation.
$y = 3x$ Simplify.

b Construct a table of values to represent the function.

Time (*x* minutes)	0	1	2	3	4
Amount of Water (*y* gallons)	0	3	6	9	12

c Graph the function.

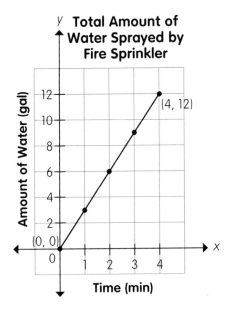

Math Note

The quantities, number of minutes and amount of water, can also be decimals. For example, after 1.2 minutes, the amount of water is $y = 3 \cdot 1.2 = 3.6$ gallons. Time can be any value starting from 0. Amount of water can be any value starting from 0. So, you should draw a line through the points to represent all possible input and output values.

TRY Practice representing functions in different forms

Solve.

1 A game shop rents out video games at $4 per game. The amount of money, *y* dollars, the shop collects is a function of the number of games, *x*, that the shop rents out.

   a Give a verbal description of the function. Then write an equation to represent the function.

   b Construct a table of values to represent the function. Use values of *x* from 0 to 3.

   c Graph the function.

2 A tank contained 8 gallons of water initially. Water was then pumped into the tank at the rate of 2 gallons per minute. The total amount of water, *y* gallons, in the tank is a function of the time, *x* minutes, after the pump was turned on.

   a Give a verbal description of the function. Then write an equation to represent the function.

   b Construct a table of values to represent the function. Use values of *x* from 0 to 3.

   c Graph the function.

3 Amelia goes to the supermarket to buy walnuts for her mother. The walnuts are sold at 15 dollars per pound. The amount of money, *y* dollars, she pays is a function of the amount of walnuts, *x* pounds, that she buys.

   a Give a verbal description of the function. Then write an equation to represent the function.

   b Construct a table of values to represent the function. Use values of *x* from 0 to 4.

   c Graph the function.

INDEPENDENT PRACTICE

Give a verbal description of each function. Then write an equation to represent the function.

1 Jesse is traveling at a constant speed of 80 kilometers per hour. The distance, d kilometers, he travels is a function of the amount of time, t hours, that he takes.

2 Mr. Cooper pays a monthly charge of $40 for a family cell phone plan. Each additional family member pays $10 every month. The total amount of money, y dollars, Mr. Cooper and his family members pay each month is a function of the number of the additional family members, x.

3 **Mathematical Habit 2** Use mathematical reasoning

For questions **1** and **2**, if a graph is drawn for each function, which graph is a straight line and which graph shows only the points? Explain.

Write an equation to represent each function. Then construct a table of values to represent the function. Use values of x from 0 to 3.

4 The members of the Robotics Club are making model windmills for a workshop. Each windmill has three blades. The total number of blades needed, y, is a function of the number of windmills, x, that they make.

5 A newly-made glass vase has an initial temperature of 580°C. Its temperature decreases at an average rate of 56°C per minute. The temperature, y °C, of the glass vase is a function of the time, x minutes, that its temperature has been decreasing.

Each of these graphs represents a function. Write an equation to represent each function.

6

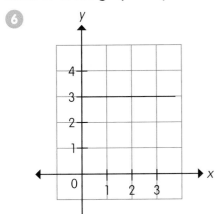

7

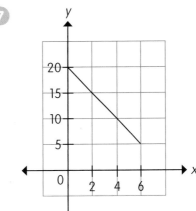

Solve.

8 The temperature, $y°C$, of a packet of food in the freezer is a function of the time, x minutes, that the packet is in the freezer. Initially, the temperature of the packet of food is 30°C. Its temperature decreases by 5°C every minute.

a **Mathematical Habit 6** **Use precise mathematical language**
Give a verbal description of the function.

b Write an equation to represent the function.

c Construct a table of values to represent the function. Use values of x from 0 to 4.

d Graph the function.

Solve. Use graph paper.

9 Sofia has $60 on her bus pass initially. Every time she rides a bus, $1.50 is deducted from the value on her pass. The amount of money, y dollars, she has on her pass is a function of the number of times, x, that she rides a bus.

a **Mathematical Habit 6** **Use precise mathematical language**
Give a verbal description of the function.

b Write an equation to represent the function.

c Construct a table of values to represent the function. Use values of x from 0 to 6.

d Graph the function. Use 1 grid square to represent 1 bus ride on the x-axis, for the x interval from 0 to 6. Use 1 grid square to represent $1 on the y-axis, for the y interval from 50.0 to 60.0.

3 Understanding Linear and Nonlinear Functions

Learning Objectives:
- Identify linear and nonlinear functions.
- Interpret the rate of change and the initial value of a linear function.
- Construct a function to model a linear relationship between two quantities.
- Describe functions.

> **New Vocabulary**
> nonlinear function
> rate of change

THINK

Give a real-world example of a nonlinear function. Name the input and output variables of the function. Describe the function qualitatively.

ENGAGE

Complete the given table to represent a linear pattern.

x	1	4		12	16
y	4		32		

How does y change in relation to x? What patterns do you notice? Explain.

LEARN Identify a linear or nonlinear function from a table

1. The ratio $\dfrac{\text{change in the first quantity}}{\text{change in the second quantity}}$ gives the rate of change of the first quantity relative to the second quantity.

The rate of change tells us how much the first quantity changes for every 1 unit change in the second quantity.

For a function, the rate of change of output relative to input is as follows:

> Rate of change $= \dfrac{\text{Change in output values}}{\text{Change in input values}}$
>
> If the rate of change of a function is constant, it is a linear function.
> If the rate of change of a function is not constant, it is a nonlinear function.

Math Talk

Consider the function relating your age in the last ten years and your height at the end of each year. Is the rate of change of your height constant? Explain.

2 You can tell whether a function represented by a table of values is linear or nonlinear by finding the rate of change.

a

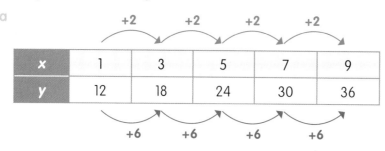

x	1	3	5	7	9
y	12	18	24	30	36

Rate of change: $\dfrac{6}{2} = 3$ $\dfrac{6}{2} = 3$ $\dfrac{6}{2} = 3$ $\dfrac{6}{2} = 3$

The rate of change is constant. So, the table represents a linear function.

b

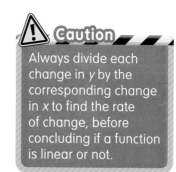

Caution

Always divide each change in y by the corresponding change in x to find the rate of change, before concluding if a function is linear or not.

x	1	2	4	7	8
y	18	12	0	−18	−24

Rate of change: $\dfrac{-6}{1} = -6$ $\dfrac{-12}{2} = -6$ $\dfrac{-18}{3} = -6$ $\dfrac{-6}{1} = -6$

The rate of change is constant. So, the table represents a linear function.

c

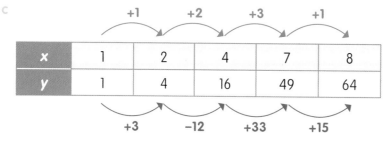

x	1	2	4	7	8
y	1	4	16	49	64

Rate of change: $\dfrac{3}{1} = 3$ $\dfrac{12}{2} = 6$ $\dfrac{33}{3} = 11$ $\dfrac{15}{1} = 15$

The rate of change is not constant.
So, the table represents a nonlinear function.

Math Note

If the rate of change is not constant, you say that the rate of change varies.

3 The table shows the recommended time, y hours, to roast a turkey as a function of the weight of a turkey, x pounds. Does the table represent a linear function? Explain.

	+5	+5	+10

Weight of Turkey (x pounds)	10	15	20	30
Time (y hours)	3.0	3.5	4.0	5.0

+0.5   +0.5   +1.0

Rate of change: $\dfrac{0.5}{5} = 0.1$ $\dfrac{0.5}{5} = 0.1$ $\dfrac{1.0}{10} = 0.1$

The rate of change is constant.
So, the table represents a linear function.

TRY Practice identifying a linear or nonlinear function from a table

Each table shows y as a function of x. Does the table represent a linear or nonlinear function? Explain.

1

x	2	4	8	10
y	3	8	18	23

2

x	−5	−3	−1	1	3
y	28	26	22	14	4

ENGAGE

A function is represented by the equation $y = 2x$. Another function is represented by the equation $y = x^2$. Are these linear or nonlinear functions? Explain using a table of values for each function.

Create an equation that represents a linear function and an equation that represents a nonlinear function. Explain your thinking.

LEARN Identify a linear or nonlinear function from an equation

① A linear function can be represented by a linear equation, which can be expressed in slope-intercept form $y = mx + b$. Since the slope, m, is $\frac{\text{change in } y}{\text{change in } x}$, m is the constant rate of change of y relative to x.

> If an equation representing a function can be expressed in slope-intercept form, the function is linear. The slope is the constant rate of change of the function.

> If an equation representing a function cannot be expressed in slope-intercept form, the function is nonlinear.

② Determine if each of these functions represented by an equation is linear or nonlinear. If the function is linear, find the constant rate of change.

ⓐ $2y = -4x + 1$

$\frac{2y}{2} = \frac{-4x}{2} + \frac{1}{2}$ Divide each term by 2.

$y = -2x + \frac{1}{2}$ Simplify.

> The slope is –2, the y-intercept is $\frac{1}{2}$.

The equation represents a linear function.
The constant rate of change is –2.

ⓑ $y = -3x$

The equation represents a linear function.
The constant rate of change is –3.

> In slope-intercept form, the equation is $y = -3x + 0$.

ⓒ $y = 4$

The equation represents a linear function.
The constant rate of change is 0.

> In slope-intercept form, the equation is $y = 0 \cdot x + 4$. y is 4 for all values of x.

ⓓ $y = 5x^2 + 1$

The equation cannot be expressed in slope-intercept form. It represents a nonlinear function.

Math Note

In slope-intercept form $y = mx + c$, x must be raised to the first power.

Determine if each of the following functions represented by an equation is linear or nonlinear. If the function is linear, find the constant rate of change.

1 $3y = x - 6$

2 $y = -\frac{1}{2}x$

3 $y = 3$

4 $y = 2x^3 + 1$

Math Talk

What does the graph of the equation $x = 3$ look like? Does $x = 3$ represent a function?

ENGAGE

Write an equation of a linear function and a nonlinear function. Sketch the two graphs. What do you notice about the differences between the two graphs?

LEARN Identify a linear or nonlinear function from a graph

1 You have learned that a linear function has a constant rate of change. You have also learned that a linear function can be represented by a linear equation. The graph of a linear equation is a straight line.

> If the graph representing a function is a straight line, the function is linear.

2 A straight line graph representing a linear function is shown. You can show that the rate of change is constant by using different pairs of coordinates to calculate the slope.

The line passes through (0, 3) and (1, 0).

$$\text{Slope } m = \frac{0-3}{1-0}$$
$$= \frac{-3}{1}$$
$$= -3$$

The line also passes through (1, 0) and (2, −3).

$$\text{Slope } m = \frac{-3-0}{2-1}$$
$$= \frac{-3}{1}$$
$$= -3$$

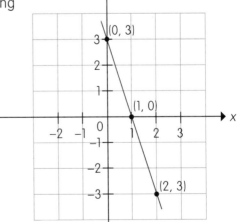

Math Talk

What is the equation of this line in slope-intercept form?

The slope of the line, which is the rate of change of the function, is a constant value.

③ The graph shows the relation between the area of a square, y square centimeters, as a function of its side length, x centimeters.

a Is the rate of change of the function constant?

The graph passes through (0, 0) and (3, 9).

Rate of change $= \dfrac{9-0}{3-0}$

$\qquad\qquad\quad = \dfrac{9}{3}$

$\qquad\qquad\quad = 3$

The graph also passes through (3, 9) and (5, 25).

Rate of change $= \dfrac{25-9}{5-3}$

$\qquad\qquad\quad = \dfrac{16}{2}$

$\qquad\qquad\quad = 8$

So, the rate of change of the function is not constant.

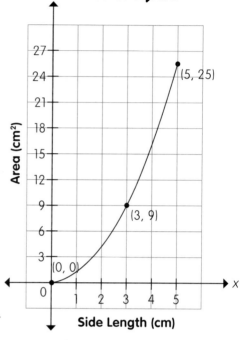

Area of Square

b Does the graph represent a linear or nonlinear function? How do you tell by looking at the graph?

The graph represents a nonlinear function because it is not a straight line.

> If the graph representing a function is not a straight line, the graph is a curve, and the function is nonlinear.

TRY Practice identifying a linear or nonlinear function from a graph

Do the following graphs represent linear functions? If so, find the rate of change of the function.

①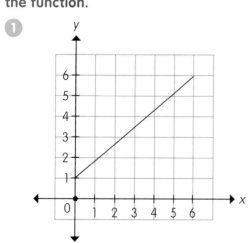

②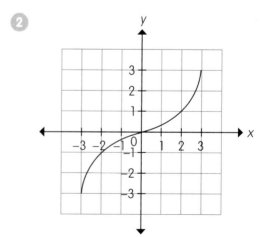

ENGAGE

The table shows the distance, *y* meters, of a bus from a bus station as a function of the time, *x* minutes, after it departed from the station.

Time (x minutes)	0	1	2	3	4
Distance (y meters)	0	250	500	750	1,000

Does the table of values represent a linear function? What does the rate of change represent? What equation can you write to model the function? Discuss.

LEARN Construct a function to model a linear relationship

1 Ashley started cycling on the main street which is a short distance away from her home. The table shows her distance, *y* meters, from home as a function of the time, *x* seconds, she spent cycling.

Time (x seconds)	0	1	2	3	4
Distance (y meters)	6	10	14	18	22

a Graph the function.

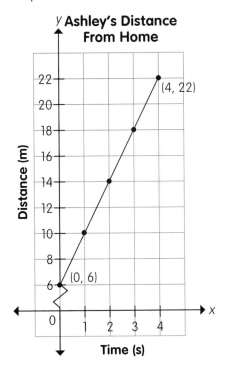

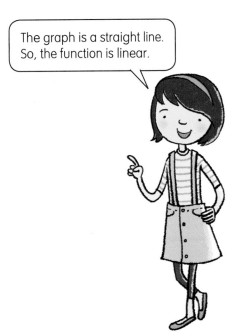

The graph is a straight line. So, the function is linear.

© 2020 Marshall Cavendish Education Pte Ltd

b Find the constant rate of change of the function.

The line passes through the points (0, 6) and (4, 22).

$$\text{Slope } m = \frac{y_2 - y_1}{x_2 - x_1} \quad \text{Use the slope formula.}$$

$$= \frac{22 - 6}{4 - 0} \quad \text{Substitute values.}$$

$$= \frac{16}{4} \quad \text{Subtract.}$$

$$= 4 \quad \text{Simplify.}$$

So, the constant rate of change is 4.

c What does the rate of change represent?

The rate of change represents Ashley's constant cycling speed, which is 4 meters per second.

d What is the initial value of y?

When $x = 0$, $y = 6$. The initial value of y is 6.

e What does the initial value of y represent?

The initial value of y represents the distance of Ashley from her home when she started cycling. The distance from home was 6 meters.

f Write a linear equation to model the function.

The linear equation is $y = 4x + 6$.

TRY **Practice constructing a function to model a linear relationship**

1 The table shows the total distance, y miles, indicated on the odometer of Tyler's car as a function of the amount of gasoline, x gallons, used on a particular day.

Amount of Gasoline (x gallons)	0	1	2	3	4
Total Distance (y miles)	1,000	1,030	1,060	1,090	1,120

a Graph the function.

b Find the constant rate of change of the function.

c What does the rate of change represent?

d What is the initial value of y?

e What does the initial value of y represent?

f Write a linear equation to model the function.

ENGAGE

The graphs below show the trips that two school buses take.

Imagine the trip that each school bus takes. What is a possible story that the graph may describe? Explain your answer.

Trips of School Buses

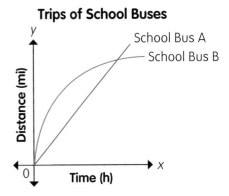

LEARN Describe functions

1. You have learned to tell whether a graph is linear or nonlinear. Now you will learn to tell whether there is an increasing or a decreasing relationship between the inputs and outputs of a function.

Increasing functions

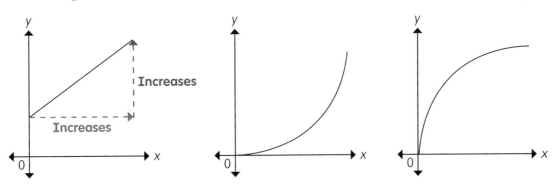

In the three graphs above, the line or curve rises. For an increasing function, as the values of x **increase**, the values of y also **increase**.

Decreasing functions

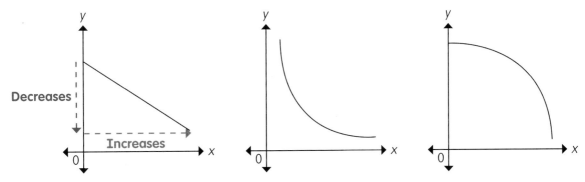

In the three graphs above, the line or curve falls. For a decreasing function, as the values of x **increase**, the values of y **decrease**.

> For a linear function with equation $y = mx + b$:
> If the slope, m, is positive, the line rises, and the function is increasing.
> If the slope, m, is negative, the line falls, and the function is decreasing.

2 Erin wants to buy some grapes from a fruit stand. Each pound of grapes costs 5 dollars. The amount of money, y dollars, that she pays is a function of the weight, x pounds, of grapes that she buys.

a Is the rate of change of the function constant? If so, explain and find its value.

Each pound of grapes costs $5. For every additional pound of grapes that Erin buys, she pays an additional $5. So, the rate of change of the function is constant. Its value is 5.

b What was the initial output value of the function? Explain.

If Erin does not buy any grapes, she spends $0. So, the initial output value was 0.

c Is the function is linear or nonlinear? Explain.

Since the rate of change is constant, the function is linear.

d Is the function increasing or decreasing? Explain.

As the weight of grapes that she buys increases, the amount of money that she pays increases. So, the function is increasing.

e Write an equation to represent the function. Sketch a graph of the function.

An equation for the function is $y = 5x$.

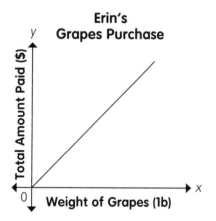

Erin's Grapes Purchase

The function is linear, increasing, and the initial values are $x = 0$ and $y = 0$. So, the graph is a rising straight line starting from the origin.

 Practice describing functions

Solve.

1 A cruise ship traveling at a constant speed consumes 4,000 gallons of gasoline per hour. Before the ship begins its journey, the fuel tank is fully filled with 330,000 gallons of gasoline. The amount of gasoline, y gallons, that is left in the fuel tank is a function of the traveling time, x hours.

a Is the rate of change of the function constant? If so, explain and find its value.

b What is the initial output value of the function? Explain.

c Is the function is linear or nonlinear? Explain.

d Is the function increasing or decreasing? Explain.

e Write an equation to represent the function. Sketch a graph of the function.

INDEPENDENT PRACTICE

Determine whether each table represents a linear or nonlinear function. Find the rate of change for each linear function.

1

x	3	5	7	9
y	6	12	18	24

2

x	−15	−10	−5	20
y	12	8	4	−16

3

x	−8	−3	8	27
y	−2	−1	2	3

State whether each graph represents a linear or nonlinear function. Find the rate of change for each linear function.

4
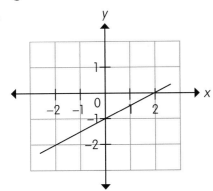

5
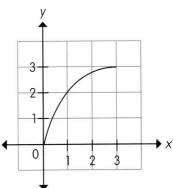

6
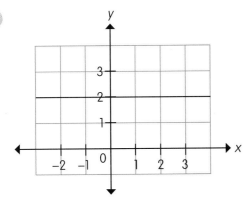

State whether each graph represents a linear or nonlinear function. State whether the function is increasing or decreasing.

⑦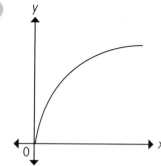

⑧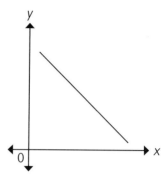

⑨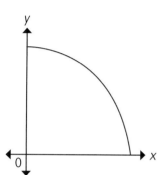

⑩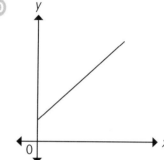

Solve.

⑪ Bruno was 100 miles from Town P. He traveled to Town P by car at a constant speed of 50 miles per hour. The distance, y miles, from Town P is a function of the traveling time, x hours.

a **Mathematical Habit 2 Use mathematical reasoning**
Is the rate of change of the function constant? If so, explain and find its value.

b **Mathematical Habit 2 Use mathematical reasoning**
What are the initial output value of the function? Explain.

c **Mathematical Habit 6 Use precise mathematical language**
Is the function linear or nonlinear? Explain.

d **Mathematical Habit 6 Use precise mathematical language**
Is the function increasing or decreasing? Explain.

e Sketch the graph of the function.

Comparing Two Functions

Learning Objective:
• Compare the properties of two functions.

THINK

Two functions, A and B, represented in different forms, are shown below. Describe the similarities and differences between the two functions.

A: $y = -2x + 3$

B:

x	1	2	3	4
y	5	7	9	11

ENGAGE

Draw a graph to show:

a a linear function

b a non-linear function

c an increasing function

d a decreasing function

Compare each type of graph. How are they alike? How are they different? Explain.

For each graph, think of a real-world example that it could describe. Share your ideas.

LEARN Compare two functions represented in the same form

1. Jessica and Isabel went on a cycling trip with the school. The graphs show the distance, *y* kilometers, traveled by each girl as a function of time, *x* hours.

   a Compare the graphs of the two functions.
      Are the functions linear or nonlinear? Are the functions increasing or decreasing?

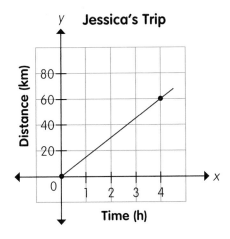

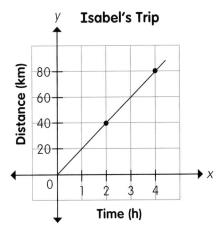

Both graphs show linear and increasing functions.

b Compare the rates of change of the functions.

To compare the rates of change, find the slopes of the graphs.

For Jessica, the line passes through the points (0, 0) and (4, 60).

Slope $m = \dfrac{60 - 0}{4 - 0}$

$ = \dfrac{60}{4}$

$ = 15$

The rate of change, given by the slope, is $\dfrac{\text{change in distance}}{\text{change in time}}$, which gives the cycling speed.

For Isabel, the line passes through the points (2, 40) and (4, 80).

Slope $m = \dfrac{80 - 40}{4 - 2}$

$ = \dfrac{40}{2}$

$ = 20$

Since 20 > 15, the function that represents Isabel's trip has a greater rate of change than the function that represents Jessica's trip.

The speeds of Jessica and Isabel, given by the rates of change, are constant. Jessica's speed is 15 km/h. Isabel's speed is 20 km/h.

c Represent the functions algebraically by using equations.

Since the y-intercept for each graph is 0, the equation for each function has the form $y = mx$.

For Jessica, the equation is $y = 15x$.
For Isabel, the equation is $y = 20x$.

 Math Talk

How can you tell from the equations that the two functions are linear and increasing?

When you compare two functions, ask yourself these questions:
(1) Are the functions linear or nonlinear?
(2) Are the functions increasing or decreasing?
(3) If both functions are linear, which function has a greater rate of change?

2 The tables show the cost of potatoes by weight at Shop A and Shop B. The total cost, y cents, is a function of the weight of potatoes, x pounds.

Shop A

Weight of Potatoes (x pounds)	1	2	3	4
Total Cost (y cents)	60	120	180	240

Shop B

Weight of Potatoes (x pounds)	1	2	3	4
Total Cost (y cents)	50	100	150	200

a Using the tables of values, find the rate of change of each function. In which shop are potatoes cheaper? Explain.

Shop A

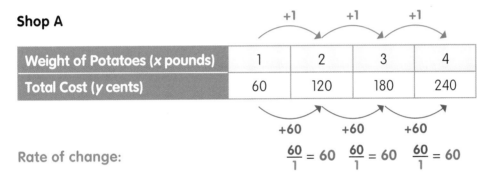

Rate of change: $\frac{60}{1} = 60$ $\frac{60}{1} = 60$ $\frac{60}{1} = 60$

The constant rate of change for Shop A is 60.

Shop B

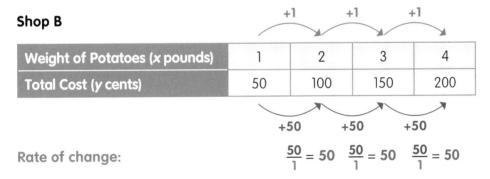

Rate of change: $\frac{50}{1} = 50$ $\frac{50}{1} = 50$ $\frac{50}{1} = 50$

The constant rate of change for Shop B is 50.
The rate of change gives the cost of 1 pound of potatoes. Shop B has a smaller rate of change. So, the potatoes in Shop B are cheaper.

b Are these functions linear or nonlinear? Explain.

Both are linear functions, because the rates of change are constant.

c Are these functions increasing or decreasing? Explain.

Both are increasing functions, because the rates of change are positive.

d Represent the functions algebraically by using equations.

If there are no potatoes ($x = 0$), there will be no cost ($y = 0$). So, the y-intercept for each graph is 0. The equations for each function has the form $y = mx$.

For Shop A, the equation is $y = 60x$.
For Shop B, the equation is $y = 50x$.

TRY Practice comparing two functions represented in the same form

Solve.

1 Water is pumped into two fish tanks, A and B. The tables show two functions relating the amount of water, y liters, and the time, x minutes, it takes to pump water into the tank.

Tank A

Time (x minutes)	5	10	20	30
Amount of Water (y liters)	70	120	220	320

Tank B

Time (x minutes)	5	10	20	30
Amount of Water (y liters)	95	170	320	470

a Using the tables of values, find the rate of change of each function. In which tank is the volume of water increasing at a faster rate? Explain.

b Are these functions linear or nonlinear? Explain.

c Are these functions increasing or decreasing? Explain.

ENGAGE

Max is looking for a new phone plan.

Plan A charges $35 dollars per month for 100 minutes of local calls and $0.20 per minute after 100 minutes.

Plan B provides unlimited text messages, and charges local calls based on the following table.

Number of Minutes (x)	100	150	200	250
Cost (y dollars)	50	75	100	125

How can Max figure out which is the better plan? Explain.

LEARN Compare two functions represented in different forms

1 Sometimes you may need to compare two linear functions that are represented in different forms. For example, you may want to compare a linear function represented by an equation with a linear function represented by a graph. One way to compare the functions is to express them in the same form, as you will learn in this example.

Jayden and David each have some savings from vacation jobs, which they started spending when they stopped working. The amount of money from their savings, y dollars, that each boy has left after x weeks is a linear function. Jayden's function is represented by a table, and David's function is represented by an equation.

Jayden's Savings

Number of Weeks (x)	0	5	15	20
Amount of Money (y dollars)	200	175	125	100

David's Savings
$y = -10x + 250$

a Find an equation representing the function for Jayden's savings.

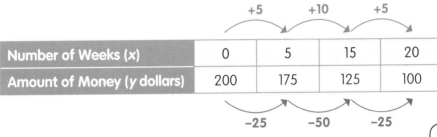

Rate of change: $\frac{-25}{5} = -5$ $\frac{-50}{10} = -5$ $\frac{-25}{5} = -5$

> The y-intercept can be read from the table. When x = 0, y = 200.

The rate of change is −5. The y-intercept is 200.
So, an equation is $y = -5x + 200$.

b Interpret and compare the rates of change of the two functions.

The rate of change gives the amount each boy spends per week. Jayden spends $5 per week. David spends $10 per week. David spends twice as much as Jayden per week.

c Interpret and compare the initial output values of the two functions.

The initial output value, given by the y-intercept, gives the initial amount each boy had in savings. Jayden had $200 in savings initially. So, David had $250 in savings initially. David had $50 more savings than Jayden initially.

d Are the two functions increasing or decreasing? Explain how you can tell from the rates of change.

Both functions are decreasing, because the rates of change are negative.

TRY Practice comparing two functions represented in different forms

Solve.

1. Two classes, A and B, raised money for a charity. The teachers in each class agreed to donate more money if students took part in a walkathon. The amount, y dollars, that the teachers in each class donated was a linear function of the distance, x miles, that the students in each class walked.

Class A

Distance Walked (x miles)	0	1	2	4
Amount Donated (y dollars)	100	115	130	160

Class B
Amount donated: $y = 20x + 50$

a Find an equation representing the function for Class A.

b Interpret and compare the rates of change of the two functions.

c Interpret and compare the initial output values of the two functions.

d Are the two functions increasing or decreasing? Explain how you can tell from the rates of change.

e If the students in each class walked 4 miles, which class raised more money? Justify your answer.

LET'S EXPLORE

1. Two identical containers, A and B, had some water in them initially. Each container is 10 inches tall. Lillian filled up container A with water from Tap A. Jayla filled up Container B with water from Tap B. Each of them recorded the depth of water in the container at the end of each minute. The equations below represent the depth of water, y inches, in each container as a function of the time, x minutes, after Lillian and Jayla turned on their taps.

Lillian: $y = \frac{1}{4}x + \frac{3}{2}$ Jayla: $y = \frac{1}{3}x + \frac{2}{3}$

a Which container had more water initially?

b Which container filled up more quickly?

c How long does it take for both containers to have the same depth of water? What is the common depth of water in both containers at this moment?

INDEPENDENT PRACTICE

Solve.

1. Determine whether the equation $y = -2x + 3$ can represent the table of values in **a** and the graph in **b**.

a

x	2	3	−1
y	−1	−3	5

b

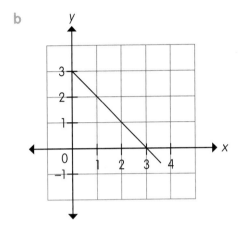

2. Determine whether the table of values can represent the equation in **a** and the graph in **b**.

x	0	1	2
y	−5	−2	1

a $y = 3x - 4$

b

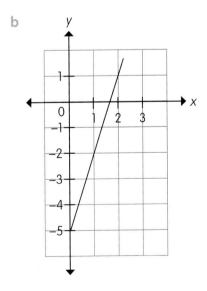

3 A pizza factory needs to grate 8,000 pounds of cheese every day. The manager of the factory wants to buy a faster cheese grating machine. She is deciding between Machine A and Machine B. For each machine, the amount of cheese to be grated, y pounds, is a function of the time, x minutes, after the machine starts grating every morning.

Machine A
The function is represented by the equation $y = 2,000 - 80x$. The initial value of 2,000 pounds represents the weight of each batch of cheese to be grated. After one batch is grated, another batch can be added to the machine.

Machine B
The function is represented by the graph below.

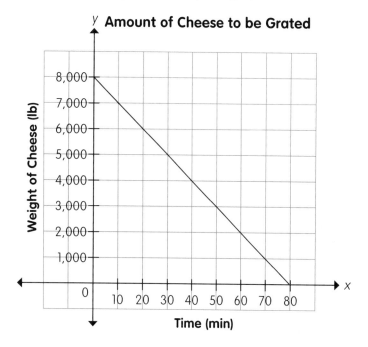

a Find an equation to represent the function for Machine B.

b **Mathematical Habit 2 Use mathematical reasoning**
Assuming that the machines are of the same quality, which machine would you recommend that the manager should buy? Explain.

4 The director of a theater group wants to rent a theater for an upcoming show. The director is given two options for paying the rent. Both options involve paying a deposit and then paying an additional charge for each ticket sold. For each option, the total rent, y dollars, is a function of the number of tickets sold, x.

Option A
The function is represented by the table below.

Number of Tickets Sold (x)	100	150	200
Total Rent (y dollars)	1,400	1,600	1,800

Option B
A deposit of $800 plus $6 per ticket sold.

a Find an equation to represent each function.

b **Mathematical Habit 2 Use mathematical reasoning**
Interpret and compare the rates of change of the two functions.

c **Mathematical Habit 2 Use mathematical reasoning**
Interpret and compare the initial output values of the two functions.

d **Mathematical Habit 2 Use mathematical reasoning**
The theater has a seating capacity of 200 people. If the director expects to sell all of the tickets, which of the two options, A or B, offers a better deal for the theater group? Explain.

Solve. Use graph paper.

5 Simone and Molly both save some money every month. The amount of money saved, y dollars, by each girl as a function of the number of months, x, that she saves, is represented by the following equations:

Simone: $y = 20x + 380$
Molly: $y = 15x + 400$

a **Mathematical Habit 2** Use mathematical reasoning
Interpret and compare the rates of change of the two functions.

b **Mathematical Habit 2** Use mathematical reasoning
Interpret and compare the initial output values of the two functions.

c Using graph paper, graph the two functions on the same coordinate plane for 8 months of savings. Use 1 grid square to represent 1 month on the x-axis, for the x interval from 0 to 8. Use 1 grid square to represent $20 on the y-axis, for the y interval from 380 to 540. For each function, draw a line through the points.

d **Mathematical Habit 2** Use mathematical reasoning
Who will have more savings over time? Explain.

Mathematical Habit 3 **Construct viable arguments**

a Give examples of the different types of linear functions you have learned. Use graphs and equations to represent your functions.

b Diego says that all straight line graphs are linear functions. Do you agree with him? Explain your answer.

Problem Solving with Heuristics

1 **Mathematical Habit 4** **Use mathematical models**
Five teachers at a school are taking a group of students to a museum.

The museum offers three different admission fee packages, A, B, and C. The total admission fee, *y* dollars, for each package is a linear function of the number of students, *x*.

Package A
Each adult ticket costs $30 and each student ticket costs $15.

Package B

Number of Students (*x*)	0	25	50
Total Admission Fee (*y* dollars)	250	600	950

Package C
Each adult ticket costs $60.

Number of Students (*x*)	10	30	50
Total Admission Fee (*y* dollars)	400	600	800

a Find an equation representing each of the three functions.

b Using graph paper, graph the three functions on the same coordinate plane.
Use 1 grid square to represent 5 students on the *x*-axis, for the *x* interval from 0 to 50.
Use 1 grid square to represent $100 on the *y*-axis, for the *y* interval from 0 to 1000.
For each function, draw a line through the points.

c Use your graph to identify the best deal for 5 teachers and 20 students. Explain.

d Use your graph to identify the best deal for 5 teachers and 50 students. Explain.

PUT ON YOUR THINKING CAP!

© 2020 Marshall Cavendish Education Pte Ltd

Chapter 6 Functions **403**

Relations Between Two Quantities

has   has

Inputs   in which each input has exactly one output are   **Outputs**

Functions   can be   Linear   has equation $y = mx + b$

Nonlinear

can be represented using

Tables   Graphs   Equations   Verbal descriptions

KEY CONCEPTS

- A relation pairs a set of inputs with a set of outputs. It can also be thought of as a rule that describes the relationship between the inputs and outputs.

- The four types of relations are one-to-one, one-to-many, many-to-one, and many-to-many.

- A function is a specific type of relation that assigns only one output to each input. All functions are either one-to-one relations or many-to-one relations.

- Functions can be represented in different ways: algebraically by using an equation, numerically by using tables of values, graphically by graphing the equation or the table of values, and by verbal descriptions.

- Functions can be linear or nonlinear.

- A linear function can be represented by an equation in the slope-intercept form $y = mx + b$. A linear function has a constant rate of change, given by the slope.

- Functions can be increasing or decreasing.

- An increasing function has a positive rate of change. A decreasing function has a negative rate of change.

Name: _____   Date: _____

Given the relation as described, identify the input and the output.

① Kylie wants to find the area of a circle given its radius.

② Mr. Davis wants to find the total cost of the items he bought at a store where every item cost him one dollar.

Given the mapping diagrams, state the type of relation. State whether the relation is a function.

③
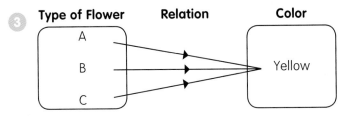

④
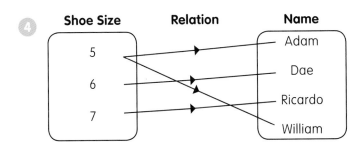

Each table below represents a relation. State whether the relation is a function.

⑤

Side Length (cm)	4	5	8	9
Perimeter (cm)	16	20	32	36

⑥

Month	Jan	Feb	May	Jul	Sep	Oct	Nov	Dec
Number of Public Holidays	2	1	1	1	1	1	2	1

Determine whether each function is linear or nonlinear, and whether it is increasing or decreasing.

⑦

Input, x	2	3	5	6
Output, y	1,500	600	150	60

⑧ The area of a circle, A square centimeters, is a function of its radius, r centimeters, where $A = \pi r^2$.

Solve.

9 During a heavy storm, reservoir engineers decided to open a floodgate to release water from the reservoir at a constant rate of 1 cubic kilometer per hour. Before they opened the gate, there were 29 cubic kilometers of water in the reservoir. The amount of water, y cubic kilometers, in the reservoir is a function of the time, x hours, that the floodgate had been opened.

    a Determine whether the function is linear or nonlinear. Then determine whether the function is increasing or decreasing. Explain.

    b Sketch a graph for the function. Explain what the y-intercept of the graph represents.

10 A scientist is checking to see whether pollutants are causing a decrease in oxygen concentration in a river near a pipe that drains water into the river. She notices that the distance, x meters, downstream from the pipe, and the oxygen concentration, y milligrams per liter, in the water can be represented by the function $y = 0.1x + 2$. The scientist also tested oxygen concentration upstream from the pipe. The graph shows the oxygen concentration as a function of the distance upstream.

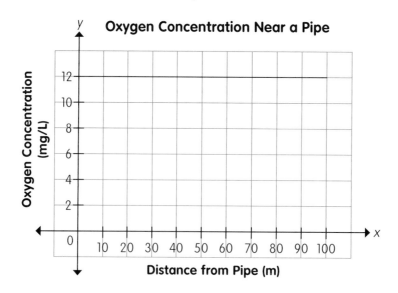

Oxygen Concentration Near a Pipe

    a Represent the function for oxygen concentration upstream using an equation. Graph the function $y = 0.1x + 2$ on the same coordinate plane.

© 2020 Marshall Cavendish Education Pte Ltd

b **Mathematical Habit** **2** **Use mathematical reasoning**
Interpret and compare the rates of change of the two functions.

c **Mathematical Habit** **2** **Use mathematical reasoning**
Give a possible reason for the difference in oxygen concentration upstream and downstream from the pipe.

d At a certain distance downstream from the pipe, the oxygen concentration is equal to the oxygen concentration upstream. What is this distance downstream?

Assessment Prep
Answer each question.

11 Which of these equations represent a linear function, where x is the input and y is the output? Choose all that apply.

Ⓐ $y = 4$

Ⓑ $x = 3$

Ⓒ $y = 3x^2$

Ⓓ $y = \dfrac{x}{3}$

Ⓔ $y = 3x + 4^2$

12 The graph represents y as a function of x.

Which additional points can be plotted so that the graph still represents y as a function of x? Choose all that apply.

Ⓐ $(-4, -1)$

Ⓑ $(-1, -4)$

Ⓒ $(0, 4)$

Ⓓ $(1, 1)$

Ⓔ $(4, 0)$

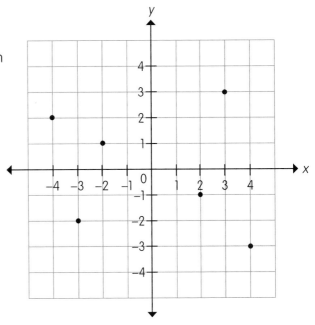

13 The graph shows *y* as a function of *x*.

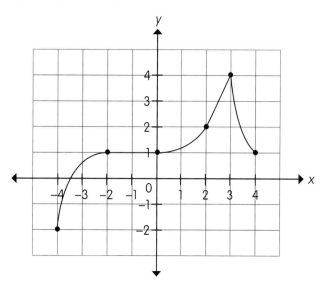

For which intervals is the function **not** increasing? Choose all that apply.

Ⓐ $-4 < x < -2$

Ⓑ $-2 < x < 0$

Ⓒ $0 < x < 2$

Ⓓ $2 < x < 3$

Ⓔ $3 < x < 4$

14 Function A is a linear function. Some values of Function A are shown in the table.

x	−2	−1	1	2
y	4	3	1	0

Function B is a linear function with a *y*-intercept of −4 and and an *x*-intercept of 2.
Which statement is true?

Ⓐ The slope of Function A is greater than the slope of Function B, and the *y*-intercept of Function A is less than the *y*-intercept of Function B.

Ⓑ The slope of Function A is less than the slope of Function B, and the *y*-intercept of Function A is greater than the *y*-intercept of Function B.

Ⓒ The slope of Function A is greater than the slope of Function B, and Function A does not have a *y*-intercept.

Ⓓ The slope of Function A is less than the slope of Function B, and Function A does not have a *y*-intercept.

Food Stands

1 Jack is selling burgers at his food stand outside a football stadium. He made 120 burgers. The table shows the profit, *y* dollars, as a function of the number of burgers sold, *x*. Negative profit represents loss.

Number of Burgers Sold (x)	10	20	30
Profit (y dollars)	−140	−100	−60

a Determine whether the table represents a linear or nonlinear function. Explain.

b What does the rate of change represent?

c Using graph paper, graph the function. Use 1 grid square to represent 5 burgers on the *x*-axis, for the *x* interval from 0 to 60. Use 1 grid square to represent $20 on the *y*-axis, for *y* interval from −200 to 0.

d Find the *x*-intercept and *y*-intercept of the graph. Explain what the values represent.

e What is the cost of making one burger? What is the profit from selling one burger?

f Write the equation representing the function. Find the number of burgers Jack would need to sell to make a profit of $200.

g Jack also bought 200 canned drinks to sell at his food stand. The profit, y dollars, from the sale of the canned drinks as a function of the number of cans sold, x, is represented by the equation $y = 1.25x - 100$. How many cans must Jack sell to recoup the cost of buying 200 canned drinks?

h Compare the rates of change and the y-intercepts of the two functions.

i Are the two functions increasing or decreasing? Explain.

Rubric

Point(s)	Level	My Performance
7–8	4	• Most of my answers are correct. • I showed complete understanding of the concepts. • I used effective and efficient strategies to solve the problems. • I explained my answers and mathematical thinking clearly and completely.
5–6	3	• Some of my answers are correct. • I showed adequate understanding of the concepts. • I used effective strategies to solve the problems. • I explained my answers and mathematical thinking clearly.
3–4	2	• A few of my answers are correct. • I showed some understanding of the concepts. • I used some effective strategies to solve the problems. • I explained some of my answers and mathematical thinking clearly.
0–2	1	• A few of my answers are correct. • I showed little understanding of the concepts. • I used limited effective strategies to solve the problems. • I did not explain my answers and mathematical thinking clearly.

Teacher's Comments

Fuel Efficiency

Have you ever shopped for cars with your family? Perhaps you have visited a car lot or shopped for cars online. In either case, you may have noticed a car's fuel efficiency rating. A car's fuel efficiency, or economy, describes a relationship between distance and fuel consumption.

In the US, a car's fuel efficiency is expressed as the distance a car travels per unit volume of fuel. The distance traveled is x miles, and the volume of fuel is y gallons. So, fuel economy is expressed as miles per gallon.

Task

Work in small groups to research the factors that affect a vehicle's fuel efficiency.

1. Choose three different car manufacturers and one car model built by each manufacturer. Select different car models, such as coupes, sedans, SUVs, and trucks. Note the fuel-efficiency rating of each car.

2. Use the fuel efficiency ratings to write equations representing the functions relating distance traveled per volume of fuel. Use graph paper to graph the functions for the three car models on the same coordinate plane.

3. Write a description of each model's fuel economy and the factors that affect it. Share your work. Discuss potential economic, social, and environmental implications of your findings as a class.

How loud is loud?

The human ear can hear a range of noises, from a soft whisper to the enormous blast of a rocket being launched into space. The intensity of sound is measured using a scale that involves powers of 10. A general rule of thumb is that if a noise sounds ten times as loud to your ears as another noise, the intensity is 10 decibels greater for the louder noise. In this chapter, you will learn how to use exponents to compare quantities such as the intensities of different noises.

How do you represent repeated multiplication of the same factor?

Name: _____ Date: _____

Interpreting the real number system

The real number system is a combination of the set of rational numbers and the set of irrational numbers.

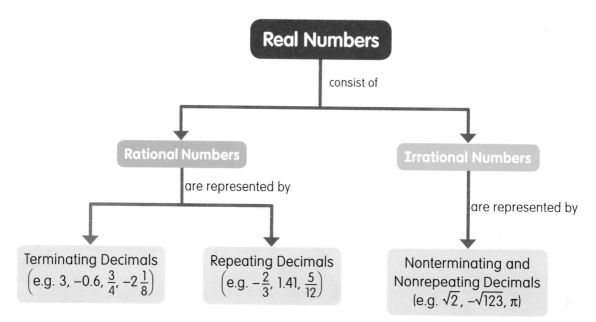

Unlike rational numbers, irrational numbers do not have exact values. You use rational approximations of irrational numbers to compare the size of irrational numbers and locate them approximately on a number line.

▶ **Quick Check**

Locate each irrational number on a number line.

 $\sqrt[3]{-47}$

 $\sqrt{19}$

Adding and subtracting integers

You can use a number line to add and subtract integers. When you add a positive integer, move to the right on the number line. When you add a negative integer, move to the left. You can also use these rules.

Adding or Subtracting Integers	Rule	Expression
Add integers with the same sign.	Add the absolute values and keep the same sign.	$3 + 5 = 8$
Add integers with different signs.	Subtract the absolute values and use the sign of the number with the greater absolute value.	$-5 + 8 = 3$
Subtract two integers.	Add the opposite of the number being subtracted.	$8 - 3$ $= 8 + (-3)$ $= 5$

▶ **Quick Check**

Evaluate each expression.

 3 $-3 + (-4)$

4 $-4 - (-2)$

Multiplying and dividing integers

You multiply or divide integers just as you do whole numbers, except you must keep track of the signs. To multiply or divide integers, always multiply or divide the absolute values, and use these rules to determine the sign of the result.

Multiplying or Dividing Integers	Rule	Expression
Multiply or divide two integers with the same sign.	Multiply or divide the absolute values of the numbers and make the result positive.	$24 \cdot 4 = 96$ $(-24) \div (-4) = 6$
Multiply or divide two integers with different signs.	Multiply or divide the absolute values of the numbers and make the result negative.	$25 \cdot (-5) = -125$ $(-25) \div 5 = -5$

▶ **Quick Check**

Evaluate each expression.

⑤ $(-7) \cdot (-3)$

⑥ $(-12) \div 3$

Finding the square of a whole number

5^2 is called the square of 5. The square of a whole number is called a perfect square. Since $5 \times 5 = 25$, 25 is a perfect square.

▶ **Quick Check**

Find the square of each number.

⑦ 9

⑧ 12

Finding the cube of a whole number

4^3 is called the cube of 4. The cube of a whole number is called a perfect cube. Since $4 \times 4 \times 4 = 64$, 64 is a perfect cube.

▶ **Quick Check**

Find the cube of each number.

⑨ 8

⑩ 11

Exponential Notation

Learning Objectives:
- Write in exponential notation.
- Expand and evaluate expressions in exponential notation.
- Use exponents to write the prime factorization of a number.

> **New Vocabulary**
> exponential notation

THINK

Lily cut a piece of paper in half and threw away the other half. She continued cutting the remaining paper in half until she had a piece of paper whose area was $\frac{1}{64}$ as large as the area of the original piece of paper. How many cuts did she make? Explain how the number of cuts made is related to the final size of the paper relative to the original size.

ENGAGE

The square of 3 is 3^2. The cube of 2 is 2^3. Which is greater, 3^2 or 2^3? Explain your reasoning. Now, compare these two numbers. Which is greater? How do you know?

a $10 \cdot 10 \cdot 10 \cdot 10 \cdot 10$

b $5 \cdot 5 \cdot 5 \cdot 5 \cdot 5 \cdot 5 \cdot 5 \cdot 5 \cdot 5$

LEARN   Write numbers in exponential notation

1. On the decibel scale, the smallest audible sound (near total silence) has an intensity of 0 decibel (dB). A lawnmower is 90 dB or 1,000,000,000 times louder than near total silence.

You can use exponential notation to describe this increase in sound intensity.

$$1{,}000{,}000{,}000 = \underbrace{10 \cdot 10 \cdot 10 \cdot 10 \cdot 10 \cdot 10 \cdot 10 \cdot 10 \cdot 10}_{9 \text{ times}}$$
$$= 10^9 \longleftarrow \text{exponent}$$
$$\underset{\text{base}}{\uparrow}$$

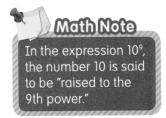

> **Math Note**
> In the expression 10^9, the number 10 is said to be "raised to the 9th power."

The expression 10^9 is written in exponential notation to show repeated multiplication of the factor 10. The exponent represents how many times the base is used as a factor.

2. Tell whether the statement $2 \cdot 2 \cdot 2 = 6^2$ is correct. If it is incorrect, state the reason.

The statement is incorrect. The base is 2, not 6, and the exponent is 3, not 2.

So, $2 \cdot 2 \cdot 2 = 2^3$.

3. Write $5 \cdot 5 \cdot 5 \cdot 5$ in exponential notation.

$5 \cdot 5 \cdot 5 \cdot 5 = 5^4$ The base is 5 and the exponent is 4.

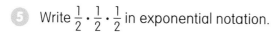
4 Write $(-3) \cdot (-3) \cdot (-3) \cdot (-3) \cdot (-3)$ in exponential notation.

$(-3) \cdot (-3) \cdot (-3) \cdot (-3) \cdot (-3) = (-3)^5$ The base is –3 and the exponent is 5.

In the expression $(-3)^5$, the base is –3 because –3 is inside the parentheses.

5 Write $\frac{1}{2} \cdot \frac{1}{2} \cdot \frac{1}{2}$ in exponential notation.

$\frac{1}{2} \cdot \frac{1}{2} \cdot \frac{1}{2} = \left(\frac{1}{2}\right)^3$ The base is $\frac{1}{2}$ and the exponent is 3.

TRY Practice writing numbers in exponential notation

Determine whether each statement is correct. If it is incorrect, state the reason.

1 $6^3 = 6 \cdot 6 \cdot 6$

2 $5 \cdot 5 = 2^5$

Write each expression in exponential notation.

3 $2 \cdot 2 \cdot 2 \cdot 2 \cdot 2 \cdot 2$

4 $(-4) \cdot (-4) \cdot (-4)$

5 $\frac{2}{3} \cdot \frac{2}{3} \cdot \frac{2}{3} \cdot \frac{2}{3}$

ENGAGE

Sebastian has a cube-shaped box with edges of length 1.2 feet. Using exponents, write an expression to find the volume of the box. Evaluate your expression.

If the volume of another cube-shaped box is 3.375 cubic feet, what is the length of each edge of the box? Explain your thinking.

LEARN Expand and evaluate expressions in exponential notation

1 Expand and evaluate 2.5^3.

$2.5^3 = 2.5 \cdot 2.5 \cdot 2.5$
$= 15.625$

2 Expand and evaluate $(-4)^2$.

$(-4)^2 = (-4) \cdot (-4)$
$= 16$

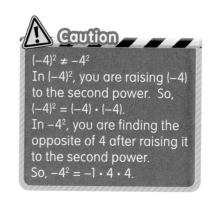

Caution

$(-4)^2 \neq -4^2$
In $(-4)^2$, you are raising (-4) to the second power. So, $(-4)^2 = (-4) \cdot (-4)$.
In -4^2, you are finding the opposite of 4 after raising it to the second power.
So, $-4^2 = -1 \cdot 4 \cdot 4$.

3 Expand and evaluate $\left(\frac{2}{3}\right)^5$.

$\left(\frac{2}{3}\right)^5 = \frac{2}{3} \cdot \frac{2}{3} \cdot \frac{2}{3} \cdot \frac{2}{3} \cdot \frac{2}{3}$
$= \frac{32}{243}$

4 Victoria deposits $100 in a bank account that earns 5% interest, compounded yearly. How much will be in her account at the end of 5 years?

> When interest is compounded yearly, a year's interest is deposited in the account at the end of the year. During the next year, interest is earned on this larger balance. Because Victoria's deposit increases to 105% of its value each year, she can use the formula $A = P(1 + r)^n$ to find out how much money she has in her account after n years when she invests a principal of P dollars at an interest rate of r%.

$A = P(1 + r)^n$
$\quad = 100(1 + 0.05)^5$ Substitute 100 for P, 5 for n and 0.05 for r.
$\quad = 100(1.05)^5$ Add within the parentheses.
$\quad \approx 127.63$ Round to the nearest hundredth.

$127.63 will be in her account at the end of 5 years.

TRY Practice expanding and evaluating expressions in exponential notation

Expand and evaluate each expression.

1 3^4

2 $(-5)^3$

3 $\left(\dfrac{3}{4}\right)^3$

 Solve.

4 Zachary, at age 25, has $2,000 in his retirement account. It will earn 6% interest, compounded yearly. How much will be in his account when he retires at age 65? Give your answer to the nearest cent.

ENGAGE

Find all of the factors of 60 and 120. Now, express each number as a product of their prime factors. How do you write them in exponential notation? Share your observations.

LEARN Use exponents to write the prime factorization of a number

1 Any composite number can be written as a product of prime factors. This prime factorization of a number can be expressed using exponents.

You may use the following divisibility rules to help you find the prime factors.

A number is divisible by	if ...
2	the last digit is even (0, 2, 4, 6, or 8).
3	the sum of the digits is divisible by 3.
5	the last digit is 0 or 5.
7	the last digit, when doubled, and then subtracted from the number formed by the remaining digits, gives a result of 0 or a number divisible by 7.

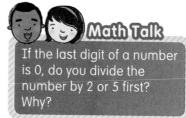

Math Talk

If the last digit of a number is 0, do you divide the number by 2 or 5 first? Why?

2 Write the prime factorization of 81 in exponential notation.

$81 = 3 \cdot 27$
$\quad = 3 \cdot 3 \cdot 9$
$\quad = \mathbf{3 \cdot 3 \cdot 3 \cdot 3}$
$\quad = 3^4$

3	81
3	27
3	9
3	3
	1

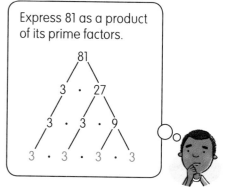

Express 81 as a product of its prime factors.

3 Write the prime factorization of 1,470 in exponential notation.

$1{,}470 = 5 \cdot 294$
$\quad\quad = 5 \cdot 2 \cdot 147$
$\quad\quad = 5 \cdot 2 \cdot 3 \cdot 49$
$\quad\quad = \mathbf{5 \cdot 2 \cdot 3 \cdot 7 \cdot 7}$
$\quad\quad = 2 \cdot 3 \cdot 5 \cdot 7^2$

5	1,470
2	294
3	147
7	49
7	7
	1

For 1,470, $1 + 4 + 7 + 0 = 12$. So, 1,470 is also divisible by 3.

TRY Practice using exponents to write the prime factorization of a number

Write the prime factorization of each number in exponential notation.

1 625

2 630

INDEPENDENT PRACTICE

Determine whether each statement is correct. If it is incorrect, state the reason.

1. $24^3 = 2 \cdot 4 \cdot 4 \cdot 4$

2. $(-2)^5 = 2 \cdot 2 \cdot 2 \cdot 2 \cdot 2$

Write each expression in exponential notation.

3. $\frac{1}{3} \cdot \frac{1}{3}$

4. $5 \cdot 5 \cdot 5 \cdot 5$

5. $(-2) \cdot (-2) \cdot (-2)$

6. $0.12 \cdot 0.12 \cdot 0.12 \cdot 0.12 \cdot 0.12$

Expand and evaluate each expression.

7. 2^3

8. $\left(\frac{3}{8}\right)^4$

9. 10^4

10. -3.4^4

Write the prime factorization of each number in exponential notation.

11 125

12 4,802

 Solve.

13 A bank account has $500 in it. Use the formula $A = P(1 + r)^n$ to find out how much will be in the account in 20 years if it earns 8% interest, compounded yearly. Give your answer to the nearest cent.

2 The Product and the Quotient of Powers

Learning Objectives:
- Use the product of powers property.
- Use the quotient of powers property.

THINK

Jupiter is 10^8 kilometers from the Sun. An asteroid is 100 times this distance from the Sun. How far is the asteroid from the Sun? The dwarf planet Eris is 10^{10} kilometers from the Sun. How many times as far as Jupiter is Eris from the Sun? Write each answer in exponential notation.

ENGAGE

Expand $2^3 \cdot 2^4$. Now, expand 2^7. What do you notice? Expand $10^2 \cdot 10^5$. Now, expand 10^7. What do you notice? Share your observations.

Write a rule for multiplying two numbers with the same base. Create another example in which your rule applies. Discuss your work.

LEARN Use the product of powers property

1. You have learned that
    $$10^6 = 10 \cdot 10 \cdot 10 \cdot 10 \cdot 10 \cdot 10$$
    and that $10^9 = 10 \cdot 10 \cdot 10 \cdot 10 \cdot 10 \cdot 10 \cdot 10 \cdot 10 \cdot 10$.

    $10^6 \cdot 10^9 = \underbrace{(10 \cdot 10 \cdot 10 \cdot 10 \cdot 10 \cdot 10)}_{\textbf{6 factors}} \cdot \underbrace{(10 \cdot 10 \cdot 10 \cdot 10 \cdot 10 \cdot 10 \cdot 10 \cdot 10 \cdot 10)}_{\textbf{9 factors}}$

    $= \underbrace{10 \cdot 10 \cdot 10 \cdot 10 \cdot 10 \cdot 10 \cdot 10 \cdot 10 \cdot 10 \cdot 10 \cdot 10 \cdot 10 \cdot 10 \cdot 10 \cdot 10}_{\textbf{15 factors}}$

    $= 10^{15}$

    So, $10^6 \cdot 10^9 = 10^{6+9}$
    $= 10^{15}$.

    Notice that 10^6 and 10^9 have the same base. You apply the same reasoning to find the product of any powers that have the same base.

    $a^4 \cdot a^3 = \underbrace{(a \cdot a \cdot a \cdot a)}_{\textbf{4 factors}} \cdot \underbrace{(a \cdot a \cdot a)}_{\textbf{3 factors}}$

    $= \underbrace{a \cdot a \cdot a \cdot a \cdot a \cdot a \cdot a}_{\textbf{7 factors}}$

    $= a^7$.

    So, $a^4 \cdot a^3 = a^{4+3}$
    $= a^7$.

When you find the product of two algebraic expressions with the same base, you add their exponents and use this exponent with the same base.

$$a^m \cdot a^n = a^{m+n}$$

2 Simplify $(-4)^2 \cdot (-4)^4$. Write your answer in exponential notation.

$(-4)^2 \cdot (-4)^4 = (-4)^{2+4}$ Use the product of powers property.

$ = (-4)^6$ Simplify.

3 Simplify $1.2 \cdot 1.2^4$. Write your answer in exponential notation.

$1.2 \cdot 1.2^4 = 1.2^{1+4}$ Use the product of powers property.

$ = 1.2^5$ Simplify.

When a number or variable does not have an exponent, it means the number or variable is raised to the first power.

Math Talk

Explain why $2^4 \cdot 3^4 \neq (2 \cdot 3)^8$.

4 Simplify $2x^4y^2 \cdot 3x^2y^6$. Write your answer in exponential notation.

$2x^4y^2 \cdot 3x^2y^6 = 2 \cdot x^4 \cdot y^2 \cdot 3 \cdot x^2 \cdot y^6$ Rewrite the product.

$ = 2 \cdot 3 \cdot x^4 \cdot x^2 \cdot y^2 \cdot y^6$ Regroup the numbers, and regroup the factors with the same bases.

$ = 6 \cdot x^{4+2} \cdot y^{2+6}$ Add the exponents of the factors with the same base.

$ = 6x^6y^8$ Simplify.

TRY Practice using the product of powers property

Simplify each expression. Write each answer in exponential notation.

1 $(-5) \cdot (-5)^5$

2 $\left(\dfrac{1}{5}\right)^3 \cdot \left(\dfrac{1}{5}\right)^4$

3 $4s^4t^3 \cdot 5s^4t^6$

ENGAGE

Expand 10^4 and 10^2. What is $10^4 \div 10^2$? Use two methods to solve.
Now, use each of your methods to solve $3^6 \div 3^4$.
How are these problems the same? How are they different? Discuss.

LEARN Use the quotient of powers property

1. How are the exponents in 5^5 and 5^2 related to the exponent of their quotient?

$5^5 \div 5^2 = (5 \cdot 5 \cdot 5 \cdot 5 \cdot 5) \div (5 \cdot 5)$

$$= \frac{\overbrace{5 \cdot 5 \cdot 5 \cdot 5 \cdot 5}^{\text{5 factors}}}{\underbrace{5 \cdot 5}_{\text{2 factors}}}$$

$= \underbrace{5 \cdot 5 \cdot 5}_{\text{3 factors}}$

$= 5^3$.

Notice that $5^3 = 5^{5-2}$. You find the exponent of the quotient by subtracting the exponent of the divisor from the exponent of the dividend.

So, $5^5 \div 5^2 = 5^{5-2}$
$\qquad\qquad = 5^3$.

$y^7 \div y^4 = (y \cdot y \cdot y \cdot y \cdot y \cdot y \cdot y) \div (y \cdot y \cdot y \cdot y)$

$$= \frac{\overbrace{y \cdot y \cdot y \cdot y \cdot y \cdot y \cdot y}^{\text{7 factors}}}{\underbrace{y \cdot y \cdot y \cdot y}_{\text{4 factors}}}$$

$= \underbrace{y \cdot y \cdot y}_{\text{3 factors}}$

$= y^3$.

So, $y^7 \div y^4 = y^{7-4}$
$\qquad\qquad = y^3$.

When you find the quotient of two algebraic expressions with the same base, you subtract the exponent of the divisor from the exponent of the dividend and use it with the common base.

$$a^m \div a^n = \frac{a^m}{a^n} = a^{m-n}, a \neq 0$$

2 Simplify $(-7)^5 \div (-7)$. Write your answer in exponential notation.

$(-7)^5 \div (-7)$
$= (-7)^{5-1}$ Use the quotient of powers property.
$= (-7)^4$ Simplify.

3 Simplify $3.5^8 \div 3.5^6$. Write your answer in exponential notation.

$3.5^8 \div 3.5^6$
$= 3.5^{8-6}$ Use the quotient of powers property.
$= 3.5^2$ Simplify.

 Math Talk

Can you use the quotient of powers property to simplify $5^4 \div 3^{20}$? Explain why.

4 Simplify $28m^7n^4 \div 7m^3n^2$. Write your answer in exponential notation.

$28m^7n^4 \div 7m^3n^2$
$= \dfrac{28m^7n^4}{7m^3n^2}$ Write the quotient as a fraction.
$= \dfrac{28}{7} \cdot \dfrac{m^7}{m^3} \cdot \dfrac{n^4}{n^2}$ Rewrite the fraction as a product of three fractions.
$= 4 \cdot m^{7-3} \cdot n^{4-2}$ Use the quotient of powers property.
$= 4m^4n^2$ Simplify.

TRY Practice using the quotient of powers property

Simplify each expression. Write each answer in exponential notation.

1 $10^8 \div 10^5$

2 $2.7^9 \div 2.7^6$

3 $63x^9y^7 \div 9x^3y^4$

Is $a^3 \cdot a \cdot a^2 = a^{3+1+2}$? Is $\dfrac{a^6}{a^3} = a^{6-3}$. Explain your thinking.

How do you simplify $\dfrac{a^3 \cdot a \cdot a^2}{a \cdot a \cdot a}$? Discuss.

Create a problem involving multiplying and dividing expressions in exponential notation. Trade with your partner. Simplify the expression. Write your answer in exponential notation.

LEARN Multiply and divide expressions in exponential notation

① You may have to use both the product of powers and quotient of powers properties together to simplify expressions.

② Simplify $\dfrac{\left(\frac{1}{4}\right)^3 \cdot \left(\frac{1}{4}\right) \cdot \left(\frac{1}{4}\right)^2}{\left(\frac{1}{4}\right) \cdot \left(\frac{1}{4}\right) \cdot \left(\frac{1}{4}\right)}$. Write your answer in exponential notation.

$$\dfrac{\left(\frac{1}{4}\right)^3 \cdot \left(\frac{1}{4}\right) \cdot \left(\frac{1}{4}\right)^2}{\left(\frac{1}{4}\right) \cdot \left(\frac{1}{4}\right) \cdot \left(\frac{1}{4}\right)} = \dfrac{\left(\frac{1}{4}\right)^{3+1+2}}{\left(\frac{1}{4}\right)^{1+1+1}}$$ Use the product of powers property.

$$= \dfrac{\left(\frac{1}{4}\right)^6}{\left(\frac{1}{4}\right)^3}$$ Simplify.

$$= \left(\frac{1}{4}\right)^{6-3}$$ Use the quotient of powers property.

$$= \left(\frac{1}{4}\right)^3$$ Simplify.

> All the numbers in the numerator and denominator have the same base. You use the product of powers property before using the quotient of powers property.

3 Simplify $\dfrac{3x^4 \cdot 5y^5 \cdot 6x^6}{2y \cdot 3x^2 \cdot 5y^3}$. Write your answer in exponential notation.

$$\dfrac{3x^4 \cdot 5y^5 \cdot 6x^6}{2y \cdot 3x^2 \cdot 5y^3} = \dfrac{3 \cdot 5 \cdot 6 \cdot x^4 \cdot x^6 \cdot y^5}{2 \cdot 3 \cdot 5 \cdot x^2 \cdot y \cdot y^3}$$
Regroup the numbers, and regroup the factors with the same bases.

$$= \dfrac{90x^{4+6}y^5}{30x^2y^{1+3}}$$
Use the product of powers property.

$$= \dfrac{3x^{10}y^5}{x^2y^4}$$
Simplify.

$$= 3(x^{10-2})(y^{5-4})$$
Use the quotient of powers property.

$$= 3x^8y$$
Simplify.

TRY **Practice multiplying and dividing expressions in exponential notation**

Simplify each expression. Write each answer in exponential notation.

1 $\dfrac{7.5^5 \cdot 7.5^3 \cdot 7.5}{7.5^2 \cdot 7.5 \cdot 7.5^4}$

2 $\dfrac{b^5 \cdot 4a^4 \cdot 9a^3}{2a^2 \cdot b^2 \cdot 6a^2}$

3 $\dfrac{\left(-\dfrac{1}{3}\right)^3 \cdot \left(-\dfrac{1}{3}\right)^6 \cdot \left(-\dfrac{1}{3}\right)^5}{\left(-\dfrac{1}{3}\right)^5 \cdot \left(-\dfrac{1}{3}\right) \cdot \left(-\dfrac{1}{3}\right)^2}$

INDEPENDENT PRACTICE

Simplify each expression. Write each answer in exponential notation.

1 $(-2)^6 \cdot (-2)^2$

2 $7.2^3 \cdot 7.2^4$

3 $\left(\dfrac{2}{3}\right) \cdot \left(\dfrac{2}{3}\right)^5$

4 $p \cdot p^8$

5 $xy^2 \cdot x^4 y^3$

6 $2.5x^3 y^6 \cdot 3x^2 y^4$

7 $(-3)^4 \div (-3)^2$

8 $\left(-\dfrac{1}{6}\right)^5 \div \left(-\dfrac{1}{6}\right)^2$

9 $h^2k^5 \div hk^4$

10 $64a^8b^5 \div 4a^3b^2$

11 $\dfrac{5^9 \cdot 5^7 \cdot 5^8}{5^3 \cdot 5^2 \cdot 5}$

12 $\dfrac{\left(\frac{4}{9}\right)^6 \cdot \left(\frac{4}{9}\right)^5 \cdot \left(\frac{4}{9}\right)^4}{\left(\frac{4}{9}\right)^3 \cdot \left(\frac{4}{9}\right)^3 \cdot \left(\frac{4}{9}\right)^4}$

13 $\dfrac{a^9 \cdot a^2 \cdot a^3}{a^6 \cdot a^3 \cdot a^4}$

14 $\dfrac{4c^6 \cdot 3b^4 \cdot 9c^5}{b^3 \cdot 6c^3 \cdot 2c^3}$

3 The Power of a Power

Learning Objective:
• Use the power of a power property.

💡THINK

It is given that $(p \cdot p \cdot p^2) = a^{12}$ and $(q \cdot q)^2 = a^{12}$. Express p and q in exponetial notation in terms of a.

How do you write $(p \cdot q)^2$ in exponetial notation in terms of a?

ENGAGE

Show the steps to solve $(2 \cdot 2)^4$. Now, solve $(2^2)^4$. How does the order of operations apply to solving these problems? What pattern can you see?

How can you make use of the pattern to solve $(5^2)^5$? Discuss.

LEARN Use the power of a power property

1. You can use the order of operations to evaluate the expression $(2^4)^3$. First, evaluate the expression inside the parentheses. Then, use 16 as a factor 3 times.

$$(2^4)^3 = (2 \cdot 2 \cdot 2 \cdot 2)^3$$
$$= (16)^3$$
$$= 16 \cdot 16 \cdot 16$$
$$= 4,096$$

You can also evaluate the expression $(2^4)^3$ by using 2 as a factor 12 times.

$$(2^4)^3 = (2 \cdot 2 \cdot 2 \cdot 2)^3$$
$$= \underbrace{(2 \cdot 2 \cdot 2 \cdot 2) \cdot (2 \cdot 2 \cdot 2 \cdot 2) \cdot (2 \cdot 2 \cdot 2 \cdot 2)}_{\text{3 groups of 4 factors}}$$
$$= \underbrace{2^{4 \cdot 3}}_{4 \cdot 3 = \text{12 factors of 2}}$$
$$= 2^{12}$$
$$= 4,096$$

You use the same method to evaluate $(n^2)^5$.

$$(n^2)^5 = (n \cdot n)^5$$
$$= \underbrace{(n \cdot n) \cdot (n \cdot n) \cdot (n \cdot n) \cdot (n \cdot n) \cdot (n \cdot n)}_{\text{5 groups of 2 factors}}$$
$$= \underbrace{n^{2 \cdot 5}}_{2 \cdot 5 = \text{10 factors of } n}$$
$$= n^{10}$$

When you raise a power to a power, keep the base and multiply the exponents.

$$(a^m)^n = a^{m \cdot n} = a^{mn}$$

2 Simplify $(3^4)^2$. Write your answer in exponential notation.

$(3^4)^2 = 3^{4 \cdot 2}$ Use the power of a power property.

      $= 3^8$ Simplify.

3 Simplify $\left[\left(\dfrac{2}{7}\right)^6\right]^4$. Write your answer in exponential notation.

$\left[\left(\dfrac{2}{7}\right)^6\right]^4 = \left(\dfrac{2}{7}\right)^{6 \cdot 4}$ Use the power of a power property.

            $= \left(\dfrac{2}{7}\right)^{24}$ Simplify.

4 Simplify $[(2a)^5]^3$. Write your answer in exponential notation.

$[(2a)^5]^3 = (2a)^{5 \cdot 3}$ Use the power of a power property.

       $= (2a)^{15}$ Simplify.

5 Simplify $[(-x)^4]^3$. Write your answer in exponential notation.

$[(-x)^4]^3 = (-x)^{4 \cdot 3}$ Use the power of a power property.

       $= (-x)^{12}$ Simplify.

       $= x^{12}$

Activity Exploring the power of a power property

Work in pairs.

In this activity, you and your partner will play a game in which you write and evaluate expressions in the form $(a^m)^n$. You will obtain a point for each expression you write. The person with the greater score wins.

1 Take three stacks of five cards, where the cards of each stack are numbered 1 to 5. Shuffle each stack of cards. You and your partner each randomly draws three cards, one from each stack.

2 **Mathematical Habit 5** **Use tools strategically**

Use your three cards to write an expression in the form $(a^m)^n$. For instance, if you draw 2, 4, and 5, you could write $(2^4)^5$, $(4^2)^5$ or another expression. Write as many expressions as you can. You may want to use a calculator to evaluate your expressions. For instance, to evaluate $(2^4)^5$, use the following keystrokes.

Press (2 ^ 4) ^ 5 ENTER.

③ Record your expressions and their values. Your partner should also record his or her expressions and their values. Check your partner's work.

④ Continue the game by replacing the cards you used and shuffling the stacks. Repeat ① to ③ several times. Find each player's score by counting the number of correct expressions that each player has written. The player with the greater score wins.

⑤ **Mathematical Habit 8 Look for patterns**
Is it correct to assume that using the greatest number drawn as the base will give an expression with the greatest possible value? Explain or give an example.

TRY Practice using the power of a power property

Simplify each expression. Write each answer in exponential notation.

1 $(2.3^4)^2$

2 $[(3p)^5]^4$

3 $[(-y)^4]^7$

ENGAGE

Is $3^4 \cdot 3^2 = 3^{4+2}$? Is $(3^6)^5 = 3^{6 \cdot 5}$? Explain your thinking.

How do you simplify $3^4 \cdot 3^2 \cdot (3^6)^5$ and $\dfrac{(3^6)^5}{3^4 \cdot 3^2}$? Discuss.

Create a problem using at least two properties of exponents. Trade with your partner. Simplify the expression. Write your answer in exponential notation.

LEARN Use properties of exponents to simplify expressions

1 You may need to use more than one property of exponents to simplify expressions.

2 Simplify $[(-4)^2 \cdot (-4)^3]^6$. Write your answer in exponential notation.

$[(-4)^2 \cdot (-4)^3]^6$
$= [(-4)^{2+3}]^6$ Use the product of powers property.
$= [(-4)^5]^6$ Simplify.
$= (-4)^{5 \cdot 6}$ Use the power of a power property.
$= (-4)^{30}$ Simplify.
$= 4^{30}$

> Follow the order of operations. First, use the product of powers property within the brackets. Then, use the power of a power property.

3 Simplify $(m^5 \cdot m)^3$. Write your answer in exponential notation.

$(m^5 \cdot m)^3$
$= (m^{5+1})^3$ Use the product of powers property.
$= (m^6)^3$ Simplify.
$= m^{6 \cdot 3}$ Use the power of a power property.
$= m^{18}$ Simplify.

④ Simplify $\dfrac{(6^4 \cdot 6^3)^4}{(6^2)^5}$. Write your answer in exponential notation.

$$\dfrac{(6^4 \cdot 6^3)^4}{(6^2)^5}$$

$= \dfrac{(6^{4+3})^4}{6^{2 \cdot 5}}$ Use the product of powers and the power of a power properties.

$= \dfrac{(6^7)^4}{6^{10}}$ Simplify.

$= \dfrac{6^{7 \cdot 4}}{6^{10}}$ Use the power of a power property.

$= \dfrac{6^{28}}{6^{10}}$ Simplify.

$= 6^{28-10}$ Use the quotient of powers property.

$= 6^{18}$ Simplify.

⑤ Simplify $(a^4 \cdot a^2)^4 \div 2a^8$. Write your answer in exponential notation.

$(a^4 \cdot a^2)^4 \div 2a^8$

$= (a^{4+2})^4 \div 2a^8$ Use the product of powers property.

$= (a^6)^4 \div 2a^8$ Simplify.

$= a^{6 \cdot 4} \div 2a^8$ Use the power of a power property.

$= a^{24} \div 2a^8$ Simplify.

$= \dfrac{a^{24-8}}{2}$ Use the quotient of powers property.

$= \dfrac{a^{16}}{2}$ Simplify.

**Math Talk**

Suppose a can be any integer in the expression $\dfrac{a^{16}}{2}$. Will the value of the expression be positive or negative? How do you know?

TRY Practice using properties of exponents to simplify expressions

Simplify each expression. Write each answer in exponential notation.

① $[(-3) \cdot (-3)^6]^2$

② $(p^4 \cdot p^2)^5$

③ $(6^3 \cdot 6^3)^7 \div 6^{10}$

④ $\dfrac{(x^8 \cdot x^4)^2}{(x^3)^6}$

INDEPENDENT PRACTICE

Simplify each expression. Write each answer in exponential notation.

1 $(2^6)^2$

2 $(3^4)^3$

3 $(25^3)^3$

4 $(x^6)^3$

5 $\left[\left(\dfrac{1}{8}\right)^3\right]^6$

6 $\left[\left(\dfrac{4}{5}\right)^2\right]^4$

7 $[(2y)^3]^8$

8 $[(57p)^4]^4$

9 $[(-6)^4]^3$

10 $[(-p)^2]^{11}$

11 $(5^5 \cdot 5^6)^2$

12 $(p^4 \cdot p^2)^6$

13 $\left[\left(\dfrac{1}{2}\right) \cdot \left(\dfrac{1}{2}\right)^3\right]^5$

14 $\left[\left(-\dfrac{4}{9}\right)^2 \cdot \left(-\dfrac{4}{9}\right)^3\right]^2$

15 $(2^2 \cdot 2^4)^3 \div 2^8$

16 $(7 \cdot 7^2)^5 \div 7^3$

17 $(s^6 \cdot s)^2 \div s^4$

18 $(t^4 \cdot t^4)^4 \div t^4$

19 $\dfrac{(8^8 \cdot 8^3)^2}{(8^5)^4}$

20 $\dfrac{(3^4 \cdot 3^2)^4}{(3^5)^2}$

21 $\dfrac{(b \cdot b^3)^5}{(b^2)^4}$

22 $\dfrac{(h^6 \cdot h^4)^2}{(h^3)^5}$

23 $(q^5 \cdot q^2)^3 \div 5q^5$

24 $(c^7 \cdot c^3)^4 \div 6c^2$

25 $\dfrac{\left(\frac{2}{3}\right)^2 \cdot \left(\frac{2}{3}\right)^6}{\left(\frac{2^2}{3^2}\right)^3}$

26 $\dfrac{\left(\frac{x}{2}\right)^3 \cdot \left(\frac{x}{2}\right)^4}{\left(\frac{x}{2}\right)^2}$

The Power of a Product and the Power of a Quotient

Learning Objectives:
- Use the power of a product property.
- Use the power of a quotient property.

THINK

Write the prime factorization of 54 in exponential notation.

If , $\frac{(2^a)^2 \cdot 3^b}{(2 \cdot 3)^a}$ what are the values of a and b?

ENGAGE

Solve $(4 \cdot 5) \cdot (4 \cdot 5) \cdot (4 \cdot 5)$ and $4^3 \cdot 5^3$.
What do you notice about your answers? What can you say about $(4 \cdot 5)^3$ and $4^3 \cdot 5^3$?
How can you use your observations to simplify $2^6 \cdot 5^6$? Discuss.

LEARN Use the power of a product property

 You can use the order of operations to evaluate the expression $(4 \cdot 5)^3$. First, evaluate the expression inside the parentheses. Then, use 20 as a factor 3 times.

$$(4 \cdot 5)^3 = (20)^3$$
$$= 20 \cdot 20 \cdot 20$$
$$= 8{,}000$$

You can also evaluate the expression $(4 \cdot 5)^3$ by using $(4 \cdot 5)$ as a factor 3 times.

$$(4 \cdot 5)^3 = (4 \cdot 5) \cdot (4 \cdot 5) \cdot (4 \cdot 5)$$
$$= \underbrace{(4 \quad \cdot \quad 4 \quad \cdot \quad 4)}_{\textbf{3 factors of 4}} \cdot \underbrace{(5 \quad \cdot \quad 5 \quad \cdot \quad 5)}_{\textbf{3 factors of 5}}$$
$$= 4^3 \cdot 5^3$$
$$= 64 \cdot 125$$
$$= 8{,}000$$

You can use the same method to evaluate $(h \cdot k)^4$.

$$(h \cdot k)^4 = (h \cdot k) \cdot (h \cdot k) \cdot (h \cdot k) \cdot (h \cdot k)$$
$$= \underbrace{(h \quad \cdot \quad h \quad \cdot \quad h \quad \cdot \quad h)}_{\textbf{4 factors of } h} \cdot \underbrace{(k \quad \cdot \quad k \quad \cdot \quad k \quad \cdot \quad k)}_{\textbf{4 factors of } k}$$
$$= h^4 \cdot k^4$$

For expressions with the same exponent, you can distribute the exponent to each base.

$$(a \cdot b)^m = a^m \cdot b^m$$

Similarly, to find the product of two algebraic expressions with the same exponent, you can multiply their bases.

$$a^m \cdot b^m = (a \cdot b)^m$$

2 Simplify $3^4 \cdot 7^4$. Write your answer in exponential notation.

$3^4 \cdot 7^4 = (3 \cdot 7)^4$　　Use the power of a product property.
　　　 $= 21^4$　　　　Simplify.

3 Simplify $\left(-\dfrac{1}{3}\right)^5 \cdot \left(-\dfrac{2}{5}\right)^5$. Write your answer in exponential notation.

$\left(-\dfrac{1}{3}\right)^5 \cdot \left(-\dfrac{2}{5}\right)^5 = \left[\left(-\dfrac{1}{3}\right) \cdot \left(-\dfrac{2}{5}\right)\right]^5$　　Use the power of a product property.

　　　　　　$= \left(\dfrac{2}{15}\right)^5$　　　　Simplify.

4 Simplify $(2r)^5 \cdot (7s)^5$. Write your answer in exponential notation.

$(2r)^5 \cdot (7s)^5 = (2r \cdot 7s)^5$　　Use the power of a product property.
　　　　 $= (14rs)^5$　　Simplify.

TRY Practice using the power of a product property

Simplify each expression. Write each answer in exponential notation.

1 $6^3 \cdot 7^3$

2 $\left(-\dfrac{5}{6}\right)^4 \cdot \left(-\dfrac{1}{4}\right)^4$

3 $(3a)^4 \cdot (4b)^4$

ENGAGE

Solve $\frac{2}{3} \cdot \frac{2}{3} \cdot \frac{2}{3} \cdot \frac{2}{3} \cdot \frac{2}{3}$ and $\frac{2^5}{3^5}$.

What do you notice about your answers? What can you say about $\left(\frac{2}{3}\right)^5$ and $\frac{2^5}{3^5}$?

How can you use your observations to simplify $8^6 \div 4^6$? Discuss.

LEARN Use the power of a quotient property

1 You can evaluate the expression $\left(\frac{2}{3}\right)^5$ by using $\frac{2}{3}$ as a factor 5 times.

$$\left(\frac{2}{3}\right)^5 = \frac{2}{3} \cdot \frac{2}{3} \cdot \frac{2}{3} \cdot \frac{2}{3} \cdot \frac{2}{3}$$

$$= \frac{\overbrace{2 \cdot 2 \cdot 2 \cdot 2 \cdot 2}^{\textbf{5 factors} \text{ of } 2}}{\underbrace{3 \cdot 3 \cdot 3 \cdot 3 \cdot 3}_{\textbf{5 factors} \text{ of } 3}}$$

$$= \frac{2^5}{3^5}$$

$$= \frac{32}{243}$$

You can use the same method to evaluate $\left(\frac{s}{t}\right)^4$.

$$\left(\frac{s}{t}\right)^4 = \frac{s}{t} \cdot \frac{s}{t} \cdot \frac{s}{t} \cdot \frac{s}{t}$$

$$= \frac{\overbrace{s \cdot s \cdot s \cdot s}^{\textbf{4 factors} \text{ of } s}}{\underbrace{t \cdot t \cdot t \cdot t}_{\textbf{4 factors} \text{ of } t}}$$

$$= \frac{s^4}{t^4}$$

For expressions with the same exponent, you can distribute the exponent to each base.

$$\left(\frac{a}{b}\right)^m = \frac{a^m}{b^m}, \ b \neq 0$$

Similarly, to you find the quotient of two algebraic expressions with the same exponent, you can divide their bases.

$$\frac{a^m}{b^m} = \left(\frac{a}{b}\right)^m, \ b \neq 0$$

You can use this property to simplify algebraic expressions like the one shown below.

$$\left(\frac{2m}{6n}\right)^3 = \frac{(2m)^3}{(6n)^3}$$
$$= \frac{8m^3}{216n^3}$$
$$= \frac{m^3}{27n^3}$$

Reduce fractions to the simplest form when possible.

2 Simplify $2^4 \div 6^4$. Write your answer in exponential notation.

$$2^4 \div 6^4 = \left(\frac{2}{6}\right)^4 \quad \text{Use the power of a quotient property.}$$
$$= \left(\frac{1}{3}\right)^4 \quad \text{Simplify.}$$

3 Simplify $(-8)^5 \div (-2)^5$. Write your answer in exponential notation.

$$(-8)^5 \div (-2)^5 = \left(\frac{-8}{-2}\right)^5 \quad \text{Use the power of a quotient property.}$$
$$= 4^5 \quad \text{Simplify.}$$

4 Simplify $(5x)^9 \div (4y)^9$. Write your answer in exponential notation.

$$(5x)^9 \div (4y)^9 = \left(\frac{5x}{4y}\right)^9 \quad \text{Use the power of a quotient property.}$$

TRY Practice using the power of a quotient property

Simplify each expression. Write each answer in exponential notation.

1 $2^5 \div 4^5$

2 $(-9)^3 \div (-3)^3$

3 $(8p)^5 \div (3q)^5$

What properties of exponents are required to simplify $\frac{6^3 \cdot 6^2}{3^2 \cdot 3^3}$?

List the properties you used in the order they were needed. Explain your thinking.

Can you do it in another way? Discuss.

LEARN Use properties of exponents to simplify expressions

1   Simplify $\frac{4^5 \cdot 4^3}{2^2 \cdot 2^6}$. Write your answer in exponential notation.

$$\frac{4^5 \cdot 4^3}{2^2 \cdot 2^6} = \frac{4^{5+3}}{2^{2+6}} \qquad \text{Use the product of powers property.}$$

$$= \frac{4^8}{2^8} \qquad \text{Simplify.}$$

$$= \left(\frac{4}{2}\right)^8 \qquad \text{Use the power of a quotient property.}$$

$$= 2^8 \qquad \text{Simplify.}$$

2   Simplify $\frac{5^5 \cdot 2^9 \cdot 5^4}{10^3}$. Write your answer in exponential notation.

$$\frac{5^5 \cdot 2^9 \cdot 5^4}{10^3} = \frac{5^{5+4} \cdot 2^9}{10^3} \qquad \text{Use the product of powers property.}$$

$$= \frac{5^9 \cdot 2^9}{10^3} \qquad \text{Simplify.}$$

$$= \frac{(5 \cdot 2)^9}{10^3} \qquad \text{Use the power of a product property.}$$

$$= \frac{10^9}{10^3} \qquad \text{Simplify.}$$

$$= 10^{9-3} \qquad \text{Use the quotient of powers property.}$$

$$= 10^6 \qquad \text{Simplify.}$$

3   Simplify $\frac{(7^2)^3 \cdot 4^6}{2^6}$. Write your answer in exponential notation.

$$\frac{(7^2)^3 \cdot 4^6}{2^6} = \frac{7^{2 \cdot 3} \cdot 4^6}{2^6} \qquad \text{Use the power of a power property.}$$

$$= \frac{7^6 \cdot 4^6}{2^6} \qquad \text{Simplify.}$$

$$= \frac{(7 \cdot 4)^6}{2^6} \qquad \text{Use the power of a product property.}$$

$$= \frac{28^6}{2^6} \qquad \text{Simplify.}$$

$$= \left(\frac{28}{2}\right)^6 \qquad \text{Use the power of a quotient property.}$$

$$= 14^6 \qquad \text{Simplify.}$$

Simplify each expression. Write each answer in exponential notation.

1 $\dfrac{6^4 \cdot 6^3}{3^2 \cdot 3^5}$

2 $\dfrac{4^6 \cdot 3^8 \cdot 4^2}{12^5}$

3 $\dfrac{(25^3)^2 \cdot 7^6}{5^6}$

You use the properties of exponents to first simplify the numerator and denominator. Look for more than one property of exponents to use.

INDEPENDENT PRACTICE

Simplify each expression. Write each answer in exponential notation.

1 $5^4 \cdot 6^4$

2 $5.4^3 \cdot 4.5^3$

3 $(2x)^5 \cdot (3y)^5$

4 $(2.5a)^6 \cdot (1.6b)^6$

5 $9^2 \div 3^2$

6 $2.8^7 \div 0.7^7$

7 $(3.3x)^9 \div (1.1y)^9$

8 $(3a)^6 \div (2b)^6$

9 $\left(\dfrac{32m^6}{4n^4}\right)^2$

10 $\dfrac{9^2 \cdot 9^7}{3^5 \cdot 3^4}$

11 $\dfrac{6^5 \cdot 2^3 \cdot 6^4}{12^3}$

12 $\dfrac{(5^4)^2 \cdot 6^8}{10^8}$

13 $\dfrac{24^9}{4^3 \cdot 6^2 \cdot 4^6}$

14 $\dfrac{9^{12}}{(3^3)^3 \cdot 3^3}$

5 Zero and Negative Exponents

Learning Objectives:
- Simplify expressions involving the zero exponent.
- Simplify expressions involving negative exponents.

THINK

Write two expressions in exponential notation that are equivalent to $\frac{x^{-8}}{x^0}$, where x is any number except zero.

ENGAGE

Use one of the properties of exponents to simplify $2^4 \div 2^2$ and $2^4 \div 2^3$.
How do you use the same property to simplify $2^4 \div 2^4$? Explain your thinking.
Discuss whether $2^0 = 1$. Create an example to justify your reasoning.

Now, choose a nonzero number. Raise it to the zero power. What is the answer? Will you have same answer if you choose other base numbers? Explain your thinking.

LEARN Simplify expressions involving the zero exponent

 Understanding the zero exponent

Work in pairs.

① Use the quotient of powers property to simplify each expression. Write each answer in exponential notation.

Expression	Exponential Notation
$\frac{3^5}{3^2}$	3^3
$\frac{3^5}{3^3}$	
$\frac{3^5}{3^4}$	
$\frac{3^5}{3^5}$	

What expression did you write for $\frac{3^5}{3^5}$? What exponent did you obtain?

② In factored form, the quotient $\frac{3^5}{3^5}$ is $\frac{3 \cdot 3 \cdot 3 \cdot 3 \cdot 3}{3 \cdot 3 \cdot 3 \cdot 3 \cdot 3}$. If you divide out all the common factors in the numerator and denominator, what is the value of $\frac{3^5}{3^5}$?

③ Based on your findings, what can you conclude about the value of 3^0?

④ **Mathematical Habit 5** Use tools strategically
Make a prediction about the value of any nonzero number raised to the zero power. Then, use a calculator to check your prediction for several numbers. For example, to raise the number –2 to the zero power, use the following keystrokes.

Press 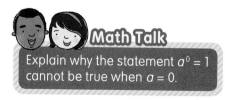.

Does your prediction hold true?

① You have seen that when a number such as 3 is raised to the zero power, its value is 1. In fact, any number except 0 raised to the zero power is equal to 1.

> A nonzero number raised to the zero power is equal to 1.
> $$a^0 = 1, \ a \neq 0$$

Math Talk
Explain why the statement $a^0 = 1$ cannot be true when $a = 0$.

© 2020 Marshall Cavendish Education Pte Ltd

2 Simplify and evaluate $7^3 \cdot 7^0$.

$$7^3 \cdot 7^0 = 7^3 \cdot 1 \qquad \text{Raise to the zero power.}$$
$$= 7^3 \qquad \text{Simplify.}$$
$$= 343 \qquad \text{Evaluate.}$$

> In this case, you can also use the product of powers property to solve.
>
> $7^3 \cdot 7^0 = 7^{3+0}$
> $\quad\quad\ = 7^3$
> $\quad\quad\ = 343$

3 Simplify and evaluate $1 \cdot 10^2 + 2 \cdot 10^1 + 3 \cdot 10^0$.

$$1 \cdot 10^2 + 2 \cdot 10^1 + 3 \cdot 10^0$$
$$= 1 \cdot 100 + 2 \cdot 10 + 3 \cdot 1 \qquad \text{Raise to the zero power.}$$
$$= 100 + 20 + 3 \qquad \text{Simplify.}$$
$$= 123 \qquad \text{Evaluate.}$$

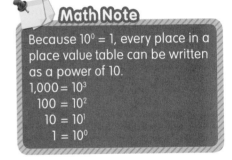

Math Note

Because $10^0 = 1$, every place in a place value table can be written as a power of 10.

$$1,000 = 10^3$$
$$100 = 10^2$$
$$10 = 10^1$$
$$1 = 10^0$$

4 Simplify and evaluate $\dfrac{4^2 \cdot 4^6}{4^8}$.

$$\frac{4^2 \cdot 4^6}{4^8} = \frac{4^{2+6}}{4^8} \qquad \text{Use the product of powers property.}$$
$$= \frac{4^8}{4^8} \qquad \text{Simplify.}$$
$$= 4^{8-8} \qquad \text{Use the quotient of powers property.}$$
$$= 4^0 \qquad \text{Simplify.}$$
$$= 1 \qquad \text{Evaluate.}$$

5 Simplify $(a^4 \div a^0) \cdot a^3$.

$$(a^4 \div a^0) \cdot a^3 = (a^4 \div 1) \cdot a^3 \qquad \text{Raise to the zero power.}$$
$$= a^4 \cdot a^3 \qquad \text{Simplify.}$$
$$= a^{4+3} \qquad \text{Use the product of powers property.}$$
$$= a^7 \qquad \text{Simplify.}$$

Simplify each expression and evaluate where applicable.

① $1.6^0 \div 0.4^2$

② $2 \cdot 10^3 + 1 \cdot 10^2 + 4 \cdot 10^0$

③ $\dfrac{3 \cdot 3^9}{3^{10}}$

④ $(t^0 \cdot t^7) \div t^5$

ENGAGE

How do you express $\dfrac{2 \cdot 2}{2 \cdot 2 \cdot 2}$ and $\dfrac{2 \cdot 2}{2 \cdot 2 \cdot 2 \cdot 2}$ in similar equivalent forms? Explain your thinking.

LEARN Simplify expressions involving negative exponents

Activity Understanding negative exponents ───────

Work in pairs.

① Use the quotient of powers property to simplify each expression.
Write each answer in exponential notation.

Expression	Exponential Notation
$\dfrac{4^5}{4^3}$	4^2
$\dfrac{4^5}{4^4}$	
$\dfrac{4^5}{4^5}$	
$\dfrac{4^5}{4^6}$	
$\dfrac{4^5}{4^7}$	

What expression did you write for $\dfrac{4^5}{4^6}$? What exponent did you obtain?

② In factored form, the quotient $\frac{4^5}{4^6}$ is $\frac{4 \cdot 4 \cdot 4 \cdot 4 \cdot 4}{4 \cdot 4 \cdot 4 \cdot 4 \cdot 4 \cdot 4}$. If you divide out all the common factors in the numerator and denominator, what is the value of $\frac{4^5}{4^6}$?

③ Repeat ② for $\frac{4^5}{4^7}$. What is the value of $\frac{4^5}{4^7}$?

④ **Mathematical Habit 8** **Look for patterns**
Suppose a represents any nonzero number. How would you write a^{-3} using a positive exponent?

① For any nonzero number that has a negative exponent, you can write it using a positive exponent.

> For any nonzero real number a and any integer n,
>
> $$a^{-n} = \frac{1}{a^n}, \ a \neq 0$$

② Simplify $13^{-7} \cdot 13^4$. Write your answer using a positive exponent.

$13^{-7} \cdot 13^4 = 13^{(-7) + 4}$ Use the product of powers property.
$\qquad\qquad = 13^{-3}$ Simplify.
$\qquad\qquad = \frac{1}{13^3}$ Write using a positive exponent.

3 Simplify $9m^{-2} \div 3m$. Write your answer using a positive exponent.

$9m^{-2} \div 3m$

$= \dfrac{9m^{-2}}{3m}$ Write the division as a fraction.

$= \dfrac{9}{3} \cdot \dfrac{m^{-2}}{m}$ Rewrite the fraction as the product of two fractions.

$= 3 \cdot m^{(-2)-1}$ Use the quotient of powers property.

$= 3m^{-3}$ Simplify.

$= 3 \cdot \dfrac{1}{m^3}$ Write using a positive exponent.

$= \dfrac{3}{m^3}$ Simplify.

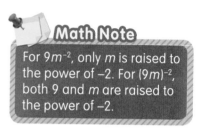

Math Note

For $9m^{-2}$, only m is raised to the power of -2. For $(9m)^{-2}$, both 9 and m are raised to the power of -2.

TRY Practice simplifying expressions involving negative exponents

Simplify each expression. Write each answer using a positive exponent.

1 $2.5^{-7} \div 2.5^{-4}$

2 $14a^{-5} \div (7a \cdot 2a^{-4})$

Usually you write your answer using a positive exponent unless asked to use a negative exponent.

INDEPENDENT PRACTICE

Simplify and evaluate each expression.

1 $8^3 \cdot 8^0$

2 $5^4 \cdot (-5)^0$

3 $\left(\dfrac{1}{3}\right)^4 \cdot \left(\dfrac{1}{3}\right)^0$

4 $7 \cdot 10^3 + 4^2 \cdot 10^2 + 5 \cdot 10^0$

5 $2.3 \cdot 10^2 + 5 \cdot 10^1 + 1 \cdot 10^0$

6 $\dfrac{7^4 \cdot 7^5}{7^9}$

7 $(9^{-3})^0 \cdot 5^2$

8 $\dfrac{(6^{-3})^{-2} \cdot 8^6}{48^6}$

Simplify each expression. Write each answer using a negative exponent.

9 $7^3 \cdot 7^{-4}$

10 $\dfrac{(-5)^{-2}}{(-5)^3}$

11 $\left(\dfrac{3}{4}\right) \div \left[\left(\dfrac{3}{4}\right)^0 \cdot \left(\dfrac{3}{4}\right)^2\right]$

12 $\left(\dfrac{2}{5}\right)^{-4} \cdot \left(\dfrac{2}{5}\right)^{-1} \div \left(\dfrac{2}{5}\right)^{-3}$

13 $\dfrac{x^0}{x^2 \cdot x^3}$

14 $\dfrac{2h^{-5} \cdot 3h^{-2}}{6h^{-3}}$

Evaluate each expression. Write each answer using a positive exponent.

15 $1.2^0 \div 1.8^2$

16 $5.2^{-3} \div 2.6^{-3}$

17 $\dfrac{(-3)^{-4}}{(-3)^2}$

18 $\left(\dfrac{5}{6}\right)^{-4} \cdot \left(\dfrac{5}{6}\right)^{-2} \div \left(\dfrac{5}{6}\right)^{-3}$

19 $\dfrac{9k^{-1} \cdot 2k^{-3}}{27k^{-6}}$

20 $\dfrac{c^{-4} \cdot c^{12}}{c^{-7}}$

Simplify each expression and evaluate where applicable.

21 $\dfrac{7^{-2} \cdot 7^0}{8^3 \cdot 8^{-5}}$

22 $\dfrac{(7^{-2})^2 \cdot 9^{-4}}{21^{-4}}$

23 $\dfrac{10^0}{2^{-2} \cdot (5^{-1})^2}$

24 $\dfrac{(3^6)^{-2}}{6^{-9}(-2^{10})}$

25 $\left(\dfrac{7m^3}{-49m^0}\right)^{-1}$

26 $\dfrac{8r^2s}{4s^{-3}r^4}$

6 Squares, Square Roots, Cubes and Cube Roots

Learning Objectives:
- Evaluate square roots and cube roots of positive real numbers.
- Solve an equation involving a variable that is squared or cubed.
- Solve real-world problems that use equations involving variables that are squared or cubed.

> **New Vocabulary**
> square root
> cube root

THINK

Use each of the numbers 1 to 9 exactly once to replace the question marks shown.

$$\frac{3^{?-?} \cdot (? + ?)^{?-?}}{\sqrt{? + ?}} = 3^{?}$$

ENGAGE

Draw a square with a side length of 4 units. Write an expression to find the area of the square. Now, draw a square with an area of 16 square units. Write an expression to find the side length. What is the relationship between the two expressions you wrote? Can you say the same relationship exists when using the negative square root of a number? Why or why not?

LEARN Find the square roots of a number

1. When you multiply a number by itself, you are squaring that number or raising it to the second power. For example, $3^2 = 9$ and $(-3)^2 = 9$.

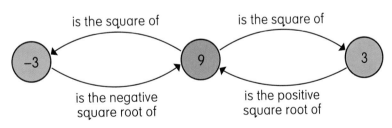

is the square of   is the square of

-3   9   3

is the negative square root of   is the positive square root of

You use $\sqrt{9} = 3$ to indicate the positive square root of 9 and $-\sqrt{9} = -3$ to indicate the negative square root of 9.

Not every number has a square root. For example, −9 has no square root as there are no two identical factors of −9. Both $(-3)^2$ and 3^2 are equal to 9.

2. Find the two square roots of 49.

$\sqrt{49} = 7$ 7 is the positive square root of 49 since $7 \cdot 7 = 49$.

$-\sqrt{49} = -7$ −7 is the negative square root of 49 since $(-7) \cdot (-7) = 49$.

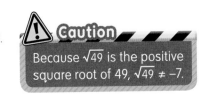

Caution
Because $\sqrt{49}$ is the positive square root of 49, $\sqrt{49} \neq -7$.

TRY Practice finding the square roots of a number

Solve.

1 Find the two square roots of 169.

ENGAGE

Sketch a cube with an edge length of 5 units. Write an expression to find the volume of the cube. Now, sketch a cube with a volume of 125 cubic units. Write an expression to find the edge length of the cube. Does this type of expression work with all rectangular prisms? Why or why not?

LEARN Find the cube root of a number

1 When you use a number as a factor three times, you are cubing that number or raising it to the third power. For example, $4^3 = 64$.

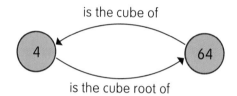

is the cube of

4 → 64

is the cube root of

Table of Cubes										
x	1	2	3	4	5	6	7	8	9	10
x³	1	8	27	64	125	216	343	512	729	1,000

$\sqrt[3]{64} = 4$ because $4 \cdot 4 \cdot 4 = 64$. So, 4 is the cube root of 64.

Notice that −4 is not a cube root of 64, because $(-4)^3 = -64$. −4 is a cube root of −64. So every number, positive, negative, or 0, has exactly one cube root.

2 Find the cube root of 343.

$\sqrt[3]{343} = \sqrt[3]{7^3}$ 7 is a cube root of 343 since $7 \cdot 7 \cdot 7 = 343$.
$\qquad = 7$ Simplify.

TRY Practice finding the cube root of a number

Solve.

1 Find the cube root of $\frac{1}{729}$.

When you solve an algebraic equation, what rules do you follow to keep the equation "balanced"? Use specific examples to explain your thinking. By making a systematic list, show how you can solve the equations $x^2 = 9$ and $y^3 = 8$.

LEARN Solve an equation involving a variable that is squared or cubed

1. To solve equations like $x^2 = 25$ and $y^3 = 125$, you need to find the value or values of the variable that make each equation a true statement. You do that by finding the square root or the cube root of both sides of the equation.

Since $4 = 2^2$, use a guess-and-check strategy to find the square root of 4.41, starting with 2.1, 2.2, and so on.

2. Solve $x^2 = 4.41$.

$x^2 = 4.41$
$x^2 = 2.1^2$ or $(-2.1)^2$ $4.41 = 2.1 \cdot 2.1$ and $4.41 = (-2.1) \cdot (-2.1)$.
$x = 2.1$ or -2.1 Show both the positive and negative square roots.

3. Solve $x^3 = 1,000$.

$x^3 = 1,000$
$x^3 = 10^3$
$\sqrt[3]{x^3} = \sqrt[3]{10^3}$ Solve for x by taking the cube root of both sides.
$x = 10$ Show the cube root.

TRY Practice solving an equation involving a variable that is squared or cubed

Solve.

1. $x^2 = 2.25$

2. $x^3 = \dfrac{1}{8}$

ENGAGE

Suppose an artist makes a cube-shaped sculpture. The area of one face of the sculpture is 121 square inches and the volume of the sculpture is 1,331 cubic inches.

How do you find the edge length of the cube? Justify your answer.

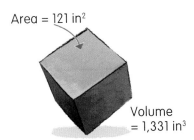

Area = 121 in^2

Volume = 1,331 in^3

LEARN Solve real-world problems involving squares or cubes of unknowns

1. You can use equations that involve squares and cubes to solve real-world problems. Sometimes, only one of the square root solutions makes sense for the problem.

2️⃣ Theresa wants to put a piece of carpet on the floor of her living room. The floor is a square with an area of 182.25 square feet. How long should the piece of carpet be on each side?

STEP 1 Understand the problem.

> What is the area of the floor?
> What do I need to find?

STEP 2 Think of a plan.
I can form an algebraic equation.

STEP 3 Carry out the plan.

Let the length of each side of the square carpet be x feet.

$$x^2 = 182.25 \qquad \text{Translate into an equation.}$$
$$\sqrt{x^2} = \sqrt{182.25} \qquad \text{Solve for } x \text{ by taking the positive square root of both sides.}$$
$$x = 13.5 \qquad \text{Use a calculator to find the square root.}$$

The length of each side of the carpet is 13.5 feet.

STEP 4 Check the answer.

> I can use the value found to find
> the area of the floor to check if
> my answer is correct.
> $13.5 \cdot 13.5 = 182.25$
> My answer is correct.

Math Talk

Why does the negative square root of 182.25 not make sense in this scenario?

3️⃣ The volume of an ice cube is 1.728 cubic meters. What is the surface area of the ice cube? Let the length of one side of the ice cube be x meters.

$$x^3 = 1.728 \qquad \text{Translate into an equation.}$$
$$\sqrt[3]{x^3} = \sqrt[3]{1.728} \qquad \text{Solve for } x \text{ by taking the cube root of both sides.}$$
$$x = 1.2 \qquad \text{Use a calculator to find the cube root.}$$

$6 \cdot 1.2 \cdot 1.2 = 8.64$

The surface area of the ice cube is 8.64 square meters.

TRY Practice solving real-world problems involving squares or cubes of unknowns

Solve.

1️⃣ A square field has an area of 98.01 square meters. Find the length of each side of the field. Let the length of each side of the field be x meters.

2️⃣ Richard bought a crystal cube that has a volume of 1,331 cubic centimeters. Find the length of a side of the crystal cube.

INDEPENDENT PRACTICE

Find the two square roots of each number. Round each answer to the nearest tenth where applicable.

1 25

2 64

 3 80

 4 120

Find the cube root of each number. Round each answer to the nearest tenth where applicable.

5 512

6 1,000

 7 999

8 $\dfrac{64}{343}$

 Solve each equation. Round each answer to the nearest tenth where applicable.

9 $a^2 = 46.24$

10 $n^2 = 350$

11 $x^3 = 74.088$

12 $x^3 = \dfrac{216}{729}$

![calculator icon] **Solve.**

13 An orchard planted on a square plot of land has 3,136 apple trees. If each tree requires an area of 4 square meters to grow, find the length of each side of the plot of land.

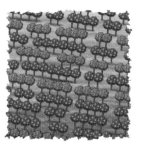

14 The volume of a cube-shaped box is 2,197 cubic centimeters. Find the area of a side of the box.

Mathematical Habit 2 Use mathematical reasoning

Jacob thinks that 57^2 is greater than 39^6 ? Is he correct? Why?

Problem Solving with Heuristics

1 **Mathematical Habit 1** **Persevere in solving problems**

Evaluate $\dfrac{4^3 \cdot 10^4}{5^2}$ without using a calculator.

2 **Mathematical Habit 1** **Persevere in solving problems**

Find the values of x and y that make the equation $\dfrac{81x^4 \cdot 16y^4}{[(2y)^2]^2} = 1{,}296$ true.

© 2020 Marshall Cavendish Education Pte Ltd

CHAPTER WRAP-UP

? How do you represent repeated multiplication of the same factor?

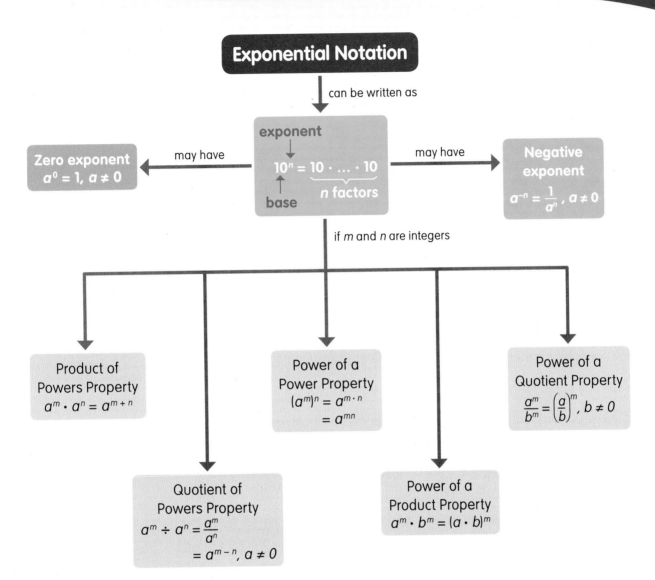

Exponential Notation

can be written as

exponent ↓
$$10^n = \underbrace{10 \cdot \ldots \cdot 10}_{n \text{ factors}}$$
↑ base

may have → **Zero exponent** $a^0 = 1, a \neq 0$

may have → **Negative exponent** $a^{-n} = \dfrac{1}{a^n}, a \neq 0$

if m and n are integers

Product of Powers Property $a^m \cdot a^n = a^{m+n}$

Quotient of Powers Property $a^m \div a^n = \dfrac{a^m}{a^n}$ $= a^{m-n}, a \neq 0$

Power of a Power Property $(a^m)^n = a^{m \cdot n}$ $= a^{mn}$

Power of a Product Property $a^m \cdot b^m = (a \cdot b)^m$

Power of a Quotient Property $\dfrac{a^m}{b^m} = \left(\dfrac{a}{b}\right)^m, b \neq 0$

KEY CONCEPTS

- You can use exponential notation to show repeated multiplication of the same factor. For example, $2^3 = 2 \cdot 2 \cdot 2$.

- A number written in exponential notation has a base and an exponent. The exponent represents how many times the base is used as a factor. For example, in the expression 9^5, 9 is the base and 5 is the exponent.

- The prime factorization of a number can be expressed using exponents. For example, $1{,}125 = 3^2 \cdot 5^3$.

- When you find the product of two algebraic expressions with the same base, you add their exponents and use this exponent with the same base, that is $a^m \cdot a^n = a^{m+n}$.

- When you find the quotient of two algebraic expressions with the same base, you subtract the exponent of the divisor from the exponent of the dividend and use it with the common base, that is $a^m \div a^n = a^{m-n}$, $a \neq 0$.

- When you raise a power to a power, keep the base and multiply the exponents, that is $(a^m)^n = a^{m \cdot n} = a^{mn}$.

- For expressions with the same exponent, you can distribute the exponent to each base, that is $(a \cdot b)^3 = a^3 \cdot b^3$ and $\left(\dfrac{a}{b}\right)^3 = \dfrac{a^3}{b^3}$, $b \neq 0$.

- A nonzero number raised to the zero power is equal to 1, that is $a^0 = 1$, $a \neq 0$.

- For any nonzero real number a and any integer n, $a^{-n} = \dfrac{1}{a^n}$.

- The square root of a number, when multiplied by itself, gives the number.

- Any positive number has a positive square root and a negative square root. You use the negative sign to distinguish them. For example, you use $\sqrt{9}$ to indicate the positive square root of 9, and $-\sqrt{9}$ to indicate the negative square root of 9.

- The cube root of a number, when used as a factor three times, gives the number.

- A number only has one cube root. For example, 4 is the cube root of 64.

© 2020 Marshall Cavendish Education Pte Ltd

Name: _____ Date: _____

Determine whether each statement is correct. If it is incorrect, state the reason.

1 $0.7^3 = 0.7 \cdot 0.7 \cdot 0.7$

2 $5^{-4} = (-5) \cdot (-5) \cdot (-5) \cdot (-5)$

Write each expression in exponential notation.

3 $2 \cdot 2 \cdot 2 \cdot 2$

4 $4.8 \cdot 4.8$

5 $\dfrac{1}{2} \cdot \dfrac{1}{2} \cdot \dfrac{1}{2}$

6 $(-1.2)(-1.2)(-1.2)(-1.2)$

Expand and evaluate each expression.

7 $(-6)^2$

8 1.1^2

9 10^5

10 $\left(\dfrac{2}{3}\right)^3$

Write the prime factorization of each number in exponential notation.

11 3,780

12 27,720

Simplify each expression. Write each answer in exponential notation.

13 $\left(\dfrac{5}{6}\right)^4 \cdot \left(\dfrac{5}{6}\right)^3$

14 $5m^3n^4 \cdot 4m^5n^2$

15 $\left(\dfrac{7}{8}\right)^3 \div \left(\dfrac{7}{8}\right)$

16 $(-h)^{15} \div (-h)^9$

Simplify and evaluate each expression.

17 $\left[\left(\dfrac{2}{3}\right)^2 \cdot \left(\dfrac{2}{3}\right)^{-1}\right]^3$

18 $\dfrac{(9^{-2})^{-2} \cdot 2^2}{9^2}$

19 $(-4)^4 \cdot (-0.5)^4$

20 $\dfrac{6^7 \cdot 56^2}{6^5 \cdot 7^2}$

Simplify each expression. Write each answer using a positive exponent.

21 $\dfrac{6^3 \cdot 15^3}{(7^0)^3}$

22 $x^8 z^5 \div x^3 z^9$

23 $25p^6 q^9 \div 45p^8 q^4$

24 $40c^5 d^3 \div 10c^9 d^2$

Simplify and evaluate each expression.

25 $\dfrac{(3^5 \cdot 3^4)^2}{(3^3)^6}$

26 $\dfrac{42^{-1}}{(2^0)^{12} \cdot 21^{-1}}$

Solve.

27 Find the two square roots of 256.

28 Find the cube root of 32.768.

Solve each equation.

29 $c^2 = \dfrac{121}{169}$

30 $t^3 = -\dfrac{27}{343}$

Solve.

31 The floor of an elevator shaft is a square with an area of 42.25 square feet. Find the length of a side of the floor.

32 The volume of a model of a puzzle Cube is 110,592 cubic inches. It is made up of 27 smaller cubes. What is the length of one side of each smaller cube?

Assessment Prep
Answer each question.

33 Which statement best describes the value of $\sqrt{18}$?

   (A) The value of $\sqrt{18}$ is between 3 and 3.5.

   (B) The value of $\sqrt{18}$ is between 3.5 and 4.

   (C) The value of $\sqrt{18}$ is between 4 and 4.5.

   (D) The value of $\sqrt{18}$ is between 4.5 and 5.

34 Which equation has both 5 and −5 as possible values of m?

   (A) $m^2 = 10$

   (B) $m^3 = 15$

   (C) $m^2 = 25$

   (D) $m^3 = 125$

35 Which expressions are equivalent to $\frac{2^{-14}}{2^{-7}}$? Choose **all** that apply.

   (A) 2^{-21}

   (B) 2^{-7}

   (C) 2^2

   (D) $\frac{1}{2^2}$

   (E) $\frac{1}{2^7}$

   (F) $\frac{1}{2^{21}}$

Name: _____   Date: _____

Intensity of Sound

1 Intensity of sound is the power of sound in watts divided by area covered in square meters. Loudness is the relative intensity of sound, above the threshold of hearing, that is perceived by a human ear. It is measured in decibels (dB). The intensity of the threshold of human hearing is about 10^{-12} watts per square meter (watts/m²), corresponding to 0 dB.

The table shows the intensity and the corresponding decibels of some common sources of sound.

Source of Sound	Intensity (watts/m²)	Loudness (dB)
Rustle of leaves	10^{-11}	10
Quiet library	10^{-8}	40
Busy street traffic	10^{-5}	70
Rock band	1	120
Jet engine, 30 m away	10^{2}	140

a Consider the sound of a quiet library and of busy street traffic. How many times is the increase in the sound intensity from 40 dB to 70 dB?

b The pain threshold of a human ear is 120 dB. Which two sources of sound in the table on page 467 should you avoid?

2 As the distance, d metres, from the source of a sound increases, the loudness, L dB, decreases according to the formula $\dfrac{L_1}{L_2} = \left(\dfrac{d_2}{d_1}\right)^2$. Sophia, who is standing 10 meters away from the loud speakers of a rock band, finds the noise unbearable. How far does she need to stand away from the loud speakers so that the noise reduces to 90 dB? Round your answer to the nearest tenth.

Rubric

Point(s)	Level	My Performance
7–8	4	• Most of my answers are correct. • I showed complete understanding of the concepts. • I used effective and efficient strategies to solve the problems. • I explained my answers and mathematical thinking clearly and completely.
5–6	3	• Some of my answers are correct. • I showed adequate understanding of the concepts. • I used effective strategies to solve the problems. • I explained my answers and mathematical thinking clearly.
3–4	2	• A few of my answers are correct. • I showed some understanding of the concepts. • I used some effective strategies to solve the problems. • I explained some of my answers and mathematical thinking clearly.
0–2	1	• A few of my answers are correct. • I showed little understanding of the concepts. • I used limited effective strategies to solve the problems. • I did not explain my answers and mathematical thinking clearly.

Teacher's Comments

STEAM

School Is Noisy

What comes to mind when you think of noise in your daily life? Voices on a school bus? A hallway crowded with students on the move? The school band's practice room? The volume on music players and phones? These noises definitely contribute to every day's noise pollution.

Builders often install acoustic insulation to reduce unwanted or excessive sound in public buildings, such as schools, restaurants, and event centers. Likewise, some people also install soundproofing products in their homes and apartments.

Engineers evaluate the effectiveness of soundproofing products and assign each product a Noise Reduction Coefficient (NRC) rating. A product with an NRC of 0 absorbs no sound, while a product with an NRC of 1 absorbs all sound.

Task

Work in small groups to investigate the costs of acoustic insulation.

1. Download a free noise app for your smart phone. Use the noise meter to measure and record the decibel levels of common daily activities in your classroom and school.

2. Calculate how many times greater the intensity of the sound with the highest decibel reading is than the sound with the lowest dB reading. Share your results with the class.

3. Investigate the acoustic insulation products available to consumers. Compare NRCs and prices. Then measure the dimensions of your classroom ceiling and determine the cost of replacing existing ceiling tiles with the best product currently available on the market.

Scientific Notation

How far away are the stars?

When you look at the stars through a telescope, you are seeing light that has traveled an enormous distance. Proxima Centauri, the star that is closest to Earth after the Sun, is 39,900,000,000,000 kilometers from Earth. Many numbers like this are so large that scientists have invented a method called scientific notation to write them. In this chapter, you will use scientific notation to describe and compare very large and very small numbers.

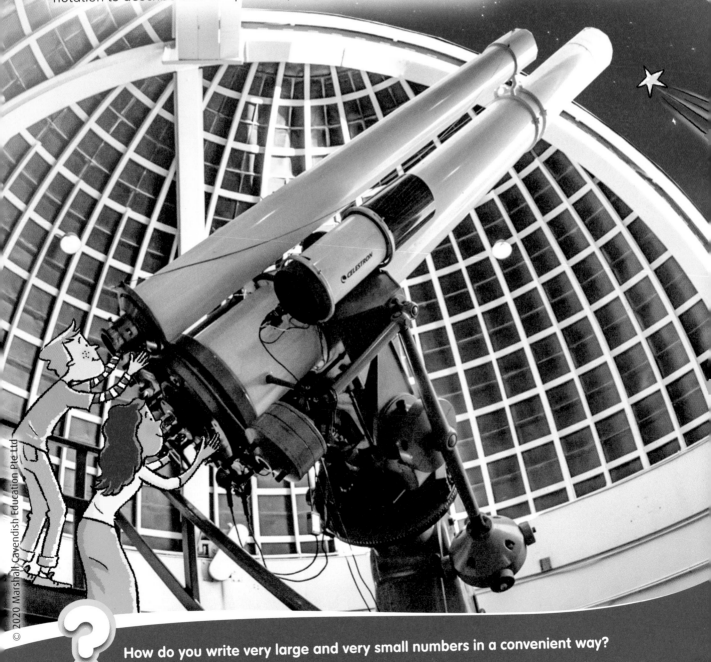

How do you write very large and very small numbers in a convenient way?

Name: _____ Date: _____

Multiplying and dividing decimals by positive powers of 10

When you multiply a decimal by a positive power of 10, the decimal point moves to the right.

Examples:

$1.47 \cdot 10 = 14.7$ Multiply by 10^1.
$1.47 \cdot 100 = 147$ Multiply by 10^2.
$-1.47 \cdot 100 = -147$ Multiply by 10^2.

When you divide a decimal by a positive power of 10, the decimal point moves to the left.

Examples:

$1.2 \div 10 = 0.12$ Divide by 10^1.
$1.2 \div 100 = 0.012$ Divide by 10^2.
$-1.2 \div 100 = -0.012$ Divide by 10^2.

▶ **Quick Check**

Evaluate each expression.

1. $1.8 \cdot 100$

2. $-0.28 \cdot 10^3$

3. $1.3 \cdot 10^4$

4. $74.5 \div 1{,}000$

5. $-3.8 \div 10$

6. $2.81 \div 10^2$

1 Understanding Scientific Notation

Learning Objectives:
- Write numbers in scientific notation or in standard form.
- Compare numbers in scientific notation.

> **New Vocabulary**
> scientific notation
> coefficient
> standard form

THINK

When visible light passes through a prism, the light waves refract, or bend, and the colors that make up the light can be seen. Each color has a different wavelength, as shown in the table.

Color	Wavelength
Green	$5.1 \cdot 10^{-7}$ m
Orange	$5.9 \cdot 10^{-5}$ cm
Red	0.00065 mm
Blue	$4.7 \cdot 10^{-10}$ km

a Shorter wavelengths refract more than longer wavelengths. Which color of light wave shows the most refraction? Which color of light wave shows the least refraction?

b The frequency of a light wave is the number of waves that travel a given distance in a given amount of time. The shorter the wavelength, the greater the frequency. List the colors by their frequencies, from least to greatest.

ENGAGE

Consider the following form of each expression.
$1,000 = 10^x$ and $90,000 = 9 \cdot 10^y$
How do you find the values of x and y?
How do you write the number 90,000,000,000,000 in a similar form? How do you write 0.0000000009? Explain your thinking.

LEARN Write numbers in scientific notation

1 Astronomers have to work with very large and very small numbers. For instance, the average distance from Earth to the moon is 380,000,000 meters.

Light from the moon travels to Earth at a speed of 300,000,000 meters per second, that is light travels 1 meter in about 0.00000000333… seconds.

It is not easy to keep track of all the zeros in such numbers. For this reason, scientists use scientific notation to represent very large and very small numbers.

2 You can write a very large number or a very small number as the product of a number between 1 and 10, inclusive of 1, and an integer power of ten.

$300{,}000{,}000 = 3 \cdot 100{,}000{,}000$
$= 3 \cdot 10^8$

$0.00000000333 = 3.33 \cdot \dfrac{1}{1{,}000{,}000{,}000}$
$= 3.33 \cdot 10^{-9}$

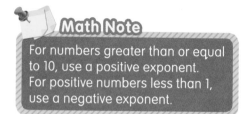

Math Note

For numbers greater than or equal to 10, use a positive exponent. For positive numbers less than 1, use a negative exponent.

Numbers written this way are said to be in scientific notation.

Any number can be written in scientific notation by expressing it in two parts: a coefficient A where $1 \le A < 10$, and a power of 10 where the exponent n is an integer.

power of 10

$A \cdot 10^n$ ← exponent

coefficient base

You can also write it as $A \times 10^n$.

3 The wavelength of infrared light is $0.01 \cdot 10^{-5}$ meter. $0.01 \cdot 10^{-5}$ is not in scientific notation as the coefficient 0.01 is less than 1. It needs to be greater than or equal to 1.

4 A field is 10×10^1 yards long. 10×10^1 is not in scientific notation as the coefficient is not less than 10.

5 Write 427.7 in scientific notation.

$427.7 = 4.277 \cdot 100$ Move the decimal point 2 places to the left and multiply by 100.
$ = 4.277 \cdot 10^2$ Rewrite 100 as a power of 10.

6 Write 0.007 in scientific notation.

$0.007 = 7 \cdot \dfrac{1}{1{,}000}$ Move the decimal point 3 places to the right and multiply by $\dfrac{1}{1{,}000}$.

$ = 7 \cdot \dfrac{1}{10^3}$ Rewrite $\dfrac{1}{1{,}000}$ as $\dfrac{1}{10^3}$.

$ = 7 \cdot 10^{-3}$ Rewrite $\dfrac{1}{10^3}$ as a power of 10.

10^{-3} has a negative exponent. You have learned that 10^{-3} can be written with a positive exponent as $\dfrac{1}{1{,}000}$.

TRY Practice writing numbers in scientific notation

Tell whether each number is written correctly in scientific notation. If it is incorrectly written, state the reason.

1 A Brazilian gold frog is $9.6 \cdot 10^0$ millimeters long.

2 Mars is $0.228 \cdot 10^7$ kilometers from the Sun.

When written in scientific notation, the coefficient should be at least 1 and less than 10.

Write each number in scientific notation.

3 856.2

4 0.06

ENGAGE

Every second, 2 million red blood cells are produced in your body. How many red blood cells are produced in one minute? Express your answer in scientific notation.

A normal white blood cell count has a maximum of $1.08 \cdot 10^4$ cells per cubic millimeter of blood. What is another way to express this number? Explain your answer.

LEARN Write numbers in scientific notation to standard form

1 You can use what you know about writing numbers in scientific notation to write them in standard form.

2 Write $7.1 \cdot 10^3$ in standard form.

$$7.1 \cdot 10^3 = 7.1 \cdot 1{,}000 \quad \text{Evaluate the power.}$$
$$= 7{,}100 \quad \text{Multiply by 1,000.}$$

3 Write $8.12 \cdot 10^{-3}$ in standard form.

$$8.12 \cdot 10^{-3} = 8.12 \cdot \frac{1}{1{,}000} \quad \text{Evaluate the power.}$$
$$= 0.00812 \quad \text{Divide by 1,000.}$$

TRY Practice writing numbers in standard form

Write each number in standard form.

1. $9 \cdot 10^4$

2. $2.5 \cdot 10^{-2}$

ENGAGE

John wrote the expression: $43 \cdot 10^2 > 5.2 \cdot 10^3$. Is he correct? Justify your thinking.

Create two expressions in scientific notation with the same powers. Trade with your partner. Explain which number is greater. Now, create two expressions in scientific notation with different powers. Trade with your partner. Explain which number is lesser.

LEARN Compare numbers in scientific notation

1. You can compare numbers easily by writing them in scientific notation. Compare the powers of 10 to determine which number is greater. If the powers are equal, compare the coefficients.

2. Identify the greater number in the pair of numbers $5.6 \cdot 10^2$ and $2.1 \cdot 10^3$.

   $10^3 > 10^2$ Compare the exponents.
   $2.1 \cdot 10^3 > 5.6 \cdot 10^2$

   So, $2.1 \cdot 10^3$ is the greater number.

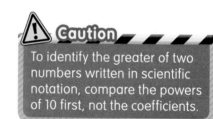

Caution
To identify the greater of two numbers written in scientific notation, compare the powers of 10 first, not the coefficients.

3. Identify the greater number in the pair of numbers $3.4 \cdot 10^{-1}$ and $1.1 \cdot 10^{-1}$.

   Because the exponents are the same, compare the coefficients.

   $3.4 > 1.1$ Compare the coefficients.

   $3.4 \cdot 10^{-1} > 1.1 \cdot 10^{-1}$

   So, $3.4 \cdot 10^{-1}$ is the greater number.

4 In 2000, Americans consumed an average of 47.2 pounds of potatoes and $5.936 \cdot 10^2$ pounds of dairy products per person. Did Americans consume more potatoes or dairy products?

▶ **Method 1**
Write the numbers in standard form and then compare the numbers.

Write the amount of dairy products consumed in standard form. Then, compare the two amounts.

$5.936 \cdot 10^2 = 593.6$

$593.6 > 47.2$

So, Americans consumed more dairy products.

▶ **Method 2**
Write the numbers in scientific notation and then compare the numbers.

Write the amount of potatoes consumed in scientific notation. Then, compare the two amounts.

$47.2 = 4.72 \cdot 10^1$

Compare $4.72 \cdot 10^1$ and $5.936 \cdot 10^2$.

$10^2 > 10^1$

$5.936 \cdot 10^2 > 4.72 \cdot 10^1$

So, Americans consumed more dairy products.

TRY Practice comparing numbers in scientific notation

Identify the lesser number in each pair of numbers.

1 $4.2 \cdot 10^2$ and $6.5 \cdot 10^1$

2 $3.6 \cdot 10^{-3}$ and $8.4 \cdot 10^{-3}$

Solve.

3 An actor has 75,126 fans on a social network. A musician has $8.58 \cdot 10^4$ fans. By writing both numbers in scientific notation or in standard form, find who has more fans on the social network.

MATH SHARING

| Mathematical Habit 6 | Use precise mathematical language

What are some other examples of very large and very small numbers. Express these numbers in scientific notation.

INDEPENDENT PRACTICE

Tell whether each number is written correctly in scientific notation. If it is incorrectly written, state the reason.

1 $71 \cdot 10^{22}$

2 $8 \cdot 10^{-2}$

3 $0.99 \cdot 10^{-3}$

4 $1.2 \cdot 10^{4}$

Write each number in scientific notation.

5 533,000

6 327.8

7 0.0034

8 0.00000728

Write each number in standard form.

9 $7.36 \cdot 10^{3}$

10 $2.431 \cdot 10^{4}$

11 $5.27 \cdot 10^{-2}$

12 $4.01 \cdot 10^{-4}$

Identify the lesser number in each pair of numbers.

13 $8.7 \cdot 10^{6}$ and $5.9 \cdot 10^{3}$

14 $4.8 \cdot 10^{3}$ and $9.6 \cdot 10^{7}$

15 $3.1 \cdot 10^{-5}$ and $7.5 \cdot 10^{-5}$

16 $6.9 \cdot 10^{-3}$ and $4.3 \cdot 10^{-3}$

Solve.

17 The table shows the populations of some countries. Write each population in scientific notation.

Country	Population
Brazil	208,000,000
Fiji	899,000
Monaco	38,000
Singapore	5,600,000

18 A caterpillar is 76 millimeters long. A praying mantis is 15 centimeters long.

a Write both lengths in millimeters in scientific notation.

b Write both lengths in centimeters in scientific notation.

c How does writing the numbers using the same unit help us compare them?

19 A technician recorded the air pressure from several pressure gauges. The table shows each air pressure reading in pascals (Pa).

Pressure Gauge	Air Pressure (Pa)
A	210,000
B	$5.2 \cdot 10^5$
C	170,000

A pascal is a unit used to measure the amount of force applied on a given area by air or other gases.

a Which pressure gauge showed the highest reading?

b Which pressure gauge showed the lowest reading?

c The atmospheric pressure when these readings were made was $1.1 \cdot 10^5$ pascals. Which gauge(s) showed a reading greater than the atmospheric pressure?

2 Adding and Subtracting in Scientific Notation

Learning Objectives:
- Add and subtract numbers in scientific notation.
- Use the prefix system.

THINK

Express each population in scientific notation. Then find the difference between the populations of any two countries. Show your findings in a table.

Country	Population
Mexico	130,000,000
Haiti	11,100,000
Costa Rica	4,950,000
United States	327,000,000

ENGAGE

Factor $3y + 3x$. How do you use what you know about factoring to simplify the expression $2.11 \cdot 10^5 + 3.5 \cdot 10^5$? Explain your thinking.

LEARN Add and subtract numbers in scientific notation with the same power of 10

1. A popular social networking site has the most members between the ages of 15 and 28. Within this age group, there are $5.11 \cdot 10^7$ student members and $9.55 \cdot 10^7$ nonstudent members. What is the total number of members in this age group? Write the answer in scientific notation.

$5.11 \cdot 10^7 + 9.55 \cdot 10^7$
$= (5.11 + 9.55) \cdot 10^7$ Factor 10^7 from each term.
$= 14.66 \cdot 10^7$ Add within parentheses.
$= 1.466 \cdot 10^1 \cdot 10^7$ Write 14.66 in scientific notation.
$= 1.466 \cdot 10^{1+7}$ Use the product of powers property.
$= 1.466 \cdot 10^8$ Write in scientific notation.

> When the powers of 10 are the same, the distributive property can be applied to the sum or difference.

So, the total number of members in this age group is $1.466 \cdot 10^8$.

If you want to find how many more nonstudent members than student members, you subtract.

$9.55 \cdot 10^7 - 5.11 \cdot 10^7$
$= (9.55 - 5.11) \cdot 10^7$ Factor 10^7 from each term.
$= 4.44 \cdot 10^7$ Subtract within parentheses.

So, there are $4.44 \cdot 10^7$ more nonstudent members than student members.

> To add or subtract numbers in scientific notation, the powers
> of 10 must be the same.

2 The thickness of a compact disc (CD) is $1.2 \cdot 10^{-3}$ meter.
A slim jewel case is $5.3 \cdot 10^{-3}$ meter thick.

a The CD is placed on top of the jewel case.
What is the total thickness of the CD and jewel case?
Write the answer in scientific notation.

$1.2 \cdot 10^{-3} + 5.3 \cdot 10^{-3}$
$= (1.2 + 5.3) \cdot 10^{-3}$ Factor 10^{-3} from each term.
$= 6.5 \cdot 10^{-3}$ Add within parentheses.

The total thickness of the CD and jewel case is $6.5 \cdot 10^{-3}$ meter.

b How much thicker is the jewel case than the CD? Write the answer in scientific notation.

$5.3 \cdot 10^{-3} - 1.2 \cdot 10^{-3}$
$= (5.3 - 1.2) \cdot 10^{-3}$ Factor 10^{-3} from each term.
$= 4.1 \cdot 10^{-3}$ Subtract within parentheses.

The jewel case is $4.1 \cdot 10^{-3}$ meter thicker than the CD.

TRY Practice adding and subtracting numbers in scientific notation with the same power of 10

Solve.

1 The population of Washington, D.C., is $5.9 \cdot 10^5$.
South Dakota has a population of $8 \cdot 10^5$.

Washington, D.C.   South Dakota

a Find the sum of the populations.
Write the answer in scientific notation.

Population: $6.9 \cdot 10^5$ Population: $8.8 \cdot 10^5$

b Find the difference between the populations. Write the answer in scientific notation.

2 The length of the smallest salamander is $1.7 \cdot 10^{-2}$ meter. The smallest lizard is $1.6 \cdot 10^{-2}$ meter long.

Salamander

Lizard

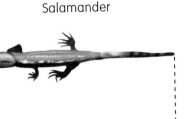 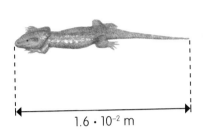

$1.7 \cdot 10^{-2}$ m

$1.6 \cdot 10^{-2}$ m

a Find the sum of the lengths. Write your answer in scientific notation.

b Find the difference between the lengths. Write your answer in scientific notation.

ENGAGE

In order to add or subtract numbers in scientific notation by factoring, what can you say about the powers of 10? Using your answer, explain how you would add $3.2 \cdot 10^7 + 4.5 \cdot 10^9$ by factoring. Share your methods with your partner. What are the similarities and difference between your methods?

LEARN Add and subtract numbers in scientific notation with different powers of 10

1 When you add or subtract numbers written in scientific notation, first check to make sure the numbers have the same power of 10. If they do not, you rewrite one or more numbers so that all the numbers have the same power of 10.

2 The area of the Pacific Ocean is $6.4 \cdot 10^7$ square miles. The area of the Arctic Ocean is $5.4 \cdot 10^6$ square miles.

a Find the sum of the areas of the two oceans. Write the answer in scientific notation.

> Rewrite one number so that the two numbers have the same power of 10 as a factor.

$6.4 \cdot 10^7 + 5.4 \cdot 10^6$
$= 64 \cdot 10^6 + 5.4 \cdot 10^6$ Rewrite $6.4 \cdot 10^7$ as $64 \cdot 10^6$.
$= (64 + 5.4) \cdot 10^6$ Factor 10^6 from each term.
$= 69.4 \cdot 10^6$ Add within parentheses.
$= 6.94 \cdot 10^1 \cdot 10^6$ Write 69.4 in scientific notation.
$= 6.94 \cdot 10^{1+6}$ Use the product of powers property.
$= 6.94 \cdot 10^7$ Write in scientific notation.

The sum of the areas of the two oceans is $6.94 \cdot 10^7$ square miles.

b How much larger is the area of the Pacific Ocean than the area of the Arctic Ocean? Write the answer in scientific notation.

$6.4 \cdot 10^7 - 5.4 \cdot 10^6$

$= 64 \cdot 10^6 - 5.4 \cdot 10^6$ Rewrite $6.4 \cdot 10^7$ as $64 \cdot 10^6$.

$= (64 - 5.4) \cdot 10^6$ Factor 10^6 from each term.

$= 58.6 \cdot 10^6$ Subtract within parentheses.

$= 5.86 \cdot 10^1 \cdot 10^6$ Write 58.6 in scientific notation.

$= 5.86 \cdot 10^{1+6}$ Use the product of powers property.

$= 5.86 \cdot 10^7$ Write in scientific notation.

The area of the Pacific Ocean is $5.86 \cdot 10^7$ square miles larger than the area of the Arctic Ocean.

> You can check that you have factored the terms correctly by multiplying again. For example, you obtain $64 \cdot 10^6 - 5.4 \cdot 10^6$ when you multiply $(64 - 5.4)$ and 10^6.

Math Talk

Can you obtain the same answer by rewriting $5.4 \cdot 10^6$ so that it has the same power of 10 as $6.4 \cdot 10^7$? Justify your answer.

3 A CD is $1.2 \cdot 10^{-3}$ meter thick. A thin coating on the CD is $7.0 \cdot 10^{-8}$ meter thick.

a How thick is the CD with the coating added? Write the answer in scientific notation.

> Choose one of the thickness measures and rewrite it so that it has the same power of 10 as the other thickness measure. In this example, the thickness of the coating is rewritten to have a power of 10^{-3}.

$1.2 \cdot 10^{-3} + 7.0 \cdot 10^{-8}$

$= 1.2 \cdot 10^{-3} + 0.00007 \cdot 10^{-3}$ Rewrite $7.0 \cdot 10^{-8}$ as $0.00007 \cdot 10^{-3}$.

$= (1.2 + 0.00007) \cdot 10^{-3}$ Factor 10^{-3} from each term.

$= 1.20007 \cdot 10^{-3}$ Add within parentheses.

The total thickness of the CD and coating is $1.20007 \cdot 10^{-3}$ meter.

b How much thicker is the CD than the coating? Write the answer in scientific notation.

$1.2 \cdot 10^{-3} - 7.0 \cdot 10^{-8}$

$= 1.2 \cdot 10^{-3} - 0.00007 \cdot 10^{-3}$ Rewrite $7.0 \cdot 10^{-8}$ as $0.00007 \cdot 10^{-3}$.

$= (1.2 - 0.00007) \cdot 10^{-3}$ Factor 10^{-3} from each term.

$= 1.19993 \cdot 10^{-3}$ Add within parentheses.

The CD is $1.19993 \cdot 10^{-3}$ meter thicker than the coating.

TRY Practice adding and subtracting numbers in scientific notation with different powers of 10

Solve.

1 The area of the continent of Australia is $9 \cdot 10^6$ square kilometers. The area of the continent of Antarctica is $1.37 \cdot 10^7$ square kilometers.

  a Find the sum of the land areas of the two continents. Write the answer in scientific notation.

  b Find the difference between the land areas. Write the answer in scientific notation.

2 An invitation card is $2.54 \cdot 10^{-4}$ meters thick. A tissue paper insert is $6.0 \cdot 10^{-6}$ meters thick.

  a The invitation card is placed inside the tissue paper insert. What is the total thickness? Write the answer in scientific notation.

  b How much thicker is the invitation card than the tissue paper insert? Write the answer in scientific notation.

ENGAGE

1,000 meters = 1 kilometer and 0.000001 meters = 1 micrometer.

Using scientific notation, how do you express 54,600 meters in terms of kilometers? How do you express 0.000546 meters in micrometers? What pattern do you notice? Describe it to your partner.

LEARN Use the prefix system

1 A prefix that precedes a basic unit of measure indicates a fraction or multiple of the unit. The table shows some of the common prefixes.

Prefix	Symbol	10^n	Standard Form	Term
Tera	T	10^{12}	1,000,000,000,000	Trillion
Giga	G	10^9	1,000,000,000	Billion
Mega	M	10^6	1,000,000	Million
kilo	k	10^3	1,000	Thousand
–	–	10^0	1	One
milli	m	10^{-3}	0.001	Thousandth
micro	μ	10^{-6}	0.000001	Millionth
nano	n	10^{-9}	0.000000001	Billionth
pico	p	10^{-12}	0.000000000001	Trillionth

The width of a human hair can be expressed as $1.76 \cdot 10^{-4}$ meters. Using the prefixes shown in the table, you can also express this measure as

$1.76 \cdot 10^{-7}$ kilometers,
$1.76 \cdot 10^{-1}$ millimeters or
$1.76 \cdot 10^{2}$ micrometers.

2 A blue whale has a mass of 190,000,000 grams. The mass of a whale shark is $2.6 \cdot 10^{4}$ kilograms. What is the sum of the masses of the blue whale and whale shark? Write the answer in scientific notation.

$190{,}000{,}000 \text{ g} = 1.9 \times 10^{8} \text{ g}$
$\phantom{190{,}000{,}000 \text{ g}} = 1.9 \times 10^{5} \text{ kg}$

Rewrite one mass so that the two masses are in the same unit.

$1.9 \times 10^{5} + 2.6 \cdot 10^{4}$
$= 19 \times 10^{4} + 2.6 \cdot 10^{4}$ Rewrite 1.9×10^{5} as 19×10^{4}.
$= (19 + 2.6) \cdot 10^{4}$ Factor 10^{4} from each term.
$= 21.6 \cdot 10^{4}$ Add within parentheses.
$= 2.16 \cdot 10^{1} \cdot 10^{4}$ Write 21.6 in scientific notation.
$= 2.16 \cdot 10^{1 + 4}$ Use the product of powers property.
$= 2.16 \cdot 10^{5}$ Write in scientific notation.

The sum of the masses of the blue whale and whale shark is $2.16 \cdot 10^{5}$ kilograms.

TRY Practice using the prefix system

Solve.

1 On average, Jupiter orbits the Sun at a distance of 778.3 gigameters. Mars's average distance from the Sun is $2.273 \cdot 10^{8}$ kilometers.

Which of the two planets is farther from the Sun? How much farther? Write the answer in scientific notation in terms of kilometres.

INDEPENDENT PRACTICE

Evaluate each expression. Write each answer in scientific notation.

1 $6.3 \cdot 10^{-2} + 4.9 \cdot 10^{-2}$

2 $7.2 \cdot 10^2 - 3.5 \cdot 10^2$

3 $3.8 \cdot 10^3 + 5.2 \cdot 10^4$

4 $8.1 \cdot 10^5 - 2.8 \cdot 10^4$

Solve.

5 The table shows the amounts of energy, in calories, contained in various foods.

a Find the total energy in chicken breast and cabbage. Write the answer in scientific notation.

Food (per 100 g)	Energy (Cal)
Chicken breast	$1.71 \cdot 10^5$
Raw potato	$7.7 \cdot 10$
Cabbage	$2.5 \cdot 10^4$
Salmon	$1.67 \cdot 10^5$

b Find the total energy in cabbage and raw potato. Write the answer in scientific notation.

c How many more Calories are in salmon than in cabbage? Write the answer in scientific notation.

6 A flight from Singapore to New York includes a stopover at Hawaii. The distance between Singapore and Hawaii is $6.7 \cdot 10^3$ miles. The distance between New York and Hawaii is $4.9 \cdot 10^3$ miles.

a Find the total distance from Singapore to New York. Write the answer in scientific notation.

b Find the difference in distance between the two flights. Write the answer in scientific notation.

7 Factories A and B produce potato chips. They use the basic ingredients of potatoes, oil, and salt. Last year, each factory used different amounts of these ingredients, as shown in the table.

Ingredient	Factory A Amount Used (lb)	Factory B Amount Used (lb)
Potato	$4.87 \cdot 10^6$	3,309,000
Oil	356,000	$5.61 \cdot 10^5$
Salt	$2.87 \cdot 10^5$	193,500

a Which factory used more potatoes? How many more pounds of potatoes did it use? Write the answer in scientific notation.

b Which factory used more oil? How much more oil did it use? Write the answer in scientific notation.

c Find the total weight of the ingredients used by each factory. Write the answer in scientific notation.

8 Angora wool, obtained from rabbits, has fibers with a width of $1 \cdot 10^{-6}$ meter. Cashmere, obtained from goats, has fibers with a width of $1.45 \cdot 10^{-5}$ meter.

a Find the total width of the two types of fiber. Write the answer in the appropriate unit in prefix form.

b How much wider is the cashmere fiber than the angora fiber? Write the answer in the appropriate unit in prefix form.

3 Multiplying and Dividing in Scientific Notation

Learning Objective:
• Multiply and divide numbers in scientific notation.

THINK

Emma wrote the following.

$$\frac{4.6 \cdot 10^8 \cdot 3.8 \cdot 10^{-4}}{2 \cdot 10^{-2}} = \frac{4.6 \cdot 3.8 \cdot 10^8 \cdot 10^{-4}}{2 \cdot 10^{-2}}$$
$$= \frac{17.48 \cdot 10^{12}}{2 \cdot 10^{-2}}$$
$$= \frac{17.48}{2} \cdot \frac{10^{12}}{10^{-2}}$$
$$= 8.74 \cdot 10^{14}$$

What mistake did she make?

ENGAGE

What is $10^3 \cdot 10^{-2}$? Next, consider $(a \cdot b) \cdot (c \cdot d) = a \cdot b \cdot c \cdot d$. How would you solve $(3 \cdot 10^3) \cdot (3.2 \cdot 10^2)$? Write another pair of numbers in scientific notation, one with a positive exponent and another with a negative exponent. Trade your numbers with your partner and multiply them. Share your working.

LEARN Multiply numbers in scientific notation

1 A rectangular swimming pool is $5 \cdot 10^1$ meters long and $2.5 \cdot 10^1$ meters wide. Find the area of the water's surface.

Area of water's surface $= 5 \cdot 10^1 \cdot 2.5 \cdot 10^1$
$= 5 \cdot 2.5 \cdot 10^1 \cdot 10^1$ Use the commutative property.
$= 12.5 \cdot 10^1 \cdot 10^1$ Multiply the coefficients.
$= 1.25 \cdot 10^1 \cdot 10^1 \cdot 10^1$ Write 12.5 in scientific notation.
$= 1.25 \cdot 10^{1+1+1}$ Use the product of powers property.
$= 1.25 \cdot 10^3 \text{ m}^2$ Write in scientific notation.

The area of the water's surface is $1.25 \cdot 10^3$ square meters.

> Multiplication and addition of numbers are commutative.

3 A rectangular field is $1.05 \cdot 10^2$ meters long and $6.8 \cdot 10^1$ meters wide. Find the area of the field. Write the answer in scientific notation.

$$
\begin{aligned}
\text{Area of field} &= 1.05 \cdot 10^2 \cdot 6.8 \cdot 10^1 \\
&= 1.05 \cdot 6.8 \cdot 10^2 \cdot 10^1 && \text{Use the commutative property.} \\
&= 7.14 \cdot 10^2 \cdot 10^1 && \text{Multiply the coefficients.} \\
&= 7.14 \cdot 10^{2+1} && \text{Use the product of powers property.} \\
&= 7.14 \cdot 10^3 \text{ m}^2 && \text{Write in scientific notation.}
\end{aligned}
$$

The area of the field is $7.14 \cdot 10^3$ square meters.

TRY Practice multiplying numbers in scientific notation

Solve.

1 In the 19th century, the Law Courts of Brussels was the largest building ever built. Its rectangular base measures $1.6 \cdot 10^2$ meters by $1.5 \cdot 10^2$ meters. Find the base area of the building. Write the answer in scientific notation.

2 The outer wall of Angkor Wat, a World Heritage site in Cambodia, encloses a rectangular area of $1.02 \cdot 10^3$ meters by $8.02 \cdot 10^2$ meters. Find the area enclosed by the outer wall. Write the answer in scientific notation.

Math Note

You can use the EE Function or 2ND on , a calculator to multiply numbers in scientific notation.

What is $\frac{10^4}{10^2}$? Next, consider $\frac{a \cdot b}{c \cdot d} = \frac{a}{c} \cdot \frac{b}{d}$. How would you solve $\frac{5.4 \cdot 10^4}{2.7 \cdot 10^2}$?

Write another pair of numbers in scientific notation, one with a positive exponent and another with a negative exponent. Trade your numbers with your partner and divide one number by the other.

Share your working.

LEARN Divide numbers in scientific notation

1. The planet Mercury has a mass of $3.3 \cdot 10^{23}$ kilograms. Mars has a mass of $6.4 \cdot 10^{23}$ kilograms. How many times as great as the mass of Mercury is the mass of Mars? Round the answer to the nearest tenth.

$$\frac{6.4 \cdot 10^{23}}{3.3 \cdot 10^{23}}$$
$$= \frac{6.4}{33} \cdot \frac{10^{23}}{10^{23}} \qquad \text{Divide the coefficients and divide the powers of 10.}$$
$$\approx 1.9 \cdot 10^{23-23} \qquad \text{Round the coefficient and use the quotient of powers property.}$$
$$= 1.9 \cdot 10^0$$
$$= 1.9 \qquad \text{Write in standard form.}$$

Mars has a mass that is approximately 1.9 times as great as the mass of Mercury.

2. The mass of an oxygen atom is $2.7 \cdot 10^{-26}$ kilograms. The mass of a silver atom is $1.8 \cdot 10^{-25}$ kilograms. How many times as great as the mass of an oxygen atom is the mass of a silver atom? Round the answer to the nearest tenth.

$$\frac{1.8 \cdot 10^{-25}}{2.7 \cdot 10^{-26}}$$
$$= \frac{1.8}{2.7} \cdot \frac{10^{-25}}{10^{-26}} \qquad \text{Divide the coefficients and divide the powers of 10.}$$
$$\approx 0.67 \cdot 10^{-25-(-26)} \qquad \text{Round the coefficient and use the quotient of powers property.}$$
$$= 0.67 \cdot 10^1$$
$$= 6.7 \qquad \text{Write in standard form.}$$

The mass of a silver atom is approximately 6.7 times as great as the mass of an oxygen atom.

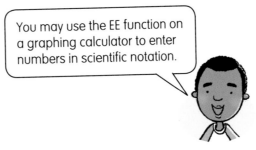

You may use the EE function on a graphing calculator to enter numbers in scientific notation.

TRY Practice dividing numbers in scientific notation

Solve.

1. The Jean-Luc Lagardère plant in France is one of the largest building in the world. It has a volume of $5.6 \cdot 10^6$ cubic meters. The NASA vehicle assembly building in Florida has a volume of $3.7 \cdot 10^6$ cubic meters. How many times as great as the volume of the NASA vehicle assembly building is the volume of the Jean-Luc Lagardère plant? Round the answer to the nearest tenth.

2. The Abraj Al-Bait towers in Saudi Arabia has a floor area of $1.5 \cdot 10^6$ square meters. The Palazzo in Las Vegas has a floor area of $6.5 \cdot 10^5$ square meters. How many times as great as the floor area of the Palazzo is the floor area of the Abraj Al-Bait towers? Round the answer to the nearest tenth.

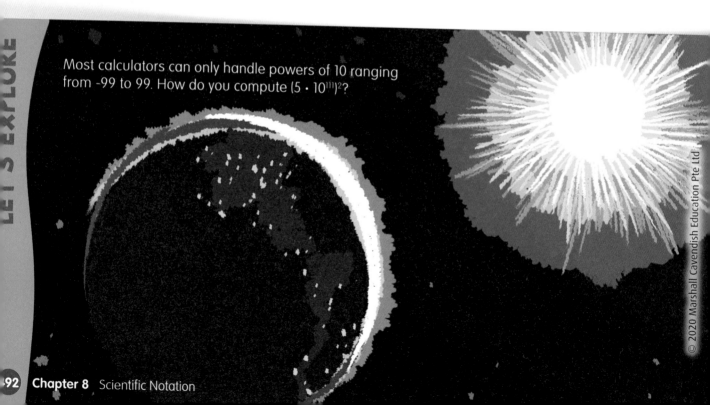

LET'S EXPLORE

Most calculators can only handle powers of 10 ranging from -99 to 99. How do you compute $(5 \cdot 10^{111})^2$?

INDEPENDENT PRACTICE

Evaluate each expression. Write each answer in scientific notation and round the coefficient to the nearest tenth where applicable.

1 $7.45 \cdot 10^6 \cdot 5.4 \cdot 10^{-6}$

2 $6.84 \cdot 10^{-5} \cdot 4.7 \cdot 10^{10}$

3 $5.75 \cdot 10^{-5} \div (7.15 \cdot 10^7)$

4 $8.45 \cdot 10^{11} \div (1.69 \cdot 10^{-8})$

Solve.

5 The table shows the volumes of some planets.

a How many times as great as the volume of Mars is the volume of Venus? Round your answer to the nearest tenth.

Planets	Volume (km³)
Venus	$9.4 \cdot 10^{11}$
Earth	$1.1 \cdot 10^{12}$
Mars	$1.6 \cdot 10^{11}$

b How many times as great as the volume of Mars is the volume of Earth? Round your answer to the nearest tenth.

c How many times as great as the volume of Venus is the volume of Earth? Round your answer to the nearest tenth.

6 Sara's digital camera has a resolution of $2560 \cdot 1920$ pixels. David's digital camera has a resolution of $3264 \cdot 2448$ pixels.

a Express the resolution of each digital camera in prefix form to the nearest whole unit. Use the most appropriate unit.

b Whose camera has a higher resolution?

7   Blake downloaded pictures of a cruise ship and a ski run from the internet. The file size of the cruise ship is 794 kilobytes while the file size of the ski run is 2.6 megabytes.

   a What is the total file size, in megabytes and in kilobytes, of the two pictures?

   b Calculate the difference between the two file sizes, in megabytes and in kilobytes.

   c To the nearest tenth, how many times as great as the file size of the ski run picture is the file size of the cruise ship picture?

   d Blake saved the two pictures on a thumb drive with a capacity of 256 megabytes. Find the remaining free capacity of the thumb drive to the nearest tenth megabyte after Blake saved the two pictures in it.

8   A rectangular aquarium is $2.63 \cdot 10^3$ inches long, $1.26 \cdot 10^2$ inches wide, and $3 \cdot 10^1$ inches deep. Find its volume. Write the answer in scientific notation.

9   The time light takes to travel one meter in a vacuum is 3.3 nanoseconds. To travel one mile it takes 5.4 microseconds. How many times longer, to the nearest tenth, does it take light to travel one mile than one meter?

Mathematical Habit 7 **Make use of structure**

The table shows some numbers written in standard form and in the equivalent scientific notation. Describe the relationship between each pair of variables.

Standard Form	Scientific Notation
0.0007	$7 \cdot 10^{-4}$
0.00182	$1.82 \cdot 10^{-3}$
1,280,000,000	$1.28 \cdot 10^{9}$
7,100	$7.1 \cdot 10^{3}$
427.7	$4.277 \cdot 10^{2}$

a The value of the positive number in standard form and the sign of the exponent when expressed in scientific notation.

b The sign of the exponent when expressed in scientific notation and the direction the decimal point moves to express the number in standard form.

Problem Solving with Heuristics

1 **Mathematical Habit** **1** **Persevere in solving problems**
Find the cube root of $2.7 \cdot 10^{10}$.

2 **Mathematical Habit** **1** **Persevere in solving problems**
Given that $a = 3 \cdot 10^3$ and $b = 4 \cdot 10^2$, find the value of each expression.

a $2a + b$

b $\dfrac{2a}{b}$

3 Solve each of the following. Write your answer in scientific notation using the basic unit.

a 80 micrograms + 200 nanograms

b 3 gigameters – 700 megameters

CHAPTER WRAP-UP

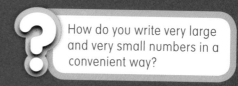

How do you write very large and very small numbers in a convenient way?

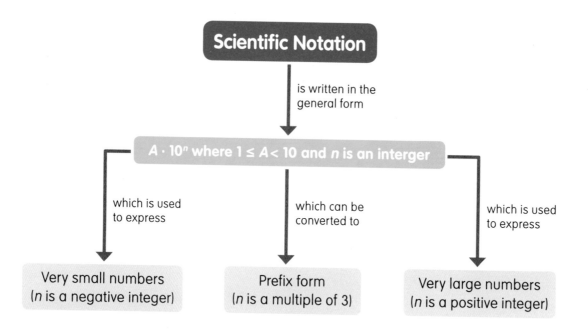

Scientific Notation

is written in the general form

$A \cdot 10^n$ where $1 \le A < 10$ and n is an interger

which is used to express

which can be converted to

which is used to express

Very small numbers (n is a negative integer)

Prefix form (n is a multiple of 3)

Very large numbers (n is a positive integer)

KEY CONCEPTS

- Scientific notation is a convenient way of writing very large or very small numbers.
- The general form of a number in scientific notation is $A \cdot 10^n$, where the coefficient A is at least 1 but less than 10, and the exponent n is any integer.
- To compare two numbers in scientific notation, first compare the powers of 10. If they are the same, then compare the coefficients.
- To add or subtract numbers in scientific notation, the numbers must be expressed using the same power of 10 before applying the distributive property.
- To multiply or divide numbers in scientific notation, multiply or divide the coefficients before multiplying or dividing the powers of 10 using properties of exponents.
- A prefix that precedes a basic unit of measure indicates a fraction or multiple of the unit. Each prefix has a unique symbol that is placed in front of the unit symbol.

Name: _____   Date: _____

Tell whether each number is written correctly in scientific notation. If it is incorrectly written, state the reason.

1   $10 \cdot 10^2$

2   $0.99 \cdot 10^{12}$

3   $1.4 \cdot 10^2$

4   $0.4 \cdot 10^{25}$

Write each number in scientific notation.

5   714,000

6   0.00087

Write each number in standard form.

7   $3.46 \cdot 10^2$

8   $5.4 \cdot 10^4$

Identify the greater number in each pair of numbers.

9   $7.8 \cdot 10^{-5}$ and $5.4 \cdot 10^{-7}$

10 $1.4 \cdot 10^{-5}$ and $6 \cdot 10^{-4}$

11 $6.5 \cdot 10^{-15}$ and $9.3 \cdot 10^{-12}$

12 $3.5 \cdot 10^{-2}$ and $4 \cdot 10^{-3}$

Evaluate each expression. Write each answer in scientific notation.

13 $2.44 \cdot 10^3 + 1.9 \cdot 10^5$

14 $3.12 \cdot 10^{-3} - 3 \cdot 10^{-3}$

15 $2.4 \cdot 10^{-2} \cdot 5 \cdot 10^{-1}$

16 $3.2 \cdot 10^8 \div (1.6 \cdot 10^4)$

Express each expression in prefix form. Choose the most appropriate unit

17 $2.8 \cdot 10^3$ meters

18 $1.5 \cdot 10^{-6}$ meters

Solve.

19 An eriophyid mite is 250 micrometers long. A patiriella parvivipara is 5 millimeters long.

a Which organism is longer?

b Express the length of the eriophyid mite in millimeters. Write the answer in scientific notation.

c Write each length in scientific notation using the basic unit.

20 The top five materials used in the automotive industry in the United States in a particular year are as shown in the table.

Material	Total Consumption (T)
Plastic	46,240
Aluminium	11,320
Steel	$9.894 \cdot 10^7$
Glass	5,417,000
Rubber	$2.86 \cdot 10^6$

a How much more plastic was used than aluminium? Write the answer in scientific notation and round the coefficient to the nearest tenth.

b How much more steel was used than glass? Write the answer in scientific notation and round the coefficient to the nearest tenth.

c Find the total consumption of these materials used by the automotive industry in that year. Write the answer in scientific notation and round the coefficient to the nearest tenth.

21 The table shows the weights of some animals.

Animal	Weight (lb)
African bush elephant	$2.706 \cdot 10^4$
Hippopotamus	$9.9 \cdot 10^3$
Walrus	$4.4 \cdot 10^3$

African bush elephant

Hippopotamus

Walrus

weight $2.706 \cdot 10^4$ lb

weight $9.9 \cdot 10^3$ lb

weight $4.4 \cdot 10^3$ lb

a How many times as heavy as the walrus is the hippopotamus? Round your answer to the nearest tenth.

b How many times as heavy as the hippopotamus is the African bush elephant? Round your answer to the nearest tenth.

Answer each question.

22 A company earns $475,000,000 in one year. What is 475,000,000 written in scientific notation?

   (A) $4.75 \cdot 10^5$

   (B) $4.75 \cdot 10^8$

   (C) $4.75 \cdot 10^9$

   (D) $4.75 \cdot 10^{11}$

23 The area of California is approximately $1.64 \cdot 10^6$ square miles. What is $1.64 \cdot 10^6$ written in standard form?

   (A) 16,400,000

   (B) 1,640,000

   (C) 164,000

   (D) 16,400

24 An atom of oxygen has a mass of $2.7 \cdot 10^{-26}$ kilograms. A gas syringe contains $9 \cdot 10^{20}$ atoms of oxygen. Find the total mass, in kilograms, of the atoms of oxygen in the gas syringe. Write the answer in scientific notation. Write your answer in the space below.

Name: _____ Date: _____

The Solar System

1 The table shows the average distance of each planet from the Sun.

Planet	Average Distance From the Sun (miles)
Mercury	$3.68 \cdot 10^7$
Venus	$6.72 \cdot 10^7$
Earth	$9.3 \cdot 10^7$
Mars	$1.416 \cdot 10^8$
Jupiter	$4.836 \cdot 10^8$
Saturn	$8.865 \cdot 10^8$
Uranus	$1.7837 \cdot 10^9$
Neptune	$2.7952 \cdot 10^9$

a Jack and Rachel want to present the planets in the solar system on a poster. They want to space out all the planets evenly. Show whether the students are correct.

b Rachel wants to calculate the distances of the planets from the Sun in Astronomical Units (au), a unit of length that measures the distance from Earth to the Sun. If Earth's distance from the Sun is 1 au, which planet is about 5 au from the Sun?

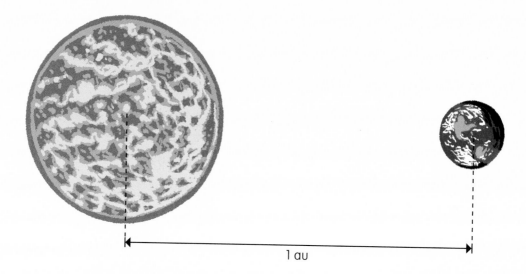

1 au

c Jack observed that to find the distance to and from Venus and the Sun in scientific notation, you would need to multiply the coefficient by 2, move the decimal point one place to the left and increase the exponent by 1. Does this strategy apply to all cases? Justify your reasoning. Use the table below to help you.

Planet	Average Distance From the Sun (miles)	Distance to and from the Sun (miles)	Application of Julio's Strategy (miles)	Does the Strategy Work?
Venus	$6.72 \cdot 10^7$	$6.72 \cdot 10^7 \cdot 2$ $= 13.44 \cdot 10^7$ $= 1.344 \cdot 10^8$	$1.344 \cdot 10^8$	Yes

Rubric

Point(s)	Level	My Performance
7–8	4	• Most of my answers are correct. • I showed complete understanding of the concepts. • I used effective and efficient strategies to solve the problems. • I explained my answers and mathematical thinking clearly and completely.
5–6	3	• Some of my answers are correct. • I showed adequate understanding of the concepts. • I used effective strategies to solve the problems. • I explained my answers and mathematical thinking clearly.
3–4	2	• A few of my answers are correct. • I showed some understanding of the concepts. • I used some effective strategies to solve the problems. • I explained some of my answers and mathematical thinking clearly.
0–2	1	• A few of my answers are correct. • I showed little understanding of the concepts. • I used limited effective strategies to solve the problems. • I did not explain my answers and mathematical thinking clearly.

Teacher's Comments

Glossary

A

- **additive inverse**

  The additive inverse of a number x is the number that, when added to x, yields zero. Example: 2 and −2 are additive inverses.

C

- **coefficient**

  A coefficient is a multiplicative factor in scientific notation.
  Example: In $5 \cdot 10^{-9}$, 5 is the coefficient.

- **complex fraction**

  A fraction in which the numerator, the denominator, or both the numerator and the denominator contain a fraction.

  Examples: $\dfrac{\left(\frac{2}{7}\right)}{8}$, $\dfrac{3}{-\left(\frac{5}{2}\right)}$, and $\dfrac{-\left(4\frac{1}{2}\right)}{-\left(1\frac{5}{16}\right)}$

  are complex fractions.

- **consistent equation**

  An equation with only one solution.

- **cube root**

  The cube root of a number, when multiplied by itself twice, gives the number.
  Example: $4 \cdot 4 \cdot 4 = 64$
  4 is the cube root of 64.

- **curve**

  A graph that is not a straight line.
  Example:

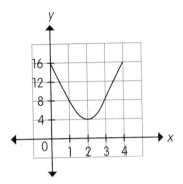

E

- **equivalent equations**

  Algebraic equations with the same solution.
  Example: $2(6 - x) = 0$ and $12 - 2x = 0$ are equivalent equations.

- **equivalent inequalities**

  Algebraic inequalities with the same solution set.
  Example: $2x < 8$ and $x - 1 < 3$ are equivalent inequalities.

- **exponential notation**

  Notation used to write a number as a base raised to an exponent.
  Example: 2^3, 3^5, and 6^9 are numbers in exponential notation.

F

- **function**

  A type of relation in which each input maps to only one output. One-to-one relations and many-to-one relations are functions.

I

- **identity**

  An equation that is true for all values of the variable.

- **inconsistent equation**

  An equation with no solution.

- **input**

  The independent variable of a relation, often denoted by x in an ordered pair (x, y).

- **irrational number**

  A number that cannot be written as $\frac{m}{n}$, where m and n are integers with $n \neq 0$.

L

- **least common denominator**

  The common multiple of the denominators of two or more fractions that has the least value.

  Example: The least common denominator of $\frac{1}{2}$ and $\frac{1}{5}$ is 10.

- **linear function**

  A function that has a constant rate of change. A linear function can be represented by a linear equation $y = mx + b$.

- **linear relationship**

  A relationship between two quantities in which there is a constant variation between the two quantities.

M

- **many-to-many**

  Describes a relation with the properties of a one-to-many relation and a many-to-one relation: one input maps to many outputs, and many inputs map to the same output.

- **many-to-one**

  Describes a relation in which many inputs map to the same output.

- **map**

  To pair an input (or a point) to an output (or another point).

- **mapping diagram**

  A diagram used to represent a relation, showing a set of inputs paired with a set of outputs.
  Example:

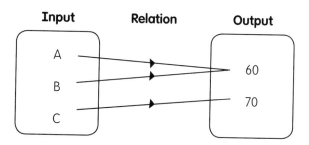

N

- **negative fraction**

  A fraction to the left of 0 on a number line.
  Examples: $-\frac{1}{2}$, $-\frac{13}{5}$, and $-\frac{10}{3}$ are negative fractions.

- **negative integer**

  An integer to the left of 0 on a number line.
  Examples: −5, −17, and −98 are
  negative integers.

- **nonlinear function**

  A function that does not have a constant rate
  of change. A nonlinear function cannot be
  represented by a linear equation $y = mx + b$.

- **one-to-many**

  Describes a relation in which one input maps to
  many outputs.

- **one-to-one**

  Describes a relation in which each input maps
  to its own unique output.

- **output**

  The dependent variable of a relation, often
  denoted by y in an ordered pair (x, y).

- **positive integer**

  An integer to the right of 0 on a number line.
  Examples: 2, 10, and 51 are positive integers.

R

- **rate of change**

  The ratio $\dfrac{\text{change in first quantity}}{\text{change in second quantity}}$, which tells
  you how much the first quantity changes for
  every 1 unit change in the second quantity.

- **rational number**

  A number that can be written as $\dfrac{m}{n}$, where
  m and n are integers with n being a nonzero
  integer.
  Examples: $8, \dfrac{7}{11}$, and $-\dfrac{63}{253}$ are
  rational numbers.

- **real number**

  A number that is either rational or irrational.
  Example: $3, -\dfrac{2}{3}$, and π are real numbers.

- **relation**

  A relation pairs a set of inputs with a set of
  outputs.

- **repeating decimal**

  A decimal that has a group of one or more
  digits that repeat endlessly.
  Examples: 0.111…, 0.030303…, and 0.16333…
  are repeating decimals.

- **rise**

  The vertical change from one point to a second point on a coordinate plane.

  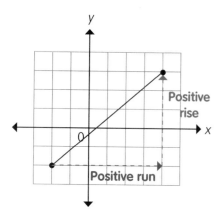

  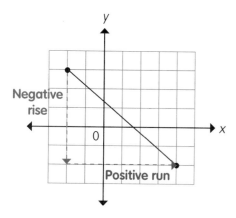

- **run**

  The horizontal change from one point to a second point on a coordinate plane.

  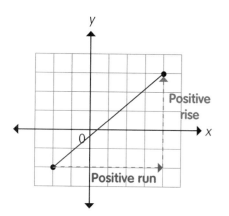

S

- **scientific notation**

  A way of expressing a large or small number in the form $A \cdot 10n$, where $1 \leq A < 10$ and n is an integer.
  Example: $1.38 \cdot 10^{-2}$ and $5.59 \cdot 10^{12}$ are numbers in scientific notation.

- **set of integers**

  The set of negative integers, 0, and positive integers: $\ldots, -4, -3, -2, -1, 0, 1, 2, 3, 4, \ldots$

- **significant digit**

  The digit that is certain or that is estimated in a number. The number of significant digits shows the precision of the estimation.
  Example: 2.506 has 4 significant digits.
  2.560 has 4 significant digits.
  0.256 has 3 significant digits.

- **slope**

  The ratio of the rise, or vertical change, to the run, or horizontal change, between any two points on a nonvertical line on the coordinate plane.
  Example:

  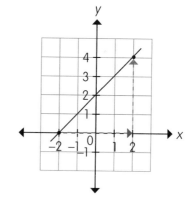

  $$\text{Slope} = \frac{\text{Rise}}{\text{Run}}$$
  $$= \frac{4 - 0}{2 - (-2)}$$
  $$= \frac{4}{4}$$
  $$= 1$$

- **slope-intercept form**

  A form of a linear equation, $y = mx + b$, where m is the slope and b is the y-intercept of the graph of the equation.

  Example: $y = \frac{5}{2}x - 3$ is a linear equation written in slope-intercept form.

- **solution set**

  A set of values that make an inequality true.

  Example: $x + 3 > 4$
  $$x + 3 - 3 > 4 - 3$$
  $$x > 1$$

  $x > 1$ is the solution set.

- **square root**

  The square root of a number, when multiplied by itself, gives the number.

  Example: 3 is the positive square root of 9.
  $$3 \cdot 3 = 9$$
  -3 is the negative square root of 9.
  $$-3 \cdot (-3) = 9$$

- **standard form**

  A way of expressing a number using the ten digits 0 to 9 and place value notation.

  Example: -0.005, 9, and 2,158 are numbers in standard form.

T

- **terminating decimal**

  A decimal that has a finite number of nonzero decimal places.

  Examples: 0.5, 0.28, and 0.75 are terminating decimals.

V

- **vertical line test**

  A test to determine if a graph represents a function.

  Example:

  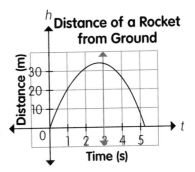

  Any vertical line intersects the graph at only one point. So, the graph represents a function.

X

- **x-intercept**

  The x-coordinate of the point where a line intersects the x-axis.

Y

- **y-intercept**

  The y-coordinate of the point where a line intersects the y-axis.

Z

- **zero pair**

  A pairing of the integers 1 and -1, whose sum is 0.

  Example: $2 + (-3)$ has two zero pairs:
  $$2 + (-3) = 1 + 1 + (-1) + (-1) + (-1)$$
  $$= [1 + (-1)] + [1 + (-1)] + (-1)$$

Index

Pages in **boldface** type show where a term is introduced.

Prefix system, 485–486, 498

Prime factorization, 420

Problem solving
  real-world problems, *see* Real-world problems

Product
  power of a, *see* Power, of product
  of powers property, 423–424, 461

Properties
  associative, *see* Associative property
  commutative, *see* Commutative property
  distributive, *see* Distributive property
  of exponents, 433–434, 441–442
  power of power, *see* Power, power of
  product of powers, *see* Product, of powers
    property
  quotient of powers, *see* Quotient, of powers
    property

Proportions, *see* Direct proportion

Q

Quantities
  combined to make zero, 47
  comparing unequal, 186

Quotient
  power of a, *see* Power, of quotient
  of powers property, 425–426, 461
  of rational numbers, 90

R

Rate of change, **379**–381, 392, 395

Rational numbers, **9,** 24, 107, 414
  adding, 83–84, 86, 92
    with different denominators, 83
    with same denominators, 83
  classifying, 17
  comparing, 18, 20
  dividing, 89–92
  multiplying, 88–89, 92
  on number line, 11–12
  as repeating decimals, **16**–18, 107, 414
  subtracting, 86–88, 92
    with different denominators, 86
    with same denominator, 86
  as terminating decimals, **15**–16, 107, 414
  writing, using long division, 15–18

Real numbers, **31,** 107, 414
  ordering, 31–32

Real-world linear relationship, 332

Real-world problems, 274, 344
  compare two slopes, 290, 291
  interpreting slopes and *y*-intercepts, 331–332,
    344, 346–347
  linear equations, 274, 331
    with one variable, 242, 274
  linear inequalities, 274
    with one variable, 268, 274
  solving
    algebraically, 203–204, 206, 208
    algebraic expressions, 167–168
    algebraic inequalities, 223–224
    algebraic reasoning for, 165–167
  squares or cubes, 455–456
  tables to organize information for, 160
  translate into algebraic expressions, 158, 160–162

Reciprocal, 6, 89–91

Recognizing
  equivalent expressions, 120
  parts of algebraic expression, 118

Relations, **357,** 404
  understand and classify, 357–358, 360

Repeated addition, 69–70
  multiplication rules using, 69

Repeating decimals, **16,** 414
  fractions as, 237, 241
  writing rational numbers as, 16–18, 107

Representing functions
  in different forms, 373–374, 376

Rise, **284**

Rounding
  decimals to significant digits, 38–39
  whole numbers to significant digits, 37–38

Rules
  divisibility, 420

Run, **284**

S

Scientific notation, **473**
  adding
    with different power of 10, 483, 485
    with same power of 10, 481–482

Photo Credits

© 2020 Marshall Cavendish Education Pte Ltd

Published by Marshall Cavendish Education
Times Centre, 1 New Industrial Road, Singapore 536196
Customer Service Hotline: (65) 6213 9688
US Office Tel: (1-914) 332 8888 | Fax: (1-914) 332 8882
E-mail: cs@mceducation.com
Website: www.mceducation.com

Distributed by
Houghton Mifflin Harcourt
125 High Street
Boston, MA 02110
Tel: 617-351-5000
Website: www.hmhco.com/programs/math-in-focus

First published 2020

ISBN 978-0-358-10294-6

Printed in Singapore

1 2 3 4 5 6 7 8   1401   25 24 23 22 21 20
4500759314   A B C D E

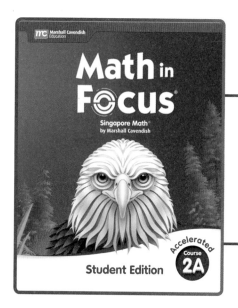

The cover image shows a bald eagle.
Bald eagles live in remote parts of North America, and northern Mexico, often near large bodies of water such as coasts and lakes. They build the largest nests of all birds, often at the top of very tall trees. They possess the natural ability to soar and glide at great heights. Their amazing eyesight allows them to prey on fish and small mammals from up to two miles away. The bald eagle is the national animal of the United States of America and appears on the seal.